Coral Reefs
and Mangroves
of the World
Coral Reefs
Mangroves

Life

A diver's guide to

Reef Life

ACKNOWLEDGEMENTS

The authors would like to express their gratitude to a few good friends who have greatly helped in the making of this book: among them Dave Behrens, Angelo Mojetta, Robert F. Myers, Massimo Boyer, Max Ammer, Jim & Cary Yanny, Steve & Miranda Coverdale, Ken Chung, Veronica Lee, Ketrick Chin, Ricky Chin, Amillson Baragus, Rodel Pepania, Honarius Basil, Ade, Otto Awom, Nikson Soor, Teri Perry, Gaspare Davi, Nino Nicoletti/Cressi Sub, Leon Joubert & Claudia Pellarini, Brigitte & Thomas Gutmann, Laria Bettini & Roberto Galli, Adam Broadbent/Scubazoo & Au Yong Seok Wun/Scubazoo, Franco Pozzi, Vanna Cammelli/Aquadiving Tours, Alan Powderham, Alexander Mustard, Kelvin Aitken, Edmund Tee, Paul Lees and Tony Wu.

Published by
Nautilus Publishing Sdn. Bhd.
Lot 38, 1st Floor, Block C, Bandar Tyng, Mile 5,
North Road, PPM 255 Elopura,
90000 Sandakan, Sabah, Malaysia
tel: 6089-673999, 674999
fax: 6089-673777

e-mail:
nautilus@streamyx.com
nautiluspub@tin.it

www.reefwonders.net

Graphic design: Daniele Clarotto
Cover design: Carla Mantero

First printing 2006

ISBN 983-2731-01-1

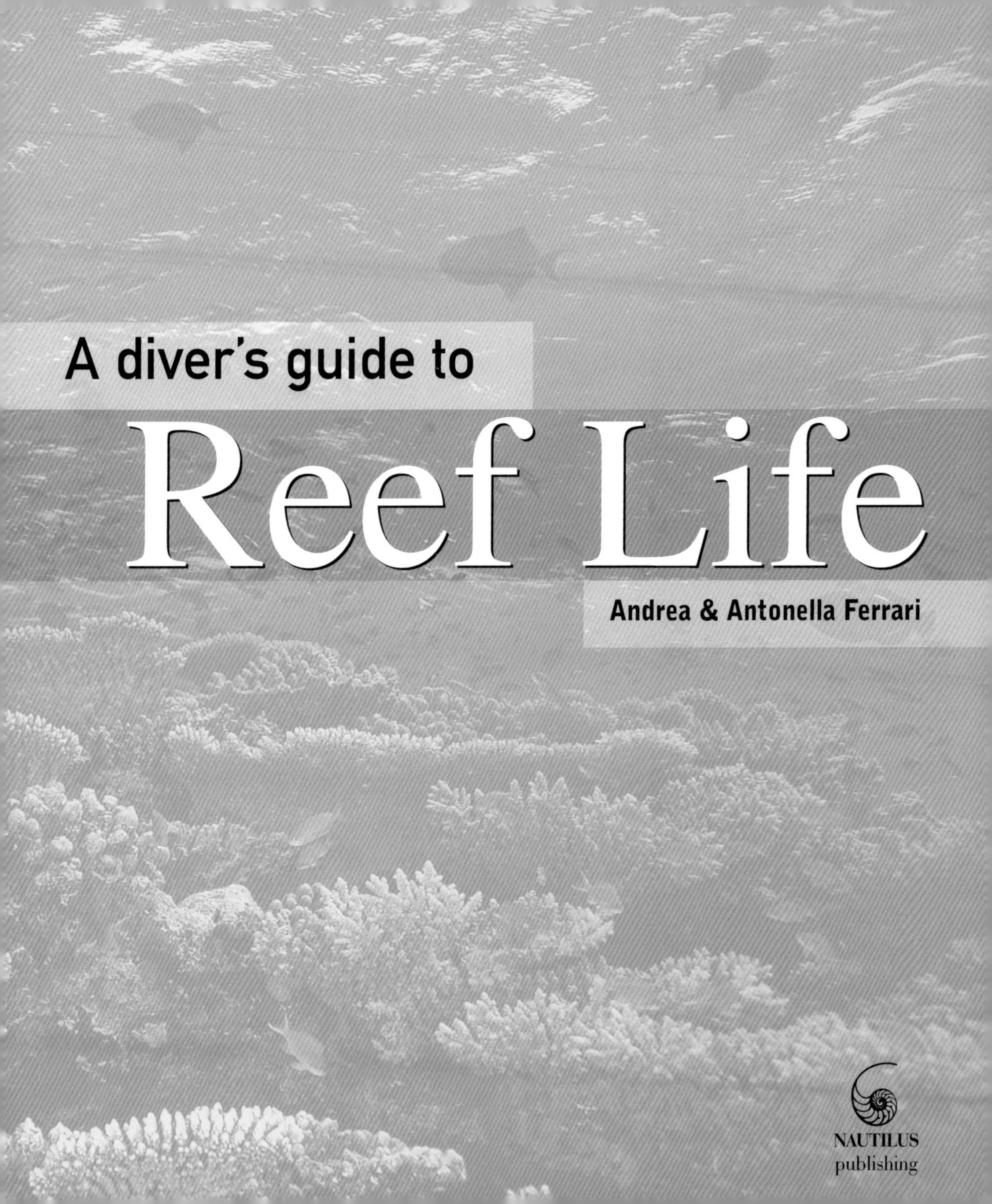

A diver's guide to

Reef Life

Andrea & Antonella Ferrari

NAUTILUS
publishing

Table of Contents

CORAL REEFS
Rainforests of the Sea

Where Life Knows No Boundaries

The numbers are simply amazing. Oceans cover more than 70% on the planet Earth and more than 90% of the living biomass of the planet is found in the sea. More than 4.000 fish species - about a quarter of the grand total - are found on tropical coral reefs. It is not a surprise, then, to discover that the coral reef is an ecosystem without equal anywhere in the world. The biggest living organism on Earth is Australia's Great Barrier Reef - 2.000 chilometers long, it is the only form of life of the planet which can be seen from the Moon! More than 90% of marine species are directly or indirectly dependant on this extraordinary environment. In our opinion, no other natural environment- not even the densest and most luxuriant tropical rainforest - can convey so deeply such an overwhelming impression of riches and vitality as an untouched and healthy coral reef. The blinding clarity of tropical waters, their high luminosity at great depths, the inexhaustible bustle of innumerable creatures in every shape and color, the surprising and often delicate architecture of madreporic colonies will never fail to astonish and fascinate even the most widely traveled divers and snorkellers.

A Maze of Corals

Persons diving on a reef are immediately confronted with one of nature's most complex environments, featuring a highly articulated physical structure. A literally infinite variety of microenvironments make up the coral reef, and every marine species living in it has adapted to it by its own peculiar evolution. Since every shape and color in nature - including the most eccentric and conspicuous ones - are ultimately dictated by laws of compliance with the environment, the richness and complexity of the reef have generated an awesome palette well known to every diver. Butterflyfish (*Chaetodontidae*) feed almost exclusively on coral polyps and thus have developed protruding mouths that work like tweezers. Their deep-bodied, laterally compressed shape allows them to flit through the dense branching of coral colonies with agility. Many species of butterflyfish are very territorial in habit, as are their close relatives, the angelfish (*Pomacanthidae*), so their appearance is most often intensely colorful and strongly recognizable by competitors. The long, narrow body of predators such as moray eels enables them to maneuver through clefts in the coral in search of prey. To protect themselves from the nocturnal stalking of moray eels - which rely primarily on their highly developed sense of smell to hunt - the parrotfish, at night embedded among the corals, have in turn evolved an unusual strategy: they secrete a cocoon of transparent and thick mucus which wholly envelops them and cuts off every olfactory trace in the water column. The striped pattern and

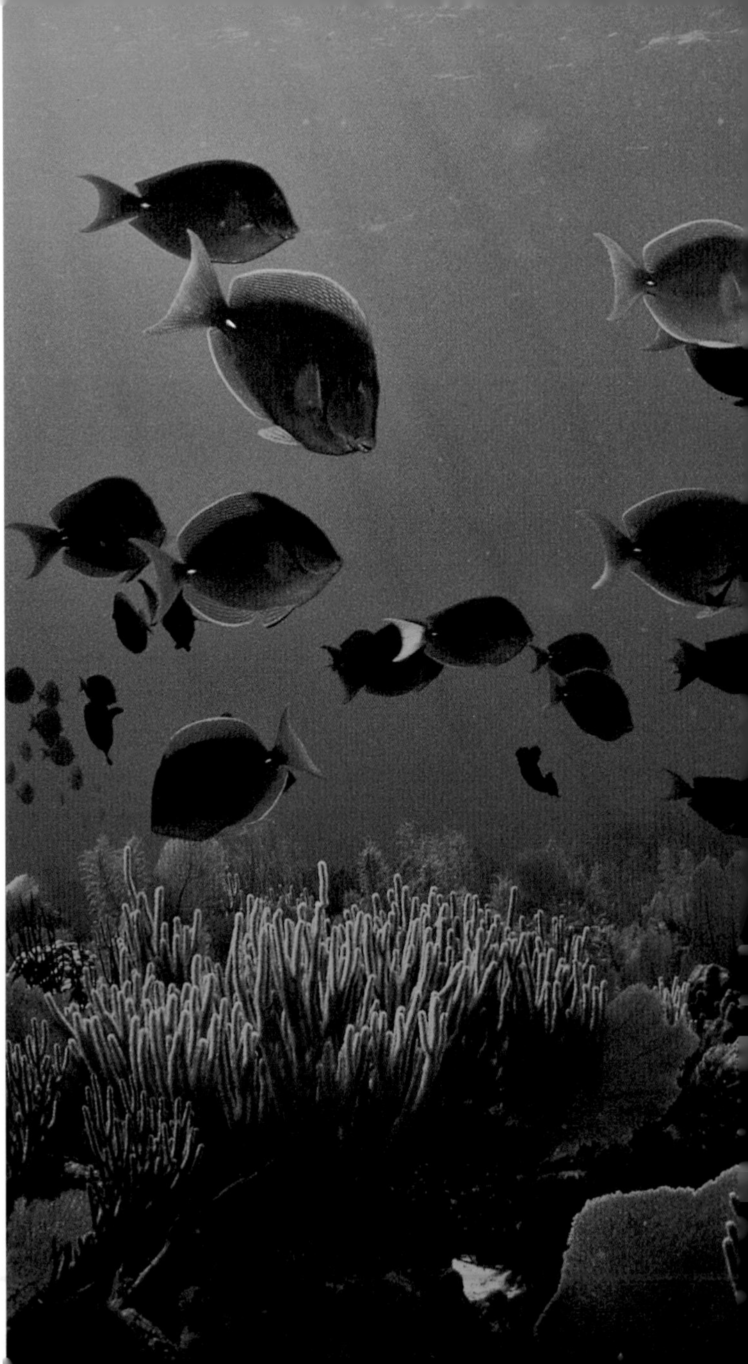

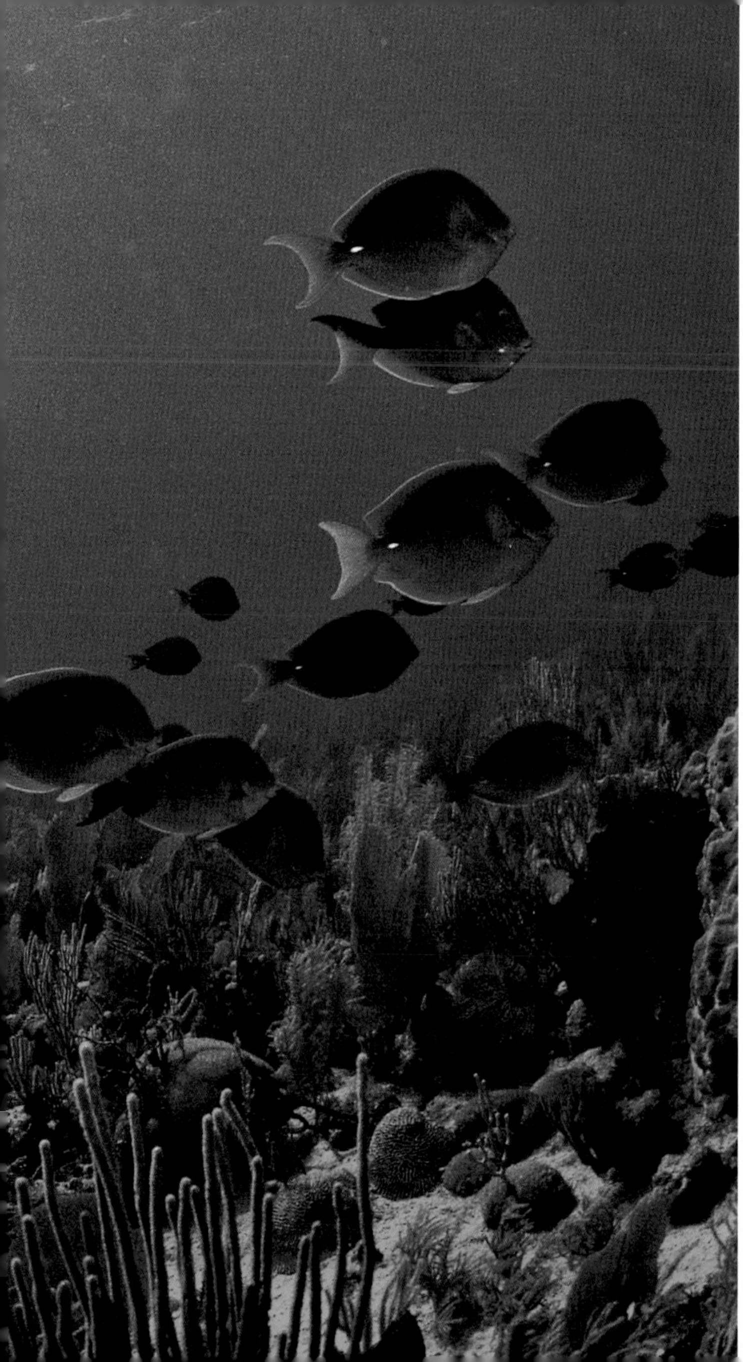

trailing banner-like fins of lionfishes may seem pointlessly sumptuous at first, but the stripes render this predator barely visible in the dappled light of coral seabeds. The large pectorals block every route of escape to the small fish which represent their prey. Every microhabitat is populated by species that are perfectly adapted to it. There are tiny fish and crustaceans that spend their entire existence within a few square centimeters, hidden and protected by the tangle of the hard coral colonies' branches. Others pass their lives fluttering nervously from one perch to another at the top of the reef, exposed to transient predators. Some other species - such as small stingrays or triggerfish - prefer instead the microenvironment offered by sand flats that interrupt the uniformity of the reef; they are more exposed to roving predators but at the same time become less vulnerable to ambush and are better able to find food. Like most fish that feed primarily on invertebrates (puffers and boxfish belong also to this group), they have evolved an especially powerful set of teeth. These are just some of the numerous examples of niche adaptation. Careful observation of each species' behavior will yield others, since we are far from having clarified all the complex ties and relationships at work among inhabitants of the reef and their surroundings. Among the first researchers to dedicate themselves to the study and classification of reef fish were the French Bernard Germain Lacépède with his

Histoire Naturelle des Poissons (1798-1803), and Georges Cuvier and Achille Valenciennes (22 volumes from 1828 to 1849), the Dutch Peter Bleeker with his *Ichthyologic Atlas of the Dutch East Indies* (1862-1877), the German Eduard Ruppell (1794-1884), and the Danish Petrus Forsskal (1775). But how many fish can normally live together in a defined expanse of coral reef? An Israeli scientific expedition has captured 2,200 specimens belonging to 128 different species with a blomass of more than 136 kg in a stretch of reef 150 meters long, 3 meters deep, and 22 meters from shore. On other occasions, between 70 and 80 species have been classified in coral masses that were no more than 3 meters in diameter.

Reef History and Ecological Needs

Coral reefs are now being severely endangered all over the world by man's activities, but they have been here much longer than us. In fact, the first traces of coral reefs date back more than 500 million years. From fossil readings we now know that their distribution has remarkably varied over time, responding in turn to phases of great geographic expansion and contraction following climatic changes that occurred during the different geological eras.
The distribution of coral reefs is presently limited to tropical seas, where reefs extend over a total area of nearly 600,000 square

kilometers. Coral colonies develop primarily between the surface and a depth of 30 meters but only in waters whose average winter temperature stays above 20°C. Other factors that limit the development of coral reefs are water salinity, which must be constant, and the intensity of ambient light. Why are these three factors - temperature, salinity and sunny exposure-so important? If we stop and think for a moment about the reef environment, we will quickly realize that the structural elements that underlie this ecosystem are the so-called corals or, more correctly, madreporic colonies. These are the wonderfully complex structures whose imperceptible growth and extraordinary fragility represent the very foundation of the reef habitat.

The Life of Corals

At their most basic level, these coelenterate organisms (*see inset 1*) can be described as innumerable and very small polyps (simple gelatinous "sacs" with an opening on top, ringed by tentacles) grouped into a hard and fragile calcareous structure built by the organisms themselves: an exoskeleton (external skeleton) whose often bizarre but always functional shapes create the actual scenery of the reef. Simply put, new polyps build new exoskeletons, progressively enlarging the coral colony. Coral polyps are broadly separated in *hermatypic* corals -

which are able to build reefs slowly as the colonies expand and propagate themselves - and *ahermatypic* corals, whose horny, elastic structure does not lend itself to the building of complex composite structures. All-important zooxanthellae are generally associated with the first kind only; they are unicellular, symbiotic algae that live in the cells of coral polyps, averaging a million for every cubic centimeter of coral. Zooxanthellae furnish the polyps with caloric substances such as sugars and aminoacids through photosynthesis (this explains the importance of ambient light). At the same time, they remove potentially harmful compounds like carbon dioxide, which could dissolve the colonies' limestone skeleton by converting it to carbonic acid when it comes into contact with water. This is the reason why the current build-up of carbon dioxide in the earth's atmosphere due to human industrial activities (the so-called Greenhouse Effect) is severely damaging and in some instances actually destroying coral reef communities which have survived for millions of years. Coral polyps are however not limited to using the zooxanthellae to procure nutrients. In fact, they sport extremely efficient weapons which allow them to paralyze and capture suspended microorganisms (plankton) carried by currents, especially at night.

Deadly stings and strange shapes

The polyps' tentacles - exactly like those of jellyfish and anemones -

are filled with bulbous cells (called *cnidoblasts*) containing a thin hollow filament that is sharp and coiled like a spring (the *nematocyst*). The instant they contact a possible prey, cnidoblasts open automatically and jab their nematocysts lightning fast into the victim's tissue, injecting a toxic compound. The tentacles of the polyp then carry the dead or paralyzed victim toward the oral cavity and ingest it.

Up close at night, it is easy to observe the tiny distended polyps that stud the surface of a coral colony by the thousands (*see inset 2*), projecting their tentacles into the current and waiting for likely prey.

Stretches of coral reef assume completely different shapes (*see inset 3*) depending on the species originating them. In a typical shallow water reef it is fairly common to observe colonies that are laminate in structure (the typical tabular madrepores of the *Acropora* genus), fingerlike (short and stubby branching, as in the *Montipora* genus), broadly branching (*Acropora* again), massive (the giant hemispherical domes of the *Porites*, *Favites* and *Favia* genera, among others), brain-shaped or labyrinthine (*Diploria*, *Platygira*, *Turbinaria*) and even non-sessile (that is, detached from the substrate, as in the flat round colonies of the mushroom corals belonging to the *Fungia* genus). Every different structure responds however to precise conditions and often presents a useful hide-out to or perch many different species of fish, mollusks and crustaceans.

Reef Structures

Not all coral reefs develop in the same way. Their shape and size vary according to wave action, the play of currents and their more or less rigid relationship with the underlying rocky substrate.
The basic structure is the so-called *fringing reef*, whose growth runs more or less parallel to the coast. In this form, the reef originates an internal lagoon with a broken rubble and sand bottom separated from the open ocean by a bar of coral whose summit lies at a very shallow depth and whose seaward outer wall (sometimes a soft slope interrupted by sandy terraces, sometimes a precipitous drop-off) hosts the highest number of species. Some of the best examples of fringing reefs can be observed in the Red Sea. So-called *barrier reefs* are instead a further evolution of this structure and are found where the continental shelf moves away from shore but continues to offer conditions that can guarantee the development of madreporic colonies. The best examples of this type of reef -

looking like a more or less oblong platform, composed of parallel structures - are found in Australia's Great Barrier Reef, in West Papua, in Papua New Guinea and in much of the Caribbean. Coral *atolls* (*see inset 4*) finally represent the third model of reef development. In their case, the progressive disappearance of a volcanic island leaves intact the fringing reef that surrounded it in remote times, originating an internal lagoon which is encircled by a more or less regular ring of coral. This type of reef structure is generally encountered in the open ocean: particularly well-known examples are found in the Maldives archipelago and in the Polynesian atolls.

The Seaward Reef Ecosystem

Be it a sand and rubble slope, a rocky wall occasionally interrupted by sandy terraces or even a precipitous vertical drop-off, the seaward or outer part of the reef represents an irresistible beacon for many large marine predators. Some of them stake out a fixed territory and end up spending their entire existence in the immediate vicinity of the reef. Others are mostly pelagic; they spend most of their existence in the open sea and approach the perimeter of the reef

only occasionally or to exploit special circumstances. Some others, finally, end up being part and parcel of the ecosystem of the coral reef, never leaving it.
The true pelagics include marine mammals such as whales and dolphins; reptiles such as turtles and sea snakes; large filter-feeders such as mantas and whale sharks, and other cartilagineous fish such as spotted eagle rays and several sharks. Their arrival to the outer reef walls is generally linked to specific phenomena such as a large concentration of their usual prey or the mating season. Several bony predator fish (especially barracudas, jacks and tarpons) and some sharks (gray reef, silvertip, blacktip) show strong territorial behavior, while others are more connected to the seabed (whitetip, nurse and leopard shark). Without exception, however, denizens of the open ocean are characterized by a powerful musculature (whose efficiency is optimized in several tuna and shark species by endothermia or "warm blood"), a spectacularly evolved hydrodynamic body shape - very different from that of reef species proper - and a sophisticated propulsive apparatus. Finally, as a general rule species coming from the open sea are much larger in size than the inhabitants of the reef itself.

A World in Balance

Rapid variations in water temperature, its transparency

(mostly due to the presence of sediments near estuaries), and its salinity (with the huge flooding of fresh water near estuaries or following torrential rains) can limit or even interrupt the development of coral reefs. These are natural occurrences which have always happened and which will naturally give rise to mixed habitats of great ecological importance like mangrove forests and brackish environments. However, irreparable damage to this exceptionally delicate ecosystem is today inextricably linked to human activities such as intensive fishing (endangered or severely depleted species include sharks, reef fishes, seahorses and sea cucumbers for the food market and Chinese traditional medicine, lobsters for the tourist industry, shrimps for export), excessive coral removal (for industrial and building uses), the immission of severely polluting substances (related to off-shore and coastal mining operations, the shipping of toxic substances, cyanide fishing for the aquarium trade, liquid sewage disposal from heavily populated coastal towns), and fishing with poison and explosives (still going on more or less unchecked throughout most of South East Asia). Plastic garbage at sea kills more than one million seabirds, at least 100.000 marine mammals and an incalculable number of fishes each year. The equivalent of more than 21 million oil barrels ends up in the oceans every year through human intervention - from factories, illegal dumping by oil tankers at sea and general industrial pollution. Collateral damage - fish and marine mammals killed and then thrown away on the spot because of no commercial interest - amounts to more than 20 million tons a year. More recently, the danger posed to coral reefs by the irrefutable climate changes taking place in our world and by ever-growing carbon dioxide immissions in the atmosphere has become even more evident. The phenomenon of "coral bleaching", in which zooxanthellae die off and the colony discolores and dies, has occasionally reached alarming proportions and is very well known to divers worldwide. In 1998 more than 75% of the world's coral reefs were affected and about 60% were wiped off - albeit temporarily. Despite several new fascinating discoveries and active scientific research being currently done on the world's reefs - *Conus* seashells venom has resulted in the production of a painkiller one thousand times stronger than morphine, deep-water sea sponges show great promise in the treatment of human tumors - the pillaging continues, and most coral reefs are not expected to survive man's folly for another century.

Coral Shapes and Structures

Calcareous coral colonies display a great variety of shapes whose surprising diversity brilliantly contributes to the reef's unmistakable look of "articulated disorder." A colony's structure is strongly influenced not only by the species it belongs to but also by the action of waves and the intensity of currents to which it is subjected. Delicately branched forms and leaf-shaped ones prefer to grow in deep and sheltered lagoons, where currents are minimal; large globular colonies - often observed where the wave action is more intense - sometimes form authentic micro-atolls several meters in diameter as the central nucleus dies off and the colony expands toward the edges. Colonies with short, robust branches that facilitate the feeding of polyps by slowing the passage of water are instead more commonly observed in shallow, surge-prone, turbulent waters, where more delicate shapes would have a hard time staying intact. Labyrinthine, brain-like structures are in fact exquisite natural engineering feats, designed to channel and slow down the passing of water, funnelling it towards the open polyps.

Detail of a branching colony of *Tubastrea micrantha* with several polyps open and feeding.

Close-up of a strongly convoluted colony of *Echinopora pacificus* with the polyps expanded.

Close-up of a rounded colony of *Favites abdita* with retracted polyps.

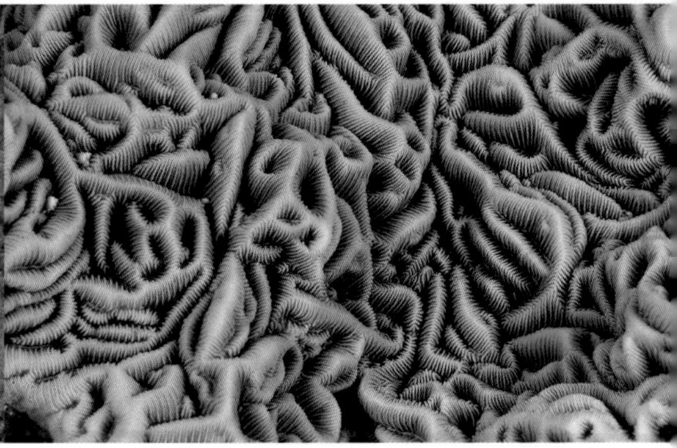

The strongly corrugate surface of an encrusting colony of *Pachyseris rugosa*.

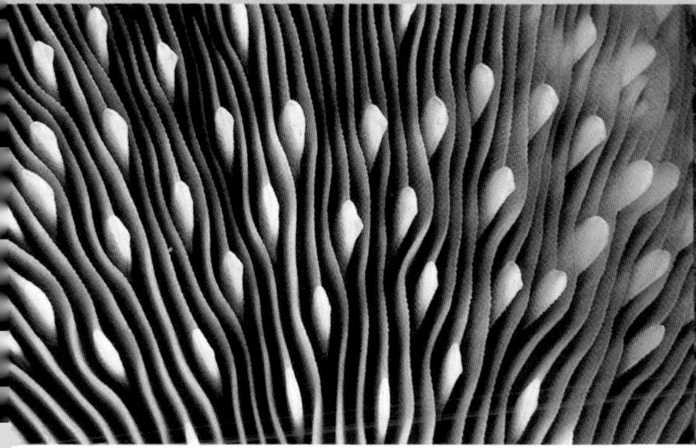

Close-up of a *Fungia* sp. colony with the polyps retracted. The channelled structure is evident.

Close-up of a *Fungia* sp. colony with the tentacles expanded in the current.

A delicate colony of the Lace Coral *Stylaster* sp. This brittle species is restricted to sheltered caves.

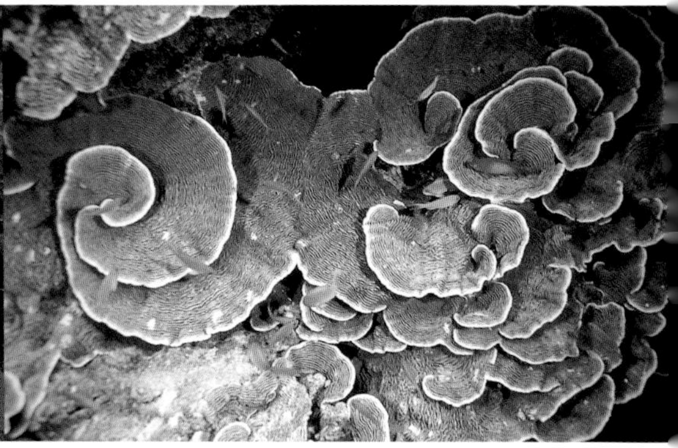

A spectacular, broad-leaved colony of *Turbinaria reniformis.*

The convolute surface of the rounded brain coral *Lobophyllia hemprichii.*

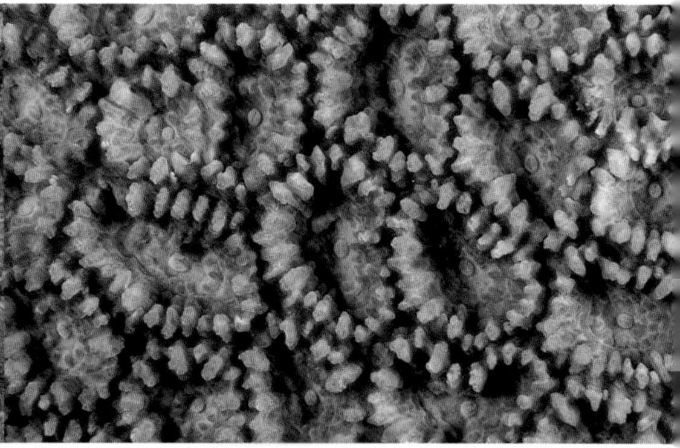

Close-up of a colony of *Favites* sp. with expanded polyps feeding in the current.

Coral Polyps

A single polyp embodies the living part of madreporic or stony coral colonies. Once inflated, it looks in section like a gelatinous sac with a mouth on top, encircled by a crown of tentacles. Specialized cells called nematocysts found on the tentacles can often deliver a powerful sting, even to humans, paralizying prey they come in contact with and carrying it to the oral opening. This activity can be clearly observed at night, particularly when currents are present. The skeletal component at the base of the polyp - into which the sac collapses during daylight - is called the calyx. Its growth basically determines the colony's rate of growth. Branching corals can grow as much as 30 centimeters a year, while roundish, dome-shaped colonies confine themselves to a few millimeters per year. Some of the bigger colonies encountered on undisturbed, remote reefs can be hundreds of thousands of years old! Observed at night and up close, coral polyps not only offer images of exceptional beauty but also essential details for recognizing the species to which the colony belongs.

Extended polyps of an encrusting colony belonging to the species *Galaxea fascicularis*.

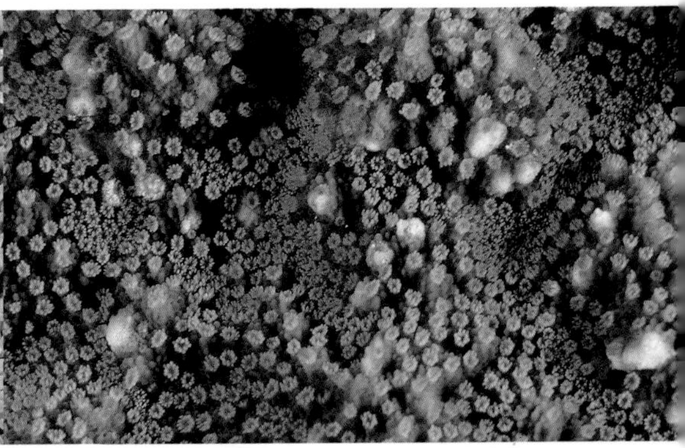

These delicately colored expanded polyps belong to a dome-shaped *Porites* sp. colony.

The abstract beauty of the inflated polyps of a *Galaxea astreata* colony.

The unmistakable, daily active, perennially pulsating "mouths" of *Xenia actuosa* colonies..

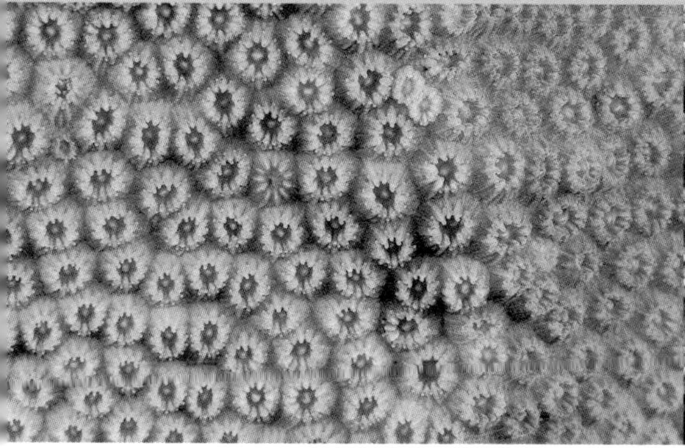

Close-up of a dome-shaped colony of *Porites lobata* with semi-open polyps.

Another example of *Galaxea* sp. polyps about to open. Coral coloration can be extremely variable.

These white-tipped coral polyps probably belong to an unidentified *Galaxea* species.

Kidney- or anchor-shaped polyps of *Euphyllia ancora* are easily identified while diving.

Multi-colored polyps belonging to several *Goniopora* species have an unmistakable flower-like appearance.

The unmistakable bright orange polyps and deep pink calyxes of *Tubastrea faulkneri* coral colonies.

Gorgonians or Sea Fans

Gorgonians - also commonly known as sea fans - feature a horny, elastic, exceptionally strong skeleton and usually tend to grow at greater depths compared to hard calcareous corals, far from the action of waves and comparatively more exposed to the play of strong, deep currents. Usually a rich red, purple or yellow, gorgonians are ahermatipic corals, meaning their colonies occur singly and are not reef-builders. Being filtering animals, the colony always grows perpendicular to the current flow to optimize its lacy, fan-like exposed surface, which sometimes exceeds 3 meters in diameter in healthy, undisturbed specimens. In fact, it is not uncommon to observe sea fans growing toward the sea floor or even horizontally because it is the current, rather than light, which determines the colony's orientation. Thin, elastic, deep-dwelling sea whips of the *Juncella* genus also belong to the gorgonian group. *Alcyonacea* (commonly known as soft corals) and gorgonians both belong to the *Octocorallia* subclass, whose colonies' polyps all have eight pinnate tentacles each.

A large sea fan possibly belonging to the genus *Subergorgia*. Sulawesi Sea, Indonesia.

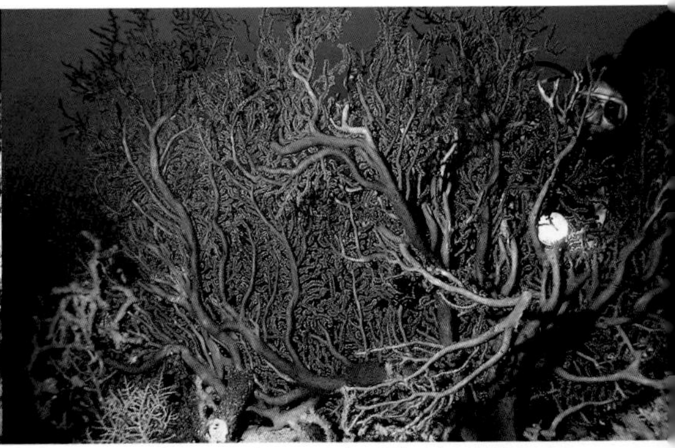

A spectacular gorgonian belonging to the genus *Subergorgia*.Tomini Gulf, Central Sulawesi, Indonesia.

Branching gorgonians and bush-like antipatharians offer shelter to a multitude of juvenile fish. Sulu Sea, Malaysia.

The expanded eight-armed polyps of a gorgonian colony are clearly visible when completely exposed at night.

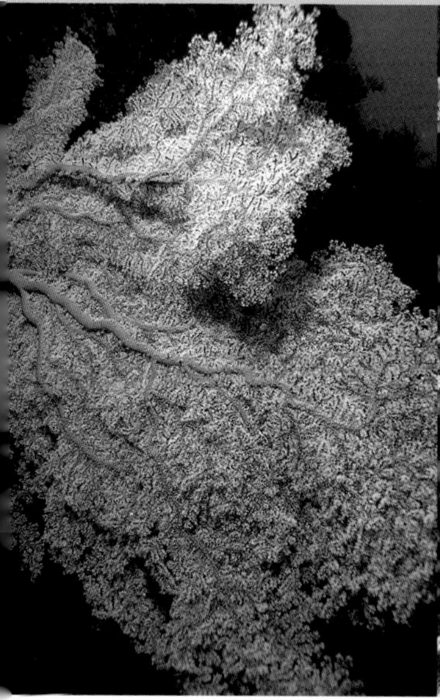

A very large unidentified gorgonian colony, South China Sea, Malaysia.

Close-up of a *Siphonogorgia* sp. colony showing calixes with retracted polyps.

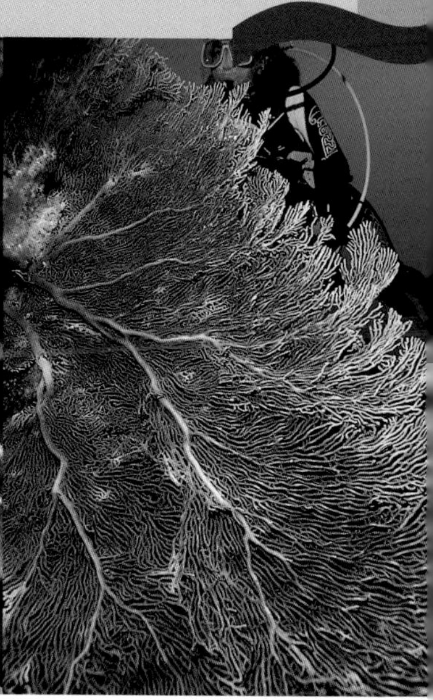

Subergorgia mollis colony, South China Sea, Malaysia.

Large *Ellisella* sp. colony, Tomini Gulf, Central Sulawesi, Indonesia.

A Melithaeid gorgonian colony, Raja Ampat, West Papua, Indonesia.

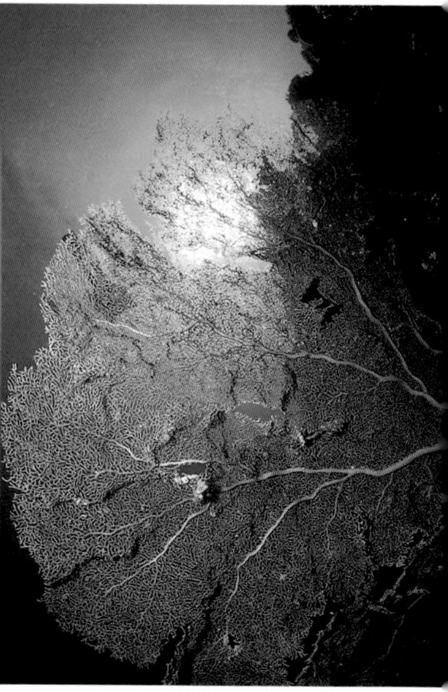

Very large *Subergorgia mollis* colony, South China Sea, Malaysia.

Gallery

The unmistakable harp-like *Ctenocella pectinata*, South China Sea, Malaysia.

Ellisella colony with expanded polyps, Sulawesi Sea, Indonesia.

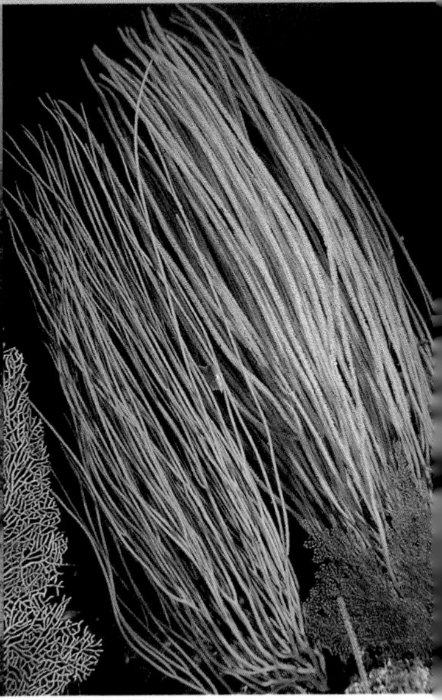

Whip-like *Ellisella* with retracted polyps, Sulawesi Sea, Indonesia.

Gorgonia ventalina colony, Jardines de la Reina, Cuba.

Melithaea sp. colony, Raja Ampat, West Papua, Indonesia.

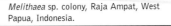

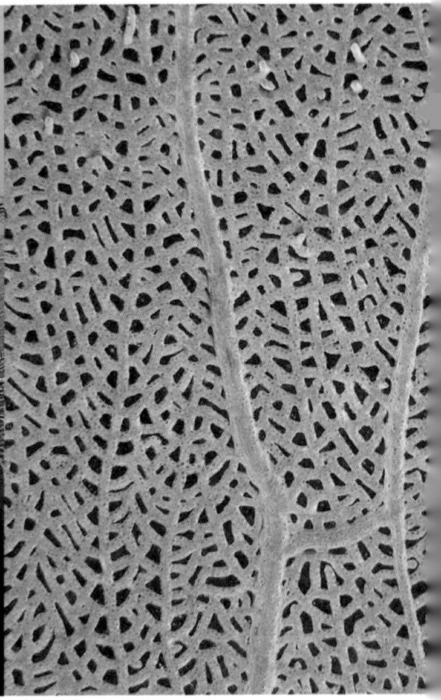

Close-up of a *Gorgonia ventalina* colony, Jardines de la Reina, Cuba.

A huge *Melithaea* sp. colony,
Raja Ampat, West Papua, Indonesia

Soft Corals

Soft corals (*Alcyonacea*) belong - together with gorgonians or sea fans - to the subclass *Octocorallia*. Like sea fans, they are not reef-builders and occur singly, often in close proximity to each other and giving rise to spectacular "living gardens", commonly found along current-swept walls or reef flats. The colonies of polyps in these organisms - often exceptionally colorful and of dazzling beauty, particularly when expanded in a strong current - are supported by a soft fleshy body whose texture is often leathery (as in the Genus *Sarcophyton* and *Sinularia*) and other times flabby and semi-transparent. In the latter case the body may be often "inflated" at will when the current is strong and rich in nutrients (as in the genus *Dendronephthya*, possibly the most often noticed by divers and photographers). In this case, the soft main body structure is reinforced by numerous calcareous spicules embedded within the tissues, which can be clearly seen with the naked eye. Soft corals defend themselves from predators by secreting toxic substances and hosting a multitude of commensal organisms.

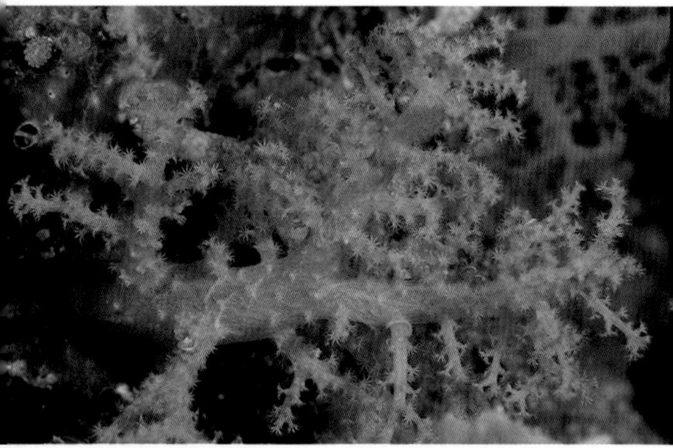

A typical *Scleronephthya sp.* colony. Raja Ampat, West Papua, Indonesia.

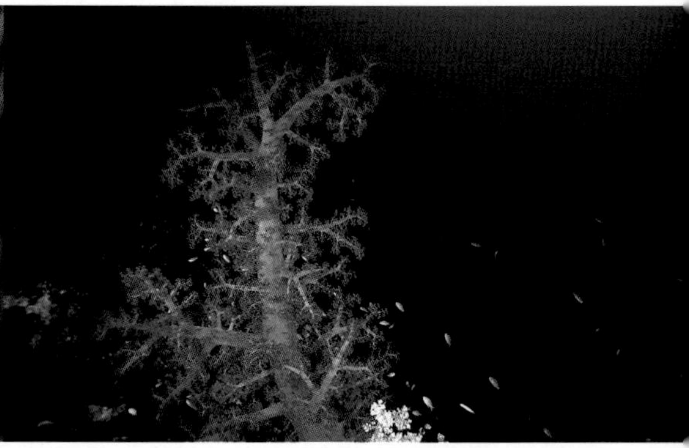

Purple *Dendronephthya* sp. colony, Southern Red Sea, Sudan.

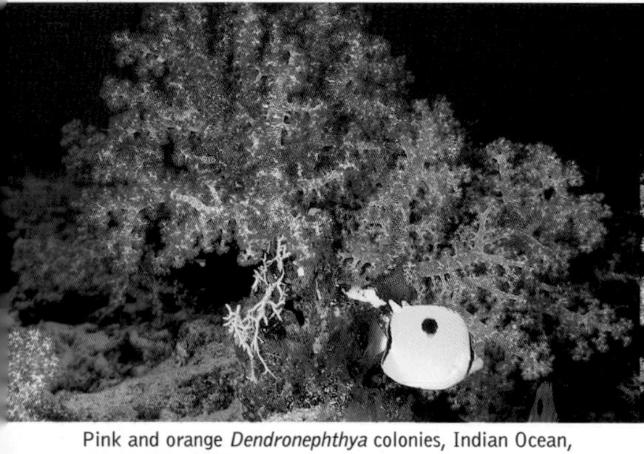

Pink and orange *Dendronephthya* colonies, Indian Ocean, Maldives Archipelago.

Pink *Dendronephthya* sp. colony, Tomini Gulf, Central Sulawesi, Indonesia.

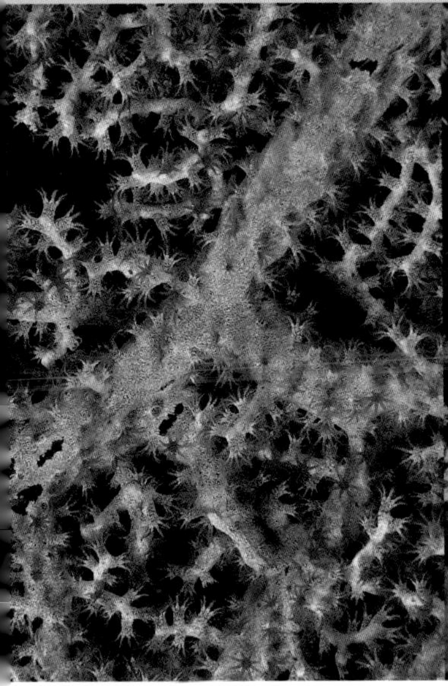

Pink *Scleronephthya* colony, Sulu Sea, Sabah, Malaysia.

Dendronephthya colonies, Northern Red Sea, Egypt.

Pink *Dendronephthya* colony, South China Sea, Malaysia.

Scleronephthya sp., Northern Red Sea, Egypt.

Unidentified species, Pulau Sipadan, Malaysia.

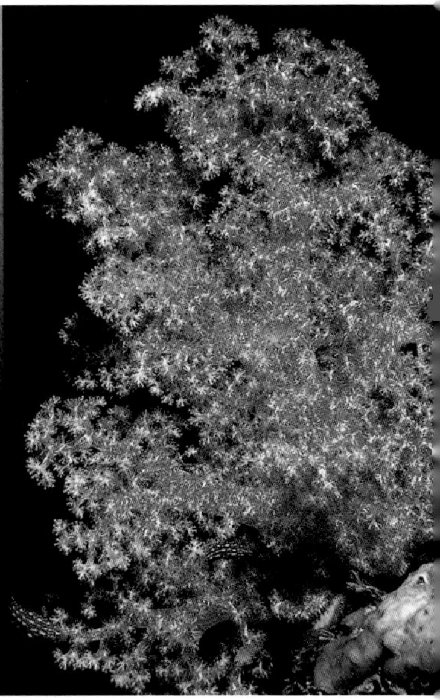

Pink *Scleronephthya* colony, Indian Ocean, Maldives.

Gallery

Expanded *Dendronephthya* sp. colonies, Southern Red Sea, Sudan.

Expanded *Dendronephthya* colony, Southern Red Sea, Sudan.

Expanded *Scleronephthya* colony, Indian Ocean, Maldives Archipelago.

Clearly visible, the calcareous spicules embedded in the tissues of soft corals are called *sclerites*.

Close-up of sclerites in a *Dendronephthya* colony, Northern Red Sea, Egypt.

Branching *Dendronephthya* colony, Pulau Sipadan, Malaysia.

Dendronephthya soft coral,
Pulau Sipadan, Sulawesi Sea, Malaysian Borneo

Sponges

Counting more than 10,000 species, almost all of them marine, sponges represent one of the most important groups of invertebrates. They compete with corals in the more brightly sunlit sections of the reef and occupy their own unique ecological niches at greater depths. They are filtering animals that ingest the surrounding water into their bodies through countless tiny holes (invisible to the naked eye and named *ostia*) and then expel it through a smaller number of bigger holes (called *oscula*) that are quite easy to discern with the naked eye. Reef sponges vary enormously in size and shape and many prove rigid and "fiberglassy" to the touch since their tissues are impregnated with needle-like spicules composed of silica. Despite being very simple beings - unchanged since the Devonian Age, about 450 million years ago - sponges are very efficient feeders: a medium sized individual is able to filter several thousand liters of water every day. Many host symbiont algae providing them with extra nutrients. Sponges are very variable and almost impossible to identify without microscopic examination of the spicules.

Leucetta sp., Indo-Pacific.

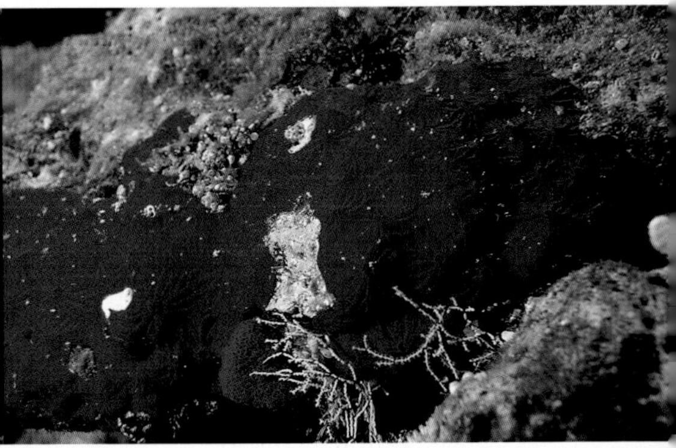

Diplastrella megastellata, Western Atlantic.

Unidentified species, Indo-Pacific.

Unidentified species, Western Atlantic.

Cribrochalina sp., Indo-Pacific.

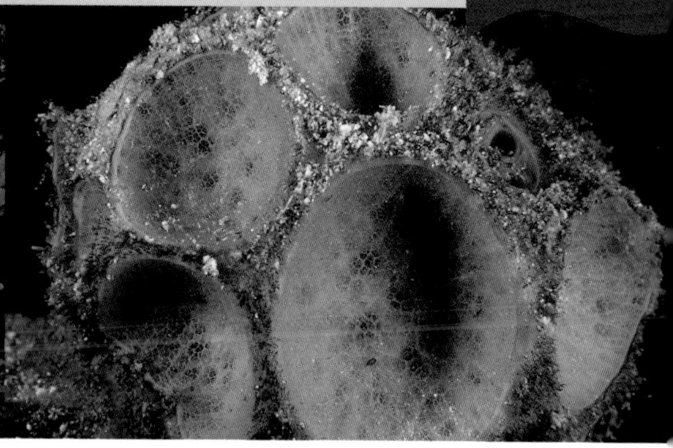

Cynachira sp., Indo-Pacific.

Niphates digitalis, Western Atlantic.

Aplysina archeri, Western Atlantic.

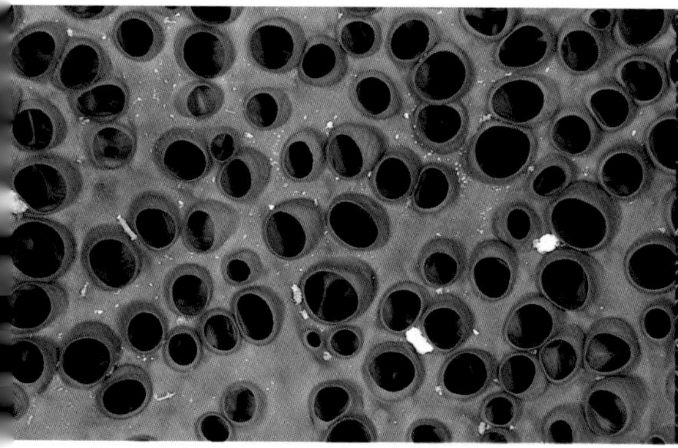

Detail close-up of *Jaspis* sp., Indo-Pacific.

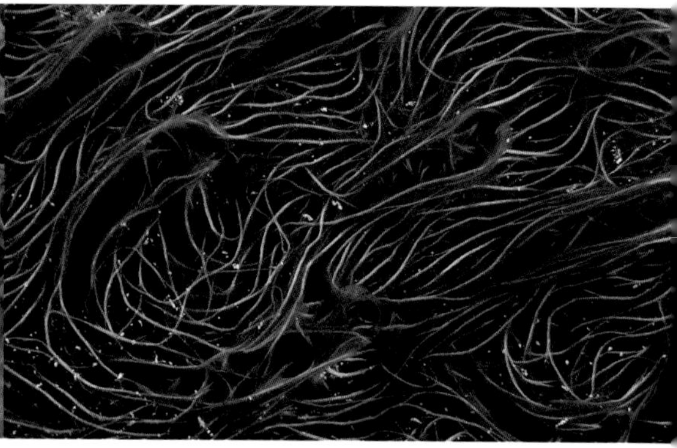

Detail close-up of *Nara nemathifera*, Indo-Pacific.

Gallery

Aplysina fistularis,
Western Atlantic.

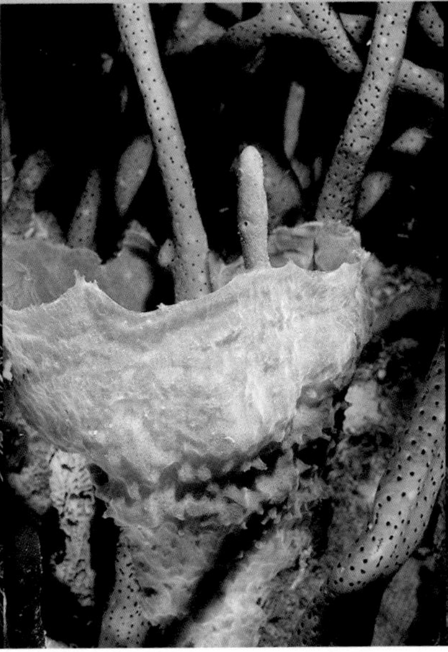

Niphates digitalis,
Western Atlantic.

Xestospongia sp.,
Indo-Pacific.

Callyspongia sp.,
Indo-Pacific.

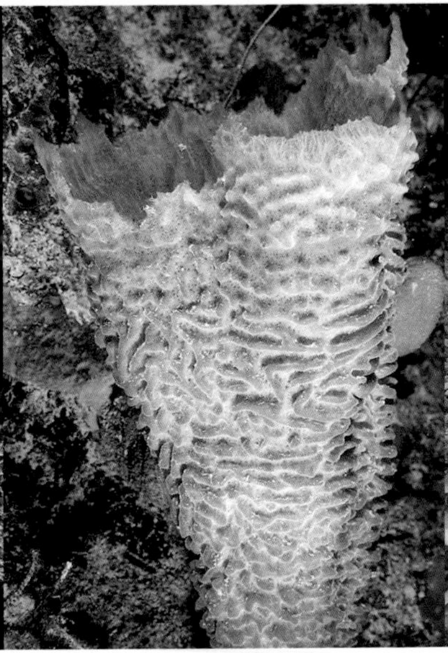

Callyspongia plicifera,
Western Atlantic.

Cribrochalina sp.,
Indo-Pacific.

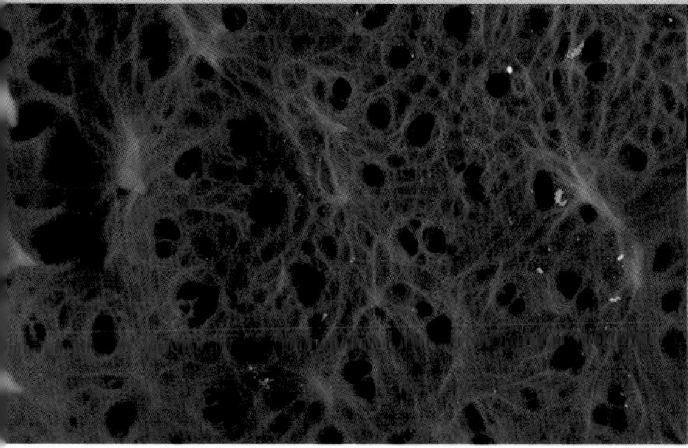

Close-up detail of unidentified species, Western Atlantic

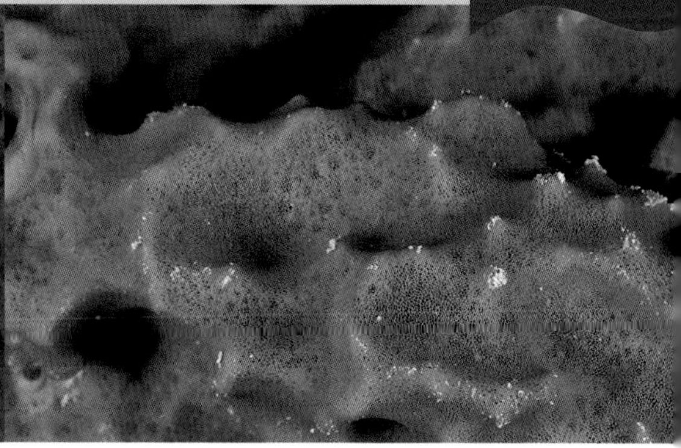

Close-up detail of *Clathria* sp., Indo-Pacific

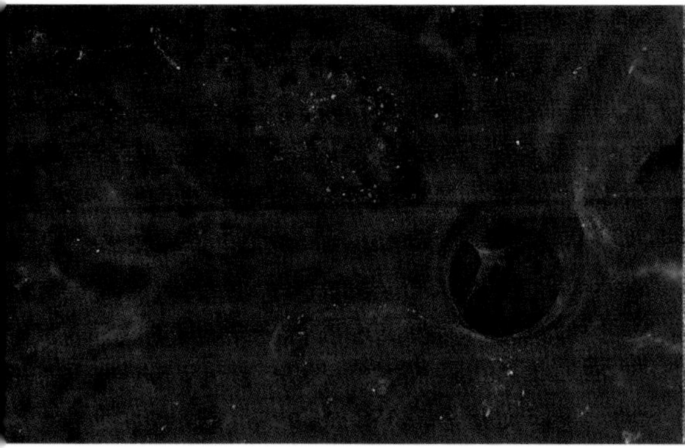

Close-up detail of *Diplastrella* sp., Western Atlantic.

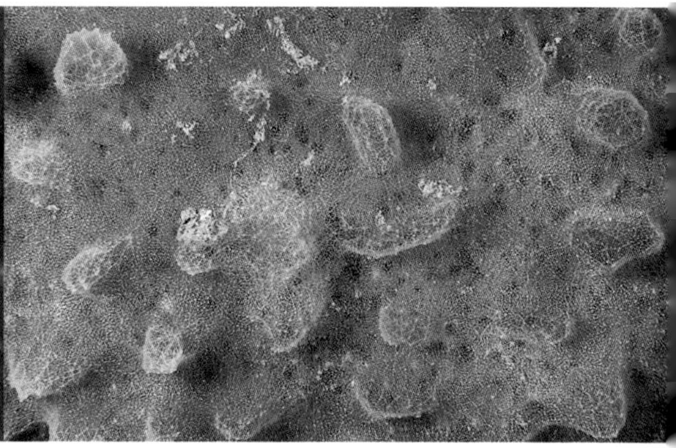

Close-up detail of *Niphates digitalis*, Western Atlantic.

Theonella cylindrica, Indo-Pacific.

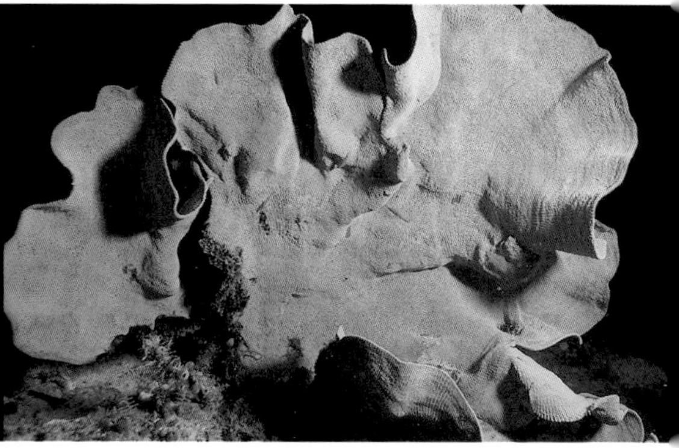

Ianthella basta, Indo-Pacific.

Unidentified species, Indo-Pacific.

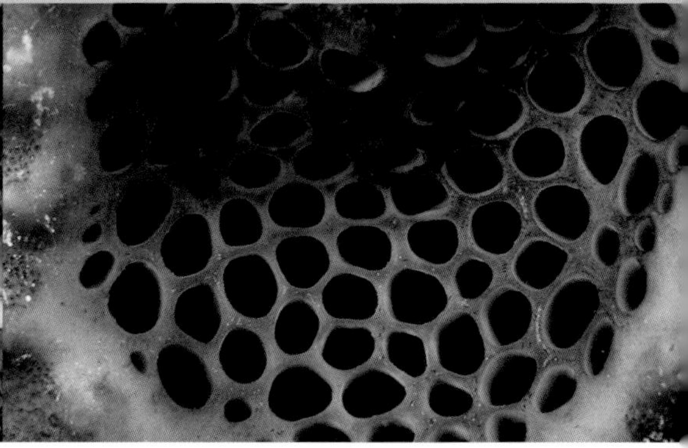

Close-up detail of *Jaspis* sp., Indo-Pacific.

Cribrochalina sp., Indo-Pacific.

Xestospongia testudinaria, Indo-Pacific.

Cribrochalina sp., Indo-Pacific.

Xestospongia testudinaria, Indo-Pacific.

Unidentified species, Indo-Pacific.

Verongula gigantea, Western Atlantic.

Haliclona sp., Indo-Pacific.

Stelletinopsis isis, Indo-Pacific.

Xestospongia testudinaria, Indo-Pacific.

Amphimedon sp., Indo-Pacific.

Ascidians or Sea Squirts

These humble and often overlooked – but extremely important - organisms can be commonly observed on coral reefs as both colonies and individuals. They are more or less solidly fixed to the substrate and are rather jelly-like to the touch, although several species are quite firm and even leathery. Generally small, ascidians come in all sorts of shapes, and even if the basic one is that of a tiny open-topped barrel, large and often quite colorful encrusting colonies can be easily mistaken for sponges or other sessile organisms. They are filtering animals, like sponges and bivalves, that ingest water through an orifice on the upper siphon, filter it through a simple pharynx, and finally expel it through the lower siphon. Water current is generated by the beating of innumerable microscopic hairs (*cilia* in scientific terms) that line the inside of the ascidian. Strange as it may sound, ascidians, commonly known as sea squirts, may be the direct ancestors of vertebrates despite their primitive character, since their larval tail is stiffened with a rod of cells just like the embryonic backbone of a vertebrate.

Atriolum robustum, Indo-Pacific.

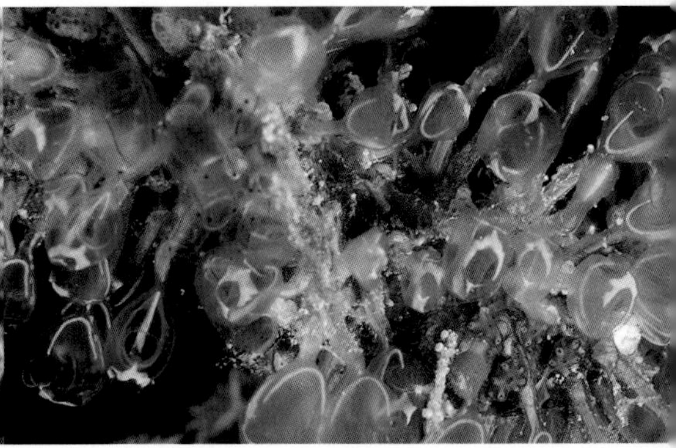

Clavelina sp., Indo-Pacific.

Clavelina robusta, Indo-Pacific.

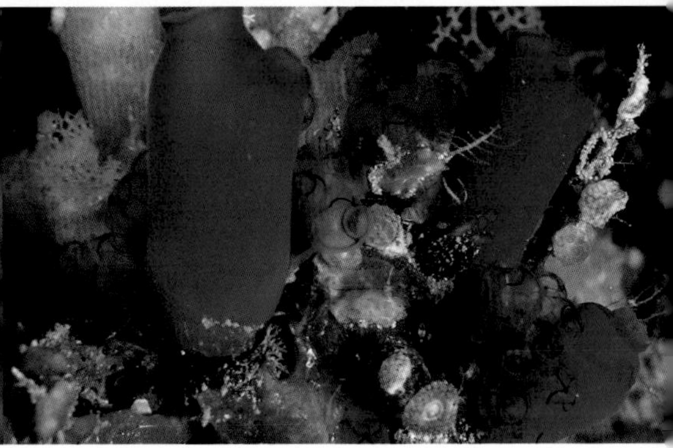

Rhopalaea crassa, Indo-Pacific.

Didemnum molle, Indo-Pacific.

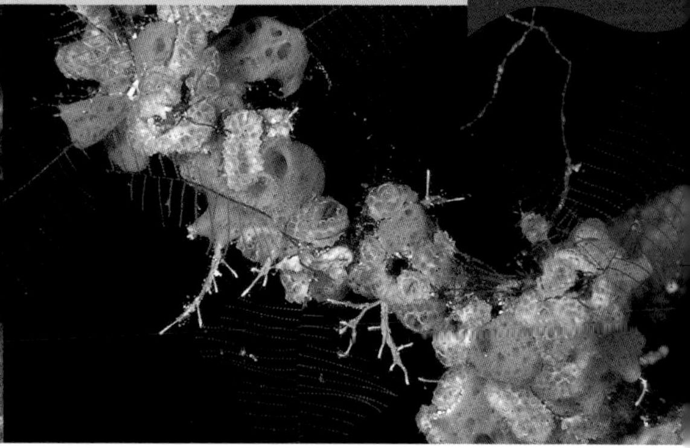

Didemnid tunicates, Indo-Pacific.

Clavelina flava, Indo-Pacific.

Didemnid tunicates, Indo-Pacific.

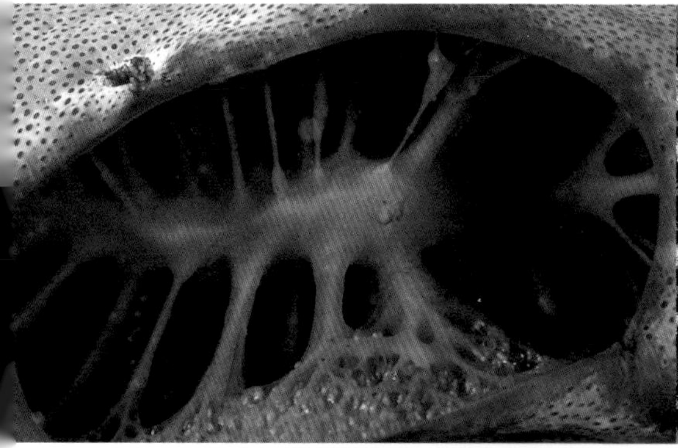

The cloacal aperture of *Didemnum molle*, Indo-Pacific.

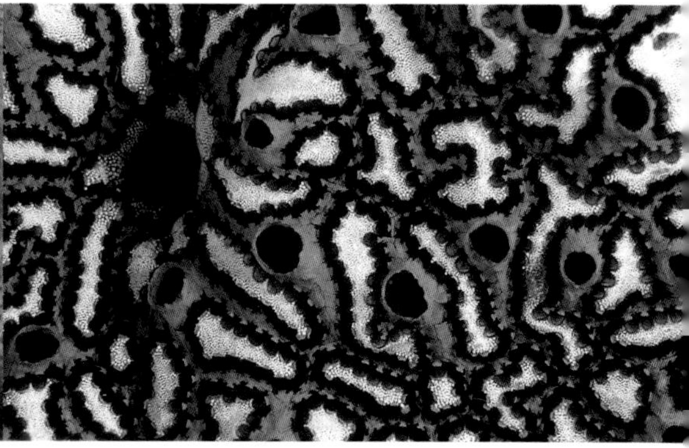

Botrylloides sp. colony, Indo-Pacific.

Rhopalaea sp.,
Indo-Pacific.

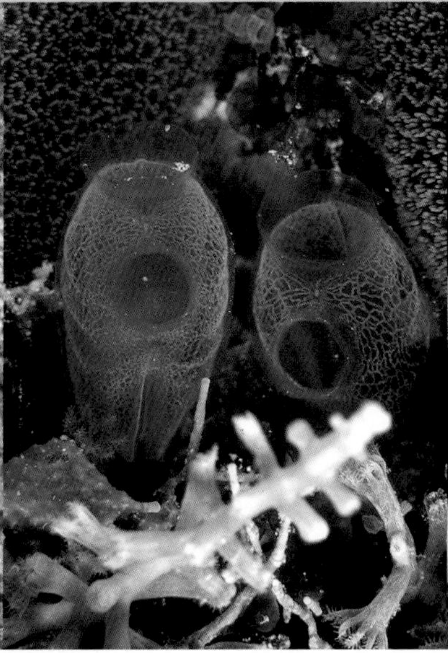
Rhopalaea sp.,
Indo-Pacific.

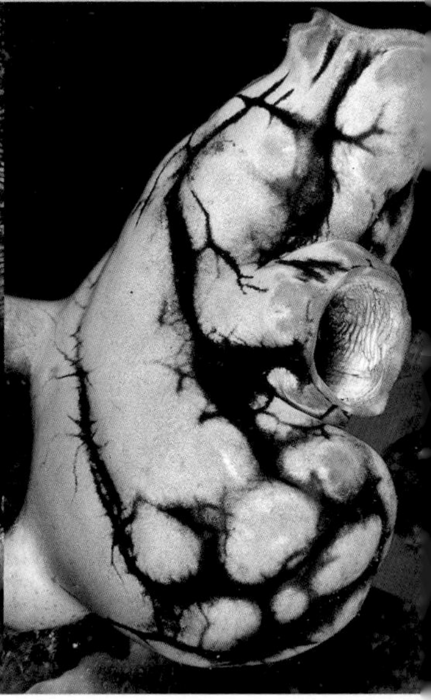
Polycarpa aurata,
Indo-Pacific.

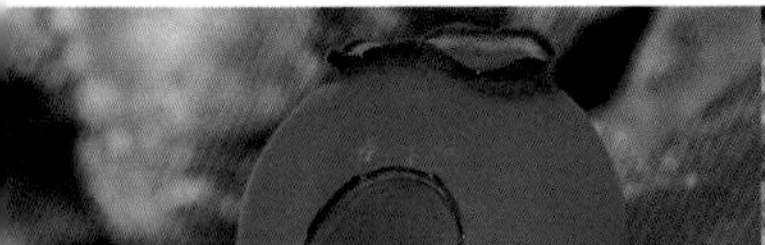
Rhopalaea sp.,
Indo-Pacific.

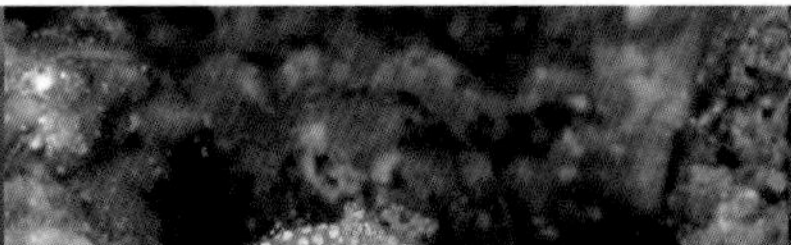
Possibly Phlebobranch ascidian,
Raja Ampat, West Papua.

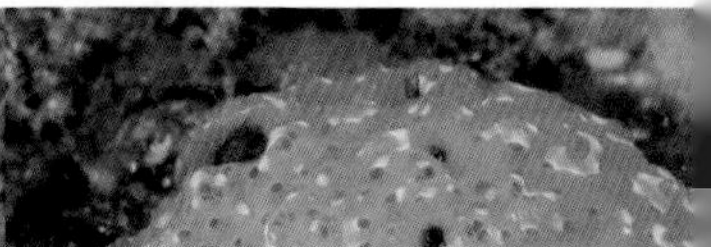
Aplidium colony,
Hawai'i.

Goby on *Rhopalaea* sp. ascidian, Pulau Lankayan, Sulu Sea, Malaysian Borneo

An Ecosystem in Danger

The reef ecosystem is currently found along the coasts of at least 109 countries in the world, yet it has been calculated that the coral reef in at least 93 of these has already been gravely damaged or even destroyed. The coral reefs distributed over 60 percent of the Indian Ocean and Red Sea, 25 percent of the Pacific Ocean, and 15 percent of the Caribbean are now severely endangered and risk disappearance. Pelagic and coastal marine life is being overexploited at a terrifying rate all over the world. The data are staggering: 94 million tons of fish globally taken yearly, with 17 million tons by China alone (the global total was just 19 million tons in 1950), 52% of commercial marine species being overexploited to the non-recovering point, 25% already having been fished beyond the no-return point, 12 of the 16 great world fishing areas to an all-time low level in harvesting with a 20% net loss since 1990. Tuna, cod, marlin, oceanic whitetip and swordfish populations have been reduced by 90% during the past sixty years. Coral reefs - and their attending environments like mangrove forests - are at the foundation of marine life and are being directly affected by this dramatic situation.

Mangroves alone act as an all-important nursery for the juveniles of more than 85% of commercial fish species in the tropics, and yet less than 0,5% of global marine environments is currently protected by law. If these environments are damaged beyond recovery they would take with them an incalculable number of species, ironically including - in the end - the very humans which are the principal cause of their spiralling rate of destruction. On the other hand, a 2006 report by the Environment Program of the United Nations has recently calculated that the cost of protecting a square kilometer of coral reef would only amount to about 775 US $ per year while generating a net gain of about 100.000 - 600.000 US $ (depending on the area) to the local economy, creating job opportunities for literally millions of people. In fact, the worldwide creation of Marine Protected Areas and the dive industry involved in the coral reef environment globally generate a direct or indirect profit of more than 30 billion US $ per year, a huge sum which has to be reckoned with by politicians and governments.

The following are a few simple suggestions to travelers and divers, which are meant to protect the reef habitat and minimize traumas to an ecosystem which is as complex as it is delicate. Remember, divers can do a lot to protect what they love most - we can and do make a difference!

How Can You Protect the Reef?

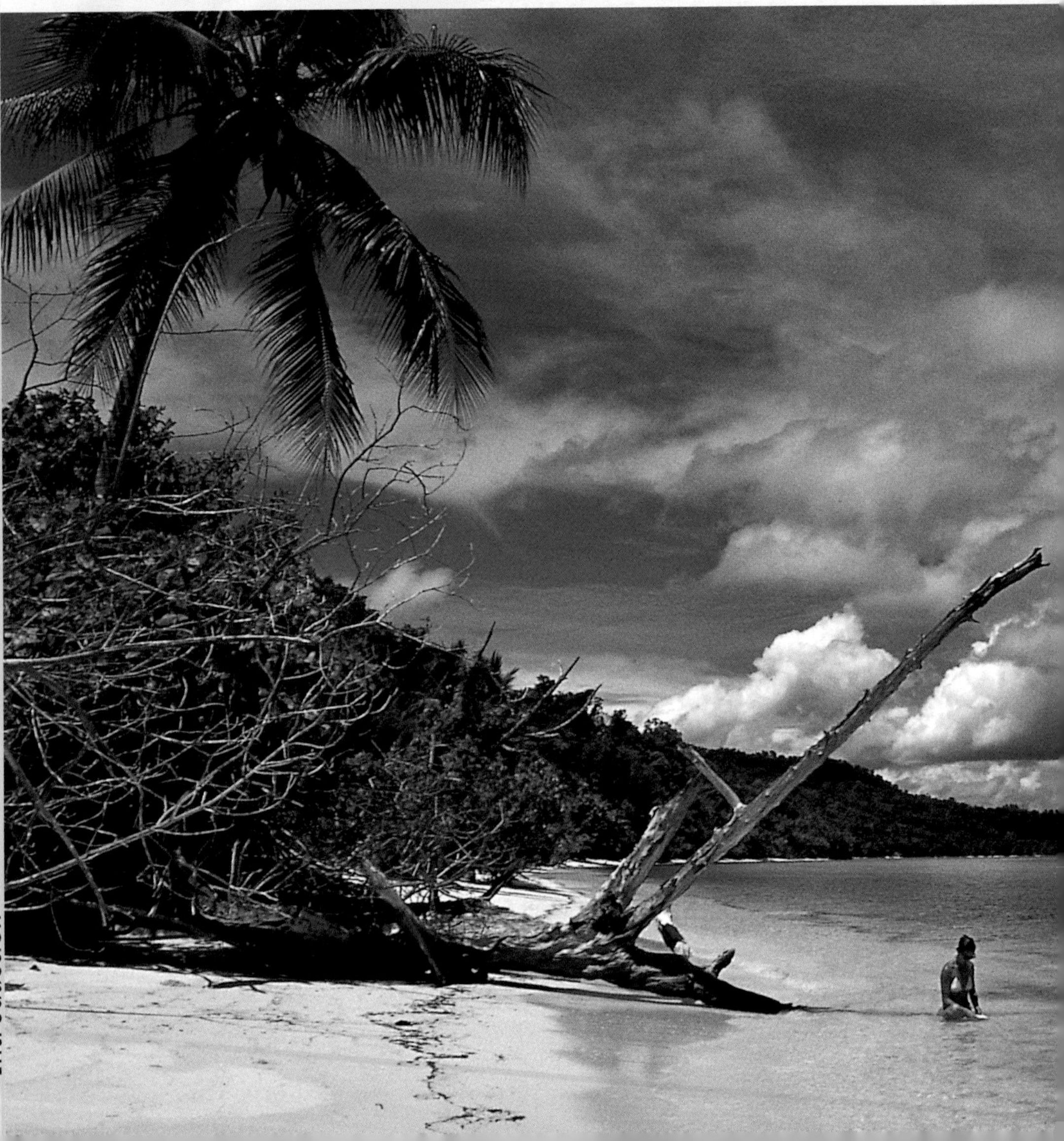

Don't buy products made from turtle shells anywhere in the world. For the same reason, avoid purchasing souvenirs made from shark jaws, shells (especially tritons) or coral.

Don't eat dishes prepared with the meat, eggs or fat of a turtle, including the infamous soup. This is especially true for travelers in Indonesia and Bali where there still exists a flourishing and semilegal trade in turtle meat, targeted exclusively at tourists.

Don't eat dishes prepared with shark meat such as the infamous sharkfin soup. Every species of shark found in tropical and subtropical waters is in grave danger from fishermen who supply the world's Chinese restaurants. Over 100 million sharks are killed every year to supply the trade in shark fins.

Don't eat lobsters in excessive quantities just because you can do so in the tropics. The appetite and provincialism of Western tourists have brought about an alarming decline of this crustacean in almost all tropical waters.

Don't buy traditional Chinese medical remedies, especially those prepared using reef animals. Beyond their doubtful efficacy (and occasional outright danger to one's health), the trade in them severely threatens many fish species, from sharks to seahorses.

Don't buy or use shark-derived medicinal products such as immunitary system boosters and the like. These are of very dubious scientifical value and a main source of shark harvesting in Central America.

Don't walk on the reef, even in rubber-soled shoes. Every step would destroy the work of millions of creatures toiling over hundreds of years. Limit romantic moonlit walks to the beach, where it is also cozier and much more comfortable – especially if you want to sit down.

Don't touch corals and reef inhabitants when diving. Besides risking an ugly wound or allergic reaction, you could destroy a stony coral colony's hundred years' labor in a few seconds. For the same reason, be very careful where you flap your fins and how you move about. Practice on your buoyancy skills!

Don't carry off living or dead organisms from a submerged reef or beach. Stuff that looks wonderful right there will quickly start to smell and become half-forgotten dead weight collecting dust at home. Corals, shells and starfish are far more beautiful left where they are and, above all, left alive.

Don't harass, disturb or endanger marine life, neither for petting nor for taking pictures. Avoid touching sleeping fish and handling marine life. You're a guest down there and none of that is yours – take away only photos, leave behind only bubbles.

CHONDRICHTHYES

Cartilaginous Fishes

Sharks and rays are cartilaginous fishes belonging to the Class Chondrichthyes, of which they form the subclass Elasmobranchii, in contrast to the Osteichthyes, or bony fishes. The structural features that distinguish the Chondrichthyes are the gills (simple slits varying in number from five to seven, whereas in bony fishes they are always protected by a bony covering), the stiff and laminar fins (without bony inner rays), the skin (a layer of derma in which are embedded innumerable enameled tooth-like placoid scales) and the skeleton (which is made up of strong cartilage rather than hard bone). Sharks and rays also lack the swim bladder and regulate their balance in water through their highly evolved body structure and their large liver, rich in oils. ~ **U/W Photo Tips:** Most of these species make spectacular if rather difficult to approach or altogether uncommon subjects. Given their average size, a lens ranging from 20 to 50mm is advisable: since most big species are framed on an open sea background, while smaller ones are often photographed among colorful corals, a measure of stealth and a judicious use of ambient light are needed.

WHALE SHARK
Rhincodon typus

Distribution: Worldwide in tropical and subtropical waters.
Size: Up to 14 meters, but on average much smaller, about 6-10 meters. May weigh up to 15 tonnes.
Habitat: Pelagic, usually close to surface but capable of diving deep; seasonally in coastal waters and in specific localities, often in large concentrations.
Life Habits: Feeds on plankton and shoals of sardines, but can ingest larger fish like tuna. A filter feeder, completely harmless to humans and severely endangered throughout its range. This is the world's largest and heaviest fish.

TASSELLED WOBBEGONG
Eucrossorhinus dasypogon

Distribution: Tropical Central Indo-Pacific. from West Papua to Australia.
Size: Up to 3 meters but usually smaller.
Habitat: Coastal and outer reefs on sand and coral rubble bottoms from 1 to 15 meters deep.
Life Habits: Body broad, with wide pectoral fins, large and flattened head, small eyes and large terminal mouth with fringe of dermal appendages. Livery in shades of brown, with broad banding and many small rosettes, originating the common name of carpet sharks. A benthic ambush predator, usually observed lying motionless on the sea bottom.

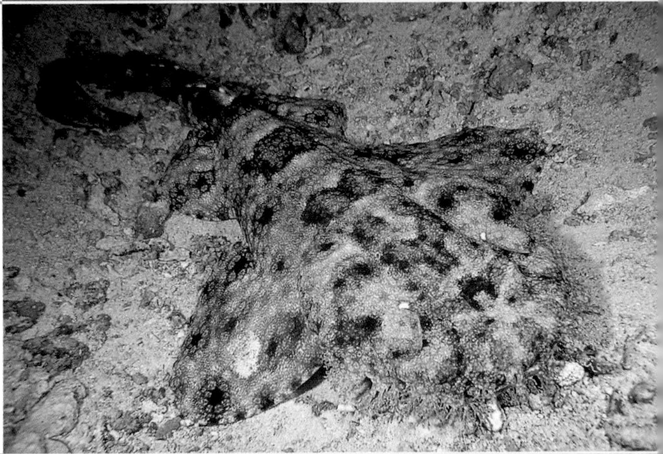

SPOTTED WOBBEGONG
Orectolobus maculatus

Distribution: Tropical Central Indo-Pacific from Southern Japan to Australia.
Size: Up to 320 centimeters.
Habitat: Coastal and outer reefs on sand and rubble bottoms from 1 to 100 meters deep, occasionally in shallow tidal pools.
Life Habits: A typical wobbegong or carpet shark which can be distinguished from the preceding species by the clustered, unbranched tendrils present on the snout. All wobbegongs are benthic ambush predators capable of inflicting severe bites and should never be molested despite their apparent laziness.

ORNATE WOBBEGONG
Orectolobus ornatus

Distribution: Tropical Western Pacific from Southern Japan to Australia.
Size: Up to 3 meters.
Habitat: A bottom dweller associated with rocky, algae-covered areas. Occasionally encountered in tidal pools and in the intertidal zone.
Life Habits: Can be identified by the flap-like tendrils at the tip of the snout; all wobbegongs have broad, flat bodies with small eyes and cryptic coloration. During the day motionless on the sea bottom, ambushing passing prey; at night more active. Responsible like all wobbegongs of unprovoked attacks on waders.

COBBLER WOBBEGONG
Sutorectus tentaculatus

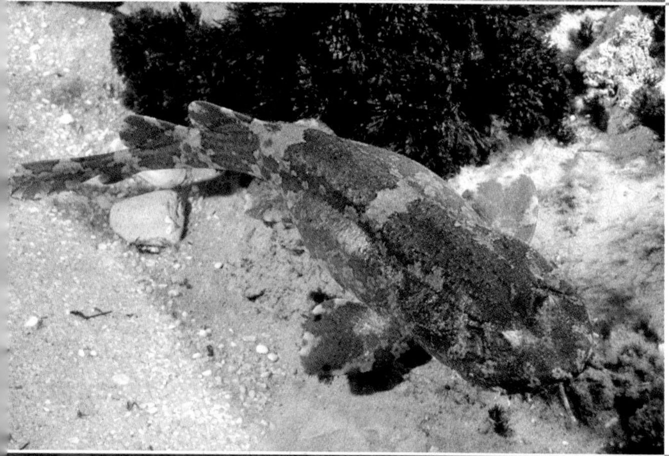

Distribution: Tropical Western Pacific, mostly in Australian waters.
Size: Up to 100 centimeters.
Habitat: Rocky reefs from 1 to 50 meters deep, often in tidal pools.
Life Habits: Smaller than other carpet sharks and with a less flattened head and body; long tendrils at the tip of the snout, body pale brown with darker saddles, wart-like bumps on head. A static, benthic ambush predator, like all other carpet sharks this species also sports long, specialized, fang-like front teeth for grasping its prey in surprise attacks.

GREY BAMBOO SHARK
Chiloscyllium punctatum

Distribution: Tropical Indo-Pacific from Japan to Australia and from India to Indonesia.
Size: Up to just over 1 meter.
Habitat: Coral reefs in shallow water and intertidal pools.
Life Habits: Commonly observed during the day under coral formations, more active at night. Feeds on small fish and crustaceans. Very shy, will however readily bite if disturbed or harassed. Juveniles sport a very distinctive, flashy, black and white banded livery.

RAJA AMPAT EPAULETTE SHARK
Hemiscyllium freycineti

Distribution: Extremely localized in Raja Ampat, West Papua, Indonesia.
Size: Up to 70 centimeters.
Habitat: Coastal reefs on sheltered sand and rubble bottoms from 1 to 5 meters.
Life Habits: One of several local races of beautiful, elegant, harmless bamboo sharks often observed at night on Indo-Pacific coastal reefs. Body elongated, with paddle-like pectoral fins, ribbon-like tail and many brown spots on a pale background. Commonly observed "ambling" on the substrate while looking for benthic crustaceans and mollusks.

EPAULETTE SHARK
Hemiscyllium ocellatum

Distribution: Very localized, in Western Pacific waters from Papua New Guinea to Northern Australia.
Size: Up to 107 centimeters.
Habitat: Sand bottoms on coastal reefs, often among corals, from 1 to 10 meters.
Life Habits: Another locally common bamboo shark commonly observed resting among branching coral colonies during the day or "walking" along the substrate while hunting at night. Like several very similar species sharing the same general area this small shark sports a darker and larger round blotch above the pectorals.

LEOPARD SHARK
Stegostoma fasciatum

Distribution: Red Sea, Indian Ocean, Central and Western Pacific.
Size: Up to 3.5 meters, half of which is tail. Usually about 2.5 meters.
Habitat: Commonly observed on sand and rubble bottoms at the foot of reefs and on terraces up to 70 meters deep.
Life Habits: Sluggish during the day, more active at night: feeds on sleeping fish, cephalopods and crustaceans. Harmless if not harassed. Juveniles sport a banded livery which is at the origin of its other common name, "zebra shark".

TAWNY NURSE SHARK
Nebrius ferrugineus

Distribution: Red Sea, Indian Ocean, Western Pacific to French Polynesia.
Size: Up to 3.5 meters, usually 2.5.
Habitat: On sand and rubble bottoms, usually in caves or under overhangs, from shallow waters to a depth of 70 meters.
Life Habits: Very sluggish during the day, more active at night. Shy and harmless if unprovoked, but capable of inflicting serious bites. Feeds on fish, cephalopods and crustaceans.In the Atlantic its place is taken by the almost identical *Ginglymostoma cirratum.*

PELAGIC THRESHER SHARK
Alopias oceanicus

Distribution: Tropical Indo-Pacific.
Size: Up to 3.5 meters; the upper lobe of the tail equals the length of the full body.
Habitat: Fully pelagic, sometimes off atolls in the open ocean, from the surface to more than 150 meters deep.
Life Habits: At least two other very similar species; all share big round black eyes, a short snout, small pectoral fins and a huge tail, with which they herd and stun the schools of fish and cephalopods on which they feed. Not aggressive, but threatened troughout its range and very rarely encountered by divers.

MAKO SHARK
Isurus oxyrinchus

Distribution: Worldwide in tropical, subtropical and temperate oceans.
Size: Up to 4 meters and 570 kgs.
Habitat: Pelagic, occasionally observed near coral atolls or outer reefs, from the surface to 150 meters deep.
Life Habits: Stiff, torpedo-shaped body with a steely blue tinge, lunate tail, pointed snout, large black eyes and curved teeth often protruding from gaping mouth. A fast predator which can reach a speed of over 40 kms/h, quite uncommon in coastal waters but responsible of several fatal attacks on humans.

CORAL CATSHARK
Atelomycterus marmoratus

Distribution: Central Indo-Pacific, from the Arabian Sea to Papua New Guinea and from the Philippines to Taiwan .
Size: Up to 70 centimeters.
Habitat: Thick coral reefs and isolated coral patches in shallow water.
Life Habits: Strictly nocturnal, almost impossible to spot in daytime, when it rests in crevices and under overhangs. An active hunter: feeds on small fish and crustaceans. Completely harmless; several more or less similar species, also belonging to different families, but all sharing the same habits and environment.

SILVERTIP SHARK
Carcharhinus albimarginatus

Distribution: Red Sea, Indian Ocean, Central and Western Pacific.
Size: Up to 3 meters.
Habitat: Isolated banks, reefs and shoals in deep water, between 30 and 800 meters deep, rarely near the coast.
Life Habits: A big, stocky deep-water reef shark with a blue-gray body and a diagnostic silver-white border and tip on all fins, including the large caudal fin. Curious and potentially dangerous, often encountered in territorial, resident groups of large females. Severely endangered throughout its range.

BLACKTIP REEF SHARK
Carcharhinus melanopterus

Distribution: Eastern Mediterranean via the Suez Canal, Red Sea, Indian Ocean, Central Indo-Pacific to Hawai'i.
Size: Up to 2 meters, usually 1.6.
Habitat: Juveniles in shallow water and in the intertidal zone; adults further out to sea, but always among coral formations.
Life Habits: Very common, but adults shy and not often seen underwater. Juveniles commonly encountered at dawn or dusk in atoll lagoons and along the shoreline, patrolling in very shallow water. May bite if harassed; unmistakable black tip of dorsal fin is diagnostic.

OCEANIC WHITETIP SHARK
Carcharhinus longimanus

Distribution: Tropical and subtropical.
Size: Up to a maximum of 4 meters.
Habitat: Strictly pelagic, from the surface to 150 meters deep. Occasionally encountered near isolated reefs in the open sea or in coastal waters.
Life Habits: A massive open sea predator, easily recognized by the bright white tip of its huge, rounded fins. Solitary and very dangerous, responsible for several attacks on shipwrecked sailors and downed WWII pilots.Once the most common of all large sized-predators on Earth, it has recently been brought to the brink of extinction by overfishing.

GREY REEF SHARK
Carcharhinus amblyrhynchos

Distribution: Red Sea, Indian Ocean, Western and Central Pacific.
Size: Up to 2.5 meters.
Habitat: Reef faces and drop-offs, sometimes on isolated coral outcrops, between 20 and 70 meters deep.
Life Habits: One of the sharks most commonly encountered by divers in the Indo-Pacific. Markedly territorial, often encountered in large groups of residential females. Potentially dangerous if harassed, will display arching its back and swimming with jerky movements before attacking the intruder in its territory .

WHITETIP REEF SHARK
Triaenodon obesus

Distribution: Red Sea, Indo-Pacific
Size: Up to 2 meters, usually smaller.
Habitat: Strictly associated with coral reefs between 8 and 40 meters. It has been sighted at more than 300 meters.
Life Habits: Very common, usually harmless if not harassed, usually resting on slopes or under coral overhangs during the day. Very active and aggressive during the night, when it actively hunts for sleeping fishes and cephalopods. Easily identified by the slim body, the squared-off blunt head, the "cat's eyes" and the white tip of its dorsal and caudal fins.

BULL SHARK
Carcharhinus leucas

Distribution: Worldwide in tropical and subtropical waters. Often encountered in rivers (Zambezi, Mississippi, Amazon) and in Lake Nicaragua.
Size: Up to 3.5 meters.
Habitat: Coastal waters, estuaries, bays, lagoons, rivers from the surface to 150 meters, often in murky water.
Life Habits: Large, powerful, aggressive and very dangerous, responsible of numerous fatal attacks on humans.Body is very stout, grey on top and paler on the belly; snout short, rounded, with small eyes. First dorsal fin large and falcate.

SILKY SHARK
Carcharhinus falciformis

Distribution: Worldwide in tropical and subtropical waters.
Size: Up to 3.3 meters, usually 2.5.
Habitat: Pelagic, from the surface to 500 meters deep. Often close to isolated rocky or coral outcrops in the open sea.
Life Habits: Very slender, with a long rounded snout and a very smooth skin. Active, fast and stubborn, occasionally aggressive, this shark often damages fishing nets pursuing its prey. Once exceptionally abundant it has become very rare due to overfishing and it is severely threatened throughout its range.

CARIBBEAN REEF SHARK
Carcharhinus perezi

Distribution: Western Atlantic from Florida to Brazil.
Size: Up to 3 meters, usually 2.5.
Habitat: Coral reefs in coastal waters from the surface to 30 meters deep.
Life Habits: Very common throughout its range. Usually encountered while it cruises along the bottom of Caribbean reefs, sometimes observed resting motionless inside caves.Feeds on bony fishes and cephalopods. Normally shy or indifferent to divers, it can become aggressive if excited or provoked.

BRONZE WHALER SHARK
Carcharhinus brachyurus

Distribution: Worldwide in tropical and subtropical waters.
Size: Up to 3 meters but usually 2.5.
Habitat: Open sea, coastal reefs, estuaries and deep-water shoals.
Life Habits: Powerful, active and speedy, potentially dangerous to divers. Back is bronze or gray with a pinkish tinge, belly is sharply separated and invariably white. It feeds on bony fishes, smaller sharks and cephalopods. Commonly encountered in the Atlantic and in Australian waters, but its biology is still not very well known.

LEMON SHARK
Negaprion brevirostris

Distribution: Tropical Atlantic from New Jersey to Southern Brazil and from Senegal to Ivory Coast; Eastern Pacific from Baja California to Ecuador.
Size: Up to 3.2 meters.
Habitat: Shallow waters and close to the surface in bays, lagoons and estuaries.
Life Habits: Yellow-brown, with a snout more broad than long. Mainly nocturnal, sometimes observed resting motionless on the bottom. Feeds on fish, cephalopods and crustaceans. Able to tolerate variations in salinity, potentially dangerous to divers and waders.

TIGER SHARK
Galeocerdo cuvier

Distribution: Worldwide in tropical and subtropical waters.
Size: Up to 8 meters, but on average between 4 and 6 meters.
Habitat: Deep during the day, in shallow water at night, from the surface to 140 meters. Coastal waters and open sea, often in harbors and turbid waters.
Life Habits: Huge, very stocky, with a big falcate caudal fin, tiger-striped when young. The snout is broad and blunt. An opportunistic, nocturnal and solitary feeder which is very rarely encountered by divers, despite being locally abundant.

SCALLOPED HAMMERHEAD
Sphyrna lewini

Distribution: Worldwide in tropical and subtropical waters.
Size: Up to 4.2 meters but usually 2.5.
Habitat: Coastal waters, often found in huge shoals around rocky outcrops far from the continental shelves.
Life Habits: The most commonly encountered hammerhead in tropical waters.Shy and easily disturbed by bubbles even if reputed potentially dangerous. Feeds on bony fishes, smaller sharks, cephalopods and large stingrays. Fished in large numbers and probably threatened throughout its range.

GREAT HAMMERHEAD
Sphyrna mokarran

Distribution: Worldwide in tropical and subtropical waters.
Size: Up to 6 meters, but on average between 4 and 5 meters.
Habitat: Pelagic and in coastal waters, usually close to coral reefs, between the surface and 80 meters.
Life Habits: Rarely encountered underwater by divers but considered by most potentially dangerous. The largest of the hammerheads, it can be identified by the almost straight front edge of the head and the huge, sickle-shaped first dorsal fin.Feeds on bony fishes, cephalopods and large stingrays.

WHITE-SPOTTED GUITARFISH
Rhynchobatus djiddensis

Distribution: Tropical Indo-Pacific.
Size: Up to 3 meters.
Habitat: Sand and rubble bottoms in coastal waters to a depth of 50 meters.
Life Habits: A very large, elongated ray which superficially looks and swims like a true shark: the two dorsal fins are tall, pointed and falcate and the snout is long, pointed and flattened. Locally common but very shy and rather difficult to approach close. Several similar but rather smaller species belonging to the same genus are found in the Atlantic and the Caribbean.

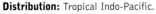

LARGE-TOOTH SAWFISH
Pristis perotteti

Distribution: Tropical Indo-Pacific, also in tropical fresh watercourses.
Size: Up to 6.5 meters.
Habitat: Benthic zones in coastal waters from 5 to 40 meters, on sand and mud beds, often in brackish estuaries and mangrove swamps and in fresh water.
Life Habits: Sawfish are large rays which look and swim like sharks.This Family numbers several species, often of great size and yet still poorly understood, all of which are very rarely encountered by divers and are gravely threatened with extinction throughout their range.

MARBLED STINGRAY
Taeniura melanospilos

Distribution: Tropical Indo-Pacific from the Red Sea and East Africa to Australia.
Size: Normally 2 meters, but can reach 3 meters including tail.
Habitat: Sand bottoms, on terraces and at the base of walls, at medium depth. Usually found at 20 meters and deeper.
Life Habits: A huge, dark-spotted grey stingray with a very thick body and tail. Two or more serrated venomous spines at the base of the tail, used for defence with a whip-like stinging action. Usually observed motionless on sand terraces; not shy and not dangerous if left unmolested.

BLUE-SPOTTED STINGRAY
Taeniura lymna

Distribution: Red Sea, Indian Ocean, Western and Central Indo-Pacific.
Size: Up to 70 cm including the tail.
Habitat: Shallow and very shallow water, tidal pools and sandy beds on coral reefs. Usually not found deeper than 30 meters.
Life Habits: Very common and often observed by divers and snorkelers. Disc rounded, yellow or yellow-green with several electric-blue spots and bright yellow eyes. Rarely digs under the sand; one or two serrated spines - connected to a poison gland - midway along the tail.

SPOTTED STINGRAY
Dasyatis kuhlii

Distribution: Tropical Indo-Pacific.
Size: Up to 40 cm including the tail.
Habitat: Sand and mud bottoms in shallow and very shallow water, sometimes in estuaries and brackish water, down to a depth of 60 meters.
Life Habits: Locally very common, often buried in the substrate. Two or more venomous spines are present on the tail and used for defense. Several similar species worldwide in tropical waters, all equally well camouflaged and all feeding on benthic organisms like gobies, crustaceans and bivalves.

SOUTHERN STINGRAY
Dasyatis americana

Distribution: Western Atlantic Ocean from New Jersey to Brazil.
Size: Up to 1.8 meters including the tail.
Habitat: Sand bottoms and coastal lagoons close to coral reefs at a depth not exceeding 25 meters.
Life Habits: A large, powerful stingray commonly observed in coastal Caribbean waters. A long serrated venomous spine is present at the base of the long tail. Often found semi-submerged in the substrate: shy but inquisitive and curious, it lets itself be approached quite closely.

ROUGHTAIL STINGRAY
Dasyatis centroura

Distribution: Temperate and subtropical Atlantic, Mediterranean.
Size: Up to 2.2 meters.
Habitat: Sand and mud bottoms in coastal waters to a depth of 60 meters and more.
Life Habits: A very large and impressive stingray, with several spiny tubercles on the back and along its tail. The body is very thick and the tail is very muscular, with two serrated spines at its base. At least two very similar species share the same environment and range.

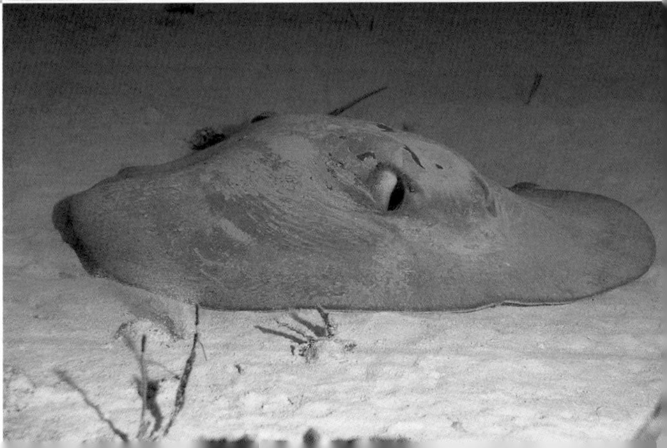

COW-TAIL STINGRAY
Pastinachus sephen

Distribution: Red Sea, tropical Indo-Pacific.
Size: Up to 3 meters including the tail.
Habitat: Sand bottoms in coastal waters and on coral reefs up to 60 meters deep.
Life Habits: Very large and rather active, uniformly brownish, with protruding eyes and large spiracles. Can be easily identified by divers by the broad ventral fin fold along the tail, which gives it an unmistakable ribbon- or flag-like appearance, especially when the stingray is swimming. Feeds on mollusks and crustaceans, mostly at night.

JENKINS' STINGRAY
Himantura jenkinsii

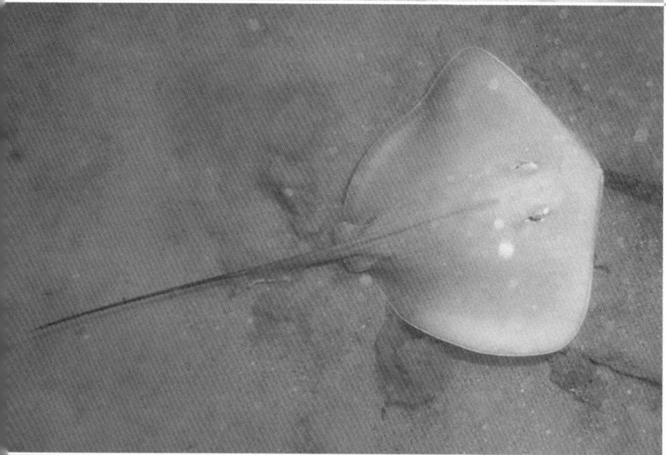

Distribution: Western and Central Indo-Pacific, from India to Malaysia.
Size: Up to 2 meters including the tail.
Habitat: Mud or sand bottoms in shallow coastal waters, often in estuaries.
Life Habits: A rather large, uniformly brownish stingray often found in brackish and turbid coastal waters. The tail is long and thin with two or more serrated venomous spines used for defense. Several very similar species worldwide, like the Tahitian Stingray *H. fai*, broadly sharing the same habitat and life habits.

MANGROVE STINGRAY
Himantura granulata

Distribution: Tropical Indo-Pacific from Indonesia to Northern Australia.
Size: Up to 1.5 meters.
Habitat: In shallow water, on sand patches in coral reefs, sand and coral rubble bottoms along beaches, mangroves.
Life Habits: A large dark gray or brownish stingray with a rounded body and a very long, whiplike, invariably white tail with one or more serrated venomous spines. Usually resting on the sea floor during the day, more active at night when it hunts for small fish, crustaceans and bivalves in the substrate.

LEOPARD WHIPRAY
Himantura undulata

Distribution: Tropical Western Indo-Pacific.
Size: Up to 5 meters including the tail.
Habitat: Sand and mud beds in shallow coastal waters and lagoon from 8 to 80 meters. Also in estauries and mangroves.
Life Habits: A very beautiful stingray easily identified by the numerous leopard-like rosettes on the pale body. Not particularly common and suspected to live in deep water, occasionally venturing in the shallows. One or more venomous spines situated halfway down its tail.

RETICULATE WHIPRAY
Himantura uarnak

Distribution: Red Sea, tropical Western Indo-Pacific as far as Micronesia.
Size: Up to 5 meters including the tail.
Habitat: Sand and mud beds in shallow coastal waters to a depth of 42 meters. Also in estuaries and mangrove swamps.
Life Habits: A spectacular large stingray identified by its busy, labyrinth-like pattern on a pale beige or brown body. Very long and thin tail, sometimes with its tip missing; often buried in sand. Easily confused with the preceding species.

PORCUPINE RAY
Urogymnus asperrimus

Distribution: Tropical Eastern Atlantic, tropical Indo-Pacific.
Size: Up to 1 meter including the tail.
Habitat: Sand and coral rubble beds especially among coral reef patches.
Life Habits: Pale grey disc with numerous thorns and pointed denticles. Tail short and sturdy without poisonous spines. Unmistakable rough appearance. Feeds on benthic invertebrates such as bivalves and crustaceans.

SPOTTED EAGLE RAY
Aetobatus narinari

Distribution: Worldwide in tropical and subtropical waters.
Size: Up to 3 meters but normally 1.5-2.
Habitat: Pelagic or in coastal waters, often on stretches of sand or close to the bottom from the surface to 60 meters .
Life Habits: A very graceful and beautiful swimmer, often encountered in small schools. Duck-billed mouth, long thin tail with several serrated spines at the base, large triangular pectoral fins similar to wings. Very fast and shy, difficult to approach underwater. Feeds on benthic organisms such as bivalves, crustaceans and bottom-dwelling fish.

MANTA
Manta birostris

Distribution: Tropical waters worldwide.
Size: Up to 9 meters wide, but normally 3-5 meters. Very large individuals are almost unknown today due to overfishing.
Habitat: Pelagic and in coastal waters from the surface to a depth of 40 meters.
Life Habits: A truly spectacular species, the biggest of the rays. Feeds on plankton that it channels towards the terminally-positioned mouth using the two cephalic lobes. Harmless, curious and gentle, once truly gigantic but today only encountered in the 2-4 meter range due to overfishing. Severely threatened of extinction throughout its range.

DEVIL RAY
Mobula tarapacana

Distribution: Worldwide in tropical waters.
Size: Up to 1.2 meters including the tail.
Habitat: Pelagic and in coastal waters, on sand beds and coral reefs in the open sea, from the surface to 20 meters deep.
Life Habits: Several similar species, often sporting one or more venomous spines near the base of the tail. Often confused with mantas, but normally found in schools and with a ventral rather than frontal mouth. A plankton feeder which favors current-prone oceanic stretches.

Open Sea Predators

Intimately connected to the chaotic universe of the coral reef itself, the daunting emptiness of the open ocean facing it hosts a variety of large predators. Which come raiding from the sea to reap a rich reward in prey

Every form in the animal world corresponds to a function, and large marine predators have developed survival mechanisms that are sometimes surprising. For example, the characteristic cephalic lobes of various species of hammerhead sharks are tied to the sharks' ability to perceive even minimal variations in the electromagnetic field, a faculty employed in their continuous search for prey. Since many hammerhead sharks feed on stingrays, the flattened contour of their nose may also facilitate the search for prey hidden on the bottom by operating like a kind of metal detector. Furthermore, in the vast immensity of the open ocean there is no need for multicolored or flamboyant costumes. Instead, robust structures and an elevated hydrodynamic coefficient, propelled by a very efficient musculature and supported by reliable instruments of predation are what is needed by pelagic species. The shark may represent evolution's apex in this sense.

Every predator has a characteristic dentition to fit its prey of choice. Thus, barracuda and open sea sharks that feed on fast fish sport long, sharp teeth to catch and hold prey better, while those that favor larger species such as turtles - as tiger

Gigantic whale sharks mostly feed on very small fish and plankton.

Hammerhead sharks have evolved electrosensitive lobed heads.

Large dogtooth tuna are often observed in front of reefs.

sharks - have evolved large heart-shaped, serrated teeth to better saw through their shells. But there are also marine species of huge dimensions - such as whales, whale sharks and mantas - that essentially have no teeth as we commonly understand them. They feed on plankton and small fish, filtering them directly from the water using the dense structures of baleen plates or gill arches. This

Grey reef sharks are strongly tied to the reef's environment.

type of feeding - enormous quantities of food secured with a minimal disbursement of energy - seems to be the most energy efficient and is the one most often adopted by massive creatures. Various marine predators, such as many tunas and several sharks, have also evolved an extra mechanism to improve their hunting skills: their body temperature is a few degrees higher than the surrounding water. This optimization of their bodily energy resources permits them to achieve higher speeds and faster reflexes when chasing prey.

Giant mantas will occasionally visit undisturbed oceanic reefs.

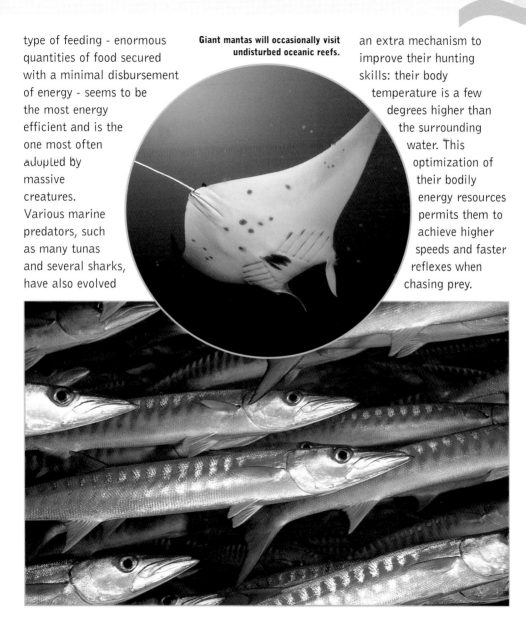

Large schools of barracudas often lurk close to oceanic reefs.

OSTEICHTHYES

Bony Fishes

Bony Fishes belong the class Osteichthyes, distinguished by having in most cases a distinct upper and lower jaw, overlapping scales covering the body, bony rays supporting the fins and a bony skeleton. Bony fishes or teleosts are considered more advanced than Chondrichthyes or cartilaginous ones (sharks, rays and chimaeras) and count more than 12.000 different marine species on a grand total of more than 23.000 freshwater and sea fish species worldwide. Due to these immense numbers a great variety in size, shape and coloration obviously exists: size for example can vary from less than 1 centimeter in some goby species to more than 5 meters and one ton in weight for the giant blue marlin. The great majority of reef species however range from very small to medium size, and are among the most colorful of all, offering a fascinating diversity in habitats and behavior. Most species belonging to this book are strictly related to the reef environment. ~ **U/W Photo Tips:** It is obviously impossible to generalize here, so more precise phototips will be given in the following pages on the Family subsection heading each series of entries.

MORAY EELS

Muraenidae

Moray eels (more than 10 genera, about 150 species) are elongated fish with a snake-like, compressed body, thick, leathery skin protected by a layer of slippery mucus and a hole-like gill opening. Most species are nocturnal and spend most of the day in their lair among rocks and corals; at night they actively roam the reef hunting for crustaceans, cephalopods and sleeping fish using their very developed sense of smell. Most species are not aggressive despite looking quite fearsome, but no moray eel is to be disturbed as most species are quite capable of inflicting painful, dangerous bites. ~ **U/W Photo Tips:** Morays are usually observed while peeking out of their holes, their large mouth rythmically gaping with every inspiration. If a slow non-threatening approach is effected it will be possible to get quite close, even to the point of taking macro shots. Try to synch with the breathing motion of the fish to click at the moment of maximum mouth aperture to show the impressing fangs of most species.

CLOUDED MORAY

Echidna nebulosa

Distribution: Tropical Indo-Pacific from the Red Sea and East Africa to Australia, Hawai'i, Panama and Southern Japan.
Size: Up to 70 centimeters.
Habitat: Shallow lagoons, dead coral areas, silty bottoms, seagrass beds.
Life Habits: Often encountered while moving around in broad daylight and in very shallow water, hunting crabs and shrimps in the intertidal zone. Easily identified by its unmistakable livery, bright white with black, evenly spread black cloudings; flat, rounded teeth indicate a diet of crustaceans.

CHAIN MORAY

Echidna catenata

Distribution: Tropical Western Atlantic from Florida to the Caribbean and Bahamas. Rare in the Western Caribbean.
Size: Up to 80 centimeters.
Habitat: Coastal and outer reefs from 1 to 15 meters deep.
Life Habits: Black or very dark brown with bright yellow chain-like markings, commonly observed among corals or peering from crevices, usually in shallow and very clear water. Feeds on crustaceans, mollusks and probably small sleeping fish, actively hunting at night.

ZEBRA MORAY
Gymnomuraena zebra

Distribution: Tropical Indo-Pacific from the Red Sea and East Africa to Southern Japan, Hawai'i and Panama.
Size: Up to 140 centimeters.
Habitat: Shallow reef flats and reef slopes down to about 50 meters.
Life Habits: Unmistakable red-brown and white banded livery; flattened, rounded teeth - evolved for breaking hard shells - indicate a staple diet of crustaceans.Very shy, almost exclusively nocturnal and usually difficult to approach, as it immediately retreats in hiding among the corals when sighted.

BLACK-CHEEK MORAY
Gymnothorax breedeni

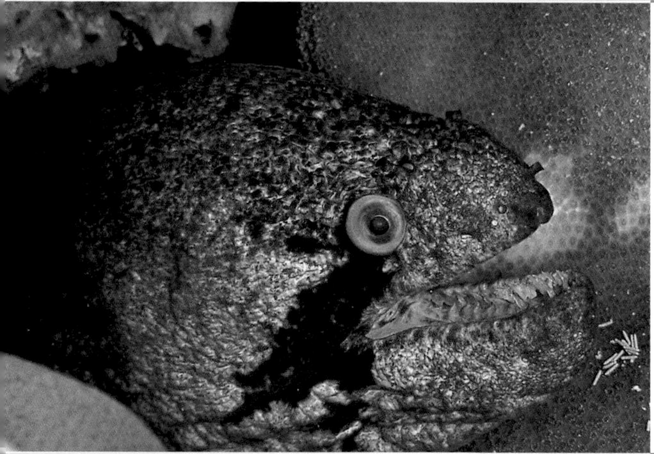

Distribution: Tropical Indo-Pacific from East Africa to French Polynesia.
Size: Up to 65 centimeters.
Habitat: Outer reef walls and slopes in healthy coral areas and clear water.
Life Habits: Small but extremely aggressive, always ready to bite even if unprovoked - never put your hand close to its lair! Easily identified by the stout head and the diagnostic black bar going from the eye to the corner of the mouth. Body is brownish, softly mottled in darker shades. Not particularly common except in oceanic, clear water locations.

SPOT-FACE MORAY
Gymnothorax fimbriatus

Distribution: Central tropical Indo-Pacific, from Indonesia to Micronesia and from Japan to Australia.
Size: Up to 80 centimeters, probably much larger.
Habitat: Coral heads, sponges and isolated outcrops on sandy bottoms.
Life Habits: A beautiful species, normally encountered between 10 and 50 meters deep around coral outcrops on flat sand beds. Lemon-yellow, black-spotted head and pale, whitish body are diagnostic; snout elongated, with big red-brown eyes. Curious, not aggressive.

YELLOW-EDGED MORAY
Gymnothorax flavimarginatus

Distribution: Tropical Indo-Pacific from the Red Sea and East Africa to Hawai'i, Southern Japan and Panama.
Size: Up to 120 centimeters.
Habitat: Coastal coral and rocky reefs from the surface to 100 meters deep.
Life Habits: Very common in its area, easily identified by the mottled yellow-brown livery and its bright yellow eyes. Often found with cleaner shrimps; peaceful, not aggressive but easily provoked if harassed and capable of inflicting deep, painful, dangerous bites.

GIANT MORAY
Gymnothorax javanicus

Distribution: Tropical Indo-Pacific from the Red Sea to Hawai'i and Japan.
Size: Up to 250 centimeters.
Habitat: Reef slopes and walls, from shallow coastal and intertidal areas to deep oceanic islands habitats.
Life Habits: Impressive and very heavy-bodied, sometimes as thick as a human thigh and reaching a weight of over 30 kgs. Usually peaceful and very easily approached, but obviously capable of inflicting very serious injuries if harassed or excited. As with other moray eels it must never be coaxed out of its lair by the offering of food.

HONEYCOMB MORAY
Gymnothorax favagineus

Distribution: Tropical Indo-Pacific from East Africa to Australia.
Size: Up to 200 centimeters.
Habitat: Outer reef walls and slopes, both in clear and murky water, from the surface to at least 50 meters deep.
Life Habits: Beautiful, quite large but not particularly common. Size and number of leopard-like spots may vary but basic livery is of a black honeycomb pattern on a white background. Feeds like most other big-sized morays on fish and cephalopods. Resident specimens are usually well-known to local dive guides.

SPOTTED MORAY
Gymnothorax isingteena

Distribution: Tropical Indo-Pacific from Sumatra to Papua New Guinea.
Size: Up to 200 centimeters.
Habitat: Reef slopes and rich coral flats, both in coastal and outer reefs, often in turbid waters.
Life Habits: Beautiful, big and usually peaceful, with large irregular black spots on a white background. Like most morays it spends most of the day being inactive in its lair, hunting and feeding on fish and crustaceans at night. Easily approached; previously identified by most as *Gymnothorax melanospilos*.

WHITE-MOUTH MORAY
Gymnothorax meleagris

Distribution: Tropical Indo-Pacific from East Africa to the Galapagos.
Size: Up to 80 centimeters, maybe more.
Habitat: Shallow water in thick coral areas but also in algae-rich rubble areas.
Life Habits: A spectacular and very beautiful species, easily identified while underwater by the bright white inside of its mouth and the finely, intricately white-spotted chocolate brown livery. Rarely observed by divers, possibly because it prefers living in tidal zones and in coastal coral rubble areas. Usually peaceful and very easily approached.

YELLOW-MOUTH MORAY
Gymnothorax nudivomer

Distribution: Tropical Indo-Pacific from the Red Sea to French Polynesia.
Size: Up to 100 centimeters, but generally smaller.
Habitat: Outer and inner reef slopes and walls, usually in clear water and thick coral formations below 30 meters.
Life Habits: Easily identified by divers underwater: the body is brownish, suffused with white spots, and the interior of the mouth is a bright yellow. Normally restricted to deep water and for this reason not commonly observed. Easily provoked and ready to bite if harassed.

BAR-TAIL MORAY
Gymnothorax zonipectus

Distribution: Tropical Indo-Pacific from East Africa to French Polynesia and from the Philippines to Australia.
Size: Up to 45 centimeters.
Habitat: Healthy coral reefs and walls, coral rubble slopes down to 40 meters.
Life Habits: A small and usually secretive but very beautiful species, easily identified underwater by the light spot between the eye and the corner of the mouth and the strongly defined, banded patter of the body. Nocturnal and usually very shy when encountered during the day but not particularly uncommon in its area.

GREEN MORAY
Gymnothorax funebris

Distribution: Western Atlantic Ocean from Massachusetts to Brazil, Caribbean and Gulf of Mexico.
Size: Up to 250 centimeters.
Habitat: Rocky and coral walls and beds from the surface to 30 meters deep.
Life Habits: A very large and impressive species, quite easily encountered by divers in the Caribbean where it is sometimes "tamed" for tourists by local dive guides. Usually peaceful, but obviously able to inflict serious injuries if harassed. Greenish-yellow, but appearing much darker in natural light; a very adaptable species found in a variety of habitats.

ATLANTIC SPOTTED MORAY
Gymnothorax moringa

Distribution: Western Atlantic Ocean from North Carolina to Brazil and the Caribbean.
Size: Up to 120 centimeters.
Habitat: Coral reefs and rubble areas from the surface down to 12 meters deep.
Life Habits: The most commonly observed moray eel in the Caribbean. Coloration very variable, but usually with many darker spots on a paler background. A middle-sized and peaceful species, easily approached during daytime. Nocturnal, it feeds on sleeping fish, crustaceans and cephalopods.

PANAMA MORAY
Gymnothorax castaneus

Distribution: Eastern Pacific from the Gulf of California to Colombia.
Size: Up to 120 centimeters.
Habitat: Rocky reefs from the surface down to 40 meters.
Life Habits: A common and thick bodied species, with a greenish-brown robust body finely dotted in white. Usually observed during the day while it rests in its lair, often in aggregations of several individuals. Aggressive if harassed: as with most true morays the numerous, sharp fangs are pointing backwards to aid in the ingestion of struggling prey.

WHITE-EYED MORAY
Siderea thyrsoidea

Distribution: Tropical Indo-Pacific from Sumatra to French Polynesia and Japan.
Size: Up to 65 centimeters.
Habitat: Silt, sand bottoms; often found in lagoons, wrecks and harbors.
Life Habits: A rather nondescript species easily identified by its startingly white eyes. Often observed with other moray species inside wrecks or among submerged rubbish such as sunken fuel drums. Harmless; probably feeds on shells and small crustaceans. A very similar species, *S. picta*, can be identified by the grey-white, finely mottled body.

BARRED SNAKE MORAY
Uropterygius fasciolatus

Distribution: Central tropical Indo-Pacific, from Indonesia to the Solomons.
Size: Up to 50 centimeters.
Habitat: Thick coral growth in coastal reefs and lagoons from 1 to 7 meters.
Life Habits: Very uncommon and rarely observed. Body is brownish with a network of fine, wavy dark lines; inside of mouth is bright orange; two extra tubular nostril openings present above the eyes. Not much is known about its habits: presumably solitary and nocturnal.

BLUE RIBBON EEL
Rhinomuraena quaesita

Distribution: Tropical Indo-Pacific.
Size: Up to 120 centimeters.
Habitat: Rubble bottoms on coastal reef tops and crests from 3 to 60 meters deep.
Life Habits: Not frequently observed but locally common; a spectacular and beautiful species, fairly long but with a pencil-thin body. Usually observed while peeking out of its lair with the frantically twisting front third of its body. Juveniles are black with a dorsal yellow stripe, mature males are blue with yellow snout and dorsal fin, terminal females (after a sex change) are all yellow and more rare.

DRAGON MORAY
Enchelycore pardalis

Distribution: Tropical Western Pacific from South Korea to French Polynesia, New Caledonia and Hawai'i.
Size: Up to 80 centimeters.
Habitat: Outer reefs in clear water from 15 to 50 meters deep.
Life Habits: Unmistakable: yellowish or pale orange with many brown-edged white spots, long tubular nostrils above the eyes, curved jaws showing fang-like teeth. Usually solitary, normally hiding in crevices during the day. Several other *Enchelycore* species sharing the same geographical distribution, all with common life habits but less showy.

SNAKE EELS
Ophichthidae

Snake eels count over 50 genera and about 250 species worldwide. These fish usually have a pointed snout and a cilindrical, pale, banded or mottled body, which they usually hide during the day in a vertical burrow, dug in the soft substrate using the stiff, pointed tail. They are more active at night, when they freely swim around the bottom hunting for crustaceans and small fish. They are all harmless but can and will bite if disturbed or handled. ~ **U/W Photo Tips:** Snake eels are commonly observed during the day with only their head poking out of their vertical burrow in the sand. A very stealthy approach is needed - usually taking several minutes - to be able to get close enough to frame the animal's snout in close-up, usually with a 105 or 60mm macro lens. Try to get as flat as possible on the substrate - digging the camera housing lens port in the sand if needed - to frame the snake eel's head as horizontally as possible .

BLACK-PITTED SNAKE EEL
Pisonophis cancrivorus

Distribution: Tropical Indo-Pacific from East Africa to Australia and Southern Japan.
Size: Up to 75 centimeters.
Habitat: Lagoons with sandy or silty bottoms, usually in shallow water.
Life Habits: Ambushing its prey during the day or actively hunting it during the night, this species feeds on cephalopds, crustaceans and small fish. Like all snake eels it lives in a vertical, mucus-coated burrow dug in the substrate using its bony tail, in which it will speedily disappear if carelessly approached. Locally common but most often overlooked by divers.

MARBLED SNAKE EEL
Callechelys marmorata

Distribution: Tropical Indo-Pacific from East Africa to Micronesia and Australia.
Size: Up to 60 centimeters.
Habitat: Silt and sand bottoms in shallow water and protected habitats to a depth of 30 meters.
Life Habits: From thinly to very densely spotted on a normally light background, with a preference for soft silty and sandy bottoms in shallow water where it can easily dig its burrow. Like all other snake eels, very fast in disappearing if carelessly approached. Feeds on crustaceand, small fish and cephalopods it hunts at night.

NAPOLEON SNAKE EEL
Ophychthys bonaparti

Distribution: Tropical Indo-Pacific.
Size: Up to 75 centimeters.
Habitat: Silt or sand soft bottoms in protected, shallow areas.
Life Habits: Very shy but spectacularly marked, especially on the head: easily identified by the golden bronze roundish spots on a pale background. As it usually happens, specimens observed on white sand are less colorful than those living on black volcanic sand. Feeds on small fish, crustaceans and cephalopods it actively hunts at night or ambushes during the daylight hours. Rarely observed by divers.

BLACK-SADDLED SNAKE EEL
Ophychthys cephalozona

Distribution: West-central Pacific, from Southern Japan to Northern Australia.
Size: Up to 100 centimeters.
Habitat: Rocky, muddy or sandy slopes in shallow water and protected areas.
Life Habits: Found not only in burrows but also in tight crevices among coral rubble. Probably mostly nocturnal like most snake eels. Snout is greyish, body yellowish: can be identified by broad white area on the neck, broken in the middle by a sharp black saddle. Feeds on benthic crustaceans and cephalopods. Probably common locally but rarely observed.

CROCODILE SNAKE EEL
Brachysomophis henshawi

Distribution: Tropical Indo-Pacific.
Size: About 100 centimeters.
Habitat: Soft, silty or sandy bottoms in shallow water down to 30 meters.
Life Habits: Very well camouflaged, a fierce-looking predator lying in ambush during the day with the body hidden in the soft substrate. Solitary, brownish or reddish, with softly mottled body. Locally common - especially in "muck" areas - but generally ignored by divers: a few very similar pale brown or whitish species with overlapping distribution.

BANDED SNAKE EEL
Myrichthys colubrinus

Distribution: Tropical Indo-Pacific.
Size: Up to 90 centimeters.
Habitat: Sandy bottoms in shallow lagoons and bays.
Life Habits: Rather common, easily observed during the day while it forages close to the shore and in very shallow water. Often confused with the Yellow-lipped or Banded Sea Krait *Laticauda colubrina* it closely mimics, but obviously a harmless fish and not a venomous snake. Width of black bands varies with geographical distribution. Feeds on benthic crustaceans and small fish.

SPOTTED SNAKE EEL
Myrichthys maculosus

Distribution: Tropical Indo-Pacific.
Size: Up to 100 centimeters.
Habitat: Coral rubble, sand and silt flats in lagoons or on the reef top.
Life Habits: A strictly nocturnal predator, sometimes observed during night dives while it forages for sleeping small fish, crustaceans and benthic cephalopods. The pattern of rounded black blotches on a white-yellow background is constant, but the shape of the spots is variable. Very rarely observed during the day.

GARDEN EELS
Heterocongridae

Garden eels are usually found in large aggregations on sandy or muddy flat bottoms close to the reef, often in deep water and in current-prone areas. Their common name derives from their swaying in the current in big numbers, with only the head and the first part of the body emerging like so many blades of grass from the substrate. These species feed on plankton brought by the current and very seldom leave their burrows. Several species still appear to be undescribed and many more doubtlessly are awaiting to be discovered. ~
U/W Photo Tips: Garden eels are some of the most difficult and frustrating subjects among the reef inhabitants, as they are always ready to slide down their burrows whenever one gets too close to them. The only way to get a good picture (with a macro lens, the only choice here) is to devote them the full dive, inching one's way closer and exhaling as little as possible waiting for them to reappear.

BIGEYE CONGER
Ariosoma anagoides

Distribution: Central Indo-Pacific from Indonesia to the Philippines.
Size: Up to 40 centimeters.
Habitat: Sand, silt or mud bottoms from 5 to 20 meters deep.
Life Habits: With a brownish body featuring a semi-transparent ribbon-like dorsal fin, this species is easily identified by the vertically elongate pupil on the large eye. Solitary and usually dug in the substrate during the day, it may be rarely observed in the open at night. Congers are closely related to garden eels.

SPOTTED GARDEN EEL
Heteroconger hassi

Distribution: Tropical Indo-Pacific from the Seychelles to Australia.
Size: Up to 40 centimeters.
Habitat: Sand flats between coral patches or along gentle slopes, always in current-swept areas.
Life Habits: Easily identified underwater by the two sharp black spots on its finely speckled body. As with all garden eels, this elegant little species lives in large colonies, partly submerged in the soft bottom and rising with the front part of its body to face the current and feed on the incoming drifting zooplankton.

LEOPARD GARDEN EEL
Heteroconger taylori

Distribution: Central tropical Indo-Pacific from Malaysian Borneo to the Philippines and Papua New Guinea.
Size: Up to 40 centimeters.
Habitat: Sand and silty habitats in quiet, shallow water.
Life Habits: A beautiful and recently described species, easily identified by the many black spots dotting its pale yellow background color. Lives in very spread-out colonies, seemingly being much less dependant on currents than other garden eel species and preferring quiet coastal waters. Less shy than other garden eels.

WHITE-SPOTTED GARDEN EEL
Gorgasia maculata

Distribution: Tropical Indo-Pacific from the Comores to Papua New Guinea.
Size: Up to 70 centimeters.
Habitat: Sand flats and gentle coral rubble slopes to at least 30 meters deep.
Life Habits: This species is often observed in huge colonies numbering hundreds of individuals living close together on fine rubble flats swept by strong currents. Not commonly encountered but easily identified by the diagnostic single row of bright pearl-like spots on the greyish side. Usually very shy and quite difficult to approach closely.

SPECKLED GARDEN EEL
Heterocongrer enigmaticus

Distribution: Very localized in Tropical Western Pacific from Indonesia to Papua New Guinea.
Size: Up to 75 centimeters.
Habitat: Fine sand beds and gentle slopes at medium depth in clear water and well-lit, current prone areas.
Life Habits: Body bluish-gray, finely dotted with countless small golden bronze spots; dorsal and anal fins clear with golden spots. Lives in large colonies counting hundreds of specimes; sometimes observed swimming out of its burrow.

EELTAIL CATFISHES
Plotosidae

Catfish species number more than 2000 worldwide, but the great majority of them is exclusively found in freshwater or brackish river mouths. Reef divers can expect to see - rarely - two species only, the enormous Giant salmon catfish *Arius thalassinus*, which can reach a length of almost two meters and is sometimes encountered inside Indo-Pacific wrecks in turbid waters, and the much more common species described here, which is differentiated by having a single, ribbon-like fin originating from the joining of the dorsal, anal and caudal fins. Striped catfish are often found in tight, ball-like schools numbering hundreds of individuals on sandy or silty sea bottoms close to the reef. ~ **U/W Photo Tips:** A large school of striped catfish makes an interesting subject, especially if framed from the front. Good close-ups can be obtained trying to click when most of the specimens have the mouth open, especially using a macro lens.

STRIPED CATFISH
Plotosus lineatus

Distribution: Tropical Indo-Pacific.
Size: Up to 35 centimeters.
Habitat: Silty coastal seabeds close to the reef, estuaries and river mouths where vegetable debris abounds.
Life Habits: Gregarious, often in ball-like schools, steam-rolling over the bottom in search of food. The younger the individuals the denser the school, which from a distance may look like a single large fish. Striped catfish are never to be handled, as they are capable of inflicting extremely painful injuries with their venomous fin spines.

GRINNERS
Harpadontidae

Grinners belong to the *Harpadontidae*, a small tropical family numbering only two genera and about 15 species. They are very common on sandy or muddy bottoms and can be easily differentiated from the very similar looking lizardfishes by their very visible small teeth. These are small, very fast ambush predators which will dart with lightning speed from the bottom to pluck their prey - usually gobies or damselfishes - from the water column, rapidly gulping it down alive tail-first. ~ **U/W Photo Tips:** Grinners and lizardfishes make good photo subjects, being more colorful than it actually seems. Very interesting shots can be obtained with extreme close-ups of their head, both frontally and in profile, but they must always be approached very slowly and stealthily and never in a straight line. If they dart away they will usually alight at a short distance, usually returning after a while to their usual perch on the substrate.

SLENDER GRINNER
Saurida gracilis

Distribution: Tropical Indo-Pacific from the Red Sea and East Africa to French Polynesia, Australia and Southern Japan.
Size: Up to 28 centimeters.
Habitat: Coral reef top and coral rubble patches from the surface to more than 100 meters deep.
Life Habits: Torpedo-shaped small ambush predator, usually perfectly still on the substrate. Can be identified underwater by the two large black saddles on the body. A "grin" of exposed, very sharp needle-like teeth in the lipless mouth idetifies all grinners.

BLOTCHED GRINNER
Saurida nebulosa

Distribution: Tropical Indo-Pacific from Mauritius to Australia and Hawai'i.
Size: Up to 16 centimeters.
Habitat: Coastal mud and sand bottoms from 1 to more than 100 meters.
Life Habits: Mostly restricted to silt and mud bottoms, usually almost completely buried in the substrate. Coloration is highly variable but normally with a series of small dark blotches on the sides. An ambushing predator which strikes at its prey from a distance with sudden unexpected bursts of speed.

LIZARDFISHES

Synodontidae
Aulopidae

Torpedo-shaped ambush predators found on the substrate on reef tops, belonging to a small family which numbers two genera and about 35 species worldwide. Can be separated from grinners underwater by their needle-like dentition, which is not bared as in members of the Family *Harpadontidae*. Fast hunters, always ready to pick weak or less alert than usual gobies and damselfishes from the water column: very attentive divers can often spot them actually catching prey and rapidly gulping it down alive, usually tail-first. ~ **U/W Photo Tips:** Very shy and difficult to approach, usually immobile on the substrate but always ready to flee a few meters away. Move slowly and do not approach directly; if the subject flees it will usually swim back to its chosen perch in a few seconds. As with grinners the use of a good macro lens is recommended, as head shots offer the most interesting opportunities.

NOSE-SPOTTED LIZARDFISH
Synodus binotatus

Distribution: Tropical Indo-Pacific from the Gulf of Aden to Taiwan and Hawai'i.
Size: Up to 20 centimeters.
Habitat: Coral reefs, on coral heads and rubble patches, usually in full view.
Life Habits: Found in shallow and well-lit clear water, usually not more than 15 meters deep. Can be identified underwater by the two small black spots at the tip of the snout and by the row of dark, evenly separated darker spots along the lower side; also by lighter first half of the torpedo-like, dark-mottled body.

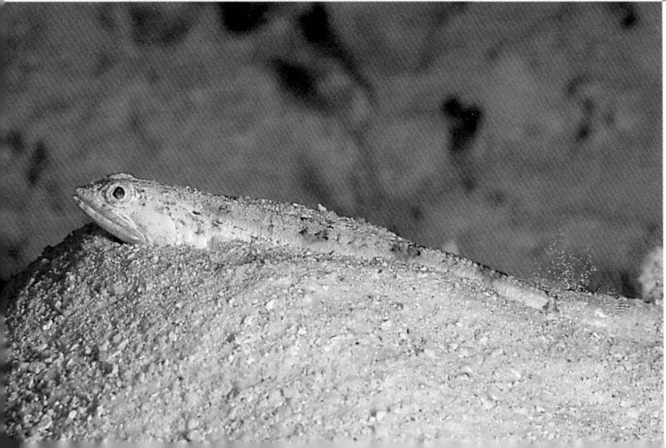

GREY-STREAK LIZARDFISH
Synodus dermatogenys

Distribution: Tropical Indo-Pacific from the Red Sea and East Africa to Australia.
Size: Up to 22 centimeters.
Habitat: Mostly on sand bottoms, close to coral heads, from 1 to 50 meters deep.
Life Habits: Usually completely or partially buried in the sand: bolts at prey with a sudden burst of speed and swallows it alive. If disturbed it will swim a short distance away and then settle on the bottom again, burying itself. Can be identified by the yellowish fins and the light blue streak on the pale grey sides.

TAIL-BLOTCH LIZARDFISH
Synodus jaculum

Distribution: Tropical Indo-Pacific from the Red Sea to French Polynesia and from Southern Japan to Australia.
Size: Up to 20 centimeters.
Habitat: Shallow coral rubble patches and undisturbed sand bottoms from 1 to 30 meters deep.
Life Habits: This species can be identified by the distinct black blotch near the base of the tail and by the showy iridescent green tinge on its back. Often observed in pairs, occasionally half-buried in the substrate. Note the large mouth typical of all grinners and lizardfishes.

CARIBBEAN LIZARDFISH
Synodus intermedius

Distribution: Western Atlantic, from North Carolina to Southern Brazil.
Size: Up to 30 centimeters.
Habitat: Reef tops or sand bottoms in clear shallow water to 25 meters deep.
Life Habits: The most common lizardfish of Florida and the Caribbean, and one of the most showy. Easily identified underwater by the bright yellow and light blue longitudinal stripes on a pale, brown-saddled background. At least three other common and rather similar species share the same general distribution area.

VARIEGATED LIZARDFISH
Synodus variegatus

Distribution: Tropical Indo-Pacific from the Red Sea to French Polynesia and from Southern Japan to Australia.
Size: Up to 25 centimeters.
Habitat: Coral reefs, coral rubble patches, coral heads from 3 to 50 meters.
Life Habits: Very colorful and rather common, normally observed singly or in pairs on the coral reef top. An alert ambush predator which can be identified by the series of elongate reddish blotches along its sides and by the generally busy pattern of its livery. Usually in the open, very seldom half-buried in the substrate.

RED-MARBLED LIZARDFISH
Synodus rubromarmoratus

Distribution: Central tropical Indo-Pacific, from Indonesia and Malaysia to Northern Australia.
Size: Up to 12 centimeters.
Habitat: Coral rubble patches from 10 to 50 meters deep.
Life Habits: Small and very colorful, this often misidentified species can be recognized by the distinct, bright red saddles on its back. Very cryptic and usually restricted to deeper waters; sometimes referred to in literature as *Synodus rubromarginatus*.

PAINTED LIZARDFISH
Trachinocephalus myops

Distribution: Circumtropical.
Size: Up to 30 centimeters.
Habitat: Soft, sandy or muddy bottoms often near estuaries, from the surface to at least 400 meters deep.
Life Habits: Large eyes, body longitudinally striped in gold and pale blue with narrow black borders, but usually found completely buried in the substrate with only the head partially showing. Extremely shy and very difficult to approach closely: it can bury itself and disappear from sight in seconds.

SERGEANT BAKER
Aulopus purpurissatus

Distribution: Subtropical and temperate waters from Western Australia to Southern Queensland and New Zealand.
Size: Up to 60 centimeters.
Habitat: Rocky reefs and sandy bottoms from 15 to 100 meters deep.
Life Habits: A very large lizardfish belonging to the Family *Aulopidae*, easily identified by the reddish body and the greatly elongated anterior rays of the first dorsal fin in males. Commonly observed by divers on rocky reefs and soft sea bottoms from Australia to New Zealand.

FROGFISHES
Antennaridae

A fascinating family of very strange, highly specialized fishes, numbering about 12 genera and at least 41 species worldwide. Frogfish (or anglerfish) sport a luring apparatus (composed by a thin ray, the illicium, and a shrimp or worm-like bit at its end, the esca) - above their eyes, which is periodically wriggled in front their mouth to attract prey. All frogfish are perfectly camouflaged to mimic their perch of choice - usually sponges - and are able to swallow in a single gulp prey as large as themselves. Most are very cryptic and walk on the substrate rather than swimming: most species look similar and are difficult to identify underwater. ~ **U/W Photo Tips:** Easy to photograph once they have been located. Very static subjects, exceptionally well camouflaged: medium focal length lenses (35-50mm) will suffice for full body shots, while a macro lens (105 or 60mm) will yield exceptional results with good close-ups of the head. Actively luring frogfish offer good photographic opportunities.

GIANT FROGFISH
Antennarius commersoni

Distribution: Tropical Indo-Pacific from the Red Sea to Japan and Central America.
Size: Up to 30 centimeters in length but very bulky.
Habitat: Reef top, overgrown piers, wrecks, large caves; usually associated with branching sponges.
Life Habits: The largest species, an exquisitely camouflaged ambush predator. Warts, general body shape, color pattern and random lines perfectly disrupt its already lumpish body. Coloration is extremely variable but always matches that of its immediate surroundings.

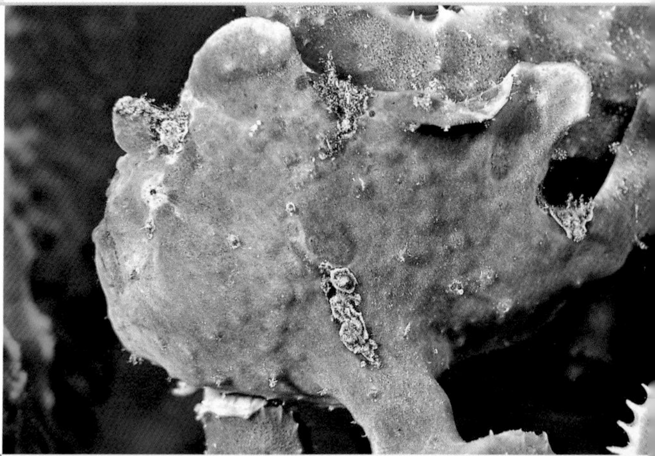

PAINTED FROGFISH
Antennarius pictus

Distribution: Tropical Indo-Pacific from East Africa to French Polynesia.
Size: Up to 16 centimeters but very bulky for its size.
Habitat: Juveniles sometimes on sand and coral rubble, adults on sponges.
Life Habits: Generally similar in body shape to *A. commersonii* but smaller and even more variable in coloration, always matching however that of the sponges on which it perches. Adult livery can be bright red, white, black, green, bright yellow; body can be spotted with ocelli mimicking holes of a sponge or not.

CLOWN FROGFISH
Antennarius maculatus

Distribution: Tropical Indo-Pacific.
Size: Up to 12 centimeters.
Habitat: Coastal reefs on sand and on sponges in shallow, often silty water.
Life Habits: The most easily identified and readily recognizable frogfish: red-brown triangular pattern on a lighter (bright white or bright yellow) body is diagnostic together with permanently erect dorsal fin first ray above the head. Juveniles are found in the open, mimicking brightly colored and poisonous nudibranches. Also called "warty frogfish" for the pores and large, very visible warts which cover its body.

STRIPED FROGFISH
Antennarius striatus

Distribution: Circumtropical.
Size: Up to 20 centimeters.
Habitat: Sandy or silty bottoms with rotting vegetable debris and sponges. Normally in shallow water but found down to 90 meters.
Life Habits: A readily identified species, usually encountered in coastal areas with lots of vegetable debris and sponges. Background coloration can be brownish, yellowish, pinkish or whitish, but elongated blotches and short darker stripes are always present. The lure looks like a large, boomerang-shaped fat worm. A rare local variation is shown below.

HAIRY FROGFISH
Antennarius striatus

Distribution: Circumtropical.
Size: Up to 20 centimeters.
Habitat: Sandy or silty bottoms with rotting vegetable debris and sponges.
Life Habits: A peculiar and locally common variation of the nominate species, showing very well developed hair-like dermal appendages. Background coloration can be brownish, yellowish, pinkish or whitish, but background blotches and stripes are always present. The lure looks like a large, boomerang-shaped fat worm. Commonly observed in the Lembeh Strait, Indonesia.

SPOTFIN FROGFISH
Antennarius nummifer

Distribution: Tropical Indo-Pacific from the Red Sea and East Africa to Central America and from Southern Japan to Australia.
Size: Up to 10 centimeters.
Habitat: Outer reef walls and slopes, often found on large sponges and wrecks.
Life Habits: Another greatly variable species which can be identified underwater by the sharp, coin-like ringed spot (*ocellus*) at the rear base of the dorsal fin. Best identification trait in frogfish is the shape of the lure (*esca*): in this species it looks like a small shrimp.

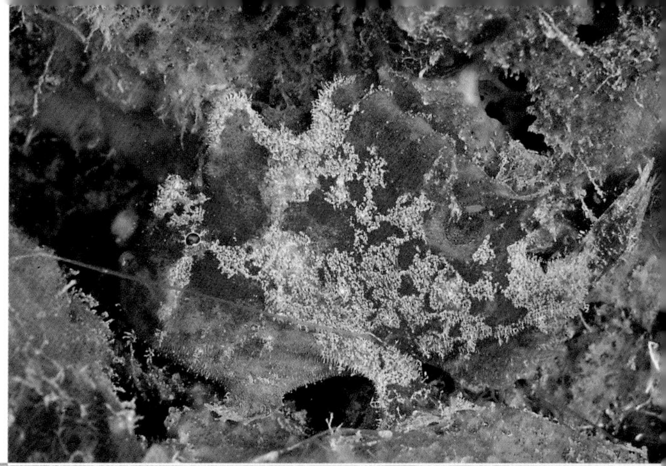

FRECKLED FROGFISH
Antennarius coccineus

Distribution: Tropical Indo-Pacific from the Red Sea and East Africa to Central America and from Japan to Australia.
Size: Up to 12 centimeters.
Habitat: Sponges, wrecks, rocky reefs, intertidal areas, usually in shallow water.
Life Habits: Small, brightly colored - usually red to orange - and lacking a distinct tailbase. Like most other frogfish, perfectly camouflaged to mimic its surroundings and rarely discovered: static, but if harassed it will quickly "walk" or swim away. Very difficult to identify correctly underwater like most frogfishes.

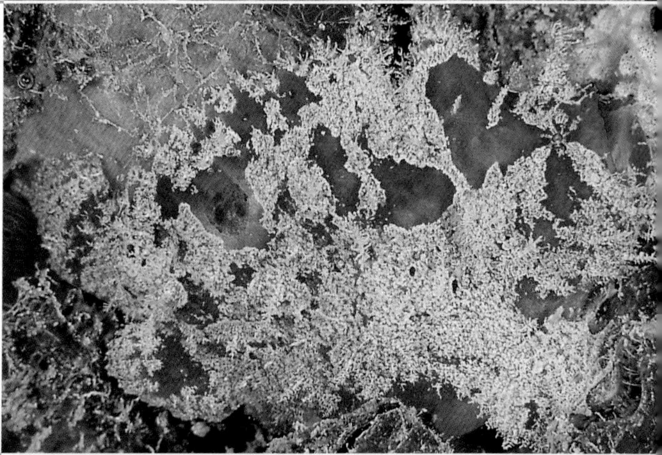

SARGASSUM ANGLERFISH
Histrio histrio

Distribution: Circumtropical but not reported from the East Pacific.
Size: Up to 15 centimeters.
Habitat: Pelagic, on drifting sargassum weed rafts; sometimes encountered in coastal areas after tropical storms.
Life Habits: Quite common in sargassum weed rafts floating on the surface but perfectly camouflaged and usually overlooked. Apparently able to survive out of the water for short periods: if chased by a predator it will jump out of the water and take refuge among the sargassum weed floating on the surface.

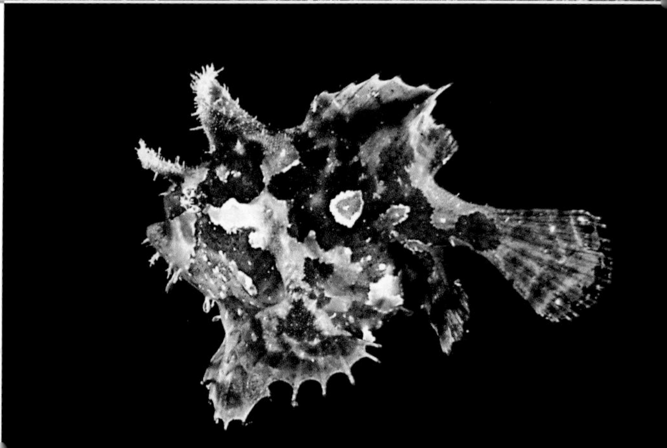

CLINGFISHES

Gobiesocidae

This large family numbers about 35 genera and more than 100 species, all of cryptic habits and small size. Clingfishes have evolved a large ventral suction cap, which originates from the fusion of their ventral fins and which they use to cling to other host organisms among which they usually take refuge, like crinoids (also known as featherstars) and long-spined sea urchins. Clingfishes lack scales and have a tough, slimy skin coated in a mucus which is sometimes quite toxic. ~ **U/W Photo Tips:** Usually very shy, ready to go into hiding and difficult to frame: a macro lens (105mm) is a must, and the help of a patient dive buddy is needed most of the times to coax the little reluctant subject in a favourable position.

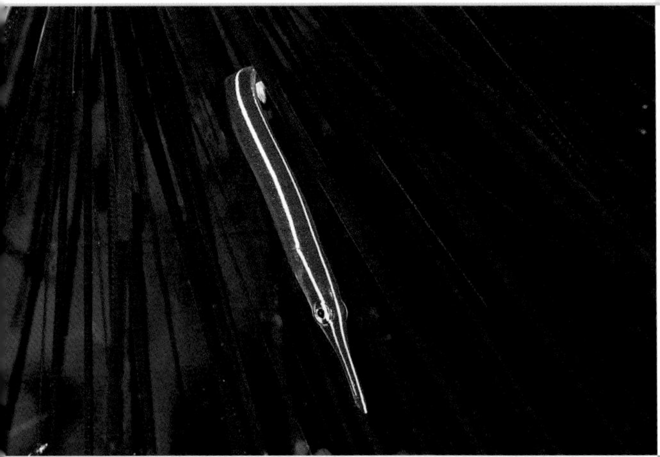

LONG-SNOUT CLINGFISH

Diademichthys lineatus

Distribution: Tropical Indo-Pacific from the Arabian Sea to New Caledonia.
Size: Up to 5 centimeters.
Habitat: Usually seen swimming in the open but always closely associated with long-spined sea urchins of the genus *Diadema*, among which it readily hides if in danger.
Life Habits: Normally observed on coastal reefs and protected inner reefs among colonies of long-spined sea urchins. Appears to be black in natural light, swimming with an undulating motion; usually unnoticed by most divers.

FEATHERSTAR CLINGFISH

Discotrema echinophila

Distribution: Tropical Indo-Pacific from Christmas Island to Fiji and Australia.
Size: Up to 4 centimeters.
Habitat: Exclusively found on crinoids.
Life Habits: This and the very similar *D. lineata* - which sports two longitudinal lines instead of one on the side - are exclusively observed on the surface of crinoids, often in pairs and hiding among the tightly rolled-up arms of the host. Fascinatingly, the coloration of this small and rather common clingfish always matches perfectly that of the featherstar on which it spends its entire life.

Frogfish Variations

Frogfish - also known as anglerfish - come in a dazzling array of sizes, shapes and colors. Rather static ambush predators quite capable of swallowing in one enormous gulp a prey even bigger than themselves thanks to their large mouth and expandable stomach cavity, they are usually found - with some luck and above all the sight of an eagle - contentedly perching among or on top of sponges, confiding in their amazing camouflage to escape detection both by possible prey and roving predator. Rather shapeless, ranging in size from a few centimeters to the dimensions of a football, with small webbed "feet" instead of proper swimming fins, a short tail and an impossibly huge mouth, they commonly choose perches of their own chromatic shade (or is it the opposite - do they subsequently develop a color identical to that of their perch?), immediately melting with the surrounding environment and becoming quite invisible to most other fishes and divers. In this remarkable endeavour they are usually helped by an array of warts, skin flaps, blotches, perfect imitations of encrusting algae or sponge holes and fascinating color variations which are only rivalled in the underwater universe by those sported by the scorpionfishes - the other great breed of ambushers. Extreme color variations are not only due to classification, but are also often surprisingly wide among members of the same species, and are presumably strongly connected to the surrounding - sandy, rocky, coralline, silty - environment. Here's just a limited example of what these amazingly collectable fish are capable of.

Clown Frogfish *Antennarius maculatus.*

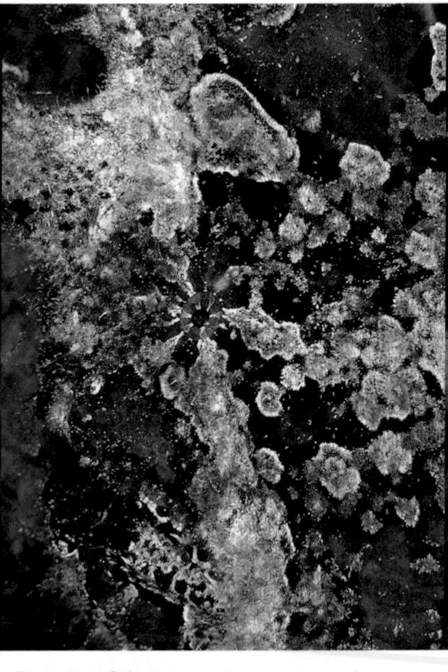

Giant Frogfish *Antennarius commersoni.*

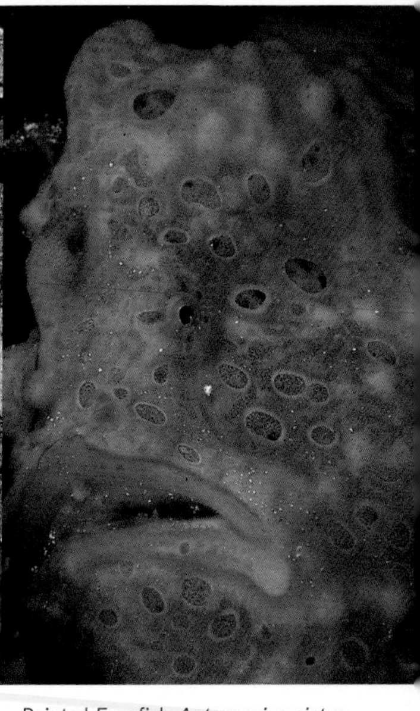

Painted Frogfish *Antennarius pictus.*

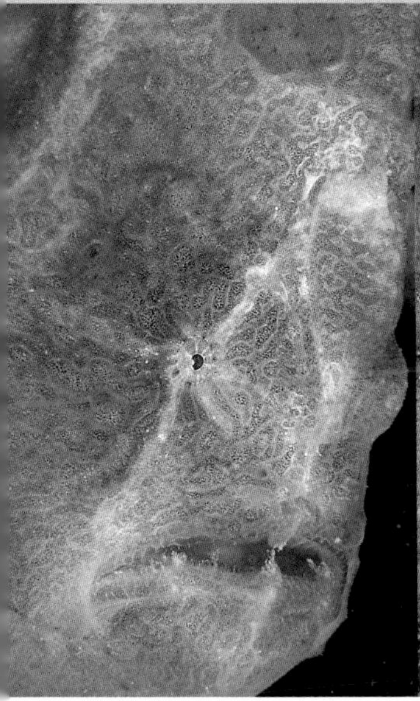

Painted Frogfish *Antennarius pictus.*

Hairy Frogfish *Antennarius striatus.*

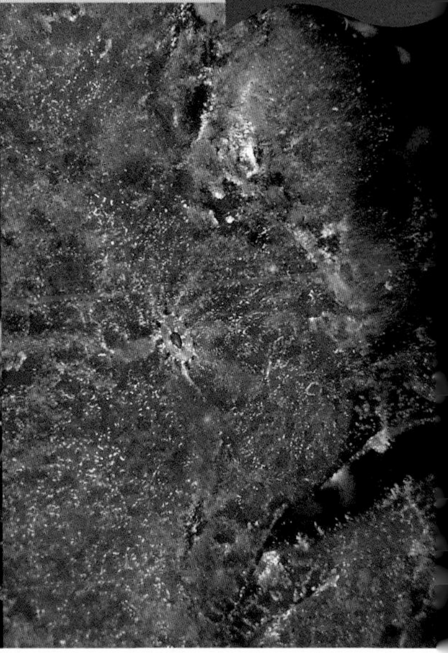

Giant Frogfish *Antennarius commersoni.*

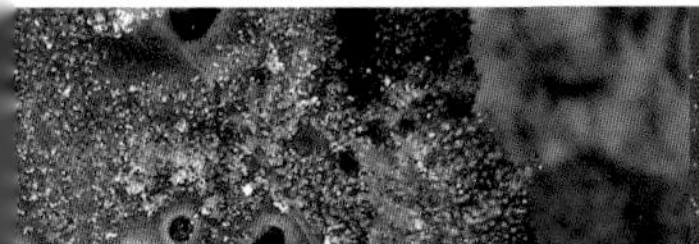

Painted Frogfish *Antennarius pictus.*

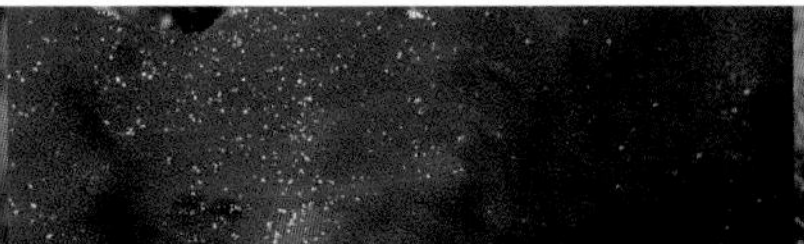

Panted Frogfish *Antennarius pictus.*

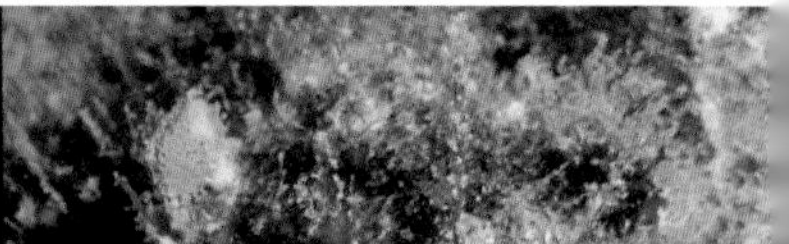

New Guinea Frogfish *Antennarius dorehensis.*

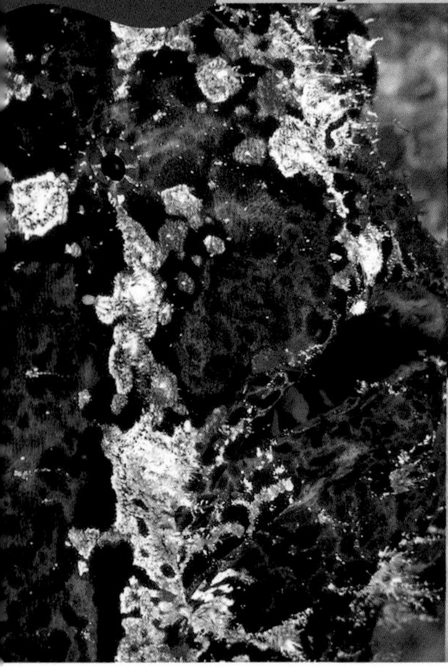

Giant Frogfish *Antennarius commersoni.*

Clown Frogfish *Antennarius maculatus.*

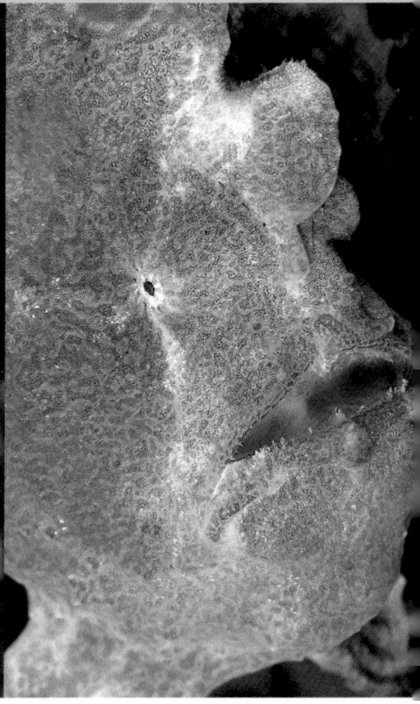

Painted Frogfish *Antennarius pictus.*

Giant Frogfish *Antennarius commersoni.*

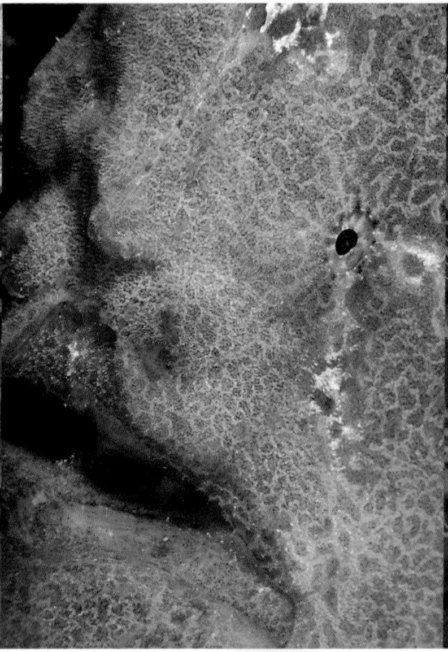

Giant Frogfish *Antennarius commersoni.*

Hairy Frogfish *Antennarius striatus.*

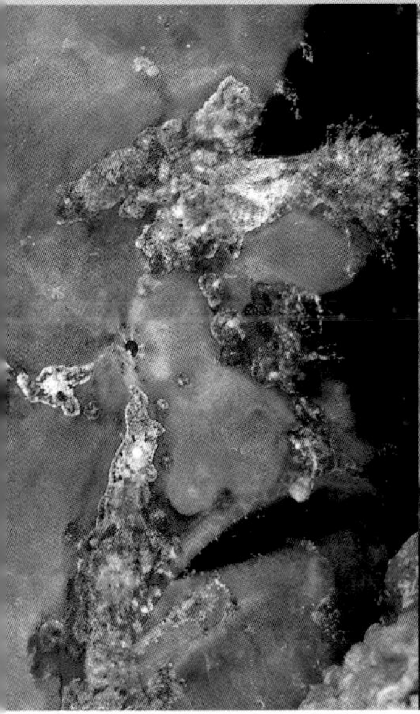

Painted Frogfish *Antennarius pictus.*

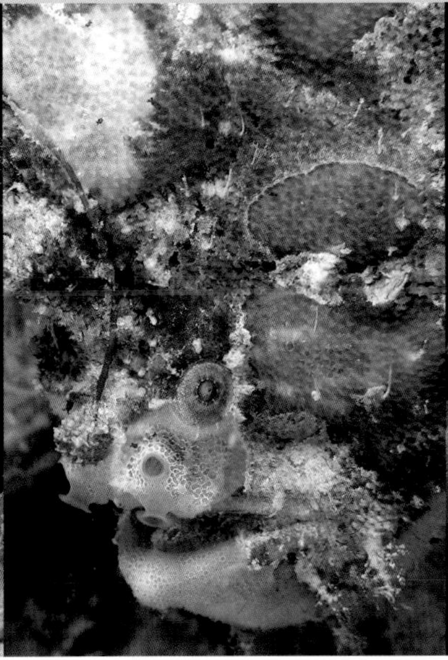

Twinspot Frogfish *Antennarius biocellatus.*

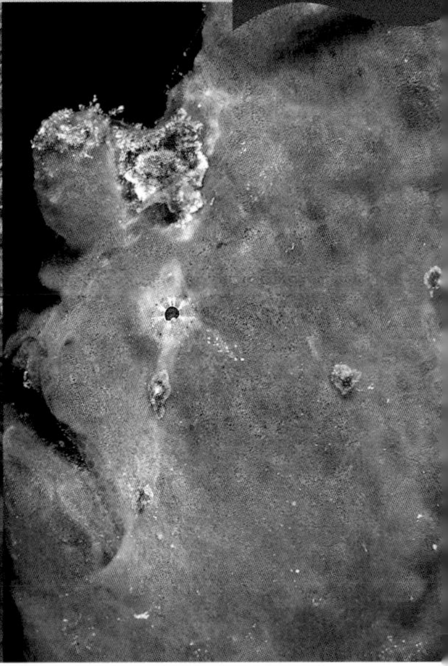

Painted Frogfish *Antennarius pictus.*

Giant Frogfish *Antennarius commersoni.*

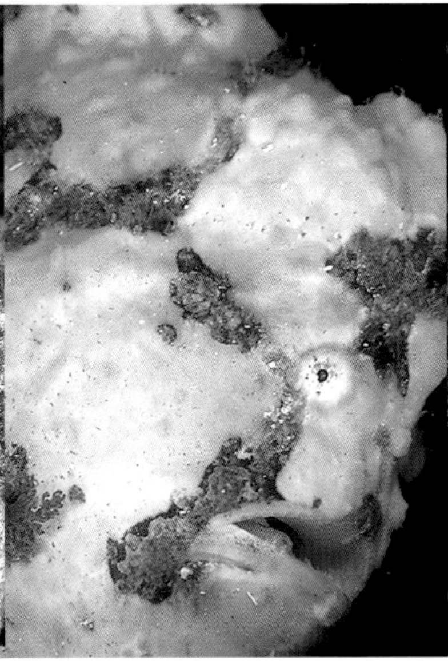

Giant Frogfish *Antennarius commersoni.*

Striated Frogfish *Antennarius striatus.*

SEA MOTHS
Pegasidae

A very strange family, numbering only 2 genera and 5 species. All have a small toothless mouth with a greatly protrusible jaw, a protruding rostrum above it and a strongly flattened body encased in hard bony plates and adapted to a life on the bottom. These small benthic fishes crawl slowly on the sandy substrate, feeding on extremely small crustaceans, and take their family's name from Pegasus, the winged horse of Greek mythology. ~ **U/W Photo Tips:** Depressed, knobbly body structure and general shape offer interesting photo opportunities, but side views are quite difficult as this small fish never leaves the bottom on which it crawls. Best shots are from the top, showing at advantage the queer shape of the animal.

SEA MOTH
Eurypegasus draconis

Distribution: Tropical Indo-Pacific from the Red Sea to French Polynesia and from Southern Japan to Australia.
Size: Up to 8 centimeters.
Habitat: Sand and rubble bottoms on coastal reefs from 5 to 90 meters deep.
Life Habits: Very strange and cryptic, perfectly camouflaged to match its surroundings. Hard body structure mimics fragments of broken skells and rubble: outer layer of skin is periodically discarded in one piece. If harassed will display flaring delicately colored broad, wing-like pectoral fins. Often in pairs.

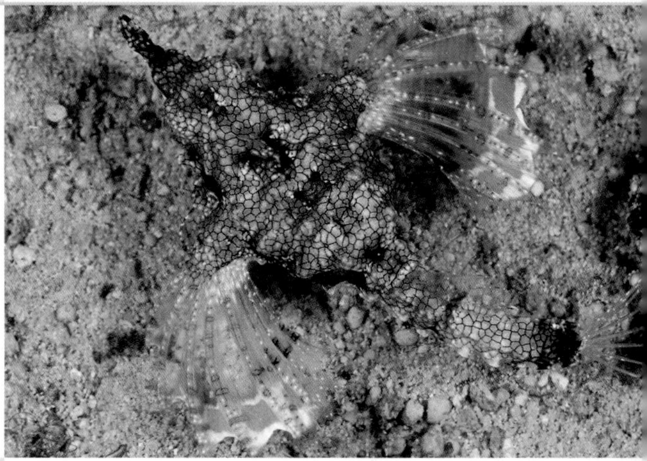

SQUIRRELFISHES
Holocentridae

A large, circumtropical family which groups squirrelfishes (subfamily *Holocentrinae*, with 3 genera all sporting a large, possibly venomous spine of the gill cover) and soldierfish (*Mypristinae*, with 5 genera and a smaller gill spine). All are reddish, big-eyed nocturnal predators usually observed hovering in mid-water in sheltered sites (caves, branching coral colonies) during the daylight hours, often in stationary groups. Most feed at night on crustaceans and small fish. ~ **U/W Photo Tips:** Middle-sized and rather stationary fish which make good subjects when met alone or in groups, usually in interesting and colorful settings like coral-encrusted caves or under overhangs. Given their usually vivid red coloration the use of powerful strobes is a must to bring out their bright colors.

WHITETIP SOLDIERFISH
Myripristis vittata

Distribution: Tropical Indo-Pacific from the Seychelles to Hawai'i and from Southern Japan to Australia.
Size: Up to 20 centimeters.
Habitat: Outer reef walls and slopes and in caves from 15 to 80 meters deep.
Life Habits: Bright orange-red and unmistakable, easily identified by the white-tipped spines of the dorsal fin and the slightly darker margin of the gill cover. Commonly encountered in large groups in caves or under coral ledges and overhangs. Easily approached.

CRIMSON SOLDIERFISH
Myripristis murdjan

Distribution: Tropical Indo-Pacific from the Red Sea and East Africa to Southern Japan and Australia.
Size: Up to 25 centimeters.
Habitat: Coastal, often silty reefs from 2 to 50 meters deep.
Life Habits: Very common, silvery white or pink with red scale margins. Readily identified by the dark brown margin of the gill cover, but often confused with similar species underwater. Generally solitary and quite secretive, sometimes observed inside wrecks or caves during the daylight hours.

YELLOWFIN SOLDIERFISH
Myripristis berndti

Distribution: Tropical Indo-Pacific from East Africa to Polynesia and Australia.
Size: Up to 30 centimeters.
Habitat: Coastal and outer reefs in clear water, inside large caves or under overhangs, from 3 to 50 meters deep.
Life Habits: White with bright red accents and fins and red scale margins: very common, easily confused with several similar-looking species but readily identified by the bright yellow spiny dorsal fin. Alone or in small stationary groups, often intermingling with other species of soldierfish under ledges or overhangs.

SHADOWFIN SOLDIERFISH
Myripristis adusta

Distribution: Tropical Indo-Pacific from East Africa to French Polynesia, Southern Japan and Australia.
Size: Up to 35 centimeters.
Habitat: Coastal and outer reefs or lagoons, in clear and deep water from 6 to 50 and more meters.
Life Habits: Can be easily identified by the wide dark margin on the rear dorsal and tail fins; otherwise quite pale, often with a greenish metallic tinge on the back. Usually solitary or in pairs in caves, generally observed under overhangs or ledges and in shadowy, protected places.

BLACKFIN SQUIRRELFISH
Neoniphon opercularis

Distribution: Tropical Indo-Pacific from the Red Sea to French Polynesia, Southern Japan and Australia.
Size: Up to 35 centimeters.
Habitat: Coastal to outer reefs in clear waters, often among staghorn corals colonies from 6 to 50 meters deep.
Life Habits: Solitary or in small groups around the 20 meter mark, it can be identified by the black dorsal fin, brightly marked with white tips and white spots along the base, which may possibly look like a toothed gaping mouth to predators when suddenly flicked open.

SPOTFIN SQUIRRELFISH
Neoniphon sammara

Distribution: Tropical Indo-Pacific from the Comores to Hawai'i, Southern Japan and Australia.
Size: Up to 35 centimeters.
Habitat: Coral patches and slopes in coastal and outer reefs from 3 to 40 meters deep.
Life Habits: Commonly observed among - or just above - branching staghorn coral colonies, usually in loose, spead-out groups. Like other squirrelfishes this species is a nocturnal predator which feeds on small fish and crustaceans.

WHITETAIL SQUIRRELFISH
Sargocentrum caudimaculatum

Distribution: Tropical Indo-Pacific from the Red Sea to French Polynesia, Southern Japan and Australia.
Size: Up to 25 centimeters.
Habitat: Coral-rich slopes, walls and drop-offs, also in coastal lagoons from 6 to 40 meters deep.
Life Habits: Easily identified by silver-white rear body and bright white stripes on head and gill cover. Usually observed in large groups during the day, sheltering inside caves and under ledges or overhangs. Locally very common and easily approached during the day like most squirrelfish species.

REDCOAT SQUIRRELFISH
Sargocentrum rubrum

Distribution: Tropical Indo-Pacific from the Red Sea and East Africa to Southern Japan and Australia.
Size: Up to 30 centimeters.
Habitat: Coastal reefs and lagoons, often in silty habitats and inside wrecks, from 5 to 90 meters deep.
Life Habits: Brassy-red and silver-white alternating stripes, blunt head. Often observed in large aggregations around coral heads at moderate to great depth. Easily confused with several rather similar-looking candy-striped species, from which it can be distinguished by the lack of any distinct black markings.

SABRE SQUIRRELFISH
Sargocentrum spiniferum

Distribution: Tropical Indo-Pacific from the Red Sea to Australia and Hawai'i.
Size: Up to 45 centimeters.
Habitat: Coastal and outer reefs in clear water from 5 to more than 120 meters.
Life Habits: The largest and possibly most impressive squirrelfish species, easily identified the large size, the pointed bony head, the orange-to-yellow belly and ventral fins and above all by the very large, possibly venomous spine on the lower gill cover. Usually alone but sometimes in groups counting more than ten individuals inside caves or cracks.

VIOLET SQUIRRELFISH
Sargocentrum violaceum

Distribution: Tropical Indo-Pacific from East Africa to Vanuatu, Southern Japan and Australia
Size: Up to 25 centimeters.
Habitat: Coastal and outer reefs in coral-rich areas from 2 to 25 meters deep.
Life Habits: Shy but unmistakable and truly beautiful: head bright red, body purplish with a bright blue streak on each scale, black rear margin of gill cover. Usually solitary, hovering close to small caves or cracks in which it will readily retreat if too closely approached.

LONGSPINE SQUIRRELFISH
Holocentrus rufus

Distribution: Tropical Western Atlantic from Florida to the Caribbean. Also found in Bermuda.
Size: Up to 28 centimeters.
Habitat: Coral patches and overhangs in clear coastal and outer reefs.
Life Habits: Commonly observed in the Caribbean and easily approached, this attractive species can be readily identified underwater by the silver-red body and the silver-white large dorsal fin.Like all squirrelfish, most active at night.

ATLANTIC SQUIRRELFISH
Holocentrus adscensionis

Distribution: Tropical Western Atlantic from North Carolina to Brazil. Also found in Bermuda.
Size: Up to 30 centimeters.
Habitat: Shallow reefs, coral patches, wall tops in clear shallow water.
Life Habits: Commonly observed in the Caribbean and from North Carolina south to Brazil, this species can be identified by its silver-red body and the yellow tinge of the large dorsal fin. Easily approached during the day and more active at night.

LONGJAW SQUIRRELFISH
Holocentrus marianus

Distribution: Tropical Western Atlantic from Florida to the Caribbean.
Size: Up to 15 centimeters.
Habitat: Usually found in deep water inside caves or close to recesses.
Life Habits: Generally uncommon in shallow water, more easily found deep. Shy, difficult to approach; a rather small but quite attractive species which can be easily identified underwater by the red and gold candy-striped body and the deeply forked tail fin.

TRUMPETFISHES
Aulostomidae

A very curious family which includes only 1 genus and 2 species, looking identical to the casual observer and which are only separated by geographical location. Trumpetfish are active and very clever predators, which can be easily identified underwater by their extremely elongate body. The head is very compressed, with a tubular, expansible long snout. The only similar species is the Cornetfish *Fistularia* sp., which is however more elongate and more of a free-swimmer, also moving around in groups. ~ **U/W Photo Tips:** Easily approached but normally very difficult to frame correctly given their peculiar body shape. Best chances are for close-ups of the head with a macro lens or full body shots from the side. Interesting behavior includes "riding" other fish to get close to intended prey or hiding and stalking vertically, head-down, among gorgonian colonies.

TRUMPETFISH
Aulostomus chinensis

Distribution: Tropical Indo-Pacific.
Size: Up to 70 centimeters.
Habitat: Reef tops and seagrass, among branching corals and soft coral colonies from 1 to 40 meters.
Life Habits: Able to change color very fast, also encountered in a xanthic (full yellow) form. Usually alone, rarely in pairs. Actively hunts during the day, stalking other fish while blending with the background or mimicking drifting weeds or gorgonian stalks. Sometimes observed "riding" other large fish such as groupers to get close unnoticed to intended prey.

ATLANTIC TRUMPETFISH
Aulostomus maculatus

Distribution: Tropical Western Atlantic from Florida and the Caribbean to Brazil.
Size: Up to 90 centimeters.
Habitat: Coastal and outer reefs in clear water from 5 to 25 meters deep.
Life Habits: Body with typically striped and spotted livery, usually kept vertically oriented with head down, hiding among gorgonians. A very adept predator, well camouflaged and often "riding" other fishes to approach prey unseen. Very common throughout its range and easily approached by divers underwater.

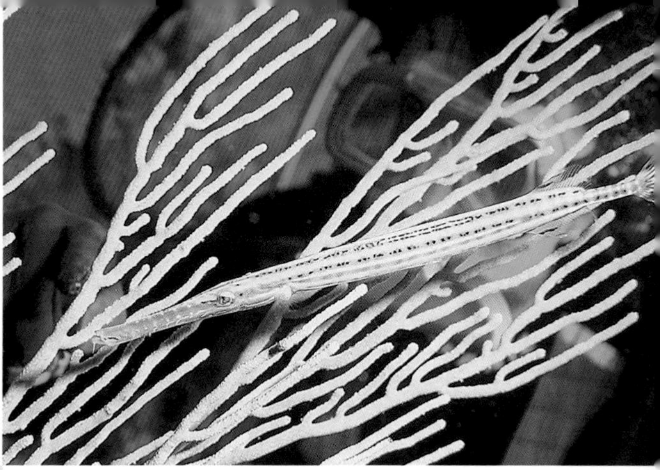

CORNETFISHES
Fistulariidae

This is a single genus family numbering just 4 circumtropical species. Cornetfishes are very long and elongated, tubular fish with a very long snout, a small mouth and a distinctive very long caudal filament. They are often observed in loose aggregations on reef tops, taking advantage of their thin bodies to "disappear" on the background of open water. Despite their delicate looks, these are cunning, stealthy and active predators. ~ **U/W Photo Tips:** Very difficul to frame correctly due to their peculiarly elongated body shape and their usually wary attitude. Can be closely approached at night while sleeping but to show their interesting shape full body shots in profile are to be preferred. Usually photographed by chance with medium focal length lenses (35-50mm) while looking for other subjects.

CORNETFISH
Fistularia commersonii

Distribution: Tropical Indo-Pacific.
Size: Up to 150 centimeters.
Habitat: Coastal reef tops and shallow lagoons in clear water from 1 to more than 100 meters deep.
Life Habits: Occasionally found in deep water, this species is commonly encountered alone or in small, loose aggregations in shallow clear water, facing the current and staying still in the water column. Not easily approached, it will readily keep its distance from approaching divers, but will occasionally come close for a fast check-up.

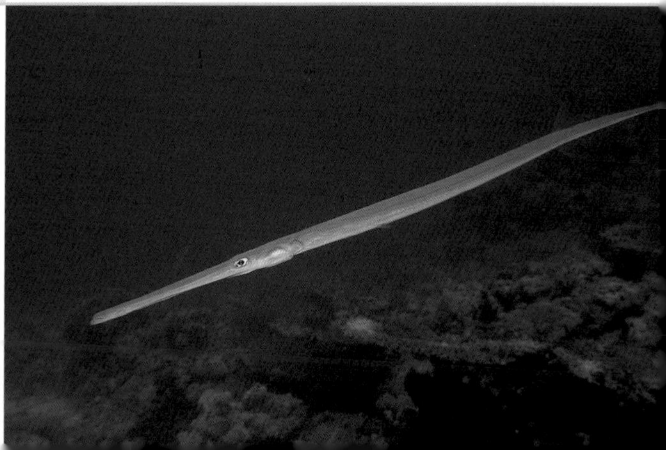

SHRIMPFISHES

Centriscidae

One family with 2 genera and 4 species, usually found in small schools with all individuals swimming together, very close to each other, head-down and very close to the bottom. The two most common species can be distinguished by the rigid or hinged large spine in the dorsal fin, not always an easy thing to do on a dive. Shrimpfish feed on tiny crustaceans (mysids) living on the substrate and have a typical metallic shine when observed underwater. ~ **U/W Photo Tips:** Normally difficult to approach close and not easily framed from a distance due to its normal head-down stance. Schools will speedily move away if carelessly approached. Occasionally single specimens will let divers come near, but best chances are at night.

CORAL SHRIMPFISH

Aeoliscus strigatus

Distribution: Tropical Indo-Pacific.
Size: Up to 14 centimeters.
Habitat: Coastal reefs and lagoons in clear water, often close to branching corals and long-spined sea urchins.
Life Habits: This species - also commonly known as razorfish - can be identified by the hinged long spine in the dorsal fin. Always head-down, swimming in synchronized fashion with other members of the school with an unmistakable swaying motion. Very small juveniles have a much shorter snout and mimic to perfection fragments of rotting vegetation hovering in mid-water.

RIGID SHRIMPFISH

Centriscus scutatus

Distribution: Tropical Central Indo-Pacific from the Seychelles to Southern Japan and Australia.
Size: Up to 14 centimeters.
Habitat: Coastal, sheltered reefs from 1 to 25 meters deep, often near sea urchins.
Life Habits: Very similar in aspect and habits to the preceding species, from which it can be distinguished by the rigid first dorsal spine, lacking a hinge. Side stripe is also more brassy, with a reddish tinge. Commonly observed in fast-moving, tight little schools hovering head-down.

GHOST PIPEFISHES

Solenostomidae

This family numbers just 1 genus and 5 or possibly more species. All have compressed, thin bodies encased in bony plates, large dorsal, ventral and caudal fins and are exceptionally well adapted to their surroundings. Females create a ventral pouch hooking ventral fins to each other to brood their clutch of eggs. These truly are among some of the most interesting, colorful and fascinating denizens of Indo-Pacific reefs. ~ **U/W Photo Tips:** Ornate and Robust Ghost pipefish offer spectacular, not-to-be missed opportunities for great macro shots, especially regarding camouflage and breeding behavior. Wait for Ornate Ghost pipefish to spread their unbelievably colorful dorsal, ventral and caudal fins before you shoot.

ROBUST GHOST PIPEFISH

Solenostomus cyanopterus

Distribution: Tropical Indo-Pacific from the Red Sea to Japan and Australia.
Size: Up to 15 centimeters.
Habitat: Sandy or silty bottoms in coastal reefs, lagoons and seagrass beds from 3 to 25 meters deep.
Life Habits: Very cryptic, perfectly mimicking a drifting piece of seagrass, including rotting spots and encrusting algae. Body thin, stiff, brown, greenish or reddish. Usually encountered in pairs, often swaying in the surge or slowly swimming head down, hunting mysids. At least two very similar species.

ORNATE GHOST PIPEFISH

Solenostomus paradoxus

Distribution: Tropical Indo-Pacific from East Africa to Micronesia and Australia.
Size: Up to 10 centimeters.
Habitat: Coral reefs and silty bottoms from 3 to 25 meters, often associated with crinoids and gorgonians.
Life Habits: Highly variable, usually very striking and including spots and stripes in black, orange, red, white and blue. Body thin, stiff, usually held vertically pointing down, its profile disrupted by a number of elaborate skin flaps. Alone, in pairs or - during mating season - in small aggregations.

DELICATE GHOST PIPEFISH
Solenostomus leptosomus

Distribution: Tropical Indo-West Pacific, from Japan to Australia. Also from Mauritius.
Size: Up to 10 centimeters.
Habitat: Usually encountered on reef edges bordering on open sand substrates at 15 meters or deeper.
Life Habits: Uncommon and easily confused with *S. cyanopterus*. Thin-bodied, pink, red or brown, usually with bushy appendage below middle of snout. Underwater identification is difficult.

ROUGH-SNOUT GHOST PIPEFISH
Solenostomus paegnius

Distribution: Tropical Indo-Pacific from Indonesia to Japan and Australia.
Size: Up to 12 centimeters
Habitat: Coral reefs on soft and algal bottoms from 10 meters and deeper.
Life Habits: Very similar to *cyanopterus* but with shorter caudal peduncle and tufts of tissue under the chin. Usually bright green or rust red, occasionally observed on soft substrates among seagrasses and algae. Correct underwater identification is generally quite difficult.

HALIMEDA GHOST PIPEFISH
Solenostomus sp.

Distribution: Tropical Indo-Pacific from East Africa to Australia.
Size: Up to 6.5 centimeters.
Habitat: Sheltered coastal reefs among *Halimeda* coralline algae from 3 to 15 meters deep.
Life Habits: Superbly camouflaged and rarely observed, mimicking to perfection the *Halimeda* coralline algae which represent its habitat. Red or bright green, always with a large head as long as the rest of the body. Still undescribed.

Color Variations

While most reef species tend to be immediately and easily recognizable thanks to their color palette and pattern, which tends to be quite constant in adults and juveniles alike, several other - mostly belonging to Ghostpipefishes and various species of scorpaenids - can be observed in a dazzling array of chromatic variations, often, but not always, depending of the type of environment they are found in. Benthic species inhabiting white sand or light grey silt bottoms tend be much paler than their counterparts living on geographically separate dark volcanic sands, while individuals belonging to the same species and geographical area but living in very different habitats (sand flats or thick seagrass beds, for instance) will commonly show extraordinarily different colorations. Yet again, greatly different liveries can be expected in several individuals belonging to the same species and living in exactly the same environment and geographical area, as it happens with the very variable Leaf Fish: these can only be attributed to a general variability within that particular species.

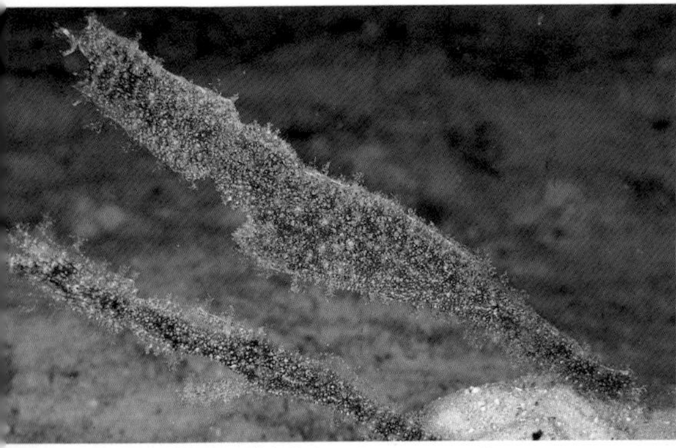

Robust Ghostpipefish *Solenostomus cyanopterus*, Pulau Mabul, Malaysia.

Robust Ghostpipefish *Solenostomus cyanopterus*, Pulau Mabul, Malaysia.

Robust Ghostpipefish *Solenostomus cyanopterus*, Pulau Mabul, Malaysia.

Robust Ghostpipefish *Solenostomus cyanopterus*, Lembeh Strait, Indonesia.

Ornate Ghostpipefish *Solenostomus cyanopterus*, Pulau Lankayan, Sulu Sea, Malaysia.

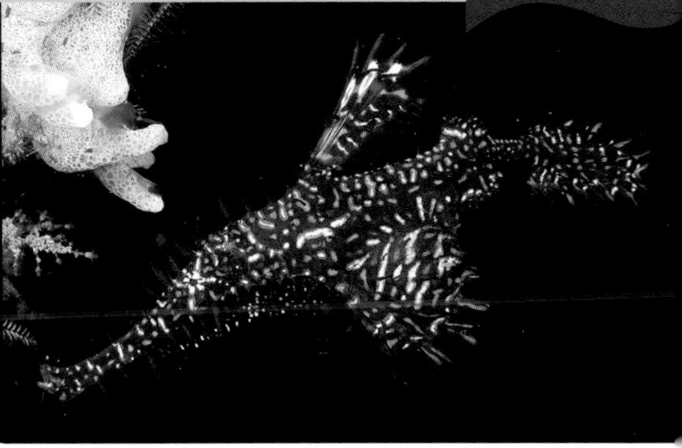

Ornate Ghostpipefish *Solenostomus cyanopterus*, Lembeh Strait, Indonesia.

Cockatoo Waspfish *Ablabys taenianotus*, Lembeh Strait, Indonesia.

Cockatoo Waspfish *Ablabys taenianotus*, Lembeh Strait, Indonesia.

Ambon Scorpionfish *Pteroidichthys amboinensis*, Lembeh Strait, Indonesia.

Ambon Scorpionfish *Pteroidichthys amboinensis*, Lembeh Strait, Indonesia.

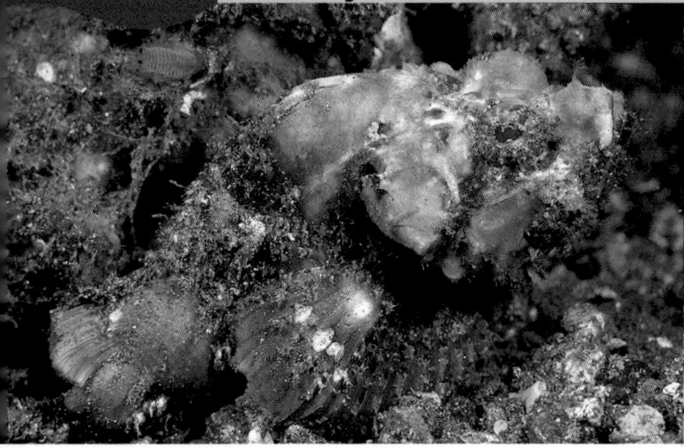

False Stonefish *Scorpaenopsis diabolus*,
Red Sea, Egypt.

False Stonefish *Scorpaenopsis diabolus*,
Pulau Mabul, Malaysia.

Dwarf Lionfish *Dendrochirus brachypterus*,
Pulau Mabul, Malaysia.

Dwarf Lionfish *Dendrochirus brachypterus*,
Lembeh Strait, Indonesia.

Devil Scorpionfish *Inimicus didactylus*,
Kapalai, Malaysia.

Devil Scorpionfish *Inimicus didactylus*,
Lembeh Strait, Indonesia

Leaf Fish *Taenianotus triacanthus*, Pulau Sipadan, Malaysia.

Leaf Fish *Taenianotus triacanthus*, Pulau Sipadan, Malaysia.

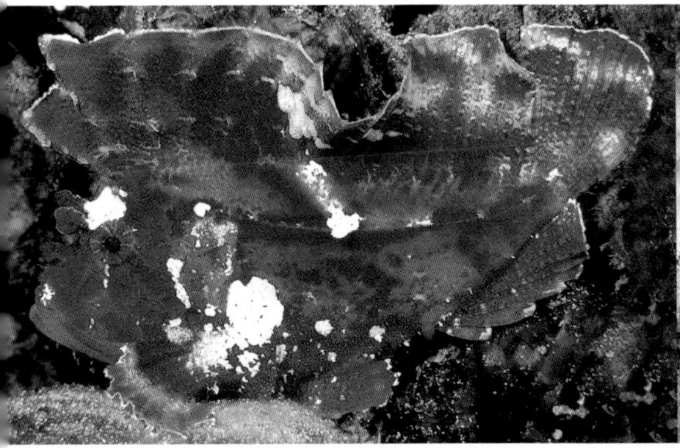

Leaf Fish *Taenianotus triacanthus*, Pulau Sipadan, Malaysia.

Leaf Fish *Taenianotus triacanthus*, Pulau Sipadan, Malaysia.

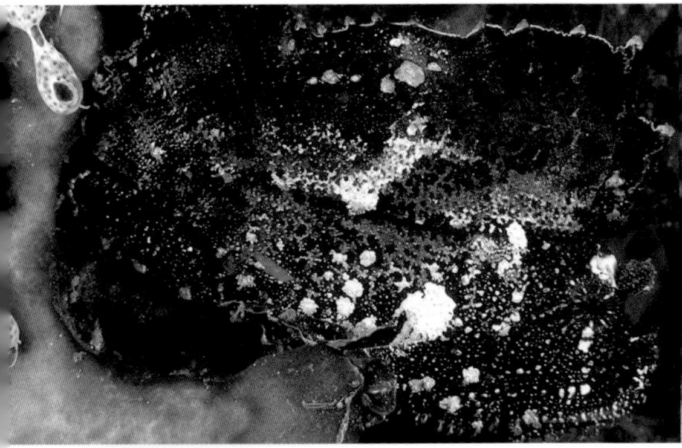

Leaf Fish *Taenianotus triacanthus*, Pulau Sipadan, Malaysia.

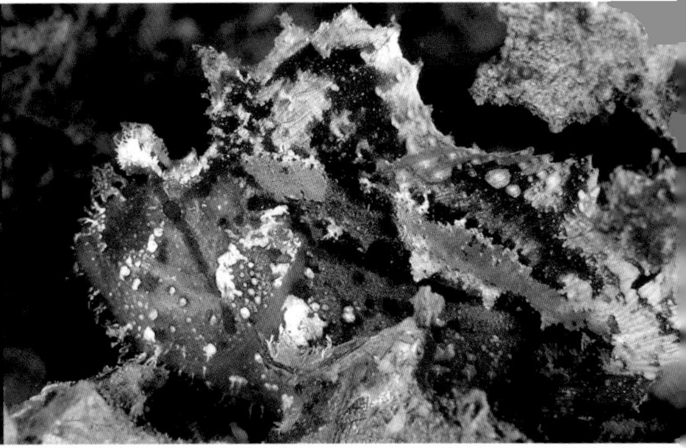

Leaf Fish *Taenianotus triacanthus*, Pulau Sipadan, Malaysia.

SEAHORSES AND PIPEFISHES

Syngnathidae

A large and interesting family numbering more than 50 genera and more than 200 species worldwide, often rather diffucult to identify underwater. They can be identified by the stiff body encased in bony plates, by the pipette-like, toothless mouth, by the enclosed gills and by the prehensile tail (in Seahorses) Most species live among corals or on seagrass beds and feed on minute benthic crustaceans. Males incubate the egg clutch in a specially evolved ventral pouch and give birth to miniature versions of their parents. Most species are severely endangered due to overcollecting for traditional Chinese medicine. ~ **U/W Photo Tips:** Easily approached once seen but not always as easily framed, due both to the peculiar shape of the body and to their tendency - especially in Seahorses - to turn their head the other way. Patience and a good macro lens are a must: the best compositions are those with animal in full profile.

ESTUARY SEAHORSE

Hippocampus kuda

Distribution: Tropical Indo-Pacific from the Maldives to Japan and Australia.
Size: Up to 28 centimeters.
Habitat: Coastal bays, harbors, lagoons, fish pens and seagrass beds at low depth.
Life Habits: Body slender, laterally compressed, encased in a series of bony rings. Coloration variable, but usually with light spots and scribbles on a dark background. Usually found in pairs or in loose aggregations in suitable habitats, clinging with its tail to debris and other objects on the substrate. Several very similar species worldwide, all difficult to differentiate for the non-specialist.

THORNY SEAHORSE

Hippocampus hystrix

Distribution: West Pacific from Japan to Indonesia.
Size: Up to 15 centimeters.
Habitat: Bays, lagoons and seagrass beds in quiet areas and in shallow water.
Life Habits: Several very similar species worldwide in tropical and subtropical waters, all featuring a long snout and spiny ridges on the body; white bands on snout are diagnostic for this species. Coloration variable, usually yellow or greenish. Quite common locally on sand with seagrass beds Like all seahorses it feeds on minute benthic crustaceans.

PYGMY SEAHORSE
Hippocampus bargibanti

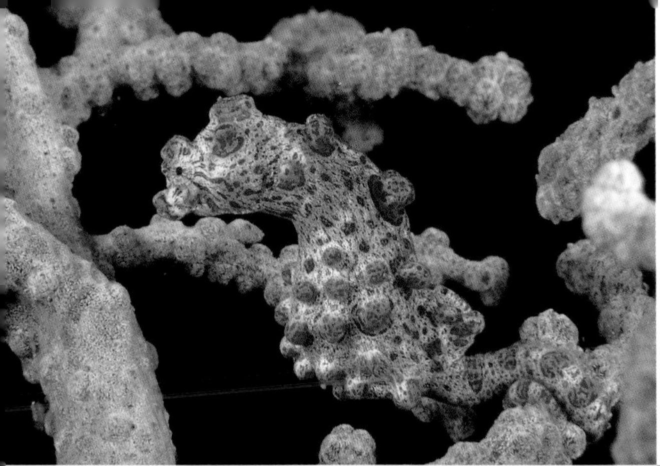

Distribution: West Pacific from Southern Japan to Indonesia.
Size: Up to 2 centimeters.
Habitat: Exclusively found in association with *Muricella* gorgonian colonies in 15 meters and deeper, often in current-prone areas.
Life Habits: Very small and exceptionally cryptic, rarely observed but locally common in suitable locations. Only recently described and not very well known; several similar and possibly still undescribed species in the same habitat.

YELLOW PYGMY SEAHORSE
Hippocampus denise

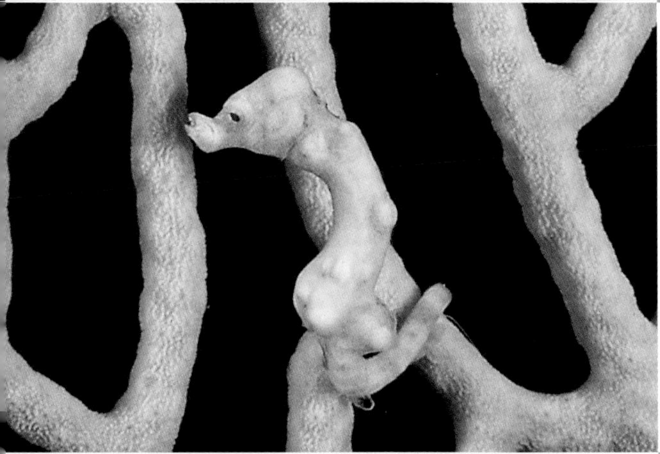

Distribution: West Pacific, but exact distribution area is still unknown.
Size: Up to 1,5 centimeters.
Habitat: Exclusively found in association with *Acanthogorgia* and *Annella* gorgonian colonies in deep water.
Life Habits: Usually orangish or yellowish, thinner and with less tubercules than the preceding species; recently described, but some still believe it simply is a juvenile form of *H. bargibanti*. Underwater identification is difficult.

PONTOH PYGMY SEAHORSE
Hippocampus "pontohi"

Distribution: West Pacific from Northern Indonesia to West Papua.
Size: Up to 1 centimeter.
Habitat: Apparently only found in association with hydroids.
Life Habits: Still undescribed, very small and whitish; unofficially named after the Indonesian dive guide who first spotted it. Several more species of Pygmy Seahorse are still waiting to be properly described in scientific literature.

DWARF PIPEHORSE
Acentronura tentaculata

Distribution: Tropical Indo-Pacific from Indonesia to Papua New Guinea.
Size: Up to 6 centimeters.
Habitat: Sand and silt bottoms, in seagrass beds and in shallow water.
Life Habits: Stationary, not uncommon but rarely noticed due to its cryptic habits. Easily identified underwater when spotted as it looks like a cross between a seahorse and a pipefish proper. Very well camouflaged, usually anchored by its prehensile tail to small sea grasses.

BROWN-BANDED PIPEFISH
Corythoichthys amplexus

Distribution: Tropical Indo-Pacific from the Seychelles to the Philippines and Australia.
Size: Up to 10 centimeters.
Habitat: Coral reef top and coral patches in shallow water and well-lit areas.
Life Habits: Several similar species worldwide, all broadly banded and short-snouted; possibly many local variations or undescribed subspecies. Often encountered in pairs, moving briskly among the coral rubble while looking for benthic crustaceans.

BLACK-THROATED PIPEFISH
Corythoichthys nigriventris

Distribution: Red Sea.
Size: Up to 12 centimeters.
Habitat: Outer reefs in clear water, often on coral patches on sand beds.
Life Habits: Endemic to the Red Sea; the almost identical *C. nigripectus* takes its place in the Indo-Pacific area from Micronesia to French Polynesia. Colorful and very active, often encountered on the bottom of large, well-lit caves: black patch in the throat area is diagnostic.

YELLOW-BANDED PIPEFISH
Corythoichthys flavofasciatus

Distribution: Red Sea and Indian Ocean from Madagascar and the Seychelles to French Polynesia, Japan and Australia.
Size: Up to 18 centimeters.
Habitat: Rubble patches on the reef top from the surface to 25 meters deep.
Life Habits: Several very similar species, all finely lined and dashed in yellow and orange on a lighter background. Underwater identification is always very difficult. Feeds on benthic crustaceans.

ORANGE-SPOTTED PIPEFISH
Corythoichthys ocellatus

Distribution: West Pacific, from the Philippines to the Solomons.
Size: Up to 12 centimeters.
Habitat: In coral rubble on reef tops and in lagoons, to about 15 meters deep.
Life Habits: Very similar to *C. schultzi*, a more common and widespread Indo-Pacific species. Small, bright orange, dark-bordered spots are diagnostic. Active and always on the move, looking for the tiny benthic crustaceans it feeds on.

BANDED PIPEFISH
Doryrhamphus dactyliophorus

Distribution: Tropical Indo-Pacific from the Red Sea to French Polynesia and from Southern Japan to Australia.
Size: Up to 20 centimeters.
Habitat: Sand and coral rubble bottoms in lagoons and bays, often associated to long-spined *Diadema* sea urchins.
Life Habits: Free-swimming and very active, often in pairs or in loose aggregations near the base of boulders, under overhangs and ledges and close to congregations of long-spined sea urchins. Will readily take refuge among the urchins' spines if disturbed.

YELLOW-BANDED PIPEFISH
Doryrhamphus pessuliferus

Distribution: Western Pacific from Indonesia to the Philippines and Australia; conspecific *D. multiannulatus* takes its place in the Indian Ocean.
Size: Up to 18 centimeters.
Habitat: Sandy and rocky slopes, under ledges, inside crevices and small caves.
Life Habits: Active, free-swimming, often encountered in pairs. Like most pipefish it is rather wary and won't let divers and photographers get too close.

ROBUST PIPEFISH
Hippichthys cyanospilos

Distribution: Tropical Indo-Pacific from the Red Sea to Fiji and from Southern Japan to Australia.
Size: Up to 16 centimeters.
Habitat: Sandy and silty bottoms in bays, lagoons, mangroves and estuaries; sometimes in brackish water.
Life Habits: Several similar species worldwide, all stout-bodied and restricted to shallow water. Often encountered among seagrasses or among rotting vegetable debris. Coloration variable, from bright yellow to dark brown.

WHISKERED PIPEFISH
Halicampus macrorhynchus

Distribution: Tropical Indo-Pacific from the Red Sea to Hawai'i and Panama.
Size: Up to 20 centimeters.
Habitat: Coral rubble patches, often among seagrass, in shallow water.
Life Habits: Exceptionally interesting and extraordinarily camouflaged: juveniles sport a series of dorsal roundish appendages mimicking round-leaved seagrasses. In adults these appendages are thinner and more thorn-like. Coral and algal encrustations are simulated by barbels, whiskers and fleshy appendages.

MUSHROOM CORAL PIPEFISH
Siokunichthys nigrolineatus

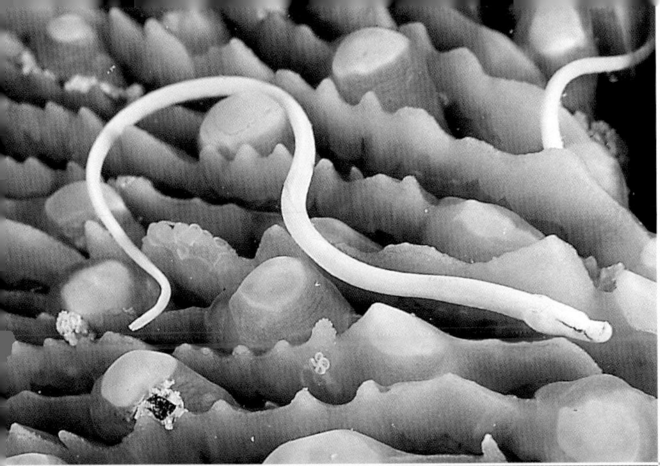

Distribution: Central Indo-Pacific from Indonesia to Papua New Guinea.
Size: Up to 8 centimeters.
Habitat: Exclusively in association with *Heliofungia* mushroom corals.
Life Habits: Observed in small groups on the top surface of *Heliofungia* mushroom corals (commonly and mistakenly identified as sea anemones by most divers) in shallow and clear water. Usually mistaken by divers for a worm, it is in fact a fascinating, highly specialized and little-known pipefish .

DOUBLE-ENDED PIPEFISH
Syngnathoides biaculeatus

Distribution: Tropical Indo-Pacific from the Red Sea to Micronesia and from Southern Japan to Australia.
Size: Up to 30 centimeters.
Habitat: Around floating weeds and in rotting large-leaved vegetable debris in quiet areas and shallow water.
Life Habits: Brownish or bright green when associated with sargassum weed rafts, usually hidden among submerged vegetation. Very cryptic and apparently able to jump out of water to escape predation. As with other pipefishes the eggs are carried and brooded by the male.

LONG-SNOUT STICK PIPEFISH
Trachyrhamphus bicoarctatus

Distribution: Tropical Indo-Pacific from the Red Sea and East Africa to Australia and New Caledonia.
Size: Up to 40 centimeters.
Habitat: Seagrass and coral rubble beds in muddy and silty habitats, often close to vegetable debris.
Life Habits: Also called - for immediately clear reasons - "broken stick pipefish". Very cryptic and slow-moving, often found in loose aggregations in current-prone areas. Brown or reddish, rarely white; possibly more than one species are involved in the complex.

SCORPIONFISHES

Scorpaenidae

This is a large and well-distributed worldwide family which numbers about 10 sub-families, two of which group the most important genera regarding divers: the *Pteroinae* or Lionfishes and the *Scorpaeninae* or Scorpionfishes. The first are more mobile and easily identified by the large, banner-like pectoral and dorsal fins; the second are more static ambush hunters and marvellously camouflaged. Both share a very large mouth, spiny heads and can inflict extremely painful injuries as their needle-like fin rays are very sharp and connected to a venom gland. Pain can be extreme and in some cases even life-threatening: the only remedy in the field is immersing the wounded limb in very hot water or applying very hot air from a hair-dryer. ~ **U/W Photo Tips:** Most lionfish and scorpionfish make easy, spectacular subjects. Static or slow-moving, they look beautiful from any angle and are a perfect beginner's subject. For best results use a macro or medium focal length lens.

CORAL SCORPIONFISH

Sebastapistes cyanostigma

Distribution: Tropical Indo-Pacific from the Red Sea and East Africa to Southern Japan and Australia.
Size: Up to 10 centimeters.
Habitat: Rich coral growth in shallow, well-lit reef tops.
Life Habits: Red or pink with bright yellow tiny spots. Difficult to spot, as it usually lives among the colonies of many different branching corals, which it will not leave even if the whole block of coral is taken out of the water. Usually several individuals sharing the same colony.

DWARF SCORPIONFISH

Scorpaenopsis macrochir

Distribution: Tropical Indo-Pacific from Mauritius to French Polynesia.
Size: Up to 10 centimeters.
Habitat: Sandy, silty or rubble bottoms in protected areas, often among rubbish.
Life Habits: One of several very similar-looking small species, all having in common a short lumpy body, an extremely large and broad head and the habit of flashing wide their brightly colored pectoral fins when in danger. All dwarf scorpionfishes are splendidly camouflaged, static ambush predators and very difficult to spot underwater. Very venomous.

SMALLSCALE SCORPIONFISH
Scorpaenopsis oxycephala

Distribution: Tropical Indo-Pacific from the Red Sea to Indonesia and Taiwan.
Size: Up to 35 centimeters.
Habitat: Healthy coral reefs, drop-offs, crevices, small caves from the surface to at least 60 meters deep.
Life Habits: The most commonly observed scorpionfish in tropical waters, often in full sight but perfectly camouflaged and most of the times ignored by divers. Skin flaps and a disruptive coloration add to its cryptic qualities. Several similar species worldwide, all equally venomous.

BLOTCHFIN SCORPIONFISH
Scorpaenodes varipinnis

Distribution: Tropical Indo-Pacific from the Red Sea to Micronesia.
Size: Up to 12 centimeters.
Habitat: Coral rubble areas along slopes and walls, under ledges and overhangs.
Life Habits: Small, shy, rather secretive and quite small, most often observed at night when it hunts for small fish and crustaceans in the open. Very difficult to spot during the day as it normally hides under ledges and overhangs or inside small caves and crevices. Several very similar-looking small species worldwide.

AMBON SCORPIONFISH
Pteroidichthys amboinensis

Distribution: Central Indo-Pacific, from Borneo to Papua New Guinea.
Size: Up to 15 centimeters.
Habitat: Sandy, silty bottoms in protected areas from 3 to 20 meters deep.
Life Habits: Uncommon and exquisitely cryptic thanks to its flourishing of dermal appendages and the two large "tendrils" growing like antlers over its eyes. Very variable, normally brown, reddish or bright yellow. Outside appearance can vary from "frilled" to "hairy" depending on the environment it lives in.

NORTHERN SCORPIONFISH
Parascorpaena picta

Distribution: Tropical Asian Pacific from Taiwan and Indonesia to Australia.
Size: Up to 15 centimeters.
Habitat: Sheltered areas on coastal reefs from 2 to 15 meters deep.
Life Habits: Very variable, mottled in reds or browns, quite colorful or very drab, but always with diagnostic barred lips. Very wary, occasionally observed hiding among corals and inside crevices . Several quite similar species, all rather difficult to identify correctly underwater.

PYGMY SCORPIONFISH
Scorpaenopsis cotticeps

Distribution: Tropical Indo-West Pacific from East Africa to Southern Japan, the Philippines and Australia.
Size: Up to 6.3 centimeters.
Habitat: Coral rubble or sand bottoms on sheltered coastal reefs from 15 to 70 meters deep.
Life Habits: Very small and exquisitely camouflaged scorpionfish, occasionally encountered by divers on sand or rubble bottoms on sheltered coastal reefs. Very similar to several other species at first sight, but small size is usually diagnostic. An ambush predator like all scorpaenids.

OBTUSE SCORPIONFISH
Scorpaenopsis obtusa

Distribution: Tropical Western Indo-Pacific from Borneo to the Philippines and Papua New Guinea.
Size: Up to 8 centimeters.
Habitat: Sand and coral rubble bottoms on sheltered coastal coral reefs from 5 to 50 meters deep.
Life Habits: Only recently described, another very small and wonderfully camouflaged scorpionfish occasionally encountered by eagle-eyed divers and photographers on rubble bottoms in sheltered coastal areas. A benthic ambush predator like most scorpionfishes.

POSS'S SCORPIONFISH
Scorpaenopsis possi

Distribution: Tropical Indo-Pacific from the Red Sea to French Polynesia.
Size: Up to 25 centimeters.
Habitat: Coastal and outer coral-rich areas from 1 to 40 meters deep.
Life Habits: A very cryptic bottom ambush predator, almost undistinguishable from the very similar *S. oxycephala* and *S. papuensis* but somewhat smaller and with a shorter snout. These three common species can only be differentiated by geographical location and a few minor taxonomical characteristics.

DWARF SCORPIONFISH
Scorpaenopsis neglecta

Distribution: Tropical Indo-Pacific from the Red Sea to French Polynesia.
Size: Up to 10 centimeters.
Habitat: Silty and rubble-strewn bottoms in very shallow water.
Life Habits: Easily confused underwater with several other small and very similar species, all exceptionally cryptic. Species belonging to this confusing complex are bottom-dwelling ambush predators, rather small, inactive and quite difficult to spot; all feature venomous fin rays.

BLACKFOOT LIONFISH
Parapterois heterura

Distribution: Tropical Indo-West Pacific from the South Africa to Japan.
Size: Up to 23 centimeters.
Habitat: Silt or sand bottoms from 15 to 300 meters deep.
Life Habits: Very colorful, with filamented tip of dorsal fin rays; broad fan-like pectorals coppery orange on the outer face and velvety black with electric blue vermiculations on the inner one. Uncommon, usually observed in deep temperate or subtropical waters and partly buried in the substrate during the day.

FALSE STONEFISH
Scorpaenopsis diabolus

Distribution: Tropical Indo-Pacific from the Red Sea to Polynesia and Australia.
Size: Up to 18 centimeters.
Habitat: Coral rubble areas, debris-filled silty bottoms in bays and lagoons.
Life Habits: One of the most commonly observed scorpionfishes in tropical waters, often confused with the much less common and much more dangerous Stonefish *Synanccia vcrrucosa* (see pag 129). Static, exceptionally cryptic, even mimicking encrusting calcareous algae. If harassed it will clumsily "hop" away or flash its colorful aposematic (advertising danger) pectoral fins. Very venomous.

RAGGY SCORPIONFISH
Scorpaenopsis venosa

Distribution: Tropical Indo-Pacific from the Arabian Sea and Sri Lanka to Southern Japan and Australia.
Size: Up to 25 centimeters.
Habitat: Coastal reefs in mixed coral-sponge areas, silty or sandy bottoms.
Life Habits: A very cryptic bottom species, identified by the multitude of dermal appendages adorning its lumpish body. Static, relying on its perfect camouflage, and very variable in coloration, but usually purplish or brownish. Well-developed skin flaps above the eyes are diagnostic. Very venomous.

COMMON LIONFISH
Pterois volitans

Distribution: Tropical Indo-Pacific.
Size: Up to 35 centimeters.
Habitat: Outer reefs, drop-offs, caves in walls from 1 to 50 meters in clear water.
Life Habits: The most commonly observed Lionfish and one of the most graceful and spectacular denizens of the reef. Mainly nocturnal, active predator which will sometimes hunt in schools herding small fish together by spreading out its huge pectoral fins and then gulping them down one by one. If observed at night it will take advantage of the diver's light to attack its sleeping prey.

SPOTFIN LIONFISH
Pterois antennata

Distribution: Tropical Indo-Pacific from East Africa to French Polynesia and from Southern Japan to Australia.
Size: Up to 20 centimeters.
Habitat: Coral reefs and coral heads from 6 to at least 60 meters deep.
Life Habits: Smaller than the Common Lionfish, easily identified by the free, long, white-tipped rays of its pectoral fins and by the blue ocelli on their basal membrane. Frilled tentacles are found above the eyes. Nocturnal, usually solitary, often observed during the day inside small caves or under overhangs. Very venomous like all lionfishes.

WHITE-LINED LIONFISH
Pterois radiata

Distribution: Tropical Indo-Pacific.
Size: Up to 20 centimeters.
Habitat: Rocky reefs and rock-algae mixed habitats, usually less than 15 meters deep.
Life Habits: Dark red-maroon body sporting regular, Y-shaped thin white lines. Pectoral fins rays white and free. Seems to prefer dead coral areas and rocky reefs, possibly because more sensitive than other lionfishes to the stinging nematocysts of living corals. Commonly encountered at night, sometimes observed during the day inside caves or under ledges and overhangs.

THREADFIN LIONFISH
Pterois mombasae

Distribution: Tropical Indo-Pacific from East Africa to Papua New Guinea.
Size: Up to 16 centimeters.
Habitat: Rubble areas in mixed coral-soft sponges habitats in sheltered reefs, usually from 10 to 80 meters.
Life Habits: Very uncommon and rarely observed, normally pale with several brownish broad bands and many large brown spots forming irregular bands at the base of the pectoral fins. The unique color phase illustrated seems to be restricted to the Lembeh Strait in Northern Sulawesi, Indonesia.

DWARF LIONFISH
Dendrochyrus brachypterus

Distribution: Tropical Indo-Pacific from the Red Sea and East Africa to Tonga and from Southern Japan to Australia.
Size: Up to 15 centimeters.
Habitat: Coastal reefs on silty bottoms, often among vegetable debris and on submerged ropes or man-made structures.
Life Habits: Often in small aggregations when resting during the day. Very cryptic and adaptable, rather common and found in a variety of environments showing a very variable coloration. If disturbed it will readily flare its brightly colored aposematic fan-like pectoral fins.

ZEBRA LIONFISH
Dendrochyrus zebra

Distribution: Tropical Indo-Pacific from the Red Sea and East Africa to Samoa and from Southern Japan to Australia.
Size: Up to 20 centimeters.
Habitat: Soft sponges and dead coral, mixed areas from 3 to 80 meters deep.
Life Habits: Smallish, nocturnal, often overlooked by divers. Occurs in a great variety of environments, usually resting in small groups or alone during the day inside large sponges or under ledges and overhangs. Like other lionfishes this species feeds on small fish and crustaceans and is very venomous.

TWO-EYED LIONFISH
Dendrochyrus biocellatus

Distribution: Tropical Indo-Pacific from Mauritius to French Polynesia and from Southern Japan to Australia.
Size: Up to 20 centimeters.
Habitat: Shallow reef flats and drop-offs in clear water from 3 to 50 meters deep.
Life Habits: Queer-looking, strictly nocturnal and rarely observed, easily identified by the two moustache-like barbels at the sides of its mouth which have earned it the nickname of "Fu Manchu Scorpionfish" in some countries. Feeds on small fish and crustaceans it actively hunts in the dark.

PADDLE-FLAP SCORPIONFISH
Rhinopias eschmeyeri

Distribution: Tropical Indo-Pacific from Mauritius to Indonesia and the Philippines.
Size: Up to 20 centimeters.
Habitat: Outer reefs in mixed coral-algae habitats, often close to sponges.
Life Habits: Uncommon and very rarely observed but much sought after by photographers due to its fascinating looks. An ambush predator, cryptic and rather static, which can be very variable in its coloration: pink, tan, orange or yellow are the most common chromatic phases. Rounded edge of dorsal fin is diagnostic.

WEEDY SCORPIONFISH
Rhinopias frondosa

Distribution: Tropical Indo-Pacific from Mauritius to Micronesia.
Size: Up to 23 centimeters.
Habitat: Outer and coastal reefs, often on rubble patches and mixed habitats.
Life Habits: Very uncommon and rarely observed but exceptionally beautiful and considered a highly desirable subject by underwater photographers. Very cryptic but rather variable and extremely colorful: can be bright yellow, orange, pink or even lilac. Deeply indented edge of dorsal fin is diagnostic.

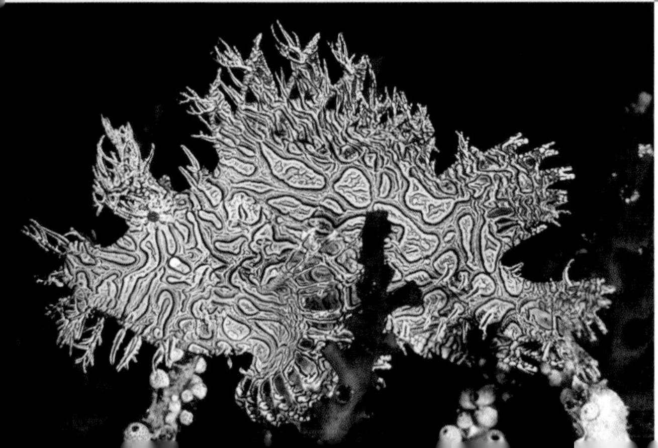

LACY SCORPIONFISH
Rhinopias aphanes

Distribution: Tropical Asian Pacific from Southern Japan to Papua New Guinea, Australia and New Caledonia.
Size: Up to 25 centimeters.
Habitat: Outer coral reefs in clear water from 5 to 30 meters deep.
Life Habits: Yet another species of the rare *Rhinopias* genus, locally common and often observed on exposed spots, close to the crinoids it apparently mimics. Maze-like pattern is diagnostic and constant but colors can vary from yellow to brown, green, tan and even black. White spot under the eye always present.

LEAF FISH
Taenianotus triacanthus

Distribution: Tropical Indo-Pacific.
Size: Up to 12 centimeters.
Habitat: Healthy reef areas, often close to sponges or perched on top of corals.
Life Habits: Leaf or Paperfish are rather common but very cryptic and easily overlooked. Leaf-thin in section, they tend to stay still, swaying rythmically as if they were decaying vegetable matter swept by the surge. Very variable, they periodically shed the outer layer of their skin in one piece to avoid a build-up of sessile organisms like hydroids and algae.

STONEFISHES
Synanceiidae

TOADFISHES
Batrachoididae

The *Synanceiidae* family numbers 5 genera and more than 9 world-wide species, all benthic, extremely cryptic and very static ambush predators. Among the most bizarre and grotesque looking denizens of coral reefs, these species are also the most venomous, being capable of injecting large doses of neurotoxins via the hollow, needle-like dorsal fin rays if stepped on. Death by cardiac arrest may occur, and treatment is very difficult and seldom available locally. Extreme care must be exercised where these species are known to be present as they are rather difficult to locate and can be a real dangers to waders. ~ **U/W Photo Tips:** Stonefish and Devilfish are easy subject which will appeal to those who like the grotesque. Easily framed, they are often not alone, so great care must be exercised to avoid putting a knee or an elbow on one while trying to photograph another. Consequences could be extremely serious indeed.

DEVIL SCORPIONFISH
Inimicus didactylus

Distribution: Tropical Indo-Pacific.
Size: Up to 20 centimeters.
Habitat: Sandy and silty habitats at the base of coral reefs and slopes, often in very shallow water from 1 to 15 meters.
Life Habits: Static, often half- or completely buried in the substrate but easily identified by the bulging eyes, the upturned sbout and the fringed, disarrayed clump of dorsal spines on the back. Coloration very variable but always exceptionally cryptic. If harassed will display flaring aposematic, brightly colored pectoral fins. Extremely venomous and a real danger to waders.

REEF STONEFISH
Synanceia verrucosa

Distribution: Tropical Indo-Pacific from the Red Sea to French Polynesia and from Southern Japan to Australia.
Size: Up to 40 centimeters.
Habitat: Silty, rubble-strewn bottoms in sheltered areas. Often below piers and in extremely shallow water.
Life Habits: Unmistakable and extremely dangerous - often deadly - if stepped on. Very static, almost shapeless, usually half-submerged in the substrate and unbelievably cryptic, with algae and hydroids growing on it and adding to its already perfect camouflage. More dangerous to waders than to divers.

PAINTED STINGFISH
Minous pictus

Distribution: Central Indo-Pacific from Indonesia to the Philippines.
Size: Up to 10 centimeters.
Habitat: Soft bottoms in sheltered bays and lagoons from 12 to 60 meters.
Life Habits: Solitary and strictly nocturnal, with small barbels on fins and free rays of pectoral fins used for "walking" on the substrate like Devilfish do. During the daylight hours usually buried in the soft, silty substrate. Feeds on small crustaceans and fish.

BANDED TOADFISH
Halophyme diemensis

Distribution: Tropical Central Indo-Pacific from the Andamans to Papua New Guinea and Australia.
Size: Up to 26 centimeters.
Habitat: Silty bottoms on sheltered coastal reefs from 1 to 20 meters deep.
Life Habits: Toadfishes belong to the *Batrachoididae* Family, numbering 19 genera and about 69 species. They are circumtropical and look rather similar to scorpionfishes, with a large mouth rimmed by fleshy tendrils.All are sluggish benthic ambush predators and some have venomous spines in the first dorsal fin.

Scorpionfish - Masters of Camouflage

The phenomena involved in mimicry and camouflage are some of the most fascinating among those encountered by observant divers on a coral reef. There is no apparent end to the ingenuity of solutions adopted by predators and prey to trick each other in their endless game for survival. Some species pass themselves off as others while others prefer to masquerade as part of their setting. To our eyes, and once artificially lit by a strobe, many scorpaenids - especially some of the most common scorpionfishes - look more gaudy than camouflaged. In fact, their bright coloration in red, yellow and brown tones, the irregular, convoluted contours of their color patterns and the large number of their dermal flaps, tendrils and warts succeed in making them magically disappear on a seabed of thick coral formations swarming with life and color. One more surprising strategy for successful hunting is clearly demonstrated for the first time in these pages. These close-ups of scorpionfish heads, all more or less taken from the same point of view - ie that of a possible prey, from the front and above - look confusing enough: but just turn the book around and look at them upside down. It doesn't take much to realize that a common pattern of light spots and darker markings suddenly conjures another pair of eyes and another mouth, perfectly reversed and pointing in exactly the opposite direction! How many surprised fish have then bolted in the wrong direction to avoid being eaten and have been abruptly gulped down by that same mouth they were tring to avoid?

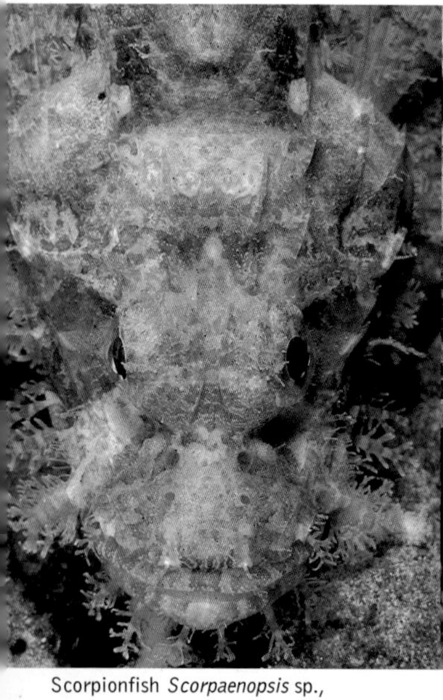
Scorpionfish *Scorpaenopsis* sp., Red Sea, Egypt.

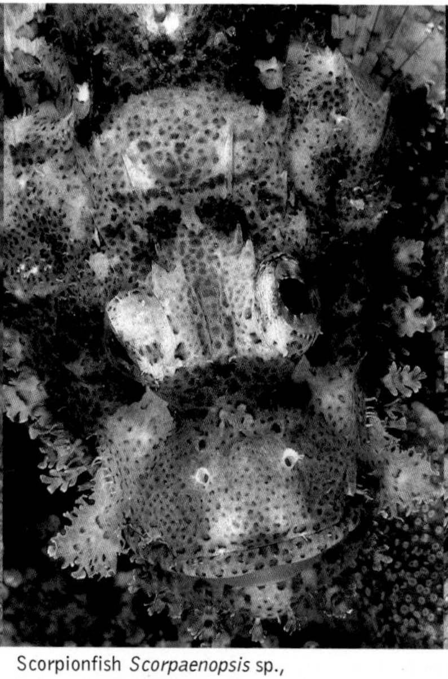
Scorpionfish *Scorpaenopsis* sp., Sulawesi Sea, Malaysia.

Scorpionfish *Scorpaenopsis* sp., Sulawesi Sea, Malaysia.

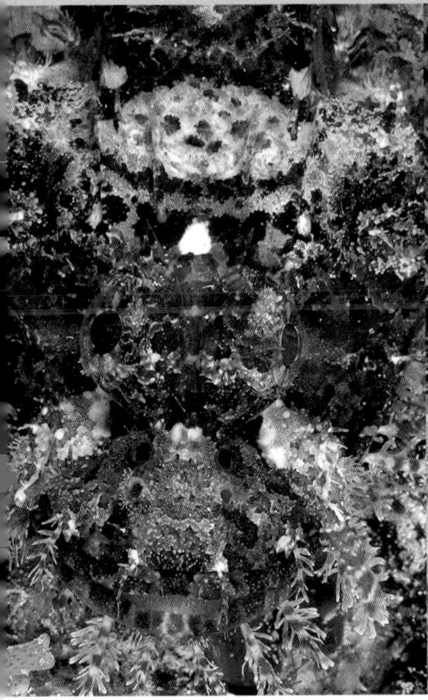

Scorpionfish *Scorpaenopsis* sp.,
Sulawesi Sea, Indonesia.

Scorpionfish *Scorpaenopsis* sp.,
Sulawesi Sea, Malaysia.

Scorpionfish *Scorpaenopsis* sp.,
South China Sea, Malaysia

Scorpionfish *Scorpaenopsis* sp.,
Sulu Sea, Philippines.

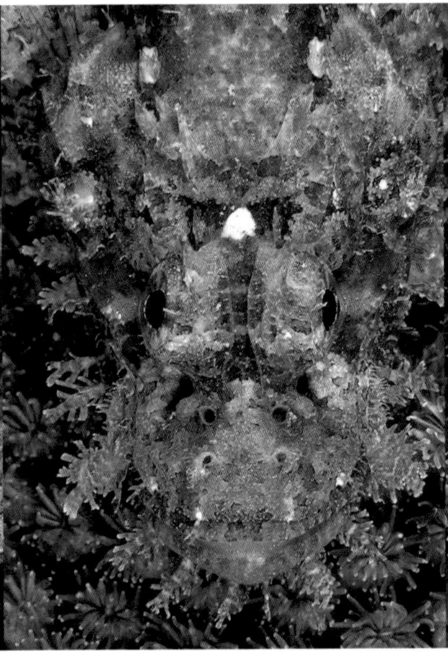

Scorpionfish *Scorpaenopsis* sp.,
South China Sea, Malaysia.

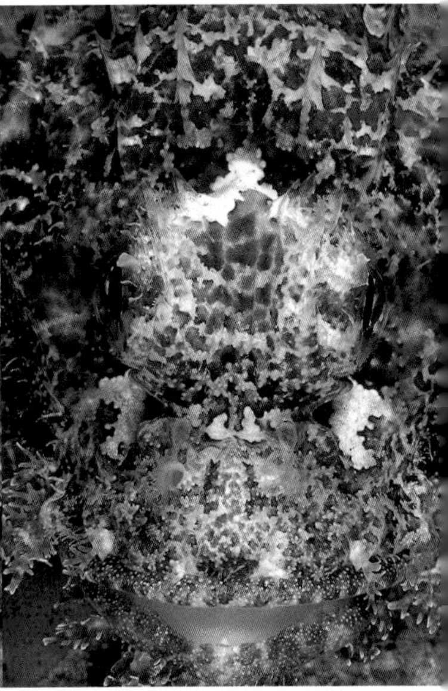

Scorpionfish *Scorpaenopsis* sp.,
Andaman Sea, Thailand.

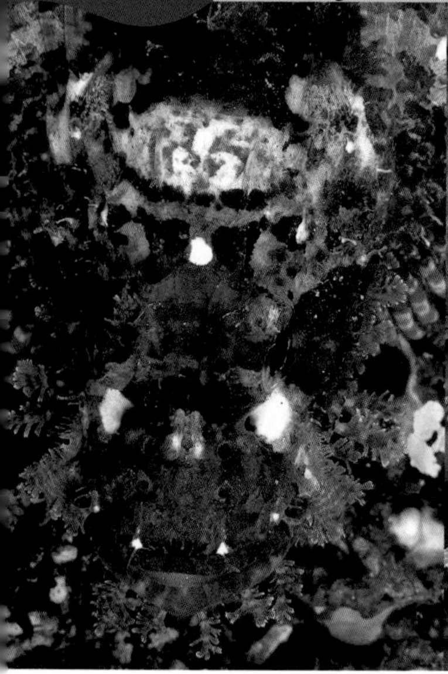

Scorpionfish *Scorpaenopsis* sp., Sulawesi Sea, Indonesia.

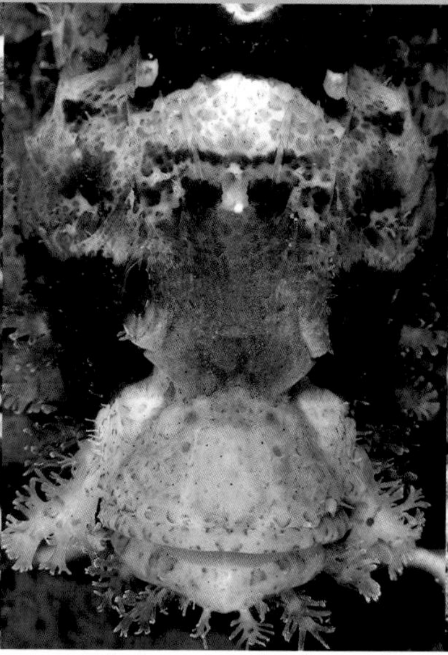

Scorpionfish *Scorpaenopsis* sp., Red Sea, Sudan.

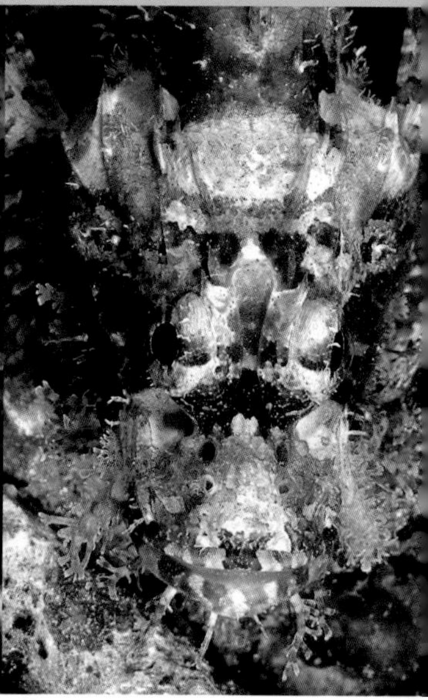

Scorpionfish *Scorpaenopsis* sp., Manado, Indonesia.

Scorpionfish *Scorpaenopsis* sp., Indian Ocean, Maldives.

Scorpionfish *Scorpaenopsis* sp., Manado, Indonesia.

Scorpionfish *Scorpaenopsis* sp., Sulu Sea, Malaysia.

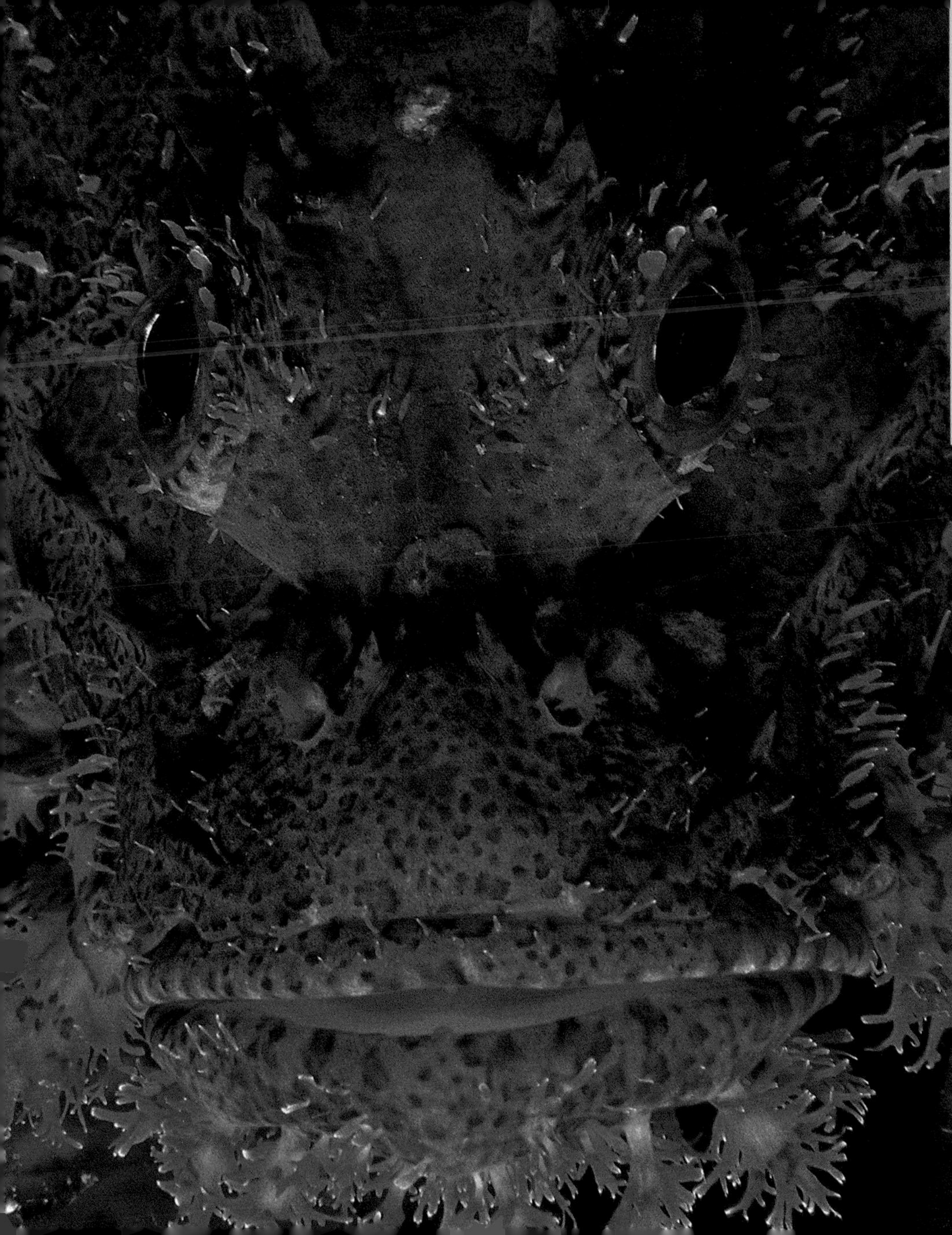

Scorpionfish *Scorpaenopsis sp.*, Pulau Sipadan, Sulawesi Sea, Malaysian Borneo

WASPFISHES

Tetrarogidae
Pataecidae

This family numbers about 15 genera and about 40 species, most of which are of no consequence to divers. All feature a large, sail-like dorsal fin originating on top of the head and giving them a typical bird-like profile. Usually rather static and very cryptic, mimicking dead vegetable matter; the two featured species are quite venomous and capable of inflicting extremely painful wounds with their needle-like hollow fin rays connected to a venom gland. ~ **U/W Photo Tips:** Waspfishes are rarely encountered by most divers due to their exceptional cryptic capabilities but make wonderful and quite underrated subjects for the discerning macro photographer, especially regarding camouflage and behavior. A macro lens (105 or 60mm) will suffice for interesting profile or frontal shots.

COCKATOO WASPFISH
Ablabys taenianotus

Distribution: Tropical central Indo-Pacific from the Andaman Sea to Fiji and from Japan to Australia.
Size: Up to 15 centimeters.
Habitat: Sand, silt or rubble bottoms in coastal reefs and shallow water.
Life Habits: Solitary or in pairs, swaying in the surge mimicking a dead leaf among submerged vegetable debris. Body laterally compressed, with tall dorsal fin. Coloration always cryptic but extremely variable, ranging from deep yellow to rusty brown or almost white.

SPINY WASPFISH
Ablabys macracanthus

Distribution: Central Indo-Pacific from Indonesia to the Philippines.
Size: Up to 18 centimeters.
Habitat: Sandy or silty bottoms in sheltered areas, bays and lagoons, usually in shallow water from 8 to 50 meters.
Life Habits: Difficult to differentiate from previous species but usually with dorsal fin margin less incised. Very cryptic, mimicking a dead leaf swaying in the surge. Solitary or in small loose aggregations among debris.

BLACKSPOT WASPFISH
Cottapistus praepositus

Distribution: Central Indo-Pacific from India to Papua New Guinea.
Size: Up to 10 centimeters.
Habitat: Coastal reefs on mud or sand from 3 to 20 meters deep.
Life Habits: A poorly known small species, rarely observed by divers. Similar to other waspfishes but less compressed laterally. Also described or possibly confused in literature as *Richardsonichthys leucogaster* or Whiteface Waspfish.

LONGSPINE WASPFISH
Paracentropogon longispinus

Distribution: Tropical Indo-Pacific from India to Australia and the Philippines.
Size: Up to 12 centimeters.
Habitat: Silty and sandy bottoms in coastal reefs from 7 to 30 meters.
Life Habits: Solitary and cryptic, rarely observed by divers, and capable of inflicting painful wounds like all waspfishes. Coloration extremely variable but often rather gaudy, going from pale brown to deep purple, often with a bright white facial mask.Hunts for small crustaceans at night.

RED INDIANFISH
Pataecus fronto

Distribution: Subtropical, endemic to Western and Southern Australia
Size: Up to 35 centimeters.
Habitat: Sponge beds, rocky reefs and estuaries from 10 to 80 meters deep.
Life Habits: Belonging to the Family *Pataecidae*, this waspfish is endemic to Australian waters and is occasionally encountered among sponges, which it closely mimics with great success. Body compressed, with very tall dorsal fin; coloration is brick red, orange or scarlet. This species periodically sheds its skin in one single piece to get rid of encrustations.

VELVETFISHES
Aploactinidae
Gnathanacanthidae

Velvetfishes are represented by a few highly specialized families in the Western Pacific and Indian Oceans, numbering about 12 genera in the family *Aploactinidae* and only one in the family *Gnathanacanthidae*. Most are benthic dwellers and are defined by having a body which is usually velvety due to the modified, prickly scales, by having knob-like spines on the head and by the unbranched fin rays. The majority of these fish are usually ignored or unseen by divers. ~ **U/W Photo Tips:** Velvetfishes are in general exceptionally well camouflaged, quite uncommon and very rarely observed by divers in tropical waters. Being very static, they are easily approached and make compliant subjects, but are of very little interest to the average, non-specialist underwater photographer.

PHANTOM VELVETFISH
Paraploactis kagoshimensis

Distribution: Central Indo-Pacific from Indonesia to Southern Japan.
Size: Up to 12 centimeters.
Habitat: Silty, soft bottoms on coastal reefs from 2 to 20 meters.
Life Habits: Grotesque but exceptionally cryptic, hardly distinguishable from a rotting piece of wood lying on the sea bottom. Body very stiff, compressed, brownish or blackish, covered in bony knobs and ridges.Will not move away if harassed, relying on camouflage to avoid predation. Probably venomous.

RED VELVETFISH
Gnathanacanthus goetzeei

Distribution: Subtropical, endemic to Australia from Victoria to Western Australia and Tasmania.
Size: Up to 30 centimeters
Habitat: Seagrass beds on sheltered coastal areas from 5 to 30 meters deep.
Life Habits: The only member of its family, this species is endemic to subtropical Australian waters and can be observed in brown, red or yellowish colorations. The body is highly compressed and the skin is covered with low papillae which give it a velvety texture. It is a mainly nocturnal species.

A family closely related to the Scorpionfishes numbering only 2 genera and 7 species. These are all bottom-dwelling and bottom- feeding medium-sized fish whose main feature are the very large pectoral fins, which when spread in alarm form an almost perfect disc and which are used for gliding away while swimming close to the bottom. A thin long dorsal fin can also be fully erected when the animal feels endangered. ~ **U/W Photo Tips:** Flying gurnards make wonderful subjects for underwater photographers once they have been detected. Best shots are taken from above with a macro or medium focal length lens when the alarmed fish is displaying its broad pectoral fins. Please always avoid unduly and frantically chasing your subject around just to take a good picture, however.

FLYING GURNARDS

Dactylopteridae
Triglidae

FLYING GURNARD

Dactyloptena orientalis

Distribution: Tropical Indo-Pacific from the Red Sea to Hawai'i and Australia.
Size: Up to 30 centimeters.
Habitat: Sand or mud bottoms with sparse seagrass in sheltered areas from 6 to over 100 meters deep.
Life Habits: Rarely noticed when camouflaged or half-buried in the substrate but truly spectacular when displaying, flaring its huge peacock-like pectoral fins. Coloration is generally subdued but large pectorals show beautiful, iridescent ocelli and scribbles; large eye is bright red. Feeds on benthic species like gobies and crustaceans.

EASTERN SPINY GURNARD

Lepidotrigla pleuracanthica

Distribution: Subtropical and temperate waters, endemic to Australia from New South Wales to Western Australia.
Size: Up to 20 centimeters.
Habitat: Sand and rubble areas in estuaries and coastal reefs from 2 to 20 meters deep.
Life Habits: This species and the closely related Spiny Gurnard *L. papilio* are endemic to subtropical and temperate Australia, where are often encountered on sand beds. If harassed, they will display raising the rounded, ocellated dorsal fin and spreading the fan-like pectorals.

FLATHEADS
Platycephalidae

This is a fairly large family numbering about 18 genera and more than 60 species, only a few of which are regularly encountered by sport divers in tropical waters. Almost all species belonging to this Family live on silty, soft bottoms, spending a great time half-buried in the substrate; all lack a swim bladder and sport a broad, flattened, alligator-like head with a large mouth and several spines and bony ridges. They are mainly ambush predators, being generally more active at night and rarely leaving the substrate on which they are normally found. ~ **U/W Photo Tips:** Flatheads are rather nondescript and rarely observed by the average diver, but Crocodile Fish are very interesting and easily approached subjects. Excellent results can be obtained using a macro lens (105 or 60mm) to take extreme close-up of their intricately ornamented livery.

CROCODILE FISH
Cymbacephalus beauforti

Distribution: Tropical Central Indo-Pacific from Malaysia to Micronesia.
Size: Up to 90 centimeters.
Habitat: Coral rubble or silty bottoms in sheltered areas from 1 to 30 meters.
Life Habits: Large, impressive but very cryptic and harmless species, often lying in ambush in the open confiding in its perfect camouflage to escape detection. Easily identified thanks to its great size, the wide head and the fine, scribbled lines which cover its bulky, flattened body. Easily approached underwater.

LONGSNOUT FLATHEAD
Thysanophrys chiltonae

Distribution: Tropical Indo-Pacific from the Red Sea and East Africa to French Polynesia and from Southern Japan to Australia.
Size: Up to 30 centimeters.
Habitat: Silty or sandy soft bottoms in sheltered areas from 6 to 30 meters.
Life Habits: Often buried in the sand and escaping detection. More active at night when it crawls on the bottom looking for prey. Several very similar species, all rather small and pale in color. Easily approached but usually ignored by divers.

A very peculiar and interesting family, numbering worldwide 8 genera and about 50 different species, all with a large upward-pointing mouth and dorsally positioned eyes on a cuboidal large head, a boxy body and two venomous spines behind the gill opening and above the pectorals. All stargazers are solitary, perfectly adapted, bottom-dwelling, ambushing predators, and some species actually sport a worm-like lure growing from the floor of the mouth which is used to attract unsuspecting prey. ~ **U/W Photo Tips:** Stargazers are not easily found as most are strictly nocturnal, and even those encountered by chance are usually carefully camouflaged. If one is discovered, however, the best shots will be taken from directly above, taking advantage of the ghastly death's head grin which is so typical of these strange and curiously interesting creatures.

STARGAZERS

Uranoscopidae

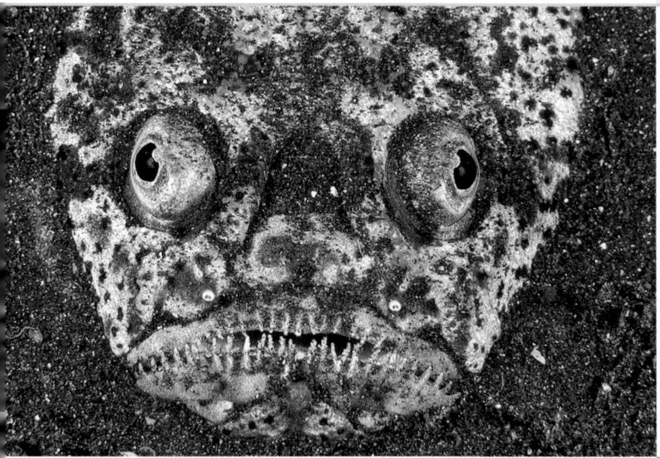

WHITEMARGIN STARGAZER

Uranoscopus sulphureus

Distribution: Tropical Indo-Pacific from the Red Sea to Micronesia.
Size: Up to 35 centimeters.
Habitat: Sand bottoms in sheltered coastal areas from 5 to 150 meters deep.
Life Habits: Strictly nocturnal, completely buried under the sand during the day; at night it rises to expose only the eyes, the mouth and a small part of the upward-facing head while it ambushes passing prey such as small fish or cephalopods. Unmistakable death's head grin emerging from the substrate - quite startling at first sight - makes for a unique photographic subject.

RETICULATE STARGAZER

Uranoscopus chinensis

Distribution: Tropical Central Indo-Pacific from Malaysia to Australia.
Size: Up to 30 centimeters.
Habitat: Soft sand and silt bottoms in sheltered coastal areas from 5 to 50 meters deep.
Life Habits: Very similar to the preceding species but with a paler backround, featuring dark brown or reddish blotches and reticulations. Usually completely immobile and buried in the substrate, emerging only with part of the head to ambush passing prey like fish or squid at twilight and during the night.

Colors and Camouflage

The art of disappearing among a riot of colors is the ultimate trick for survival in the highly competitive environment of the reef. But hiding in the endless visibility of the open water of the ocean is even more difficult

At first glance, the world of coral reefs may look like a kingdom of gaudy costumes and flamboyant colors. In reality, however, many of its inhabitants deftly employ sophisticated camouflage techniques to make themselves as inconspicuous as possible, both to procure food and to avoid becoming food for predators. These aims are frequently linked to one another. Even the large pelagic species that frequent the seaward outer reef adopt this trick. Sharks and manta rays immediately come to mind when one thinks of the technique called *countershading*, adopted by man for air superiority camouflage on military aircraft. Viewed from above, the animal's dark grey or bluish back blends well with the shadowy depths beneath, while its pale or white belly makes it nearly invisible against the backdrop of the surface when the animal is seen from below, against the

Ambushing lionfish often lurk among gorgonians.

light of the sun's rays. Several pelagic predators - tunas, barracuda and jacks among others - hunting in shallow water have instead adopted a typically "chrome-plated" and shiny coloration, interrupted by dark vertical bands. They rely on sudden bursts of speed, and this coloration helps them blend effectively into the mottled shadows of the shallows, where the sun's penetration and surge action are more intense. Large pelagic hunters generally adopt countershaded but substantially uniform liveries since the monochromatic backdrop of the open ocean would not offer any special advantages to spotted or striped patterns, which in fact would make the animal easier to spot. On the other hand, stripes and mottles prove far more advantageous to species with more sedentary habits. A *somatolitic* livery enables the animal to literally disappear by obscuring its contours against an equally kaleidoscopic backdrop. Among families that distinguish themselves in the application of this formula, the true masters are lionfish and scorpionfish (*Scorpaenidae*), ghost pipefish (*Syngnathidae*) and frogfish (*Antennariidae*). These creatures often combine the advantages offered by a striped and mottled livery to those provided by skin flaps and by a body that - in the most extreme cases - looks like anything but a fish. The effectiveness of camouflage

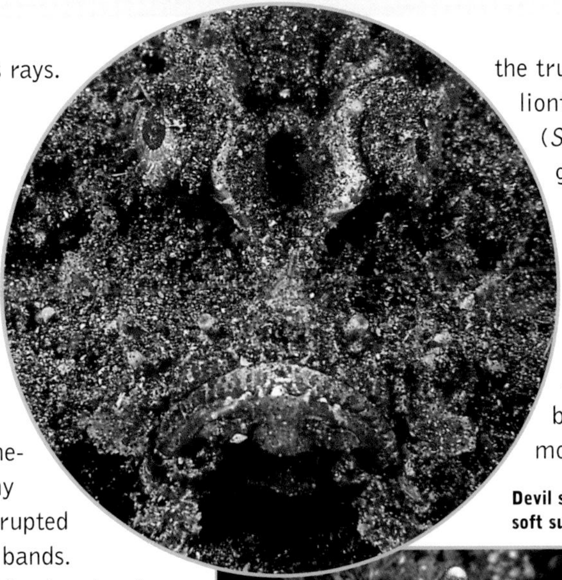

Devil scorpionfish often hide in the soft substrate.

Frogfish perfectly mimic the sponges among which they live.

Zoom

Grey reef sharks are countershaded to hunt in open water.

is optimized in several species by habits, posture and by the animal's bodily structure. *Synanceia verrucosa* stonefish maintain such a scrupulous immobility that they usually end up almost covered with algae and hydroids contributing to their camouflage; ghost pipefish, *Solenostomus* spp., stand in a head-down, vertical position; flounders and soles are distinctively flattened, while frogfish have evolved pawlike pectoral fins to better grip sponges. If these techniques and camouflage are largely typical of species that try to disappear in the environment surrounding them for hunting purposes, there are many occasions when a species uses the so-called Batesian mimicry - a theory named after H.W. Bates, one of the first scientists to study it (1862) - to pass itself off for another. The little predatory blenny *Aspidontus taeniatus* gets close to its victims by making itself look like the harmless common cleaner wrasse *Labroides dimidiatus*; and the larval stage of the sea cucumber *Bohadschia graeffei* assumes a color and shape nearly identical to the inedible and poisonous nudibranch *Phyllidia varicosa*. Examples of this mimicry are numerous and intriguing. It will also be useful to remember the effective and surprising function carried out by the chromatophores or specialized skin cells in many species. They ultimately determine the animal's coloration and may sometimes be dilated or contracted at will, allowing the animal to change its own coloration.

Stingrays often hide under the sand.

Barracudas commonly prowl among the reflections of shallow water.

Diver and Coral Grouper *Cephalopholis miniata*, Raja Ampat, West Papua, Indonesia.

GROUPERS AND BASSLETS

Serranidae

This is one of the most important, best known and most varied families in the community of coral reefs, numbering almost 50 genera and more than 400 species, often divided in a confusing array of subfamilies. *Epinephelinae* are the true groupers, generally medium-sized or large fish, usually very colorful and closely associated to the corals; *Anthiinae* group the small plankton-eating basslets, often found in enormous numbers in the water column; *Grammistinae* group instead the so-called soapfishes, secretive and with a slimy skin covered in toxic mucus. ~ **U/W Photo Tips:** Groupers are usually rather shy and can be approached only with some difficulty when resting under ledges during the day, while basslets are very active and found in dense schools in the water column. Both are wonderful and normally very colorful subjects but require a degree of patience and a bit of cunning to get close to.

SLENDER GROUPER

Anyperodon leucogrammicus

Distribution: Tropical Indo-Pacific from the Red Sea to Southern Japan and Australia.
Size: Up to 40 centimeters.
Habitat: Among branching corals and under ledges in healthy coral reef and clear water from 5 to 50 meters deep.
Life Habits: Rather wary but unmistakable, solitary, often hiding among branching or soft coral colonies. Body pale green-gray with many fine red or orange spots, snout elongated. Juveniles sport a very different striped livery mimicking that of harmless *Halichoeres* wrasses, which they use to approach prey unnoticed.

REDMOUTH GROUPER

Aethaloperca rogaa

Distribution: Tropical Indo-Pacific from the Red Sea to Fiji and Australia.
Size: Up to 60 centimeters.
Habitat: Inside caves or under ledges in coral-rich areas on outer reefs from 3 to 50 meters deep.
Life Habits: This is a solitary, wary, not easily approached species. The body is brown or blackish, clearly more rounded than that of other groupers; the inside of the mouth is bright red and diagnostic. Feeds on fish, crustaceans and cephalopods like most groupers.

PEACOCK GROUPER
Cephalopholis argus

Distribution: Tropical Indo-Pacific from the Red Sea to Australia and Southern Japan.
Size: Up to 45 centimeters.
Habitat: Coastal and outer reefs in clear water from 1 to 20 meters deep in coral rich areas.
Life Habits: Wary and rather difficult to approach closely but very colorful, often observed freely swimming among branching corals on reef crests and tops. Sometimes in loose aggregations or pairs. Coloration is vivid but its intensity can be greatly varied at will, often displaying several pale bars on rear body.

BLUESPOTTED GROUPER
Cephalopholis cyanostigma

Distribution: Central Indo-Pacific from Eastern Malaysia to the Great Barrier Reef in Australia.
Size: Up to 35 centimeters.
Habitat: Coastal and outer reefs, often under overhangs from 1 to 50 meters.
Life Habits: Wary, not easily approached; commonly observed while sneaking among branching coral formations, most of the times close to the substrate. Body is reddish, often mottled, with many small black-edged pale blue spots. Juveniles are dark gray or brown with yellow fins and tail.

BLUELINED GROUPER
Cephalopholis formosa

Distribution: Tropical Indo-Pacific from India to North-West Australia.
Size: Up to 34 centimeters.
Habitat: Sheltered silty or dead reefs, also close to river mouths.
Life Habits: Solitary and very wary, difficult to approach; often observed among thick branching coral formations. Thick body is brown or yellowish with many horizontal bright blue lines on head, body and fins. Feeds on crustaceans, cephalopods and other fish.

CHOCOLATE GROUPER
Cephalopholis boenak

Distribution: Tropical Indo-Pacific from East Africa to Southern Japan.
Size: Up to 26 centimeters.
Habitat: Silty or dead reefs in sheltered areas from 4 to 40 meters deep.
Life Habits: Usually solitary but often locally very abundant and in loose aggregations; body dark or pale brown depending on mood with several paler vertical bands, margin of dorsal, ventral and caudal fins yellow and blue. Feeds mainly on crustaceans.

LEOPARD GROUPER
Cephalopholis leoparda

Distribution: Indo-Pacific from East Africa to French Polynesia and Australia.
Size: Up to 25 centimeters.
Habitat: Coastal and outer reefs, on healthy slopes and reef crests in clear water from 3 to 40 meters deep.
Life Habits: One of the smallest reef groupers, usually solitary, very shy and not readily approached or identified. Body reddish, mottled, with many orangish or pinkish red spots.Dark small saddle at the base of the tail is diagnostic.

FLAGTAIL GROUPER
Cephalopholis urodeta

Distribution: Tropical Indo-Pacific from East Africa to French Polynesia.
Size: Up to 27 centimeters.
Habitat: Coastal and outer reef crests with rich soft and hard coral growth from 1 to 60 meters deep.
Life Habits: Solitary and usually wary, often observed while sneaking among soft and hard corals. Body brown to deep red, with diagnostic white bands across corners of the tail, missing however in the Indian Ocean form.

CORAL GROUPER
Cephalopholis miniata

Distribution: Tropical Indo-Pacific from the Red Sea and East Africa to Southern Japan and Australia.
Size: Up to 40 centimeters.
Habitat: Coral-rich areas on coastal and outer reefs, in clear water from 5 to more than 50 meters deep.
Life Habits: One of the most commonly observed reef groupers, generally solitary but occasionally in small aggregations. Often encountered on drop-offs or inside wrecks. Body is bright orange to red with many bright blue, dark edged round spots. Not particularly wary and possibly for this reason often captured by local fishermen.

SADDLED GROUPER
Cephalopholis sexmaculata

Distribution: Indo-Pacific from East Africa to French Polynesia and Japan .
Size: Up to 45 centimeters.
Habitat: Coastal and outer reef drop-offs in clear water from 10 to 150 meters deep, often inside caves and crevices.
Life Habits: Wary and solitary but very beautiful, usually observed upside down inside caves or crevices or positioned vertically on walls. Body is bright orange-red with several pale saddles which become bars on the sides and several bright blue spots. Feeds on small fish, mostly cardinals and basslets, and crustaceans.

TOMATO GROUPER
Cephalopholis sonnerati

Distribution: Indo-Pacific from East Africa to Southern Japan and Australia.
Size: Up to 65 centimeters.
Habitat: Coastal reefs with rocks or corals, often on silty bottoms.
Life Habits: Rounded body, bright red with a dense network of darker red spots on the head. Usually solitary, not particularly wary and sometimes easily approached. Often observed being serviced by cleaner shrimp: large adults usually encountered deep.

HARLEQUIN GROUPER
Cephalopholis polleni

Distribution: Tropical Indo-Pacific from South East Africa to South West Japan.
Size: Up to 43 centimeters.
Habitat: Outer reef walls, drop-offs and steep walls usually below 30 meters.
Life Habits: A solitary and shockingly beautiful reef grouper, not too wary but restricted to deeper water. Body is bright yellow-green with several horizontal bright blue or violet stripes on body, head and fins. Active during the day but rarely encountered by divers.

OCELOT GROUPER
Epinephelus dermatolepis

Distribution: Eastern Pacific from the Gulf of California to Ecuador.
Size: Up to 90 centimeters.
Habitat: Rocky reefs, caves in clear water from 3 to 200 meters deep.
Life Habits: Very wary and not easily approached, usually encountered in deeper waters. The almost identical *E. inermis* takes its place in the Atlantic from Florida to the Caribbean; also in Bermuda. Easily identified underwater by the steep head profile, the white-mottled and spotted tall body and the yellow-margined fleshy fins.

AREOLATE GROUPER
Epinephelus areolatus

Distribution: Tropical Indo-Pacific from the Red Sea to to North-West Australia.
Size: Up to 40 centimeters.
Habitat: Muddy, silty bottoms in sheltered areas from 6 to 200 meters.
Life Habits: Whitish to gray with several rounded brownish spots; narrow white diagnostic straight margin on truncate tail. Solitary but rarely found in small, loose aggregations resting on the bottom.Easily confused underwater with several other many-spotted species.

BLEEKER'S GROUPER
Epinephelus bleekeri

Distribution: Tropical Indo-Pacific from Oman to Taiwan and Australia.
Size: Up to 65 centimeters.
Habitat: Coastal reefs on silty bottoms from 1 to 50 meters deep.
Life Habits: Variable background, dark grey to pale whitish body with numerous medium sized orange spots, white margin often present on darker tail. Usually solitary on shallow flats or muddy slopes.

FLAG GROUPER
Epinephelus labriformis

Distribution: Eastern Pacific from the Gulf of California to Colombia.
Size: Up to 100 centimeters.
Habitat: Rocky reefs and caves in clear water from 5 to 70 meters deep.
Life Habits: Usually encountered on rocky reefs and walls. Easily identified underwater by the ten dark bands on the sides and by the bright blue and orange spots on the head. Feeds on crustaceans, smaller fish and cephalopods .

GREASY GROUPER
Epinephelus tauvina

Distribution: Tropical Indo-Pacific from the Red Sea to French Polynesia and from Southern Japan to the Great Barrier Reef.
Size: Up to 75 centimeters.
Habitat: Coastal and outer reefs, also sheltered lagoons and sand bottoms.
Life Habits: Solitary and quite common. Several similarly spotted species: can be identified underwater by the whitish, mottled body with several reddish brown small spots. Sometimes darker saddles are present on the back and sides.

HIGHFIN GROUPER
Epinephelus maculatus

Distribution: Tropical Indo-Pacific from East Africa to Samoa.
Size: Up to 60 centimeters.
Habitat: Open sand bottoms at the base of coastal and outer reefs in water 2 to 100 meters deep.
Life Habits: Solitary, often observed and rather easily approached on open sand. Body pale brown covered in orange-brown polygonal spots; two bright white saddles often "flashed" on the forehead and in the middle of the back. Juveniles on sand, often mimicking nudibranchs.

WHITESTREAKED GROUPER
Epinephelus ongus

Distribution: Tropical Indo-Pacific from East Africa to Australia.
Size: Up to 35 centimeters.
Habitat: Inside caves or under ledges in coastal reefs and sheltered lagoons from 5 to 25 meters deep.
Life Habits: Solitary, very wary, occasionally and locally common. Secretive and cryptic, sometimes near large sponges. Easily identfied by darker head and finely, densely spotted brownish-greenish body. Juveniles black with white bright spots and yellow pectoral fins, often observed among branching corals.

ORANGE-SPOTTED GROUPER
Epinephelus coioides

Distribution: Tropical Indo-Pacific from East Africa to Samoa.
Size: Up to 100 centimeters.
Habitat: Estuaries, coastal lagoons and sheltered bays often in turbid water from 1 to 100 meters deep
Life Habits: An impressive species, often encountered on large bommies and coral outcrops or inside wrecks. Massive, pale, with several orangish spots on head, body and fins and four irregular dark saddles or H-shaped bars on sides.

BLACKTIP GROUPER
Epinephelus fasciatus

Distribution: Tropical Indo-Pacific from the Red Sea to French Polynesia and from Southern Japan to Australia.
Size: Up to 40 centimeters.
Habitat: Rocky outcrops and coral bommies in healthy reefs or silty coastal environments from 1 to 150 meters deep.
Life Habits: Very common, often observed in loose aggregations of several individuals resting on the bottom or on coral heads and sponges. Coloration extremely variable, from almost white to strongly banded, but always with very sharply defined facial markings. Black tips of dorsal spines are diagnostic.

LONGFIN GROUPER
Epinephelus quoyanus

Distribution: Tropical Indo-Pacific from East Africa to Indonesia.
Size: Up to 50 centimeters.
Habitat: Coastal and estuarine reefs from 1 to 70 meters deep.
Life Habits: Body robust and pale with polygonal darker spots and brownish diagonal bands; also pair of dark bands under gill cover. Quite common, easily confused with several other species all similarly spotted. Usually solitary, often observed and rather easily approached while resting on the bottom leaning against corals or rocks.

HONEYCOMB GROUPER
Epinephelus merra

Distribution: Tropical Indo-Pacific from East Africa to French Polynesia.
Size: Up to 32 centimeters.
Habitat: Coastal and outer reefs in sheltered lagoons and bays from 1 to 50 meters deep, usually in shallow water.
Life Habits: Easily confused with the preceding species and similarly spotted but devoid of any diagnostic distinctive markings. Solitary, often observed resting on the bottom, leaning against rocks.

CAMOUFLAGE GROUPER
Epinephelus polyphekadion

Distribution: Tropical Indo-Pacific from the Red Sea to French Polynesia and from Southern Japan to Australia.
Size: Up to 65 centimeters.
Habitat: Coastal and outer reefs and walls in clear water 1 to 50 meters deep.
Life Habits: Body very fat and robust, mottled in a confusing pattern of white and brownish shades with several small spots on head. Like most groupers can change colors and their intensity in a very short time. Solitary and rather wary, seldom observed by sport divers.

PANAMA GROUPER
Epinephelus panamensis

Distribution: Eastern Pacific Ocean from the Gulf of California to Peru.
Size: Up to 50 centimeters.
Habitat: Rocky outcrops and wall cracks in clear water from 5 to 30 meters deep.
Life Habits: Exceptionally well camouflaged, often sitting in the open but unnoticed by divers. Body light olive with darker diagonal bands, finely dotted with many well-distanced light blue spots. Feeds on crustaceans, cephalopods and small fish.

GRAYSBY
Epinephelus cruentatus

Distribution: Western Atlantic Ocean from Southern Florida to Brazil. Also in Caribbean and Bermuda.
Size: Up to 30 centimeters.
Habitat: Coral reefs and small caves in clear water from 3 to 20 meters deep.
Life Habits: One of the most commonly observed groupers in the Caribbean. Wary, often encountered resting on the bottom. Background color is light brown or gray with a fine pattern of roundish orange-red spots on the head, body and fins. Can pale or darken in a few seconds.

BARRAMUNDI COD
Cromileptes altivelis

Distribution: West Pacific from Eastern Malaysia to Australia and New Caledonia.
Size: Up to 70 centimeters.
Habitat: Coastal, silty, often dead reefs and slopes from 1 to 40 meters deep.
Life Habits: Unmistakable: body pale grey-greenish with numerous widely spaced black spots; compressed body with broad fins and elongated, sloping snout. Juveniles are bright pure white with larger black spots (see page...). Often found hovering close to crevices or among thick branching coral colonies.

TIGER GROUPER
Mycteroperca tigris

Distribution: Western Atlantic Ocean from Florida to Brazil. Also Bahamas, Caribbean, Bermuda and Gulf of Mexico.
Size: Up to 60 centimeters.
Habitat: Reefs and walls in clear water from 1 to 15 meters deep.
Life Habits: Unmistakable: impressive, stout body with bright reddish "tiger stripes" over light background. Like all groupers can dramatically pale or darken in a matter of seconds. Usually wary but occasionally curious like most large members of the same Family.

SQUARETAIL CORAL GROUPER
Plectropomus areolatus

Distribution: Tropical Indo-Pacific from the Red Sea to Australia and Japan.
Size: Up to 80 centimeters.
Habitat: Coastal and outer reefs from 2 to 20 meters deep, also lagoons.
Life Habits: Large, robust body with a whitish or pale grey background and many dark-edged blue spots all over. Often darker saddles on back, edge of caudal fin dusky and straight. Usually solitary, occasionally - like all groupers - in large loose aggregations. Feeds on fish, crustaceans and cephalopods .

HIGHFIN CORAL GROUPER
Plectropomus oligacanthus

Distribution: Central Indo-Pacific, from Indonesia to the Philippines, Micronesia and Australia.
Size: Up to 75 centimeters.
Habitat: Deep drop-offs and steep walls in clear water from 5 to 150 meters.
Life Habits: Unmistakable: body reddish to violet with numerous bright blue lines and dots all over. Spectacular and very colorful but solitary, very wary and rarely observed, also difficult to approach. Juveniles mimic harmless *Cheilinus* sp. wrasses to get close to prey unnoticed.

SPOTTED CORAL GROUPER
Plectropomus maculatus

Distribution: Central Indo-Pacific from Eastern Malaysia to Papua New Guinea.
Size: Up to 125 centimeters.
Habitat: Silty coastal reefs, bays, lagoons and algal slopes from 5 to 50 meters deep.
Life Habits: Locally common, usually solitary but occasionally in large, loose aggregations, especially during the mating season. Body robust, reddish, brownish or olive green with numerous round light blue spots which become elongate on the head. Often caught by local fishermen.

BLACKSADDLE CORAL GROUPER
Plectropomus laevis

Distribution: Indo-Pacific from East Africa to French Polynesia and Australia.
Size: Up to 125 centimeters.
Habitat: Coastal and outer reefs in a variety of habitats from 5 to 100 meters.
Life Habits: Very variable, sometimes white with black saddles and yellow tail. Also known for this reason as "Footballer Cod". The illustrated color phase is possibly only restricted to mature males. An aggressive, dominant feeder often observed close to slopes and coral rubble terraces at medium depth. Wary but occasionally curious.

LEOPARD CORAL GROUPER
Plectropomus leopardus

Distribution: Central Indo-Pacific from the South China Sea to Australia.
Size: Up to 70 centimeters.
Habitat: Coastal and outer reefs in rich coral growth from 3 to 100 meters deep.
Life Habits: Very variable coloration, but usually red or brownish with several small blue spots on head, body and fins; easily confused with several similarly marked species. Usually solitary, rarely in small loose aggregations during mating season, often observed resting under large table corals. Feeds on reef fish, crustaceans and cephalopods.

ROVING CORAL GROUPER
Plectropomus pessuliferus

Distribution: Tropical Indo-Pacific from the Red Sea to Indonesia.
Size: Up to 120 centimeters.
Habitat: Coastal, outer reef tops in clear water from 10 to 150 meters deep.
Life Habits: Large, thick-set and impressive: body is brown, orangish or olive green with numerous, small, vertically elongate bright blue spots; dark saddles on back occasionally present. An aggressive and dominant feeder, usually solitary and occasionally curious.

YELLOW-EDGED LYRETAIL
Variola louti

Distribution: Tropical Indo-Pacific from the Red Sea to Australia and Polynesia.
Size: Up to 80 centimeters.
Habitat: Coastal and outer reef tops with rich coral growth, in clear water 3 to 250 meters deep .
Life Habits: One of the most beautiful reef groupers, easily identified by the bright violet to orange body with many violet to blue spots and by the unmistakable lyre-shaped tail with a bright yellow margin. Solitary but occasionally encountered in loose aggregations during mating season.

YELLOWBACK ANTHIAS
Pseudanthias evansi

Distribution: Indian Ocean from East Africa to the Andaman archipelago.
Size: Up to 10 centimeters.
Habitat: Rich coral areas, steep walls and drop-offs in clear water from 5 to 40 meters deep.
Life Habits: Usually encountered in large schools in the water column close to the reef wall, feeding on plankton. Body from pale to bright violet with yellow back; red stripe across eye. Dominant males more colorful than females.

SQUARE-SPOT ANTHIAS
Pseudanthias pleurotaenia

Distribution: West Pacific from Indonesia to Samoa and Australia.
Size: Up to 20 centimeters.
Habitat: Rich coral areas, steep walls, slopes and drop-offs in clear water from 5 to 180 meters deep.
Life Habits: One of the larger basslets, usually observed in very loose aggregations in deep water below 30 meters. Males are bright magenta with square violet spot on the side; females are golden orange with yellow fins and violet stripes going from the eye to the tail base.

REDFIN ANTHIAS
Pseudanthias dispar

Distribution: West Pacific from Indonesia to the Philippines and Australia.
Size: Up to 9 centimeters.
Habitat: Rich coral areas, reef tops and drop-offs in clear water from 1 to 15 meters deep.
Life Habits: Commonly encountered in large schools along the upper edge of drop-offs, feeding in the water column. Males often observed displaying to each other erecting the dorsal fin, females more subdued, uniform peach to orange.

PURPLE ANTHIAS
Pseudanthias tuka

Distribution: West Pacific from Indonesia to the Great Barrier Reef.
Size: Up to 12 centimeters.
Habitat: Rich coral areas, steep walls and drop-offs in clear water from 2 to 40 meters deep.
Life Habits: Commonly encountered in large schools along the edge of steep drop-offs in clear water and current-swept areas, feeding in the water column. Males (illustrated) exceptionally colorful, females more subdued and with a bright yellow stripe at the base of the dorsal fin.

THREADFIN ANTHIAS
Pseudanthias huchti

Distribution: West Pacific from Indonesia to the Great Barrier Reef.
Size: Up to 12 centimeters.
Habitat: Rich coral areas, reef tops and drop-offs in clear water from 2 to 20 meters deep.
Life Habits: Commonly observed in small schools feeding on plankton in the water column. Like all *Anthias*, this species lives in harems with several females and a dominant male; when the male dies one of the dominant females changes sex and takes its place. Females, always more numerous, are a dull greenish yellow.

STOCKY ANTHIAS
Pseudanthias hypselosoma

Distribution: West Pacific, from the Maldives to the Great Barrier Reef.
Size: Up to 19 centimeters.
Habitat: Coral heads in silty habitats on sheltered reefs from 2 to 40 meters.
Life Habits: Rather variable in coloration but generally pinkish with red head and right red spot on dorsal fin; tail rounded, dorsal and ventral fins very developed. Often encountered in large aggregations above isolated coral bommies in silty, sheltered habitats.

SCALEFIN ANTHIAS
Pseudanthias squamipinnis

Distribution: Tropical Indo-Pacific from the Red Sea to Australia and Fiji.
Size: Up to 15 centimeters.
Habitat: Rich coral areas, steep walls, slopes and drop-offs in clear water from 2 to 20 meters deep.
Life Habits: Commonly observed in huge, thick schools along drop-offs, feeding in the water column close to the reef wall. Males rather variable from red to orange but always very colorful, sporting elongate first ray of dorsal fin; females, always much more numerous, a bright orange with violet-edged stripe from eye to pectoral fin base.

RANDALL'S ANTHIAS
Pseudanthias randalli

Distribution: West Pacific from Indonesia to Micronesia and Japan.
Size: Up to 7 centimeters.
Habitat: Rich coral areas, steep walls and drop-offs in clear water from 15 to 120 meters deep, usually in caves or under ledges.
Life Habits: Very colorful but wary, ready to hide inside caves or under ledges and difficult to approach; also normally encountered in deep water. Males are red to lavender with variable, longitudinal violet stripes.

HAWK ANTHIAS
Serranocirrhitus latus

Distribution: West Pacific from Indonesia to Fiji and New Caledonia.
Size: Up to 13 centimeters.
Habitat: Under ledges and overhangs along steep walls and drop offs in clear water from 15 to 70 meters deep.
Life Habits: Beautiful but extremely wary and very difficult to approach; also normally encountered in deep water. Often observed singly or in small groups, swimming upside down under ledges or inside caves. Body is yellow and bright pink with yellow and pink stripes radiating from eye and on gill cover.

HARLEQUIN BASS
Serranus tigrinus

Distribution: Atlantic Ocean, from Florida to the Caribbean; also in Bermuda.
Size: Up to 10 centimeters.
Habitat: Seagrass and coral rubble areas from 1 to 40 meters deep.
Life Habits: Unmistakable, curious and easily approached, often found in seagrass areas and above coral rubble patches, always close to the substrate and looking for small crustaceans.

DOUBLE-BANDED SOAPFISH
Diploprion bifasciatum

Distribution: Tropical Indo-Pacific from India and the Maldives to Papua New Guinea and from Southern Japan to Australia.
Size: Up to 25 centimeters.
Habitat: Coastal reefs and sheltered lagoons, in turbid waters from 1 to 20 meters deep. Also in estuaries.
Life Habits: Soapfishes have a slimy skin covered in a toxic mucus. This species is occasionally observed, alone or in small groups, in coastal, sheltered areas. Specimens encountered in clear water or on volcanic sand are a much brighter yellow.

SIX-LINED SOAPFISH
Grammistes sexlineatus

Distribution: Tropical Indo-Pacific from the Red Sea to French Polynesia and from Southern Japan to Australia.
Size: Up to 25 centimeters.
Habitat: Coastal bays, lagoons and reefs in sheltered areas from 1 to 150 meters.
Life Habits: Unmistakable and easily identified, usually solitary and under ledges or close to any kind of shelter. Like all soapfishes it has a slimy skin covered in toxic mucus which is copiously secreted if the fish is harassed. In larger adults, usually found in deeper water, the yellow lines break up into dashes.

GREATER SOAPFISH
Rypticus saponaceus

Distribution: Atlantic Ocean from Florida to Brazil. Also in Bermuda.
Size: Up to 30 centimeters.
Habitat: Reef tops and coral patches from 3 to 20 meters deep.
Life Habits: Solitary, nocturnal, generally inactive and often observed resting on the bottom, leaning against a rock or a coral head. Not particularly attractive but easily approached. Secretes a toxic mucus from its skin when feeling endangered like all soapfishes.

ARROW-HEAD SOAPFISH
Belonoperca chabanaudi

Distribution: Tropical Indo-Pacific from East Africa to Samoa and from Southern Japan to Australia.
Size: Up to 15 centimeters.
Habitat: Outer reef walls and drop-offs from 5 to 50 meters deep.
Life Habits: Common but usually unnoticed by divers, often hiding or retreating under ledges or in dark crevices. Solitary and very wary, easily identified by pike-like body shape, blue-gray general coloration, bright yellow spot on tail base and blue-rimmed black spots on dorsal and ventral fins.

FAIRY BASSLET
Gramma loreto

Distribution: Western Atlantic Ocean in the Caribbean and Bahamas. Also in Bermuda, not found in Florida.
Size: Up to 5 centimeters.
Habitat: Around or inside caves and recesses in the reef face and clear water from 1 to 70 meters deep.
Life Habits: Beautiful, jewel-like species belonging to the Family *Grammatidae*, closely related to groupers. Often observed inside recess and swimming upside down, close to the ceiling of small caves and crevices. Very wary, not easily approached.Feeds on zooplankton.

INDIGO HAMLET
Hypoplectrus indigo

Distribution: Atlantic Ocean, in the Caymans, Cuba, Bahamas and Belize.
Size: Up to 13 centimeters.
Habitat: Reef tops in clear water from 1 to 40 meters deep.
Life Habits: Hamlets are easily observed in several locations of the Caribbean and offer a great degree of variation, but several researchers believe these to be all local phases of one single species, *H. unicolor*. Most are very colorful and shy, but occasionally display interest in divers.

DOTTYBACKS
Pseudochromidae

A large, complicated family numbering at least 6 genera and over 70 tropical species, mostly including small and usually very colorful fish noted for their partiality to crevices, cracks and dark hiding places in general. Dottybacks are usually solitary, most often observed along reef walls and slopes - often among intricate coral branching colonies - usually in clear water but invariably close to shelters or inside small caves. Most are aggressive and territorial, living a solitary existence and chasing away competitors from their home range.
~ **U/W Photo Tips:** Dottybacks are invariably very colorful and very difficult subjects, being always exceptionally wary and ready to hide if approached. A good macro lens (105mm is the best choice here) and a lot of patience are needed to take reasonably good shots.

PURPLE DOTTYBACK
Pseudochromis fridmani

Distribution: Red Sea.
Size: Up to 6 centimeters.
Habitat: Outer reefs in clear water from 6 to 70 meters, often near ledges and close to the opening of small caves.
Life Habits: This brightly colored species is endemic to the Red Sea, its place being taken further east by the Magenta Dottyback *P. porphyreus*, ranging from the Philippines to Southern Japan. It can be often observed in the open, always close to the substrate and ready to bolt into its lair if too closely approached.

PURPLEBACK DOTTYBACK
Pseudochromis diadema

Distribution: West Pacific from Malaysia to the Philippines.
Size: Up to 6 centimeters.
Habitat: Along the base of outer reef walls and drop-offs in clear water from 5 to 25 meters deep.
Life Habits: A very beautiful, jewel-like small species, often observed in the open and close to the substrate but always ready to dash into the closest crevice if approached. Locally common but often unnoticed by divers. Solitary and territorial.

TWO-TONE DOTTYBACK
Pseudochromis paccagnellae

Distribution: West Pacific from Indonesia to Papua New Guinea and Melanesia.
Size: Up to 5 centimeters.
Habitat: Coastal and outer reefs at the base of drop-offs and walls in clear water from 10 to 50 meters deep.
Life Habits: Easily identified underwater but very shy and not easily approached. Most dottyback species have a bright purple coloration in parts of the body which appears dark blue in natural light, disrupting their general shape to avoid predation. Solitary and territorial.

LONGFIN DOTTYBACK
Pseudochromis polynemus

Distribution: West Pacific from Indonesia to the Philippines and Palau.
Size: Up to 12 centimeters.
Habitat: Among corals and sponges on coastal and outer reefs in clear water from 10 to 30 meters deep.
Life Habits: Exceptionally shy, rarely observed while it dashes from one shelter to the next with an unmistakable, undulating swimming motion.Solitary and territorial; orange blotch at the base of pectoral fin is diagnostic.

DUSKY DOTTYBACK
Pseudochromis fuscus

Distribution: Tropical Central Indo-Pacific from India to the Solomons and from Taiwan to Australia.
Size: Up to 9 centimeters.
Habitat: Coastal and outer reefs in thick coral growth from 1 to 30 meters deep.
Life Habits: Usually observed like most dottybacks in close proximity to crevices, recesses and hideouts, commonly encountered in a dark brown or, more rarely, bright yellow and blue spotted (illustrated) color phase. Solitary and rather wary, not easily approached.

SPLENDID DOTTYBACK
Pseudochromis splendens

Distribution: Very localized Central Indo-Pacific, from West Papua to Northern Australia.
Size: Up to 13 centimeters.
Habitat: Coastal reefs in thick coral and sponge growth from 5 to 40 meters deep.
Life Habits: Grey with yellow spots and black mask on white snout: unmistakable, extraordinarily beautiful and extremely active, often briefly glimpsed while swimming from one hideout to the next. Usually observed among corals and tubular sponges, inside which it will often hide. Very localized but locally common, as in Raja Ampat, West Papua.

FIRETAIL DEVIL
Labracinus cyclophthalmus

Distribution: West Pacific from Malaysia to the Philippines and Australia.
Size: Up to 20 centimeters.
Habitat: Reef crests and tops among live or dead coral in shallow water to 15 meters deep.
Life Habits: Large, active and very variable, from olive green to bright red, usually with paler vertical stripes. Often observed in very shallow water on reef crests among algae-covered corals in surge-swept areas. Very shy and not easily approached, always ready to hide.

BIGEYES
Priacanthidae

This is a rather small family numbering 4 genera and about 17 species, all tropical or subtropical and quite distinctive. Their large round eyes are indicative of a strictly nocturnal existence, and during the day they can be often observed in sheltered areas, alone or in small groups, resting before the coming of darkness. All species are silvery or reddish, often with a brassy sheen, being able to pale or darken in a matter of seconds, and sport a distinctly oblique, large mouth. ~ **U/W Photo Tips:** Very compliant subjects, easily approached during daytime when reasonably inactive and encountered drifting around coral heads or under reef ledges.

GLASSEYE
Priacanthus blochii

Distribution: Tropical Western Indo-Pacific from the Gulf of Aden to the Philippines and Australia.
Size: Up to 30 centimeters.
Habitat: Coastal or outer reef tops in clear water 15 to 100 meter deep.
Life Habits: Nocturnal, feeding on small fish and crustaceans in the water column. Often encountered alone or in small groups during the day, most of the times inactive, hovering close to coral heads or under reef ledges. *P. hamrur* a very similar species, also in the same area, with a well-defined crescent tail.

BLOTCHED BIGEYE
Heteropriacanthus cruentatus

Distribution: Circumtropical.
Size: Up to 35 centimeters.
Habitat: Coastal and outer reef tops in clear water 3 to 20 meters deep.
Life Habits: Variable red to silvery, showing a typical metallic sheen, often with mottled fins. Solitary or in small groups during the day, most of the times inactive, hovering close to coral heads or under reef ledges. Feeds on small fish and tiny crustaceans at night.

CARDINALFISHES
Apogonidae

A very large and important family of very common tropical coastal fishes, numbering about 26 genera and an astounding 250 species. Most are small and rather secretive, usually spending daylight hours among thick branching coral colonies or inside caves and dark shelters in shallow water, coming out at night to feed in the water column. Cardinalfish practice oral brooding, with the male incubating the clutch of eggs in its mouth for about a week before hatching occurs. ~ **U/W Photo Tips:** Very easily approached and photographed with a 105mm macro lens just before twilight, when they start to forage in the open, leaving the thick branching coral colonies among which usually spend the day. Exciting (but not easy) close-ups are offered by brooding specimens, so always try to take a good look and see if they are carrying eggs in their mouth.

TIGER CARDINALFISH
Cheilodipterus macrodon

Distribution: Tropical Indo-Pacific from the Red Sea to French Polynesia and from Southern Japan to Australia.
Size: Up to 22 centimeters.
Habitat: Coastal reefs, rocky estuaries, mangroves from 3 to 30 meters deep.
Life Habits: One of the largest cardinalfish, easily identified by the longitudinal striped pattern, the pale bar on the base of the tail and the golden yellow stripes across the eye. Very secretive, usually among corals or inside small caves and dark shelters.

FIVE-LINE CARDINALFISH
Cheilodipterus quinquelineatus

Distribution: Tropical Indo-Pacific from the Red Sea to French Polynesia and from Southern Japan to Australia.
Size: Up to 10 centimeters.
Habitat: Coastal reefs and outer reef crests from 3 to 40 meters deep.
Life Habits: Can be identified by the five longitudinal stripes on the pale body and by the black spotted yellow blotch on the caudal peduncle. Secretive during the day, often found in small loose aggregations among branching corals. Easily confused with the very similar *C. isostigma.*

RING-TAIL CARDINALFISH
Apogon aureus

Distribution: Tropical Indo-Pacific from East Africa to Micronesia and from Southern Japan and Australia.
Size: Up to 14 centimeters.
Habitat: Coastal reef crests and slopes among branching corals or under overhangs from 1 to 50 meters.
Life Habits: Often observed in thick, stationary schools among large branching staghorn coral colonies. Pink-orange body, distinctly marked with electric blue spots and stripes on the snout and a sharp black band at the base of the tail.

CHEEK-SPOT CARDINALFISH
Apogon chrysopomus

Distribution: Central Indo-Pacific, from Malaysia to Indonesia and the Philippines.
Size: Up to 11 centimeters.
Habitat: On coastal reefs and in very shallow water, hovering above or among thick coral colonies.
Life Habits: Usually with clearly marked orange spots on gill cover and cheek. Body pale yellow, with two longitudinal dark stripes, often very faint. Many local variations observed in different geographical localities all over its wide distribution area.

YELLOW-LINED CARDINALFISH
Apogon chrysotaenia

Distribution: Central Indo-Pacific, from Eastern Indonesia to Papua New Guinea.
Size: Up to 10 centimeters.
Habitat: Reef flats, lagoons and slopes to 10 meters deep.
Life Habits: Usually solitary or in small schools in shallow water. Body is yellowish or pinkish, with pale bronze longitudinal stripes and very bright electric blue stripe across lower cheek. Second dorsal fin is very tall.

BLACK-LINED CARDINALFISH
Apogon nigrofasciatus

Distribution: Tropical Indo-Pacific from the Red Sea to French Polynesia and from Southern Japan to Australia.
Size: Up to 10 centimeters.
Habitat: Coastal and outer reefs among corals or in crevices from 3 to 50 meters.
Life Habits: Very common, usually in small aggregations. Easily identified by the four bright yellow longitudinal stripes on a black-brown background. The very similar *A. angustatus* can be identified by a very small black spot at the base of the tail.Fins are pinkish in both species.

ORANGE-LINED CARDINALFISH
Apogon cyanosoma

Distribution: Tropical Indo-Pacific from Western Indonesia to Australia and Southern Japan.
Size: Up to 9 centimeters.
Habitat: Coastal and outer reefs among branching corals from 1 to 35 meters.
Life Habits: Very common. Body and fins are silver-pinkish with several bright golden orange longitudinal stripes. Upper snout usually darker than the rest of the body. Several very similar species easily confused with this one.

BLUE-SPOT CARDINALFISH
Apogon compressus

Distribution: Central Indo-Pacific from Malaysia to the Great Barrier Reef.
Size: Up to 12 centimeters.
Habitat: Among branching coral colonies in shallow water from 1 to 20 meters.
Life Habits: Older individuals usually alone or in small loose aggregations under overhangs or among branching coral colonies. Larger than most species, with a coppery, pinkish robust body and large electric blue eyes. A night feeder like most cardinalfish species.

EYE-BAR CARDINALFISH
Apogon exostigma

Distribution: Tropical Indo-Pacific from the Red Sea to French Polynesia and from Southern Japan to Australia.
Size: Up to 12 centimeters.
Habitat: Lagoons and sheltered bays, often on sand bottoms close to coral heads in shallow water from 1 to 10 meters deep.
Life Habits: Many similar species in the area, most with a dark longitudinal stripe on a pale pinkish body. Colors however fade dramatically at night (see photo) when all cardinalfishes slowly forage in the open for zooplankton.

FROST-FIN CARDINALFISH
Apogon hoevenii

Distribution: Central Indo-Pacific from Malaysia to Micronesia and Japan.
Size: Up to 5 centimeters.
Habitat: Silty bottoms, often among debris, rotting vegetable matter and sea urchins from 3 to 30 meters deep.
Life Habits: Quite common locally, easily identified by the metallic copper-orangish tinge of the laterally compressed body and the bright white posterior edge of the first dorsal fin. Often observed in schools.

BAR-GILL CARDINALFISH
Apogon sealei

Distribution: Central Indo-Pacific from Malaysia to North-West Australia.
Size: Up to 9 centimeters.
Habitat: Coastal reefs in sheltered, shallow, often silty water from 2 to 25 meters deep.
Life Habits: Often observed in small schools among *Acropora* branching corals or sheltering among long-spined *Diadema* sea urchins. Body is pale yellow, with a small black spot on tail base, two brownish longitudinal stripes and a line of orange spots running along the side. Cheeks are barred or spotted.

REDSTRIPE CARDINALFISH
Apogon margaritophorus

Distribution: Central Indo-Pacific from Indonesia to the Solomon Islands.
Size: Up to 5 centimeters.
Habitat: Silty bottoms in shallow water, often among debris from 1 to 5 meters.
Life Habits: Uncommon, occasionally observed in small aggregations around coral heads or among weeds and rotting vegetable matter. Body is reddish with a distinct coppery tinge; segmented pearl-necklace like markings on lower side are diagnostic. Male pictured is brooding eggs in greatly extended gular pouch.

HARTZFELD'S CARDINALFISH
Apogon hartzfeldii

Distribution: Tropical West Pacific from Malaysia to Papua New Guinea and the Great Barrier Reef in Australia.
Size: Up to 10 centimeters.
Habitat: Coastal reefs and sheltered lagoons from 1 to 10 meters deep.
Life Habits: Uncommon, large, usually solitary or in mixed groups with other cardinalfish species. Body robust, bronze or silver-brown with large, clearly visible scales, black spot at the base of the tail; bright white lines on the back and across the eye.More active at night.

SPINY-HEAD CARDINALFISH
Apogon kallopterus

Distribution: Tropical Indo-Pacific from the Red Sea to French Polynesia and from Southern Japan to Australia.
Size: Up to 15 centimeters.
Habitat: Sheltered spots in shallow surge areas on coastal and outer reefs from 3 to 45 meters deep.
Life Habits: Body pinkish-brown, with dark mid-lateral stripe and sharp dark spot at the base of the caudal fin. Bright yellow front edge of first dorsal fin is diagnostic. Often observed in small loose aggregations. The specimen illustrated is being parasitized by a large isopod.

PAINTED CARDINALFISH
Archamia fuchata

Distribution: Tropical Indo-Pacific.
Size: Up to 10 centimeters.
Habitat: Lagoons and sheltered areas with rich coral growth from 2 to 60 meters, often in caves.
Life Habits: One of the most beautiful cardinalfish species, often observed in small aggregations among thick branching coral colonies. Body is bright coppery pink with several vertical thin orange stripes; head is golden with two blue stripes across the eye; black spot present at the base of the tail.

CORAL CARDINALFISH
Archamia zosterophora

Distribution: Central Indo-Pacific from Malaysia to the Philippines.
Size: Up to 10 centimeters.
Habitat: Thick branching coral in clear shallow water and in sheltered areas from 1 to 10 meters.
Life Habits: A very beautiful species, easily identified underwater by the two bright orange "slashes" on the cheek and by the broad dark band halfway its shiny chrome-silver body. Schooling in great numbers, often observed among thick branching coral colonies.

PAJAMA CARDINALFISH
Sphaeramia nematoptera

Distribution: Central Indo-Pacific from Indonesia to the Great Barrier Reef.
Size: Up to 8.5 centimeters.
Habitat: Thick branching corals in shallow clear water and in sheltered areas from 1 to 25 meters deep.
Life Habits: Spectacular but very shy, occasionally observed in loose, large aggregations among staghorn or branching coral colonies. Juveniles usually observed in twos or threes. Not easily approached but very distinctly marked.

POLKA-DOT CARDINALFISH
Sphaeramia orbicularis

Distribution: Tropical Indo-Pacific from East Africa to Kiribati and from Southern Japan to New Caledonia.
Size: Up to 10 centimeters.
Habitat: Mangroves, lagoons, very close to the surface under piers and not deeper than 3 meters.
Life Habits: Silver-gray body with a narrow dark band at midbody and several brownish spots posteriorly. Commonly observed in loose, stationary aggregations under jetties or close to pier pylons, often in very shallow water. Quite shy and not easily approached during the day.

HARBOR CARDINALFISH
Foa fo

Distribution: Tropical Indo-Pacific from the Maldives to French Polynesia and from Southern Japan to Australia.
Size: Up to 5 centimeters.
Habitat: Sheltered areas on sand or silt bottoms, among seaweeds and soft corals from 5 to 50 meters deep.
Life Habits: Uncommon and rarely observed by divers, usually superbly camouflaged. Body is brownish with numerous irregular white spots. Specimens illustrated are both brooding males with greatly enlarged mouth cavity.

BANGGAI CARDINALFISH
Pterapogon kauderni

Distribution: Endemic to the Banggai Island in Central Sulawesi, Indonesia; imported population in the Lembeh Strait in Northern Sulawesi, Indonesia.
Size: Up to 6.5 centimeters.
Habitat: Rubble areas in sheltered bays from 2 to 16 meters deep.
Life Habits: Unmistakable; possibly the most beautiful cardinalfish species. Strictly endemic but locally common, usually observed while sheltering among long-spined *Diadema* sea urchins or among tentacles of sea anemones, to which it is apparently immune.

Distribution: Central Indo-Pacific from Indonesia to Papua New Guinea.
Size: Up to 4 centimeters.
Habitat: Sheltered coastal reefs from 1 to 20 meters deep.
Life Habits: Usually observed taking shelter among long-spined *Diadema* or *Asthenosoma* fire urchins. Usually silver-white with dark longitudinal stripes but can darken in a few seconds. Small white dots on rear of dorsal fins separate this species from the very similar but more common *S. versicolor*, distributed from the Gulf of Oman to Southern Japan.

LONGFINS
Plesiopidae

This small family numbers 6 genera and about 20 species, most being small and very secretive. The most commonly observed and better known species belonging to this family is the Comet, a very shy but spectacular cave-dwelling fish often seen in tropical salt-water aquaria. Other species are poorly known and of little interest to the average diver. ~ **U/W Photo Tips:** Comets are very difficult subjects, being very wary and usually only observed inside deep, dark caves. When lit by a torch or approached by a photographer they will invariably retreat to the deeper recesses of the cave and disappear in the darkness, so a macro lens used as a tele (105mm) should be used if possible. Comets will usually re-appear after a short time, however, and will slowly learn to tolerate the presence of divers, so a lot of time and patience are needed.

Distribution: Tropical Indo-Pacific from the Red Sea to Australia and Japan.
Size: Up to 20 centimeters.
Habitat: Caves and crevices in drop-offs on coastal and outer reefs from 3 to 50 meters deep.
Life Habits: Very wary, generally unnoticed but occasionally observed hovering motionless at entrance of cave, slowly retreating if approached. Solitary, also in silty areas on dead reefs. White spots decrease in size but get more numerous in large adults.Livery apparently mimicks head of moray eel.

TILEFISHES
Malacanthidae

This small family numbers only 2 genera and 11 species, all tropical or subtropical. Tilefishes are generally small and rather slender plankton feeders, occasionally filtering mouthfuls of sand for food, usually encountered alone or in pairs on sand and mud flats, hovering close to the substrate and always ready to dash with lightning speed down their burrow if approached or threatened. ~ **U/W Photo Tips:** Tilefishes are usually ignored by divers and photographers giver their very shy nature, which has them disappearing in their burrow as soon as they feel they're being approached. They will occasionally let divers close, but good images will require time and patience. Given their usually small size a macro lens is a must.

FLAGTAIL BLANQUILLO
Malacanthus brevirostris

Distribution: Tropical Indo-Pacific from the Red Sea to Panama and from Southern Japan to Australia.
Size: Up to 30 centimeters.
Habitat: Coastal reefs in sheltered areas on sand or silt flats from 6 to 50 meters.
Life Habits: Pale, ribbon-like body with two sharp black stripes along the tail; usually observed from a distance, hovering close to the bottom, alone or in pairs. Territorial, with many similar-looking species worldwide. Feeds on zooplankton and small benthic invertebrates.

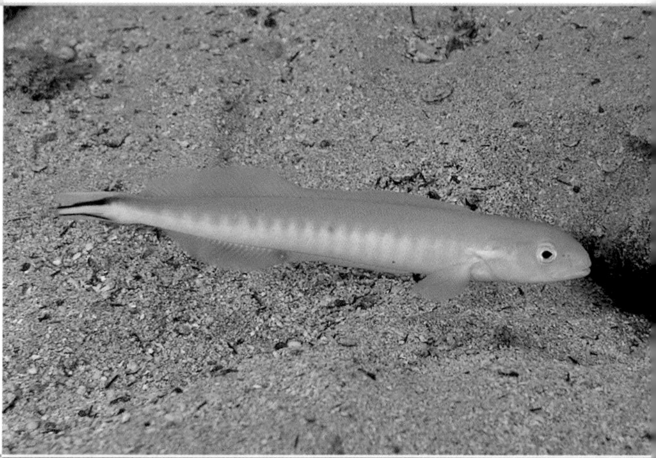

BLUE BLANQUILLO
Malacanthus latovittatus

Distribution: Tropical Indo-Pacific from the Red Sea and East Africa to French Polynesia, Southern Japan and Australia .
Size: Up to 35 centimeters.
Habitat: Coastal reefs on sand and coral rubble bottoms from 5 to 30 meters deep.
Life Habits: Body very elongated, often in a sinuous motion, with a blue head and a blue green back; a black mid-lateral stripe runs from the gill opening to the tail. Alone or in pairs, not particularly shy like other members of the Family: if approached will swim away, keeping its distance, without diving into a burrow.

BLUE-HEAD TILEFISH
Hoplolatilus starcki

Distribution: Central Indo-Pacific from Indonesia to Australia and Fiji.
Size: Up to 15 centimeters.
Habitat: Reef flats and slopes on sand and silt from 20 to 100 meters deep.
Life Habits: Possibly the most distinctive tilefish species, usually encountered in deep water. Body is yellow, tail is bright yellow and head is bright blue. Commonly observed in pairs. Feeds on zooplankton and small benthic invertebrates.

COBIAS
Rachycentridae

This family numbers just one monospecific genus, the cobia itself: frequently encountered by divers, boatmen and anglers in the Atlantic and Indo-Pacific, these large fish have an elongate body with a distinctly depressed head. Six to nine short free spines preceede the long dorsal fin. Cobias look superficially like sharks - especially when seen from the front - and feed on crustaceans, fishes, and squids: they are reputed to be an excellent food and gamefish. ~ **U/W Photo Tips:** Cobias have the disconcerting habit of suddenly appearing from the open ocean, pointing straight at the diver and looking exactly like a very determined grey shark. In fact, once seen from the side they just look like the bony fishes they are, and as such do not make particularly appealing subjects for the camera, lacking bright colors and being of a generally very dull appearance.

COBIA
Rachycentron canadum

Distribution: Circumtropical.
Size: Up to 2 meters.
Habitat: Pelagic, occasionally visiting coastal reefs.
Life Habits: A single pelagic species belonging to the Family *Rachycentridae*, usually striped when young but a dirty grey-brown in large adults, which occasionally "buzzes" divers in open water or along coastal reefs. Large specimens swim fast and are quite impressive, closely resembling a shark when seen from the front. Adults are occasionally encountered in small groups (2-6) in coastal shallow waters.

REMORAS
Echeneididae

This is a small but very peculiar and interesting family numbering 4 genera and 8 species. Remoras and sharksuckers are identified by a large dorsal sucking disc found on the head and nape, evolved from a highly modified first dorsal fin, which using its traverse mobile laminae enables these curious fish to attach themselves to large moving objects like sharks, rays and sometimes even boats. These large fish eat the scraps and leftovers from the feeding host, but will occasionally also keep it clean from external isopod parasites. ~ **U/W Photo Tips:** Sharksuckers are easy but not extremely interesting subjects, while larger and less colorful remoras tend to be observed while attached to large, fast-swimming species such as whale sharks and as such are more difficult subjects. For both a medium focal length lens (28-50mm) will suffice.

SLENDER REMORA
Echeneis naucrates

Distribution: Circumtropical.
Size: Up to 1 meter.
Habitat: Coastal or pelagic, shallow or deep depending on the host.
Life Habits: Usually observed attached to sharks (also commonly named sharksucker), large rays, mantas and turtles. Body grey-green on the back and belly, longitudinally striped in black and yellow, elongate, small scaled, with distinctly protruding lower jaw and large, mobile eyes. Always remember that remoras attach themselves *dorsally* to their host, so what you are seeing is in fact their upturned ventral surface.

JACKS AND TREVALLIES
Carangidae

A large circumtropical family numbering about 25 genera and more than 140 different species, all exquisitely adapted to an open sea, wide-ranging existence. Most are pelagic, streamlined, very strong and very fast predators, often encountered while hunting in schools close to reef walls or on reef tops, some reaching an impressive size and weight. Most are silvery or steely in appearance and many are regularly fished. ~ **U/W Photo Tips:** Like most pelagic species jacks and trevallies are fast swimmers which are not easily approached. Usually encountered in open water, they will only allow for a few shots before departing towards the blue, so fast reflexes and a wide-angle (20mm) are mandatory. Impressive images can be obtained photographing large schools with a fish-eye (15 or 16mm).

AFRICAN POMPANO
Alectis ciliaris

Distribution: Circumtropical.
Size: Up to 130 centimeters.
Habitat: Pelagic, often close to deep drop-offs down to 100 meters.
Life Habits: Chrome-like, often with a greenish or bluish tinge. Body deep, very robust, with a steep profile and deeply forked tail. Juveniles diamond shaped, with exceptionally long thread-like filaments from dorsal and anal fins. Adults most often solitary or in small free-ranging schools.

GOLD-SPOTTED TREVALLY
Carangoides fulvoguttatus

Distribution: Tropical Indo-Pacific from the Red Sea to Northern Australia.
Size: Up to 130 centimeters.
Habitat: Pelagic, often along coastal reefs and lagoons to 100 meters deep.
Life Habits: Solitary or in small schools; body silvery, with a metallic sheen and several golden or brassy spots on the sides. Adults often with three or four dark blotches along lateral line.

BARCHEEK TREVALLY
Carangoides plagiotenia

Distribution: Tropical Indo-Pacific from the Red Sea to Micronesia and Australia.
Size: Up to 42 centimeters.
Habitat: Pelagic, often along drop-offs from 2 to 200 meters deep.
Life Habits: Silvery, with a metallic sheen; body elongated, with a narrow dark bar on gill cover. Usually solitary or in small schools; a fast-swimming predator like all members of the Family.

ORANGE-SPOTTED TREVALLY
Carangoides bajad

Distribution: Tropical Indo-Pacific from the Red Sea to Papua New Guinea.
Size: Up to 60 centimeters.
Habitat: Pelagic, often along coastal reefs and walls from 2 to 70 meters.
Life Habits: Unmistakable: body oval with deeply forked tail, brassy silver to metallic yellow-orange with several orange small spots on sides. Usually solitary or in small loose aggregations.

COACHWHIP TREVALLY
Carangoides oblongus

Distribution: Tropical Indo-Pacific from East Africa to Fiji and Australia.
Size: Up to 45 centimeters.
Habitat: Coastal reefs, bays and lagoons, usually on sand bottoms from 2 to 50 meters.
Life Habits: Solitary or in small schools. Body silvery, with lower lobe of tail, anal and pectoral fins occasionally yellowish. Rear dorsal fin usually elongate. Commonly observed in small groups while skimming sea bottom looking for prey.

BLUE TREVALLY
Carangoides ferdau

Distribution: Tropical Indo-Pacific from the Red Sea to New Caledonia.
Size: Up to 70 centimeters.
Habitat: Outer reefs and lagoons, often on sand bottoms from 2 to 60 meters.
Life Habits: Body silvery, with rear dorsal, anal and caudal fins often displaying a yellowish tinge; the only species in the Family featuring from 5 to 7 vertical dark bars on sides. Commonly observed in large, fast-moving schools.

BLACK JACK
Caranx lugubris

Distribution: Circumtropical.
Size: Up to 75 centimeters.
Habitat: Pelagic, usually on offshore reefs and in deep water, from 20 to 70 meters deep.
Life Habits: A large, impressive species, usually solitary or encountered in small schools. Body silvery, steely gray or brownish-black; rear dorsal, anal and rear part of caudal fins dusky. A fast-moving, aggressive reef predator like all members of the Family.

BLUEFIN TREVALLY
Caranx melampygus

Distribution: Tropical Indo-Pacific from the Red Sea to Australia and Japan.
Size: Up to 1 meter.
Habitat: Outer reefs from the surface to 200 meters, often along drop-offs.
Life Habits: Possibly the most commonly observed trevally in the Indo-Pacific, locally abundant and easily identified by divers. Body silvery-blue with a greenish tinge, iridescent, densely spotted above; fins light to dark blue.Often encountered in small loose groups, raiding the reef face for weakened or wounded fish prey.

BIGEYE TREVALLY
Caranx sexfasciatus

Distribution: Tropical Indo-Pacific from the Red Sea to Australia and Japan.
Size: Up to 1 meter.
Habitat: Pelagic, on outer reefs and drop-offs in clear water from 2 to 50 meters deep.
Life Habits: Another commonly observed species, often encountered in enormous aggregations taking the shape of a living, shimmering, tornado-like vortex. Bright, shiny silver, with white tip of rear dorsal fin; males turn almost black when courting and mating (see photo).

GIANT TREVALLY
Caranx ignobilis

Distribution: Tropical Indo-Pacific from the Red Sea to Japan and Australia.
Size: Up to 165 centimeters.
Habitat: Pelagic, often along walls and drop-offs on outer reefs from 2 to 80 meters deep.
Life Habits: Very large, impressive and powerful: body is silvery with a steely tinge and featuring several scattered small dark spots. Large size and steep profile of the head are diagnostic; usually solitary in deep water, often encountered on offshore reefs.

ALMACO JACK
Seriola rivoliana

Distribution: Circumtropical and subtropical.
Size: Up to 90 centimeters.
Habitat: Pelagic, occasionally on offshore reefs; often observed under floating rafts and objects.
Life Habits: Silvery, elongated, with a high back profile and an unmistakable dark band running from the upper lip across the eye to the base of the dorsal fin. Solitary or in small schools.

SNUBNOSE POMPANO
Trachinotus blochi

Distribution: Tropical Indo-Pacific from the Red Sea to Japan and Australia.
Size: Up to 65 centimeters.
Habitat: On coastal and outer reefs from 10 to 50 meters deep, often very shallow in surge areas.
Life Habits: Pompanos are easily identified during a dive by the blunt, broadly rounded snout, by the elongate lobes of the rear dorsal and anal fins and by the deeply forked tail. Body silvery, fins occasionally yellow or orange. Solitary or in small schools.

GOLDEN TREVALLY
Gnathanodon speciosus

Distribution: Tropical Indo-Pacific.
Size: Up to 140 centimeters.
Habitat: Coastal reefs, lagoons often in silty water from 2 to 20 meters.
Life Habits: Easily identified underwater by the large size, the drooping forehead profile, the yellow lips and the black bars on the sides. Large adults (pictured) rarely observed; juveniles bright silvery yellow with 7-11 vertical black stripes, commonly encountered accompanying large pelagics (mantas, whale sharks) or close to jellyfishes.

PILOTFISH
Naucrates ductor

Distribution: Circumtropical.
Size: Up to 75 centimeters.
Habitat: Pelagic, normally accompanying large sharks or mantas.
Life Habits: Silver with 5 to 7 wide black bars, commonly observed schooling in small groups in association with large, free-ranging pelagics like open sea sharks and "riding" their pressure wave. Juveniles occasionally observed close to jellyfishes, taking shelter among venomous tentacles, an interesting behavior commonly observed in several immature *Carangidae* species.

YELLOWTAIL SCAD
Atule mate

Distribution: Tropical Indo-Pacific.
Size: Up to 30 centimeters.
Habitat: Coastal reefs, bays, mangroves from 2 to 30 meters deep.
Life Habits: Common, often encountered in small schools swimming fast over sandy or silty substrates, looking for food. Body rather elongate, silvery with yellow tail. Many similar species, all restricted to coastal, shallow, often turbid waters. Often fished for local consumption.

Schooling for Life

A quarter of marine fish species live in schools: to find protection against roving predators, to have better chances in mating, to find food more easily. But successfully living in a group calls for special strategies

Thick schools of glassfish are commonly found inside caves.

Divers often come across spectacular schools (or shoals) composed of thousands of fish. Few natural spectacles in the world can deliver the same raw dramatic impact as a large assembly of fish: today the ocean is the last place on Earth where humans can admire such impressive concentrations of individuals belonging to a single species. But for how long? Fish gather in schools for different reasons: to hunt, to escape their predators, to reproduce, or to migrate. The results are always spectacular, but nowadays often terribly dangerous for the fish themselves: with the advent of ultrasonic sounding gear, commercial fishing fleet can now net thousands of individuals in a single stroke. This group strategy improves however each individual's odds of survival in the natural and highly competitive environment of the coral reef. Weak or small species

Bigeye jacks often school in undisturbed oceanic locations.

Schooling bannerfish are a frequent sight in the Indian Ocean.

often adopt it, but so do big and clearly very efficient predators. It is not by chance that more than half of marine fish species live in schools as juveniles and at least a quarter of the total continue to do so as adults. Pelagic hunters that prowl the seaward reef - especially dolphins, jacks and trevallies, tunas and barracudas, but also (on and off) several species of shark - regularly adopt schooling strategies to hunt their prey. After methodically surrounding a victim, they attack in force with coordination and precision. However, it is anything but simple for a large predator to select and focus its attack on a single prey in the face of a "living wall" made up of thousands of individuals which are perfectly coordinated to the split second in their movements. In fact, one of the most amazing aspects of large schools is the extraordinary synchrony of separate individuals coordinating their movements and generating as a result a sort of single "superfish" of gigantic proportions. Recent research indicates the important role of the so-called lateral line in this behavior: this line of pores runs horizontally along the fishes' sides and is used by individuals to register microvariations of pressure in their surroundings. Species that spend the better part of their existence in shoals also feature metallic colorations with distinctive iridescent reflections. Observed underwater, this coloration will polarize depending upon the fish's position in relation to

Silversides school in the thousands to escape predation.

Large schools of scads and silversides are often found in the shade of jetties.

the incidence of ambient light. In a split second, the school's silvery curtain may become a confused and blurry fog. Thus, a school of fish under attack by one or more predators will deploy fast, slanting

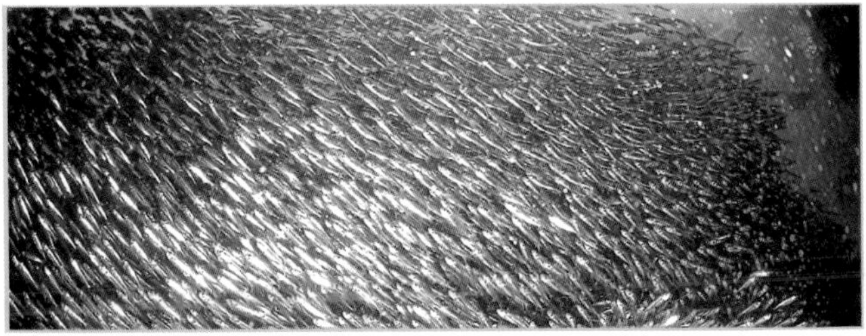

The polarizing of light aids the schools in confusing predators.

A pack of roving trevallies attacks a tight school of silversides.

actions and furiously change course to confound the onslaught. Another strategy involves keeping the formation tight while opening a space around the attacker - only to reunite instantly on the other side. To capture its quarry, the predator must then focus on the slowest individuals, which usually gravitate to the edges of the school, or it must succeed in slamming into the school at lightning speed, stunning its members with the mere force of the strike and picking off wounded or dazed individuals. Tresher sharks *Alopias* sp. are thought to use their enormously elongate upper tail lobe as a whip, first herding their prey together and then slashing it among the tight school to kill and wound their prey (but it must be stressed that this behavior has not been yet documented). Several other species, finally, simply school when resting during the day, dispersing at night to feed.

Bigeye jacks often school in tightly turning, tornado-like shoals.

SNAPPERS

Lutjanidae

This is a very large and important family, numbering 17 genera and more than 100 species worldwide including some of the fishes most commonly observed on tropical reefs. Found in a variety of habitats - juveniles seem to favor brackish or even fresh waters - they are commonly observed alone or in large schools, usually very close to the bottom. Snappers are active predators, feeding on a variety of other benthic organisms, and they are hunted in turn by man for their firm, tasty flesh. Larger and older specimens are however often responsible for ciguatera poisoning, caused at the origin of the food chain by a toxic dinoflagellate (*Gambierdiscus toxicus*) living on dead coral. ~ **U/W Photo Tips:** Snappers are common and they are not difficult to photograph properly. They usually allow a fairly close, slow, cautious approach and are often found in schools. A medium lens (24-50mm) or a wide angle (20mm) will suffice.

SMALLTOOTH JOBFISH

Aphareus furca

Distribution: Tropical central Indo-Pacific from Indonesia to the Great Barrier Reef in Australia.
Size: Up to 80 centimeters.
Habitat: Reefs and rocky bottoms from 10 to 100 meters deep.
Life Habits: Can be identified underwater by elongate body shape, dark bars on gill cover and deeply furcate tail. A fast and voracious feeder, rather shy and not easily approached by divers.

DOG SNAPPER

Lutjanus jocu

Distribution: Atlantic Ocean from Massachusetts to Florida, the Caribbean, Bermuda and Brazil.
Size: Up to 90 centimeters.
Habitat: Rocky areas, wrecks from 10 to 30 meters deep.
Life Habits: Occasionally observed in shadowy areas, under overhangs or inside wrecks. Can be identified by a pale triangular area under the eye. Very wary and ready to keep a distance from divers if approached underwater.

SCHOOLMASTER
Lutjanus apodus

Distribution: Tropical Western Atlantic Ocean from Massachusetts to Bermuda, the Caribbean, the Gulf of Mexico and Southern Brazil. Also Eastern Atlantic.
Size: Up to 60 centimeters.
Habitat: Reef tops in shallow water from 3 to 25 meters deep.
Life Habits: Usually observed in small groups sheltering under large branching corals or among large gorgonians. Body silvery or coppery, with coppery eyes and bright yellow fins. Usually rather wary.

HUMPBACK SNAPPER
Lutjanus gibbus

Distribution: Tropical Indo-Pacific from the Red Sea to New Caledonia.
Size: Up to 50 centimeters.
Habitat: Lagoons, passes or reef slopes from 1 to 150 meters deep.
Life Habits: Solitary (usually older mature specimens) or in large stationary schools.Body color is very variable, from gray to red; tail is maroon with rounded lobes, back is distinctly arched; a bright orange spot is present at the base of the pectoral fins.

RED EMPEROR SNAPPER
Lutjanus sebae

Distribution: Tropical Indo-Pacific.
Size: Up to 100 centimeters.
Habitat: Deep, sandy bottoms from 30 to 100 meters deep.
Life Habits: Solitary, easily identified by brightly marked livery with red-brown and white stripes which becomes entirely deep red in older specimens living in very deep water. Juveniles very sharply marked, often observed on sandy or muddy bottoms in association with long-spined sea urchins.

BLUESTRIPE SNAPPER
Lutjanus kasmira

Distribution: Tropical Indo-Pacific.
Size: Up to 35 centimeters.
Habitat: Found in a variety of habitats, from reef tops to deep water on coastal and outer reefs from 5 to 265 meters.
Life Habits: Commonly observed in large, stationary and spectacular schools close to coral outcrops and facing the current. Body is bright yellow with four neon-blue longitudinal stripes; belly is white. The schools presumably disperse at night when the individuals forage for food.

SPANISH FLAG SNAPPER
Lutjanus carponotatus

Distribution: Central Indo-Pacific from India to Papua New Guinea and from Southern China to the Great Barrier Reef.
Size: Up to 40 centimeters.
Habitat: Coastal reefs and lagoons from 1 to 35 meters deep.
Life Habits: Solitary or in loose aggregations on top of the reefs, usually close to shelters. Body is white with 5-9 yellow to brown longitudinal stripes; small black spot at the base of the pectoral fins.

TWO-SPOT SNAPPER
Lutjanus biguttatus

Distribution: Tropical Indo-West Pacific from the Maldives to the Great Barrier Reef in Australia and Fiji.
Size: Up to 20 centimeters.
Habitat: Coastal reefs, slopes and lagoons from 5 to 30 meters deep.
Life Habits: Often observed in small or occasionally large aggregations sheltering among table corals. Body is elongate, with grey back and reddish sides: two or three white spots on back and one thick bright white longitudinal stripe along the sides; fins are bright yellow .

BROWNSTRIPE SNAPPER
Lutjanus vitta

Distribution: Tropical Indo-Pacific.
Size: Up to 40 centimeters.
Habitat: Lagoons, coastal reefs or sand areas between coral bommies from 10 to 40 meters deep.
Life Habits: Usually solitary or in small groups. Body whitish or silvery with yellow back and yellow, brown or blackish longitudinal stripe from the eye to the base of the tail. Juveniles occasionally observed in association with anemones.

ONESPOT SNAPPER
Lutjanus monostigma

Distribution: Tropical Indo-Pacific from the Red Sea to French Polynesia and New Caledonia.
Size: Up to 60 centimeters.
Habitat: Sheltered areas along outer reefs from 5 to 60 meters deep.
Life Habits: Large, silvery, usually unmarked but with yellow fins. Solitary or in small loose aggregations, a large and powerful reef predator usually encountered inside caves or wrecks. Rather wary like most large snappers and not easily approached underwater.

BUTTON SNAPPER
Lutjanus boutton

Distribution: Central Indo-Pacific from Indonesia to the Philippines and Papua New Guinea.
Size: Up to 30 centimeters.
Habitat: Coastal reefs and lagoons from 5 to 50 meters deep.
Life Habits: Solitary or in very large stationary schools which disperse at night. Body is yellow or brownish with maroon fins, but may fade or darken at will and in a few seconds like many other species. Usually lacks any specific markings.

BLACKTAIL SNAPPER
Lutjanus fulvus

Distribution: Tropical Indo-Pacific from the Red Sea to French Polynesia and South East Australia.
Size: Up to 40 centimeters.
Habitat: Coastal reefs, lagoons and outer slopes from 6 to 40 meters.
Life Habits: Body from silvery to pale yellow with black, light-blue bordered tail and second dorsal fin. Pectoral, ventral and anal fins yellow. A widely dispersed species, occasionally observed in the deeper parts of the reef close to caves and sheltered areas. Juveniles in brackish water and estuaries.

RED SNAPPER
Lutjanus bohar

Distribution: Tropical Indo-Pacific from the Red Sea to Australia and French Polynesia.
Size: Up to 75 centimeters.
Habitat: Lagoons and outer reefs from 5 to 150 meters deep.
Life Habits: A large, unmistakable, impressive predator. Body red or reddish grey and very robust, with large yellow eye. Strong canine teeth visible in gaping mouth. Often observed deep, solitary or in large schools. Commonly fished for human consumption, but larger and older individuals may be ciguatoxic.

CHECKERED SNAPPER
Lutjanus decussatus

Distribution: Tropical Central Indo-Pacific from India to Western Papua.
Size: Up to 30 centimeters.
Habitat: Reef tops in coastal and outer reefs from 3 to 30 meters deep.
Life Habits: Unmistakable "grilled" look with several black-brown intercrossing bars and stripes on white background; black spot at the base of the tail. Solitary or in small groups along reef crests, sheltering among table corals.

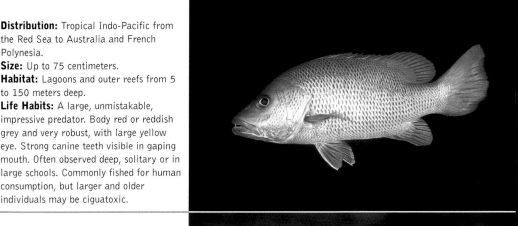

STAR SNAPPER
Lutjanus stellatus

Distribution: Subtropical Asian Pacific, from Southern Japan to Hong Kong.
Size: Up to 55 centimeters.
Habitat: On coastal coral and rocky reefs from 5 to 50 meters deep.
Life Habits: Locally common but very localized. Body is silvery or coppery with yellow fins, a white spot usually visible just above the lateral line below the first soft ray of the dorsal fin. Solitary or in small groups, generally of little interest to divers or underwater photographers.

FIVE-LINE SNAPPER
Lutjanus quinquelineatus

Distribution: Tropical Indo-Pacific from the Arabian Gulf to Australia.
Size: Up to 40 centimeters.
Habitat: Coastal reefs, lagoons and outer reef slopes from 2 to 40 meters deep.
Life Habits: Usually encountered in large, milling schools often numbering hundreds of individuals close to coral outcrops. Body yellow with five neon-blue longitudinal stripes, dark spot often present on rear back. Easily confused underwater with *L. kasmira*, which however has four blue stripes along the flank instead of five.

BIGEYE SNAPPER
Lutjanus lutjanus

Distribution: Tropical Indo-Pacific from the Red Sea and East Africa to the Solomons and from Southern Japan to Australia.
Size: Up to 30 centimeters.
Habitat: Coastal reefs and slopes from 10 to 90 meters deep.
Life Habits: Body silvery with yellow or orange longitudinal stripe from eye to yellow tail; several yellow thin stripes below. Often encountered in large schools numbering hundreds of individuals, occasionally - as illustrated - mingling with other common snapper species.

MIDNIGHT SNAPPER
Macolor macularis

Distribution: Tropical Indo-West Pacific from the Maldives to New Caledonia.
Size: Up to 60 centimeters.
Habitat: Walls, drop-offs along outer reefs from 5 to 50 meters deep.
Life Habits: Commonly observed in large loose aggregations, seldom solitary, usually rather inactive by day. Body pale, grey-yellowish, with many scribbled markings; large golden eye. Juveniles are boldly marked in black and white with greatly elongated ventral fins.

CHINAMANFISH
Symphorus nematophorus

Distribution: Central Indo-Pacific from Southern Japan to Northern Australia and New Caledonia.
Size: Up to 80 centimeters.
Habitat: Coastal reefs from 5 to 50 meters deep.
Life Habits: Body brownish to olive with numerous thin, longitudinal, irregular blue stripes; dorsal fin often filamented; able to pale or darken dramatically in a few seconds. Solitary or in small groups, locally fished for human consumption but often ciguatoxic.

SAILFIN SNAPPER
Symphorichthys spilurus

Distribution: Tropical Central Indo-Pacific from Indonesia to New Caledonia.
Size: Up to 60 centimeters.
Habitat: Outer reefs on sand open bottoms, often close to coral bommies, from 5 to 60 meters deep.
Life Habits: Beautiful, easily identified. Body from pale to bright yellow with several irregular pale blue longitudinal stripes; profile of head in adults very steep, almost vertical. Often long trailing filaments from tip of dorsal fin in sub-adults and juveniles.

GRUNTS

Pomadasyidae

This is a basically Atlantic family numbering more than 4 common genera and about 15 common species. Their generic name comes from the noise these fish can make grinding their pharyngeal teeth, greatly amplified by the resonating swim bladder. Most species are nocturnal feeders and can be easily observed in very large, closely packed schools during the day, often sheltering among table or branching corals on the reef top and along slopes. ~ **U/W Photo Tips:** Grunts are among the most easily compliant and most colorful subjects on Caribbean reefs, often encountered in large schools which can be closely approached. Use a macro lens (60 or 105mm) for single individuals, but move to a wide-angle (28 or 20mm) for striking images of shimmering, colorful schools hovering among the corals.

FRENCH GRUNT

Haemulon flavolineatum

Distribution: Atlantic Ocean from Florida to the Caribbean, Bermuda, Gulf of Mexico and Brazil.
Size: Up to 30 centimeters.
Habitat: Coral reefs in shallow water from 4 to 18 meters deep.
Life Habits: Commonly observed in large schools which may number thousands of individuals, often sheltering among staghorn or elkhorn corals along reef crests. Body is silvery-blue with many irregular longitudinal yellow stripes.

BLUESTRIPED GRUNT

Haemulon sciurus

Distribution: Atlantic Ocean from Florida and the Caribbean to Brazil.
Size: Up to 45 centimeters.
Habitat: Reef crests and drop-offs in clear water from 4 to 15 meters deep.
Life Habits: Commonly observed in small schools among large gorgonians or sheltering below staghorn or elkhorn corals. Body yellow-gold with several irregular bright blue longitudinal stripes. Dark tail and rear dorsal fin are diagnostic. Wary, not easily approached.

FLYING FISHES
Exocoetidae

A very interesting family, numbering about 7 genera and more than epipelagic and circumtropical species. All can be identified by the silvery, torpedo-shaped body, by greatly enlarged lower lobe of the tail and by the wing-like greatly extended pectoral fins, which enable these fish to escape attacking predators by jumping above the water and glide above the surface for great distances. ~ **U/W Photo Tips:** Adults skimming on the surface are frequently observed from the bow of dive boats but are almost impossible to photograph if one is not very lucky. Very small juveniles like the specimen pictured below are rarely encountered in small groups in coastal waters, on the surface, after tropical storms.They look like tropical butterflies and make exceptionally interesting but difficult subjects.

FLYING FISH
Cypselurus sp.

Distribution: Circumtropical.
Size: Up to 27 centimeters.
Habitat: Just under the surface in oceanic waters, normally offshore.
Life Habits: Adults have silvery, torpedo-like body with silver-blue pectoral fins; juveniles sport four very large and exceptionally colorful pectoral and ventral fins which make them look like tropical butterflies when observed from above. Usually observed from dive boats while "flying" skimming the surface, very rarely encountered underwater.

CORAL BREAMS
Nemipteridae

A small family numbering about 5 genera and a total of 65 species, several of which are restricted to deep water. Coral, Whiptail or Threadfin breams are small, unassuming benthic fish of nocturnal habits, usually observed during the day while resting on the sand and among the corals, somewhat motionless and very close to the substrate, often in small loose aggregations.They are very common but not being brightly colored or strangely shaped are usually ignored by divers and photographers . ~ **U/W Photo Tips:** Coral or Threadfin breams are very common and easily approached but are usually ignored by divers and photographers due to their modest coloration and rather uninteresting shape. Those wishing to photograph them will be able to get reasonable results with a 105 or 60 mm lens.Beware: artificial light often washes out their already pale colors.

DOUBLE WHIPTAIL
Pentapodus emeryii

Distribution: Central Indo-Pacific from Indonesia to the Philippines and Australia.
Size: Up to 35 centimeters.
Habitat: Silty coastal reefs from 2 to 35 meters deep.
Life Habits: Body elongate, blue or lavender with yellow longitudinal stripe on back and on flank. Snout pointed, tail lunate with greatly elongated lobes. Often encountered swimming above sand or mud flats, feeding in the water column; possibly the most colorful species belonging to this genus.

BRIDLED MONOCLE BREAM
Scolopsis bilineatus

Distribution: Tropical Indo-West Pacific from the Maldives to New Caledonia.
Size: Up to 25 centimeters.
Habitat: Sand and rubble bottoms from 5 to 25 meters deep.
Life Habits: Dark gray back, white belly separated by crescent-shaped black-edged white band; yellow stripes on head. Solitary or in small loose aggregations close to the substrate; rather inactive during the day, occasionally taking mouthfuls of sand to sift small benthic invertebrates. Locally very common.

PEARLY MONOCLE BREAM
Scolopsis margaritifer

Distribution: Western Pacific from Sumatra in Indonesia to Micronesia and Northern Australia.
Size: Up to 25 centimeters.
Habitat: Sand and rubble bottoms from 2 to 25 meters deep.
Life Habits: Body pearly gray, often with rows of small yellow spots on the lower flank; solitary or in small groups, motionless, always hovering very close to the bottom and near shelters. Feeds on a variety of small benthic invertebrates.

MONOGRAM MONOCLE BREAM
Scolopsis monogramma

Distribution: West Pacific from Sumatra to Papua New Guinea and Australia.
Size: Up to 38 centimeters.
Habitat: Sand and rubble bottoms in lagoons from 2 to 50 meters deep.
Life Habits: Body pale gray, with a pale blue band between the eyes; tail yellow with pale blue edge, elongate brown blotch often present on the flanks. Occasionally observed very close to the substrate in sheltered, quiet areas. Feeds on benthic invertebrates.

SILVER BATFISHES
Monodactylidae

This is a small tropical family numbering 3 genera and a total of 5 species only. The *Monodactylidae* - commonly known as Silver Batfishes, Diamondfish or Fingerfish - usually inhabit brackish river estuaries and frequently venture into both fresh and marine habitats. Silver Batfishes are schooling fish which live in the coastal regions of Africa, Southeast Asia and Australia. These are silvery, tall, disc-shaped, laterally compressed fish with a small head and mouth; the eyes are large and have a black band running through them. The dorsal and anal fins are green to orange and almost opposite one other. ~ **U/W Photo Tips:** Silver Batfishes are commonly encountered in large, thick schools under jetties: while not particularly colorful they make pleasing subjects with a strong sun in the background, as their shape and reflective silver livery create interesting patterns.

SILVER BATFISH
Monodactylus argenteus

Distribution: Tropical Indo-Pacific from the Red Sea and East Africa to Micronesia and from Southern Japan to Australia.
Size: Up to 27 centimeters.
Habitat: Silty coastal reefs, estuaries and brackish waters from 1 to 10 meters.
Life Habits: Silvery, diamond-shaped, laterally compressed, with greenish or yellow opposed dorsal and ventral fins: commonly observed in thick schools under jetties or in harbors, where it feeds on floating algal matter and zooplankton.

Diver and Tallfin Batfish *Platax teira*,
Raja Ampat, West Papua, Indonesia

EMPERORS

Lethrinidae

A medium-sized family of tropical fish, numbering about 5 genera and about 39 species. All are medium-sized to rather large, plainly colored benthic predators, usually observed hovering close to the bottom or in the water column, being rather inactive during the day. Solitary or in small groups, emperors are regularly fished by man but are often ciguatoxic - like their close relatives, the snappers - as most reef predators at the apex of the food chain. ~ **U/W Photo Tips:** Emperors are most of the times very wary and plain silver-colored, being as such not really much sought-after subjects. Since they will not allow a close approach, a medium focal length (24-50mm) is the lens of choice .

STRIPED BIGEYE BREAM

Gnathodentex aureolineatus

Distribution: Tropical Indo-Pacific from East Africa to Japan and Australia.
Size: Up to 30 centimeters.
Habitat: Coastal reefs, lagoons and outer reef drop-offs from 3 to 20 meters deep.
Life Habits: Body silvery gray to brownish with a row of small yellow spots on the sides; bright, stoplight-like yellow spot on the rear back at the base of second dorsal fin. Usually in large stationary aggregations along reef crests, often mixed with other species.

HUMPNOSE BIGEYE BREAM

Monotaxis grandoculis

Distribution: Tropical Indo-Pacific from the Red Sea to French Polynesia, Australia and New Caledonia.
Size: Up to 60 centimeters.
Habitat: Coastal and outer reefs close to drop-offs from 1 to 60 meters deep.
Life Habits: Body chunky, silvery or grayish, often with yellow accents on the head. Often observed in large groups during the day, dispersing at night to feed on the substrate in deeper waters.

GRAY BIGEYE BREAM
Gymnocranius griseus

Distribution: Eastern Indo-Pacific from the Andamans to Southern Japan.
Size: Up to 35 centimeters.
Habitat: Sand and coral rubble bottoms from 15 to 80 meters deep.
Life Habits: Body compressed, silvery gray with several irregular brownish stripes. Solitary or in small aggregations, usually unnoticed by divers. Feeds at night on benthic invertebrates.

ORANGE-STRIPED EMPEROR
Lethrinus obsoletus

Distribution: Indo-West Pacific from the Red Sea to Japan, Micronesia and New Caledonia.
Size: Up to 50 centimeters.
Habitat: Coastal reefs on seagrass beds and rubble bottoms from 2 to 30 meters.
Life Habits: Body pale gray with a yellow stripe running from the base of the pectoral fin to the tail; otherwise nondescript. Solitary or in small groups, often among segrasses. Feeds on benthic invertebrates and small fishes like most emperors.

SMALLTOOTH EMPEROR
Lethrinus microdon

Distribution: Tropical Indo-Pacific from the Red Sea to Papua New Guinea.
Size: Up to 70 centimeters.
Habitat: Coastal sand slopes and reef patches close to drop-offs from 5 to 30 meters deep.
Life Habits: Body elongate, with long pointed snout and dark lines radiating from the eye to the mouth. Generally pale, but able to rapidly switch to a mottled pattern when feeding or afraid. Feeds on a variety of benthic organisms. Normally very wary, difficult to approach closely.

YELLOWFIN EMPEROR
Lethrinus erythracanthus

Distribution: Tropical Indo-Pacific from East Africa to French Polynesia and the Great Barrier Reef in Australia.
Size: Up to 70 centimeters.
Habitat: Deep lagoons and outer reef drop-offs from 15 to 120 meters.
Life Habits: Large, stocky; head grey to bluish, body dark grey with yellowish fins. Solitary, uncommon; occasionally observed close to drop-offs and easily identified by body shape and large size. Very shy, not easily approached.

LONGFIN EMPEROR
Lethrinus erythropterus

Distribution: Tropical Indo-Pacific from East Africa to Papua New Guinea.
Size: Up to 50 centimeters.
Habitat: Reef tops, lagoons and coral rubble flats from 2 to 25 meters deep.
Life Habits: Possibly the most colorful among all emperors, easily identified by the rust-red or olive green body showing pale bars on the tail base. Head marked with red and yellow, but very variable, may pale or darken dramatically in a very short time. Solitary and close to the bottom, feeding on a variety of benthic invertebrates and small fish.

LONGFACE EMPEROR
Lethrinus olivaceus

Distribution: Tropical Indo-West Pacific from the Red Sea to Micronesia, Australia and New Caledonia.
Size: Up to 100 centimeters.
Habitat: Lagoons and outer reefs from 1 to 190 meters deep.
Life Habits: Body elongate, gray to olive, often faintly mottled, with very long and pointed snout; the largest member of the Family. Usually solitary, actively swimming above the bottom, scanning for prey. Large size and lack of distinct markings are diagnostic underwater.

Ribbon Sweetlips *Plectorhynchus politaenia*, Raja Ampat, West Papua, Indonesia

FUSILIERS
Caesionidae

Numbering only 4 genera and about 20 species, this small family is mostly restricted to tropical waters of the Indo-Pacific region, where its members are fished in the hundreds of thousands by trawlers belonging to commercial fleets. Closely related to snappers (*Lutjanidae*), these are fast-swimming, torpedo-shaped small fish moving rapidly about in very large schools, continuously feeding on plankton drifting in the water column. Often very colorful, they are not always easy to differentiate underwater but all are equally beautiful. ~ **U/W Photo Tips:** Given their schooling habits and their fast way of swimming, fusiliers are more easily photographed using wide-angle lenses and as a school rather than as lone specimens. Exciting opportunities are offered when predators on the prowl - such as trevallies - scythe thru the big fusilier schools.

BLUESTREAK FUSILIER
Pterocaesio tile

Distribution: Tropical Indo-Pacific from East Africa to French Polynesia and New Caledonia.
Size: Up to 25 centimeters.
Habitat: Coastal and outer reef slopes and walls in clear water from 2 to 60 meters deep.
Life Habits: One of the most common species, easily identified by the silvery blue body sporting an iridescent, broad blue band on the side. The lower half of the body turns bright red at night, when these fish hide among the corals to sleep.

RANDALL'S FUSILIER
Pterocaesio randalli

Distribution: Central Indo-Pacific from the Andamans to the Philippines.
Size: Up to 25 centimeters.
Habitat: Coastal and outer reef slopes and drop-offs in clear water from the surface to 30 meters deep.
Life Habits: Body silvery or bluish; elongate bright yellow blotch on forebody is diagnostic underwater. Often encountered in very large schools, frequently mixing with other fusilier species. Feeds on plankton.

BLUE AND YELLOW FUSILIER
Caesio teres

Distribution: Tropical Indo-Pacific from East Africa to Micronesia and the Great Barrier Reef in Australia.
Size: Up to 40 centimeters.
Habitat: Coastal and outer reef slopes and walls from the surface to 30 meters.
Life Habits: One of the largest fusilier species, often encountered in large schools mixing with other members of Family. Body silvery blue, yellow from back to all of tail; black pectoral fin base.Feeds on plankton drifting in the water column.

LUNAR FUSILIER
Caesio lunaris

Distribution: Tropical Indo-Pacific from the Red Sea to Australia and Fiji.
Size: Up to 40 centimeters.
Habitat: Coastal and outer reef slopes and walls from the surface to 30 meters.
Life Habits: A large species, often observed in large schools mixing with other fusiliers. Body silvery blue; distinct black tail tips are diagnostic underwater. Commercially fished in enormous quantities and probably severely endangered like all fusilier species.

SCISSORTAIL FUSILIER
Caesio caerularea

Distribution: Tropical Indo-Pacific from the Red Sea to Micronesia and the Great Barrier Reef in Australia.
Size: Up to 35 centimeters.
Habitat: Coastal and outer reef slopes and drop-offs in clear water from the surface to 30 meters deep.
Life Habits: Body silvery blue with distinct yellow longitudinal stripe running from head to tail. Often encountered in large schools mixing with other fusiliers. Intensively fished for human consumption and probably endangered.

TRIPLETAILS
Lobotidae

A circumtropical family numbering just one monospecific genus. Tripletails are little-studied fish which can be identified by the rounded caudal fin and the triangular head. In particular the anal and soft dorsal fins sport a rounded posterior lobe which makes the fish the fish look triple-tailed. Juveniles float sideways - often among sargassum rafts - like leaves as a form of camouflage. Adults reach about 1 m maximum length. ~ **U/W Photo Tips:** None of importance as adults are very rarely encountered. Juveniles make very interesting subjects when found floating on their side - mimicking to perfection a dead leaf - but are almost never observed by divers.

TRIPLETAIL
Lobotes surinamensis

Distribution: Circumtropical.
Size: Up to 100 centimeters.
Habitat: Pelagic, often under floating objects or sargassum rafts.
Life Habits: Sluggish, with juveniles usually floating on the side near the surface. Adults lightly mottled, brownish or greenish, juveniles mimicking to near perfection dead leaves. The only species belonging to this monospecific genus; some also recognize *L. pacificus* in the Eastern Pacific from Nicaragua to Peru.

SWEETLIPS
Haemulidae

This is a large family, numbering about 18 genera grouping more than 120 different species. Most are stationary reef dwellers, observed singly or in small aggregations under ledges and overhangs during the day. As adults they can be easily identified underwater by their large mouths with thick, fleshy lips; all juveniles however greatly differ from the adults and most of the times look completely different, swimming in a frantic, greatly exaggerated and undulating motion. ~ **U/W Photo Tips:** Sweetlips make wonderful subjects as they are very colorful and often rather easily approachable, both alone or in schools. Side views take advantage of their vivid coloration and sharp pattern, but frontal or three-quarter head close-ups are equally interesting, especially when the fish are schooling.

DIAGONAL-BANDED SWEETLIPS
Plectorhynchus lineatus

Distribution: Tropical West Pacific from Indonesia to the Great Barrier Reef.
Size: Up to 60 centimeters.
Habitat: Coral-rich areas on coastal and outer reef slopes and flats from 3 to 50 meters deep.
Life Habits: Silver-white with many oblique black bands; lips yellow, dorsal, anal and caudal fins yellow spotted in black. Often encountered in small groups hovering under ledges during the day; more active at night when drifting out, foraging for food in the open.

ORIENTAL SWEETLIPS
Plectorhinchus vittatus

Distribution: Central Indo-Pacific from East Africa to Australia.
Size: Up to 85 centimeters.
Habitat: Coastal and outer reefs on current-prone, coral-rich slopes from 3 to 50 meters deep.
Life Habits: Body bright white with longitudinal black stripes, lips and fins bright yellow; spotted dorsal, anal and caudal fins. Common on outer reefs: often encountered during the day in large, stationary schools, often facing strong currents. At night schools disperse and single individuals drift out foraging for food.

STRIPED SWEETLIPS
Plectorhynchus lessonii

Distribution: Tropical Central Indo-Pacific from Malaysia to New Caledonia.
Size: Up to 48 centimeters.
Habitat: Coastal and outer reefs, lagoons from 1 to 50 meters deep.
Life Habits: Body white with 4-5 brownish darker longitudinal stripes on back and sides. Lips yellow, dorsal, anal and caudal fins yellowish and spotted. Less commonly encountered than other similar species, usually observed alone or in small loose aggregations.

RIBBON SWEETLIPS
Plectorhynchus polytaenia

Distribution: Central Indo-Pacific from Indonesia to Papua New Guinea.
Size: Up to 40 centimeters.
Habitat: Coastal reefs in current-prone areas from 3 to 50 meters deep.
Life Habits: Body yellow with several longitudinal black-edged white or pale blue stripes. Unmistakable, possibly the most beautiful of all sweetlips. Usually encountered alone or in small groups under overhangs or inside small see-through passages in deep water.

GOLD-SPOTTED SWEETLIPS
Plectorhynchus flavomaculatus

Distribution: Tropical Indo-Pacific from the Red Sea to Papua New Guinea.
Size: Up to 60 centimeters.
Habitat: Coastal, often silty reefs in sheltered areas from 2 to 25 meters.
Life Habits: Coppery or gray with small orange spots all over, augmented by bright blue stripes on head. Solitary or in small groups, but encountered less often and possibly less common than other sweetlips in the region.

MAGPIE SWEETLIPS
Plectorhynchus picus

Distribution: Tropical Indo-Pacific from Seychelles to French Polynesia.
Size: Up to 85 centimeters.
Habitat: Outer reefs on sand bottoms among coral heads from 10 to 30 meters.
Life Habits: Adults are whitish or greyish peppered with a multitude of small black spots; sub-adults (illustrated) with black back, white belly, two bright white saddles on back and a white ring around the base of the tail. Usually solitary and rather uncommon.

MANY-SPOTTED SWEETLIPS
Plectorhynchus chaetodonoides

Distribution: Tropical Indo-Pacific from the Maldives to Fiji and Australia.
Size: Up to 70 centimeters.
Habitat: Coastal and outer reefs close to drop-offs from 10 to 30 meters deep.
Life Habits: One of the most commonly observed sweetlip species, often encountered alone or in small stationary groups along deep drop-offs on outer reefs, sheltering under ledges or overhangs. Body greenish with unmarked white belly and a multitude of small roundish black or dark brown spots all over.

RED SEA SWEETLIPS
Plectorhynchus gaterinus

Distribution: Western Indian Ocean from the Red Sea to Natal and Madagascar.
Size: Up to 50 centimeters.
Habitat: Coral rich outer reef slopes in clear water from 3 to 30 meters deep.
Life Habits: Body silvery with many small black spots; tail and fins yellow, spotted in black. Usually observed during the day in small stationary groups, sheltering under *Acropora* table corals. Schools disperse at night when individuals spread out to forage for food.

GIANT SWEETLIPS
Plectorhynchus obscurus

Distribution: Tropical Indo-Pacific from the Red Sea to Australia and Fiji.
Size: Up to 100 centimeters.
Habitat: Deep coastal and outer reefs, offshore reefs, often inside wrecks, from 20 to 60 meters deep.
Life Habits: The largest sweetlip, uniformly greyish with dusky fin tips. Usually solitary, occasionally observed close to deep wrecks or at the base of steep drop-offs. Uncommon and rarely encountered by the average sport diver.

GOLDSTRIPED SWEETLIPS
Plectorhinchus chrysotaenia

Distribution: Tropical Indo-Pacific from Indonesia to New Caledonia and from Southern Japan to the Great Barrier Reef.
Size: Up to 50 centimeters.
Habitat: Coastal reefs in coral-rich areas from 5 to 60 meters deep.
Life Habits: Body silvery-blue with several longitudinal bright yellow stripes and bright yellow fins. Solitary or in small groups during the day and formerly classified as *P. celebicus*. Quite beautiful but rather localized: one of the less commonly encountered sweetlips species.

INDONESIAN SWEETLIP
Diagramma sp.

Distribution: Tropical Central Indo-Pacific, but only from Malaysia, Indonesia and the Philippines.
Size: Up to 50 centimeters.
Habitat: Sand bottoms in lagoons or along coastal reefs from 3 to 40 meters.
Life Habits: Pale gray with fine black spots all over; yellow dorsal and caudal fins, black ventral and anal fins. Easily identified underwater but still undescribed in literature.

PAINTED SWEETLIP
Diagramma pictum

Distribution: Tropical Indo-Pacific from the Red Sea to New Caledonia and from Southern Japan to Australia.
Size: Up to 95 centimeters.
Habitat: Coastal reefs and lagoons on sand bottoms from 5 to 40 meters.
Life Habits: Body steely grey with many small orange spots; very old specimens almost uniform grey. Solitary or in small groups on sand or mud bottoms with isolated coral bommies.

GOATFISHES

Mullidae

A smallish tropical and temperate family numbering 6 genera and 35 species, all easily distinguished by the pair of barbels always present on their chin. Body is elongate, with large scales, triangular fins and a forked tail. Goatfishes move around alone or in fast-swimming, "messy" schools, frantically digging in the substrate for food and using their chin barbels to locate the small invertebrates they eat, often accompanied by wrasses and sometimes even small jacks ready to take advantage of the opportunity. ~ **U/W Photo Tips:** Goatfishes are always on the move and very close to the bottom, so they are not easy subjects. One has to take advantage of their short and frequent stops to feed (which offer a great opportunity to photograph the several species of wrasses always showing up on such occasions). At night they are easier to approach, but keep in mind their colors and even patterns change radically while sleeping.

YELLOWFIN GOATFISH

Mulloidichthys vanicolensis

Distribution: Tropical Indo-Pacific from the Red Sea to Hawai'i and Easter Island.
Size: Up to 38 centimeters.
Habitat: Coastal reefs, lagoons, outer reef slopes from 5 to 100 meters deep.
Life Habits: Body bluish-white, with yellow fins and back and a yellow longitudinal stripe from eye to tail base. Commonly observed in large stationary schools during the day, often mixed with snappers, which disperse at night to feed.

DOUBLEBAR GOATFISH

Parupeneus bifasciatus

Distribution: Central Indo-Pacific from Indonesia to Japan and Australia.
Size: Up to 35 centimeters.
Habitat: Outer and coastal reefs, slopes and lagoons from 1 to 140 meters deep.
Life Habits: Very variable, rapidly changing from white to purple, always with orange spots and two blackish short bars at the base of the second dorsal fin and on the caudal peduncle. Generally encountered alone, resting on the bottom, or in small groups.

GOLDSADDLE GOATFISH
Parupeneus cyclostomus

Distribution: Tropical Indo-Pacific, from the Red Sea to French Polynesia.
Size: Up to 50 centimeters.
Habitat: Coastal and outer reefs, lagoons and slopes from 1 to 100 meters deep.
Life Habits: Very variable, often purplish, grey or completely xanthic (yellow, illustrated). Blue lines radiating from the eye normally present, often a yellow saddle on the tail base in purple specimens. A large species, occasionally encountered in fast-moving schools.

MANYBAR GOATFISH
Parupeneus multifasciatus

Distribution: Central Indo-Pacific from Indonesia to Hawai'i and Australia.
Size: Up to 30 centimeters.
Habitat: Coral rubble and sand bottoms near the base of reefs from 1 to 140 meters deep.
Life Habits: Light grey, yellowish or purplish, with two black bars and occasionally white ones on the posterior half of the body.Usually solitary, actively feeding on small benthic invertebrates on the bottom during the day.

DASH-DOT GOATFISH
Parupeneus barberinus

Distribution: Tropical Indo-Pacific from East Africa to Polynesia, Japan and Australia.
Size: Up to 50 centimeters.
Habitat: Coastal reefs and lagoons on sand and rubble bottoms from 5 to 100 meters deep.
Life Habits: White with grey or yellow back, with a thin black stripe running from the eye to the second dorsal fin and a round spot at the base of the tail. Usually encountered alone or in small groups, actively feeding on benthic invertebrates which are flushed out rummaging in the substrate.

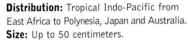

FRECKLED GOATFISH
Upeneus tragula

Distribution: Tropical Indo-Pacific from East Africa to Japan and New Caledonia.
Size: Up to 30 centimeters.
Habitat: Sand and rubble bottoms on coastal reefs from 1 to 30 meters deep.
Life Habits: Tan or whitish, heavily mottled in brown, able to rapidly switch to a bright red phase; bright brick-red spots at the tip of dorsal fins, dark mid-lateral stripe. Often observed in small groups, resting or feeding on the bottom.

TARPONS
Elopidae

This small family numbers just one genus and 5 species, one of which is illustrated here being the most relevant to reef divers. Members of this family are chiefly marine but commonly enter estuaries and freshwater, especially as juveniles. Most are found worldwide in tropical and subtropical waters. The body is generally fusiform, oval and slightly compressed. The eyes are big, partially covered with adipose eyelids. The mouth is terminal, with the upper jaw extending to the posterior border of eyes, and a typically prominent lower jaw. ~ **U/W Photo Tips:** Tarpons are large and extremely easy subjects. Slow, careful swimmers can drift within the schools and approach single animals quite closely: their plate-like, strongly reflecting scales request however a very careful balance of artificial and natural light.

TARPON
Megalops atlanticus

Distribution: Atlantic Ocean from Virginia to Florida, Bermuda, the Caribbean and Brazil.
Size: Up to 240 centimeters.
Habitat: Canyons and crevices in clear water on coastal reefs from the surface to 12 meters deep.
Life Habits: Unmistakable: very large, elongate body with chrome-plated appearance, big deeply falcate tail and strongly upturned mouth. Commonly observed in large groups schooling in specific dens during the day. Unafraid, will allow a close approach if unmolested.

SWEEPERS
Pempherididae

A small family numbering only 2 genera and about 20 species, ranging from tropical to temperate seas. Commonly observed singly (generally *Pempheris*) or in very large schools - numbering thousands of semi-transparent individuals - sheltering in caves or under overhangs, where the sound made by their syncronous swimming is clearly audible. During the night the schools disperse and the fish feed singly in the water column. ~ **U/W Photo Tips:** A favorite subject of wide-angle underwater photographers, sweepers are particularly impressive when portrayed in large, thick schools. Single specimens are equally interesting and easily approached using a macro lens. Always beware however of their highly reflective, glittering bodies.

VANIKORO SWEEPER
Pempheris vanicolensis

Distribution: Tropical Indo-Pacific, from the Red Sea to the Philippines, Vanuatu and Samoa.
Size: Up to 20 centimeters.
Habitat: Caves and overhangs in coastal reefs from 2 to 30 meters deep.
Life Habits: Body compressed and hatchet-like, coppery, with a deep belly and a black margin to the anal fin. Usually observed alone or in small, loose aggregations under ledges and overhangs, hiding in the shadows if approached. Several similar species, all difficult to distinguish underwater.

COPPER SWEEPER
Pempheris oualensis

Distribution: Tropical Indo-Pacific from East Africa to the Philippines and the Great Barrier Reef in Australia.
Size: Up to 15 centimeters.
Habitat: Under ledges and overhangs in coastal reefs from 3 to 40 meters deep.
Life Habits: Silvery or coppery, often with a greenish tinge and a strong iridescence. Commonly observed in small loose aggregations under overhangs, hiding in shadow if approached. Several very similar species, all difficult to distinguish underwater.

GOLDEN SWEEPER
Parapriacanthus ransonneti

Distribution: Tropical Indo-Pacific, from Indonesia to New Caledonia. A virtually identical species in the Red Sea.
Size: Up to 10 centimeters.
Habitat: Caves or under table corals, ledges and underhangs in coastal and outer reefs from 3 to 30 meters deep.
Life Habits: Often observed in thick, cloud-like schools numbering thousands of fish, moving in unison while sheltering inside caves or under large ledges. Body semi-transparent with a golden tinge; schools disperse at night to feed.

~

DRUMMERS
Kyphosidae

A small family accounting for 3 genera and 10 species. Drummers - also known on West Atlantic coasts as Sea Chubs - are rather non-descript reef fishes found in shallow coastal areas, where they mostly feed on drifting algae and the small invertebrates found on them. Congregating in large schools, they are occasionally fished by locals but are often discarded as their flesh is not held in great esteem and sometimes believed hallucinogenic. ~ **U/W Photo Tips:** None of importance as most members of this Family are rather uninspiring subjects. Drummers are mostly very drab and also tend to live in shallow coastal waters, often in mediocre visibility.

SNUBNOSE DRUMMER
Kyphosus cinerascens

Distribution: Tropical Indo-Pacific from the Red Sea and East Africa to French Polynesia and from Southern Japan to Australia.
Size: Up to 45 centimeters
Habitat: Shallow coastal coral and rocky reefs, lagoons and reef flats from 1 to 25 meters deep.
Life Habits: Ash-colored or silver grey, with a distinctly rounded rear dorsal fin. Often encountered in schools in high-energy areas on coastal reefs, feeding on drifting algal matter in the water column.

BATFISHES
Ephippidae

This is a small but important and impressive family, of which the genus *Platax* - numbering 5 species - is the most commonly observed by divers. All batfish are fairly large, highly compressed, slow-moving animals, with a silvery, shining body more or less distinctly barred in black and a very calm demeanor. In some open-sea locations they can occur in immense schools which are very impressive to behold. They all feed on algae, vegetable matter and a variety of small invertebrates~ **U/W Photo Tips:** Batfishes are very beautiful and easily approached subjects, both alone or in schools. Take advantage of their stately poses and silvery bodies framing them against the blue of the sea for great compositions, but do not forget to look everywhere for juvenile specimens, often unbelievably different from the adults of the species they belong to see page 216.

ROUND BATFISH
Platax orbicularis

Distribution: Tropical Indo-Pacific, from the Red Sea to Australia, Japan and New Caledonia.
Size: Up to 30 centimeters.
Habitat: Outer reefs on walls and slopes from 2 to 40 meters deep.
Life Habits: Body large, highly compressed, silvery, with two dark bars on the front of the body - one across the eye and the other across the pectoral fin. Slow moving, peaceful; can be distinguished by similar species by the small black flecks on the sides. For the juvenile form see page 217.

PINNATE BATFISH
Platax pinnatus

Distribution: Western Pacific, from Sumatra to the Solomons, Australia and New Caledonia.
Size: Up to 37 centimeters.
Habitat: Coastal and outer reefs, often in wrecks, from 2 to 25 meters deep.
Life Habits: Less commonly observed than other similar species: body silvery, highly compressed, with more elongate dorsal and ventral fins than other batfishes. Slightly but distinctly protruding snout is diagnostic. For the juvenile form see page 216.

ZEBRA BATFISH
Platax batavianus

Distribution: Western Pacific from Malaysia to Papua New Guinea.
Size: Up to 50 centimeters.
Habitat: Coastal, inshore reefs from 15 to 60 meters deep.
Life Habits: Less commonly observed than other batfish species; very large, impressive body is a dull silver with one black bar across the eye and fainter second one behind. Many dark spots scattered all over. Usually observed alone or in small loose aggregations in coastal, often turbid waters. Older adults feature a very distinct hump on the forehead.For the juvenile form see page 217.

TALLFIN BATFISH
Platax teira

Distribution: Tropical Indo-Pacific from the Red Sea to the Great Barrier Reef in Australia.
Size: Up to 40 centimeters.
Habitat: Clear water along drop-offs on outer reefs from 2 to 30 meters deep.
Life Habits: Very commonly observed by divers, often in large, free-swimming schools. Body highly compressed, silvery, with yellowish fins and two black bars on the front. Can be identified underwater by the steep profile of the forehead and by the distinct black blotch behind and above the base of the ventral fin.

BOERS BATFISH
Platax boersii

Distribution: Tropical Indo-Pacific, from the Red Sea to Papua New Guinea.
Size: Up to 45 centimeters.
Habitat: Clear water along coastal and outer reefs drop-offs from 3 to 30 meters.
Life Habits: Silvery, often with a yellowish tinge; darker markings are usually fainter than in other batfish species. Commonly observed along drop-offs in clear water on outer reefs, often in very large, fast-moving, compact schools. Easily confused underwater by most divers with *P. teira* but less commonly encountered.

Juveniles

One of the most interesting phenomena of reef life is the occasionally enormous difference in shape, pattern and coloration between adult specimens and their juvenile phase. In several cases the two look so much different that it is not uncommon to believe they in fact belong to two completely separate species (this has happened many times in scientific descriptions in the past), and several very young juveniles which have been clearly documented photographically have not been allocated to a species yet - no one really knows what the adult looks like since no intermediate phases have been photographed or described yet! Since very young juveniles can be exceptionally small and may be completely unable to defend themselves from predators, they may often mimic well-known poisonous organisms (baby groupers, frogfish and even sea cucumbers will try to pass themselves as toxic nudibranchs); in other cases they will try to camouflage themselves, trying to simply disappear in the surrounding environment (see the Coral Shrimpfish masquerading as floating bits of vegetable debris below).

Clown frogfish *Antennarius maculatus*, 2 centimeters.
See page 93.

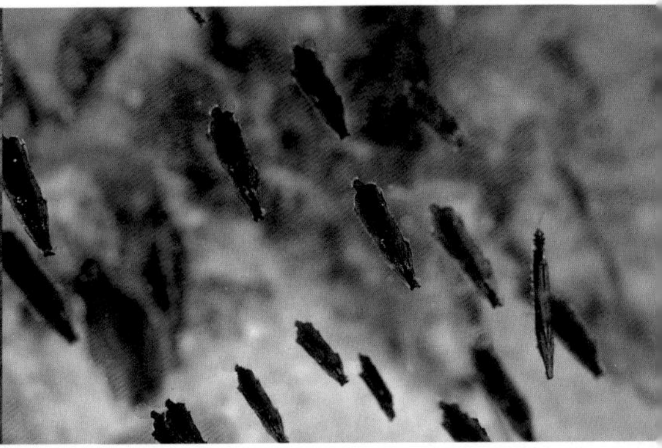

Coral Shrimpfish *Aeoliscus strigatus*, 0.5 centimeters.
See page 107.

Common Lionfish *Pterois volitans*, 4 centimeters.
See page 124.

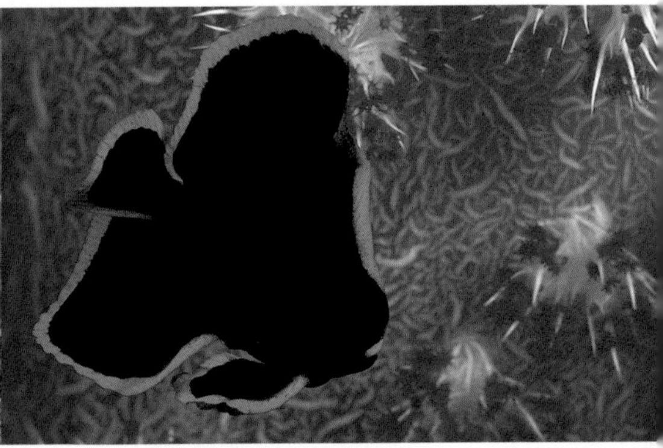

Pinnate Batfish *Platax pinnatus*, 4 centimeters.
See page 214.

Zebra Batfish *Platax batavianus*, 10 centimeters.
See page 215.

Round Batfish *Platax orbicularis*, 20 centimeters.
See page 214.

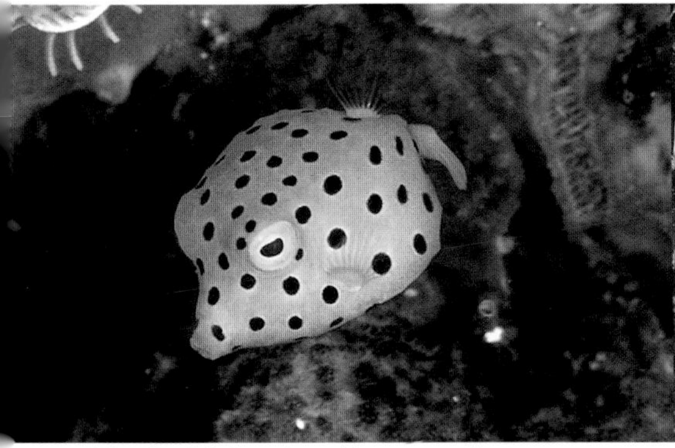

Yellow Boxfish *Ostracion cubicus*, 2,5 centimeters.
See page 371.

Unidentified Boxfish or Trunkfish, 2,5 centimeters.
See page 370.

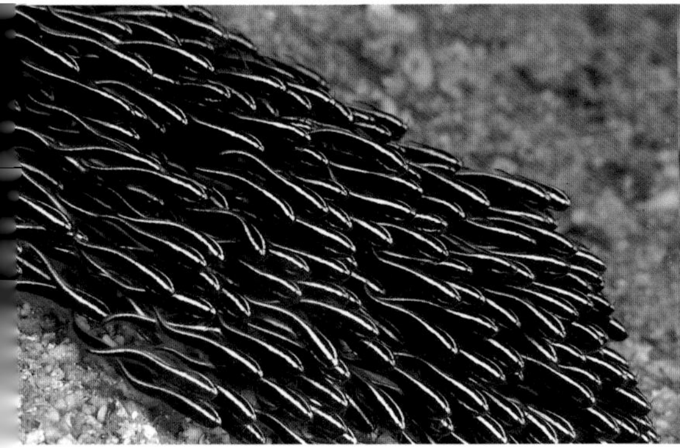

Striped Catfish *Plotosus lineatus*, 4 centimeters.
See page 87.

Cockatoo Waspfish *Ablabys taenianotus*, 2 centimeters.
See page 134.

Weedy Scorpionfish *Rhinopias frondosa*, 5 centimeters. See page 127.

Ornate Ghostpipefish *Solenostomus paradoxus*, 4 centimeters. See page 108.

Sea Cucumber *Bohadschia graeffei*, 4 centimeters, mimicking poisonous nudibranch *Phyllidia coelestis*. See page 416.

Blue Triggerfish *Pseudobalistes fuscus*, 6 centimeters. See page 361.

Clown Triggerfish *Balistoides conspicillum*, 4 centimeters. See page 361.

Yellow-Margin Triggerfish *Pseudobalistes flavimarginatus*, 4 centimeters. See page 362.

Star Pufferfish *Arothron stellatus*, 6 centimeters. See page 373.

Spotted Drum *Equetus punctatus*, 5 centimeters. See page 222.

Barramundi Cod *Chromileptes altivelis*, 4 centimeters. See page 154.

Emperor Angelfish *Pomacanthus imperator*, 9 centimeters. See page 244.

Yellowtail Damselfish *Neoglyphidodon nigroris*, 4 centimeters. See page 253.

Crocodile Fish *Cymbacephalus beauforti*, 1,3 centimeters. See page 138.

Rockmover Wrasse *Novaculichthys taeniourus*, 3 centimeters. See page 289.

Yellowtail Coris *Coris gaimard*, 3 centimeters. See page 273.

Unidentified sole *Aseraggodes* sp., 3 centimeters. See page 359.

Unidentified sole *Soleichthys* sp., 3 centimeters. See page 359.

Highfin Grouper *Epinephelus maculatus*, 3,5 centimeters. See page 151.

Whitestreaked Grouper *Epinephelus ongus*, 6 centimeters. See page 151.

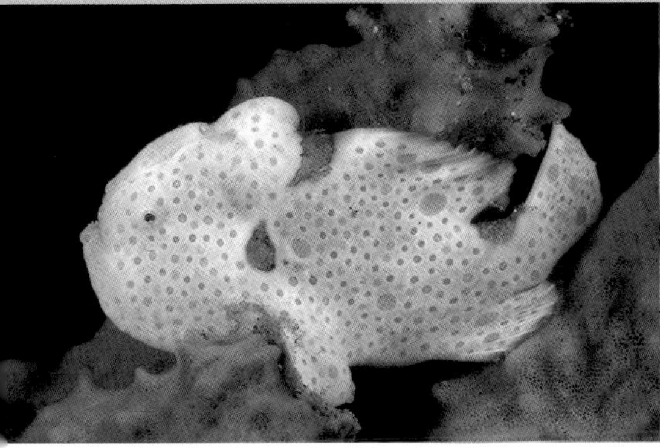

Painted Frogfish *Antennarius pictus*, 4 centimeters
See page 92.

Fingered Dragonet *Dactylopus dactylopus*,
1,5 centimeters. See page 314.

Kuiter's Dragonet *Dactylopus kuiteri*, 1,3 centimeters.
See page 314.

Many-spotted Sweetlips *Plectorhynchus chaetodonoides*,
5 centimeters. See page 207.

Bicolor Parrotfish *Cetoscarus bicolor*, 4 centimeters.
See page 295.

Greater Soapfish *Rypticus saponaceus*, 5 centimeters.
See page 161.

DRUMS
Sciaenidae

A small but rather interesting family, of which the genus *Equetus* is the best known. Croakers or drums - so called because of their ability to produce low-frequency but clearly audible underwater sounds by vibrating their swim bladder - are rather common in the Caribbean, being generally unafraid and easily approached. *Equetus* species in particular are well-known due to the striped, showy livery and the elongated fins of the juveniles and sub-adults. ~ **U/W Photo Tips:** Croakers or drums in general cannot be said to be exceptionally flamboyant subjects, but juveniles and sub-adults of the *Equetus* genus make very interesting and rewarding subjects. Generally unafraid and very easily approached, they will need a good macro lens (60-105mm) to be properly framed up close.

SPOTTED DRUM
Equetus punctatus

Distribution: Atlantic Ocean, from Southern Florida to the Caribbean.
Size: Up to 30 centimeters.
Habitat: Under ledges and overhangs from 3 to 30 meters deep.
Life Habits: Easily identified thanks to the brightly marked, black and white livery, striped in the front and dotted on the back. Commonly and easily observed under ledges or overhangs, usually swimming in well-defined and repeated circuits. *E. lanceolatus* is quite similar but less brightly marked. For the juvenile stage see page 219.

BUTTERFLYFISHES
Chaetodontidae

A large family, numbering 10 genera and about 120 species which count some of the most beautiful and better-known species of tropical coral reef fishes. Most butterflyfish are extremely colorful and are commonly observed in shallow water on the reef top, very often in pairs paired for life or in small loose aggregations, feeding on small invertebrates and coral polyps they pick off the coral colonies using their small, protrusible mouth. The greatest concentration of species occurs in Indonesian waters. ~ **U/W Photo Tips:** Butterflyfishes are some of the most beautiful and colorful subjects one can hope to ever meet on a reef. Usually skittish but sometimes surprisingly easy to get close to, they are quite unpredictable and behave just like...butterflies. A good macro lens (60 or 105mm) is a must for smallish, erratic, fast-swimming subjects such as these.

FOUREYE BUTTERFLYFISH
Chaetodon capistratus

Distribution: Atlantic Ocean from Massachusetts to Florida, Bermuda, the Gulf of Mexico and the Caribbean.
Size: Up to 12 centimeters.
Habitat: Reef top in clear, brightly lit water from 3 to 12 meters deep.
Life Habits: Possibly the most commonly observed butterflyfish of the Caribbean. Body silver-grey, marked with numerous diagonal, dark, thin lines; black ocellus ringed in white on the rear of the body, near the base of the tail. Commonly observed in territorial pairs: wary, not easily approached.

YELLOWRIMMED BUTTERFLYFISH
Chaetodon guentheri

Distribution: Central Indo-Pacific from Northern Sulawesi to Japan, Papua New Guinea and the Great Barrier Reef.
Size: Up to 14 centimeters.
Habitat: Coral-rich slopes and rocky reefs from 5 to 40 meters deep.
Life Habits: Body silvery white with numerous dark dots; upper and rear parts rimmed in rich yellow. Less commonly observed than most other butterflyfish species; often encountered alone or in small loose aggregations in deeper water and near cool upswellings.

DOTTED BUTTERFLYFISH
Chaetodon semeion

Distribution: Tropical Indo-Pacific from Sri Lanka to Indonesia, Polynesia and the Great Barrier Reef in Australia.
Size: Up to 24 centimeters.
Habitat: Coral-rich coastal and outer reefs from 2 to 50 meters deep.
Life Habits: Large, bright yellow with horizontal rows of small spots and bright blue forehead. Rear dorsal fin with thread-like filament. Usually in pairs on reef crests and channels, but rather shy, less regularly observed than other more common butterflyfish species and not easily approached.

MEYER'S BUTTERFLYFISH
Chaetodon meyeri

Distribution: Tropical Indo-Pacific from East Africa to the Great Barrier Reef.
Size: Up to 18 centimeters.
Habitat: Coral-rich areas along coastal and outer reefs from 2 to 25 meters deep.
Life Habits: Bluish with curving black stripes converging to the base of the pectoral fin; yellow rim encircling body. Solitary or in pairs, commonly observed along reef crests, nibbling on coral polyps. A very beautiful species with a velvety look, occasionally intergrading throughout its range with the following one.

ORNATE BUTTERFLYFISH
Chaetodon ornatissimus

Distribution: Tropical Indo-Pacific from the Maldives to French Polynesia.
Size: Up to 18 centimeters.
Habitat: Coral-rich areas along crests and tops on coastal and outer reefs from 2 to 35 meters deep.
Life Habits: Bluish with orange diagonal bands, yellow rim encircling body, black bands crossing face. Usually in pairs, feeding off coral polyps it nibbles flitting on top of the reef. Occasionally intergrading with *C. meyeri*.

REDFIN BUTTERFLYFISH
Chaetodon lunulatus

Distribution: Tropical Western Pacific, from Indonesia to the Great Barrier Reef. The very similar *C. trifasciatus* occurs from East Africa to Indonesia.
Size: Up to 15 centimeters.
Habitat: Coral-rich areas on crests and reef tops on coastal and outer reefs from 2 to 20 meters deep.
Life Habits: Oblique purplish stripes on a pale yellow background, dark red anal fin, black stripe across eye. Usually observed in pairs, flitting along the reef top, feeding on coral polyps.

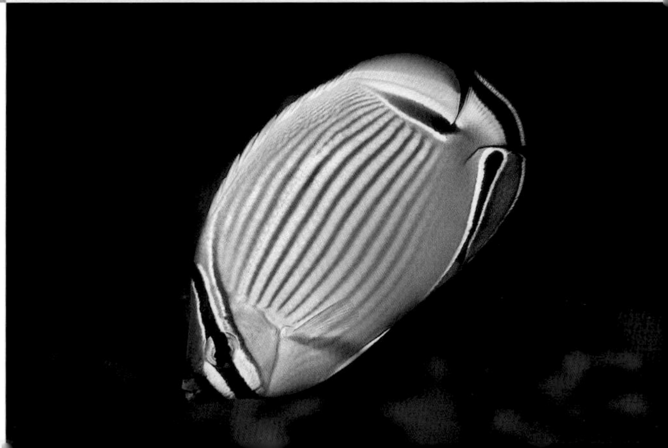

INDIAN PINSTRIPED BUTTERFLYFISH
Chaetodon trifasciatus

Distribution: Indian Ocean, from East Africa to Bali in Indonesia.
Size: Up to 15 centimeters.
Habitat: Coral-rich areas in coastal and outer reefs from 2 to 20 meters deep.
Life Habits: Body pale, yellowish in the front and bluish posteriorly, with many longitudinal purplish stripes; orange-red anal fin and base of caudal fin; black bar crossing eye. Often a small elongate black spot on the upper side. Replaced further east by the very similar *C. lunulatus*.

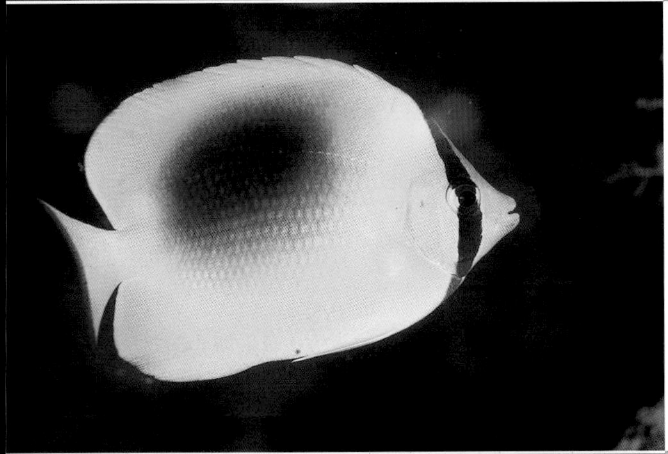

OVAL-SPOT BUTTERFLYFISH
Chaetodon speculum

Distribution: Western Pacific from Indonesia to Papua New Guinea, Southern Japan and Australia.
Size: Up to 18 centimeters.
Habitat: Coral-rich areas in coastal and outer reefs from 5 to 35 meters deep.
Life Habits: Body bright yellow featuring a large oval black spot on the upper side; black bar crossing the eye. Rather shy, usually observed in pairs, flitting erratically among corals and occasionally feeding off their polyps.

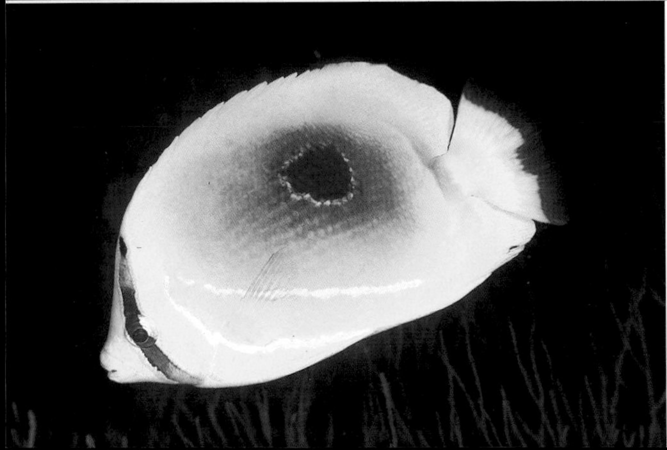

BENNETT'S BUTTERFLYFISH
Chaetodon bennetti

Distribution: Tropical Indo-Pacific from East Africa to French Polynesia, Japan and the Great Barrier Reef in Australia.
Size: Up to 18 centimeters.
Habitat: Coral-rich areas in coastal and outer reefs from 5 to 35 meters deep.
Life Habits: Body bright yellow with large blue-bordered black ocellus on rear side, two light blue lines on lower body. Solitary or in pairs, often encountered in deeper water on drop-offs and close to gorgonian colonies. Feeds on coral polyps.

TEARDROP BUTTERFLYFISH
Chaetodon unimaculatus

Distribution: Tropical Pacific from Indonesia to Polynesia and Hawai'i.
Size: Up to 20 centimeters.
Habitat: Lagoons and outer reefs in coral-rich areas from 10 to 60 meters.
Life Habits: Body bright white with lemon-yellow dorsal, anal and ventral fins; black ocellus ringed in white on rear back; large black band crossing eye. Solitary or more commonly in large groups flitting around the reef top and erratically feeding on coral polyps.

KLEIN'S BUTTERFLYFISH
Chaetodon kleinii

Distribution: Tropical Indo-Pacific from East Africa to Southern Japan, Hawai'i and Australia.
Size: Up to 14 centimeters.
Habitat: Rocky reefs and coral-rich areas in outer reefs and passes from 5 to 60 meters deep.
Life Habits: Body yellow-brown, with bright blue "forehead" and dirty white face. Blackish lips and ventral fins. One of the less striking butterflyfish species, often however observed in impressive, enormous schools in deep water, feeding on coral polyps.

BURGESS' BUTTERFLYFISH
Chaetodon burgessi

Distribution: Central Indo-Pacific, from Indonesia to Papua New Guinea.
Size: Up to 14 centimeters.
Habitat: Drop-offs on outer reefs from 20 to 80 meters deep.
Life Habits: Unmistakable livery, with black diagonal band on the side and broad black diagonal area on the white rear body. Occasionally observed alone or in pairs under ledges and overhangs along vertical drop-offs in deep water, usually below 40 meters. Very wary, not easily sighted or approached.

CROSS-HATCH BUTTERFLYFISH
Chaetodon xanthurus

Distribution: Central Indo-Pacific from the Gulf of Thailand to the Philippines.
Size: Up to 14 centimeters.
Habitat: Coral-rich areas in coastal and outer reefs from 10 to 50 meters deep.
Life Habits: Body silvery with cross-hatch darker pattern, broad yellow-orange band on rear body and tail. Often observed in pairs along drop-offs on outer reefs and easily confused with the very similar *C. mertensii* or Yellowback Butterflyfish, which has a more chevron-like darker pattern on the body.

RED-BACK BUTTERFLYFISH
Chaetodon paucifasciatus

Distribution: Red Sea.
Size: Up to 12 centimeters.
Habitat: Coral-rich areas on coastal and outer reefs from 2 to 40 meters.
Life Habits: Body silver-white with darker chevrons, bright blood-red rear body and tail rear end. Usually observed in pairs or small loose aggregations, flitting around the reef and feeding on coral polyps. Endemic to the Red Sea and ranging to the Gulf of Aden.

SPECKLED BUTTERFLYFISH
Chaetodon citrinellus

Distribution: Tropical Indo-Pacific from East Africa to French Polynesia, Japan and Australia.
Size: Up to 13 centimeters.
Habitat: Reef flats on coastal and outer reefs from 1 to 3 meters deep.
Life Habits: Body pale yellow or whitish with many rows of blue spots. Commonly observed on reef flats exposed to surf and in very shallow water, rarely below 15 meters. Generally encountered in pairs or in small loose aggregations flitting around and feeding off coral polyps.

SPOT-BANDED BUTTERFLYFISH
Chaetodon punctatofasciatus

Distribution: Central Indo-Pacific from Indonesia to Taiwan and the Great Barrier Reef in Australia.
Size: Up to 12 centimeters.
Habitat: Coral-rich areas in coastal and outer reefs from 5 to 45 meters deep.
Life Habits: Body yellowish with seven grey bars on upper body and rows of dark spots below; tail base suffused with bright orange. Usually observed in pairs or in small loose aggregations, occasionally mixing and intergrading with the very similar *C. pelewensis* or Dot & Dash Butterflyfish.

RETICULATED BUTTERFLYFISH
Chaetodon reticulatus

Distribution: Central Indo-Pacific from Sulawesi in Indonesia to French Polynesia and Australia.
Size: Up to 16 centimeters.
Habitat: Coral rich-areas on outer reefs from 2 to 30 meters deep.
Life Habits: Body deep, velvety black with a pale pearly grey spot on each scale; margin of tail grey and yellow with black edge; large, yellow-rimmed black band crossing eye. Solitary, very impressive, often observed in well-lit, open areas on shallow reefs .

COLLARED BUTTERFLYFISH
Chaetodon collare

Distribution: Indo-Pacific from the Arabian Peninsula to the Philippines.
Size: Up to 16 centimeters.
Habitat: Coral-rich areas on rocky, boulder-strewn reefs from 2 to 30 meters.
Life Habits: Superficially similar to the preceding species *C. reticulatus* from which it can be readily distinguished by the bright white "collar" marking behind the head and the bright blood-red tail. Often observed in large aggregations; very common in Thai waters.

PANDA BUTTERFLYFISH
Chaetodon adiergastos

Distribution: Central Pacific from Indonesia and Malaysia to the Philippines, Japan and Australia
Size: Up to 16 centimeters.
Habitat: Coral-rich areas on coastal and outer reefs from 3 to 25 meters deep.
Life Habits: Unmistakable: bright white with many diagonal dark stripes, orange-yellow fins and a round black blotch on eye. A smaller black spot is also present on nape. Commonly observed in pairs or in small aggregations, usually sheltering under large *Acropora* table corals.

RED SEA RACCOON BUTTERFLYFISH
Chaetodon fasciatus

Distribution: Red Sea.
Size: Up to 24 centimeters.
Habitat: Coral-rich areas on coastal and outer reefs from 2 to 30 meters deep.
Life Habits: Body golden yellow with several diagonal dark stripes and a mask-like black and white marking on the head. Very similar to the following species *C. lunula* which takes its place further east and from which it can be distinguished by the lack of black on the caudal peduncle. Very common in proximity of soft corals and endemic to the Red Sea.

RACCOON BUTTERFLYFISH
Chaetodon lunula

Distribution: Tropical Indo-Pacific from East Africa to Hawai'i and Galapagos.
Size: Up to 21 centimeters.
Habitat: Lagoons, coastal and outer reefs from 1 to 30 meters deep.
Life Habits: Body golden yellow, faintly banded with diagonal stripes, with a black and white "mask" across the head; diagonal black stripe from this marking to the dorsal fin. A very common species with a broad-ranging distribution, usually observed in pairs or in huge aggregations.

MASKED BUTTERFLYFISH
Chaetodon semilarvatus

Distribution: Red Sea.
Size: Up to 23 centimeters.
Habitat: Coral-rich areas on coastal and outer reefs from 2 to 25 meters deep.
Life Habits: A striking species: body is a rich golden yellow with several vertical dark orange stripes and a bright blue "eyepatch". Easily approached and commonly observed during the day in small to large aggregations, sheltering almost motionless under large *Acropora* table corals. Endemic to the Red Sea and ranging to the Gulf of Aden.

BLACK-BACKED BUTTERFLYFISH
Chaetodon melannotus

Distribution: Tropical Indo-Pacific from the Red Sea to the Philippines, Papua New Guinea and Australia.
Size: Up to 15 centimeters.
Habitat: Coral-rich areas on coastal and outer reefs from 2 to 20 meters deep.
Life Habits: Body white with many diagonal black lines, yellow rim encircling the body, small black saddle at the base of the tail. Easily confused with the almost identical Tail-spot Butterflyfish *C. ocellicaudus,* with which it probably intergrades. Often observed in small schools, feeding on coral polyps.

TAIL-SPOT BUTTERFLYFISH
Chaetodon ocellicaudus

Distribution: Tropical Indo-Pacific from the Andamans to Papua New Guinea and the Great Barrier Reef in Australia.
Size: Up to 14 centimeters.
Habitat: Coral-rich areas in coastal and outer reefs from 3 to 50 meters deep.
Life Habits: Almost identical to the preceding species - with which it probably intergrades in many areas - but with a black spot at the base of the tail. Commonly observed in channels on the reef top, often in small, fast-swimming schools feeding on coral polyps.

PACIFIC DOUBLE-SADDLE BUTTERFLYFISH
Chaetodon ulietensis

Distribution: Western Pacific from Cocos-Keeling to French Polynesia and from Southern Japan to Australia.
Size: Up to 15 centimeters.
Habitat: Coral-rich areas in lagoons and outer reefs from 5 to 30 meters deep.
Life Habits: Body whitish with several darker vertical lines and two blackish saddles; rear part of body and tail bright yellow. Usually encountered in pairs or in small groups, feeding on coral polyps and small benthic invertebrates. Saddleback Butterflyfish *C. falcula* similar but with yellow back and sharper saddles.

LINED BUTTERFLYFISH
Chaetodon lineolatus

Distribution: Tropical Indo-Pacific, from East Africa to Southern Japan and French Polynesia.
Size: Up to 30 centimeters.
Habitat: Lagoons and coastal reefs from 2 to 170 meters deep.
Life Habits: Body white with several thin vertical black lines, rear body and fins bright yellow, broad black band - enclosing white spot on nape - crossing eye. With a maximum length of 30 cm this is the largest butterflyfish species, commonly encountered alone or in pairs.

SPOT-NAPE BUTTERFLYFISH
Chaetodon oxycephalus

Distribution: Tropical Indo-Pacific from the Maldives to Papua New Guinea and from the Philippines to Australia.
Size: Up to 25 centimeters.
Habitat: Coastal and outer reefs in coral-rich areas from 10 to 40 meters deep.
Life Habits: Body bright white with several thin vertical black lines, bright yellow dorsal, caudal and anal fins with black rear upper body: superficially similar to Lined Butterflyfish *C. lineolatus* but with black patch on nape distinctly separated from black eye bar.

YELLOW-DOTTED BUTTERFLYFISH
Chaetodon selene

Distribution: Central Indo-Pacific, from Malaysia to Papua New Guinea.
Size: Up to 16 centimeters.
Habitat: Sand or coral rubble bottoms on coastal reefs from 10 to 50 meters.
Life Habits: Body white with numerous yellow spots in diagonal rows, fins a rich yellow, black trim on rear body. Feeds on coral polyps and presumably small benthic invertebrates. Usually in pairs, less commonly observed than other butterflyfish species.

SADDLED BUTTERFLYFISH
Chaetodon ephippium

Distribution: Tropical Indo-Pacific from Sri Lanka to French Polynesia and from Southern Japan to Australia.
Size: Up to 23 centimeters.
Habitat: Coral-rich areas in lagoons and outer reefs from 5 to 30 meters deep.
Life Habits: One of the most striking butterflyfish species. Body is pearly grey with blue lines on the lower front and a large, white-trimmed rear black portion; chin is orange, rear dorsal fin often thread-like. Commonly observed in pairs, very territorial and easily approached.

LATTICED BUTTERFLYFISH
Chaetodon rafflesi

Distribution: Tropical Indo-Pacific from Sri Lanka to French Polynesia and from Southern Japan to Australia.
Size: Up to 15 centimeters.
Habitat: Coral-rich areas in coastal and outer reefs from 2 to 15 meters deep.
Life Habits: Body a bright, uniform lemon yellow with a delicate network of grey lines; blue patch on forehead. Solitary or in pairs for life, occasionally observed on silty environments.Feeds principally on coral polyps.

THREADFIN BUTTERFLYFISH
Chaetodon auriga

Distribution: Tropical Indo-Pacific from the Red Sea to French Polynesia and from Southern Japan to Australia.
Size: Up to 23 centimeters.
Habitat: Coastal and outer reefs from 2 to 40 meters deep.
Life Habits: Body white with chevron-like darker markings, rear part bright yellow with black spot on rear dorsal fin, also sporting thread-like filament in adults. Commonly observed alone or in pairs among soft and hard corals and occasionally on sand and rubble bottoms. Feeds mostly on coral polyps.

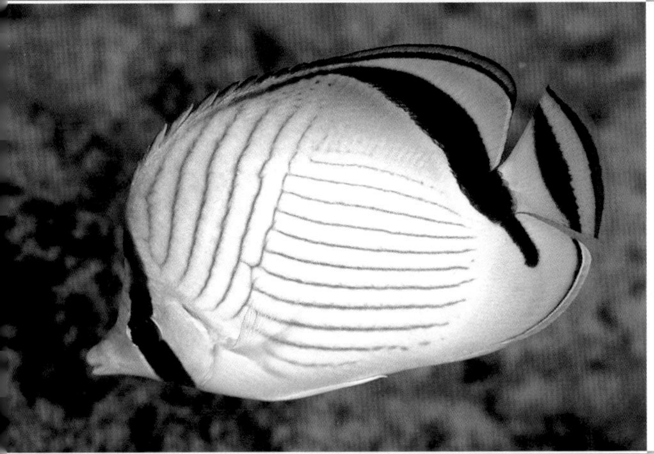

VAGABOND BUTTERFLYFISH
Chaetodon vagabundus

Distribution: Tropical Indo-Pacific from East Africa to Hawai'i and from Southern Japan to Australia.
Size: Up to 23 centimeters.
Habitat: Coastal and outer reefs from 5 to 30 meters deep.
Life Habits: Body white, fading to yellow, with chevron-like pattern of fine darker lines. Territorial like most butterflyfishes, often observed alone or in small loose groups on coral rubble slopes in current-prone areas near drop-offs. Feeds on coral polyps and small benthic invertebrates.

CHEVRONED BUTTERFLYFISH
Chaetodon trifascialis

Distribution: Tropical Indo-Pacific from the Red Sea to Hawai'i and from Southern Japan to Australia.
Size: Up to 18 centimeters.
Habitat: Coral-rich areas on coastal and outer reefs from 3 to 12 meters deep.
Life Habits: Body silvery white with busy chevron black markings, tail black with orange-yellow margin. Body more elongate than average compared to other butterflyfish species. Territorial and usually solitary; feeds on coral polyps.

EASTERN TRIANGULAR BUTTERFLYFISH
Chaetodon baronessa

Distribution: Tropical Eastern Indo-Pacific from Cocos-Keeling to the Great Barrier Reef in Australia. The very similar *C. triangulum* takes its place from East Africa to Indonesia.
Size: Up to 15 centimeters.
Habitat: Shallow plate and table corals from 1 to 10 meters deep.
Life Habits: Beautiful but extremely shy and very difficult to approach, often observed flitting in pairs above *Acropora* table corals in very shallow, well-lit clear water. Feeds on coral polyps exclusively.

EIGHT-BANDED BUTTERFLYFISH
Chaetodon octofasciatus

Distribution: Central Indo-Pacific from Sri Lanka to Papua New Guinea.
Size: Up to 12 centimeters.
Habitat: Coral-rich areas in coastal reefs from 3 to 20 meters deep.
Life Habits: Body from white to rich yellow with eight narrow black vertical bars. Often observed alone or in small loose aggregations while sheltering among branching corals, occasionally in silty and turbid water. Feeds on coral polyps only.

TINKER'S BUTTERFLYFISH
Chaetodon tinkeri

Distribution: Very localized, Central Pacific from Marshalls and Hawai'i.
Size: Up to 15 centimeters.
Habitat: Steep slopes on outer reefs from 27 to 160 meters deep.
Life Habits: Body white with several small black dots, yellow bar crossing eye, black diagonal area on rear body. Usually bserved sheltering among black coral colonies or gorgonians in pairs or small aggregations. At least two other similar species (*C. flavocoronatus* and *C. declivis*) in the same general distribution area.

TWO-EYED CORALFISH
Coradion melanopus

Distribution: Central Indo-Pacific from Indonesia to Papua New Guinea.
Size: Up to 15 centimeters.
Habitat: Coastal and outer reefs from 10 to 30 meters deep.
Life Habits: Body white with orange-brown vertical bars and a pair of ocellated black spots on rear dorsal and anal fins. Generally observed alone or in pairs, very often in sponge-rich habitats. Less frequently encountered than other butterflyfish species.

ORANGE-BANDED CORALFISH
Coradion chrysozonus

Distribution: Central Indo-Pacific from the Andamans to the Solomons and from Southern Japan to Australia.
Size: Up to 15 centimeters.
Habitat: Coral-rich areas in coastal reefs from 3 to 60 meters deep.
Life Habits: Body white with two wide rust-orange bars and a single black ocellus on rear dorsal fin. Usually solitary. This is the most commonly observed *Coradion* species in the Central Indo-Pacific area, often encountered in silty and turbid environments.

HIGH-FIN CORALFISH
Coradion altivelis

Distribution: Central Indo-Pacific from the Andamans to the Solomons and from Southern Japan to Australia.
Size: Up to 20 centimeters.
Habitat: Coastal reefs in sponge-rich habitats from 3 to 15 meters deep.
Life Habits: Easily confused underwater with the two preceding *Coradion* species, but has a longer and more pointed dorsal fin and adults (a sub-adult is illustrated) lack the ocellus.Rather uncommon and very seldom observed by divers.

EYE-SPOT BUTTERFLYFISH
Parachaetodon ocellatus

Distribution: Western Pacific from Indonesia to Fiji and from Southern Japan to Australia.
Size: Up to 18 centimeters.
Habitat: Sponge-rich areas in coastal and outer reefs from 5 to 40 meters.
Life Habits: Body is markedly rhomboidal, silvery-white with five bright orange vertical stripes and a black spot in the middle of the dorsal fin. Very wary, not easily approached and rather uncommon. Very seldom observed.

BEAKED CORALFISH
Chaetodon (Chelmon) rostratus

Distribution: Central Indo-Pacific from the Andamans to Papua New Guinea and from Southern Japan to Australia.
Size: Up to 20 centimeters.
Habitat: Coastal reefs from 2 to 25 meters deep.
Life Habits: Body distinctly triangular, bright chrome-like or silvery white, with four bright orange vertical bars - one across the eye - and a long, beak-like snout. Often observed in pairs in turbid water on silty bottoms on inner reefs. Mostly known as *Chelmon rostratus*.

LONGNOSED BUTTERFLYFISH
Forcipiger longirostris

Distribution: Tropical Indo-Pacific from East Africa to Hawai'i and from Southern Japan to Australia.
Size: Up to 22 centimeters.
Habitat: Coral-rich areas on outer reefs from 5 to 60 meters deep.
Life Habits: Body bright yellow with black and silvery-white head and a very long, beak-like snout. Usually solitary or in pairs, flitting among the corals and using its tweezers-like long mouth to pick exposed coral polyps and small benthic invertebrates. Very common in its area.

FORCEPSFISH
Forcipiger flavissimus

Distribution: Tropical Indo-Pacific from the Red Sea to Central America and from Southern Japan to Australia.
Size: Up to 22 centimeters.
Habitat: Coral-rich areas on coastal and outer reefs from 2 to 110 meters deep.
Life Habits: Almost identical to the preceding species but with a comparatively shorter snout. Commonly observed flitting among the corals, feeding on exposed polyps using its tweezers-like long mouth.

SCHOOLING BANNERFISH
Heniochus diphreutes

Distribution: Tropical Indo-Pacific from the Red Sea to Australia and from Japan to Hawai'i.
Size: Up to 21 centimeters.
Habitat: Outer reef slopes and drop-offs in oceanic locations from 5 to 20 meters.
Life Habits: Usually encountered in very large aggregations, schooling in front of drop-offs or along steep slopes and feeding on plankton in the water column. Easily identified by the striped livery and the very elongated dorsal fin filament.

LONG-FIN BANNERFISH
Henicchus acuminatus

Distribution: Tropical Indo-Pacific from the Red Sea to French Polynesia and from Southern Japan to Australia.
Size: Up to 25 centimeters.
Habitat: Lagoons and outer reef walls and drop-offs from 2 to 75 meters deep.
Life Habits: Very similar to the preceding species but never in such large schools and more closely tied to the reef environment; snout also slightly longer. Commonly encountered alone or in small groups feeding on plankton and on small benthic invertebrates.

RED SEA BANNERFISH
Heniochus intermedius

Distribution: Red Sea.
Size: Up to 18 centimeters.
Habitat: Coral-rich areas on slopes and reef tops from 2 to 50 meters deep.
Life Habits: This species is endemic to the Red Sea and replaces in the region the preceding one, *H. acuminatus*. Very similar but with a strong yellow tinge on the silvery body. Very commonly observed in pairs or in small groups, especially where soft corals are present.

SINGULAR BANNERFISH
Heniochus singularius

Distribution: Tropical Indo-Pacific from the Maldives to Samoa and from Southern Japan to Australia.
Size: Up to 23 centimeters.
Habitat: Coastal and outer reefs from 2 to 250 meters deep.
Life Habits: Body thick-set, black, with bright yellow dorsal and caudal fin; first ray of dorsal fin white and filamented; horn-like bump above eyes. Usually alone or in pairs, often motionless, sheltering under ledges and overhangs along vertical walls and drop-offs.

MASKED BANNERFISH
Heniochus monoceros

Distribution: Tropical Indo-Pacific from East Africa to French Polynesia and from Southern Japan to Australia.
Size: Up to 23 centimeters.
Habitat: Coastal and outer reefs in coral-rich areas from 2 to 30 meters deep.
Life Habits: Body white with sharp black band running down the side and yellow rear; bump on nape, black mask on snout, curved white filamented dorsal fin. Usually observed in pairs or in small schools, often stationary or slow moving, hovering around coral colonies.

PENNANT BANNERFISH
Heniochus chrysostomus

Distribution: Central Indo-Pacific from Cocos-Keeling to French Polynesia and from Southern Japan to Australia.
Size: Up to 18 centimeters.
Habitat: Coastal and outer reefs from 3 to 50 meters deep.
Life Habits: Body striped in black and white and distinctly triangular due to raised, feather-like dorsal fin. Usually encountered alone or in pairs, occasionally in small groups sheltering under ledges or overhangs during the day.

HUMPHEAD BANNERFISH
Heniochus varius

Distribution: Central Indo-Pacific from Indonesia to French Polynesia and from Southern Japan to Australia.
Size: Up to 19 centimeters.
Habitat: Coral-rich areas in coastal and outer reefs from 2 to 30 meters.
Life Habits: Body distinctly triangular due to raised, feather-like dorsal fin; pair of horn-like protrusions above the eyes; concave area between eyes and nape. A queer-looking butterflyfish, usually observed alone or in pairs while sheltering motionless among corals.

PYRAMID BUTTERFLYFISH
Hemitaurichthys polylepis

Distribution: Central Indo-Pacific from Cocos-Keeling to French Polynesia and from Southern Japan to Australia.
Size: Up to 18 centimeters.
Habitat: Reef walls and drop-offs in clear water from 2 to 120 meters deep.
Life Habits: Unmistakable pyramid-like white marking on yellow body with deep brown head. Locally common, often observed in enormous schools, feeding on plankton in the water column in front of steep walls and drop-offs.

ANGELFISHES
Pomacanthidae

A medium-sized family numbering 7 genera and about 80 species, accounting for some of the most spectacularly beautiful animals one can ever see on a coral reef. They are generally medium-sized fish, often capable of producing clearly audible grunting sounds underwater, commonly seen in pairs and of very territorial habits, regularly patrolling their range. Closely related to butterflyfishes, they can be easily identified by the large spine on the lower corner of their branchial plate. ~ **U/W Photo Tips:** Angelfishes are some of the most beautiful and easily approached subjects on a tropical reef. Take advantage of their territorial habits and try to shoot at the moment they are displaying, presenting their colorful side to the intruder. A good macro or medium (25-50mm) lens will do in most cases, but angelfishes are also wonderful in a wider reef setting.

MULTI-BARRED ANGELFISH
Paracentropyge multifasciata

Distribution: Tropical Indo-Pacific from Cocos-Keeling to French Polynesia, Japan and the Great Barrier Reef in Australia.
Size: Up to 10 centimeters.
Habitat: Drop-offs and steep walls on outer reefs from 20 to 70 meter deep.
Life Habits: Body roundish, with alternated black and white stripes. Lower part often tinged with bright yellow. Commonly observed under ledges and overhangs, sometimes swimming upside down. Extremely wary and not easily approached, usually mistaken by divers and photographers for a butterflyfish.

THREE-SPOT ANGELFISH
Apolemichthys trimaculatus

Distribution: Tropical Indo-Pacific from East Africa to Samoa, Southern Japan and the Great Barrier Reef in Australia.
Size: Up to 25 centimeters.
Habitat: Coral-rich areas on steep slopes and drop-offs from 15 to 60 meters deep.
Life Habits: Unmistakable: body bright yellow with blue lips; wide black trim on anal fin. Usually solitary or in pairs. Feeds mostly on algae and benthic invertebrates scraping them from sponges, rocks and corals. Common in its area.

TWO-SPINED ANGELFISH
Centropyge bispinosa

Distribution: Tropical Indo-Pacific from East Africa to French Polynesia, Southern Japan and Australia.
Size: Up to 10 centimeters.
Habitat: Coral-rich areas on outer reefs and lagoons from 5 to 45 meters deep.
Life Habits: Extremely colorful: bright, velvety blue with orange "burning through". Solitary or in small loose aggregations, very shy, always ready to take shelter among corals or under ledges. Very territorial; feeds on algal matter and small benthic invertebrates.

PEARL-SCALED ANGELFISH
Centropyge vroliki

Distribution: Western Indo-Pacific from Indonesia to Vanuatu, Southern Japan and Australia.
Size: Up to 12 centimeters.
Habitat: Coral-rich areas on coastal and outer reefs from 5 to 25 meters.
Life Habits: Pearly grey, gradually becoming black on rear body. Solitary or in small loose aggregations; very wary, always ready to hide among the corals. Quite common and territorial; feeds on algae and small benthic invertebrates.

FLAME ANGELFISH
Centropyge loricula

Distribution: Central Indo-Pacific from Papua New Guinea to French Polynesia, with isolated populations in West Pacific and Indonesia.
Size: Up to 10 centimeters.
Habitat: Coral-rich areas on outer reefs from 5 to 60 meters deep.
Life Habits: Body bright orange with five or six black bars, bright blue stripes on rear of dorsal fins. Shy, always ready to hide among corals; rarely found on coastal reefs, relatively more common in pelagic locations.

BICOLOR ANGELFISH
Centropyge bicolor

Distribution: Western Pacific from Indonesia to Samoa, Southern Japan and Australia.
Size: Up to 15 centimeters.
Habitat: Coral-rich areas and rubble bottoms on outer reefs and in lagoons from 10 to 25 meters deep.
Life Habits: Unmistakable, often observed in pairs or in small groups: head bright yellow with blue spot on nape, body bright deep blue, tail yellow. Truly beautiful and easily approached; very territorial. Feeds on algae, sponges and small benthic invertebrates.

KEYHOLE ANGELFISH
Centropyge tibicen

Distribution: Western Pacific from Indonesia to New Caledonia, Southern Japan and Australia .
Size: Up to 18 centimeters.
Habitat: Coastal reefs and lagoons from 4 to 35 meters deep.
Life Habits: Dark blue or blackish with unmistakable keyhole-shaped bright white blotch on side; margin of anal fin bright yellow. Solitary or in small groups, often observed among coral rubble. Feeds on algae, small sponges and small benthic invertebrates. Territorial and very wary.

VERMICULATED ANGELFISH
Chaetodontoplus mesoleucus

Distribution: Central Indo-Pacific from Indonesia to the Solomons, Southern Japan and Northern Australia.
Size: Up to 18 centimeters.
Habitat: Coral-rich areas on coastal reefs and lagoons from 5 to 20 meters.
Life Habits: Body pearly grey with many fine white vermiculations, tail yellow, black bar across eye. Locally very common, usually observed in pairs. Feeds mostly on sponges and tunicates like the majority of angelfishes. A possibly different species - yet undescribed by scientific literature - has a grey tail.

QUEENSLAND ANGELFISH
Chaetodontoplus meredithi

Distribution: Localized Indo-Pacific from Great Barrier Reef to Lord Howe Island in Australia.
Size: Up to 25 centimeters.
Habitat: Coastal reefs with flat bottoms and isolated bommies and boulders from 6 to 50 meters deep.
Life Habits: Body black with bluish vermiculated head with white bar behind, bright yellow tail and chest. Solitary or in pairs, with a very localized distriburion and endemic to Australian waters. Feeds on sponges, tunlcates and invertebrates.

PEWTER ANGELFISH
Chaetodontoplus dimidiatus

Distribution: Central Indo-Pacific from Indonesia to West Papua and Japan.
Size: Up to 20 centimeters.
Habitat: Coastal and outer coral and rocky reefs from 5 to 30 meters deep.
Life Habits: Body light velvety grey with blkack dorsal fin and belly; yellow vermiculations on snout, bright yellow tail and yellow margins of dorsal and anal fins. Solitary or in pairs, with a very localized distribution but locally common. Feeds on sponges, tunicates and benthic invertebrates on coral and rocky reefs.

LAMARCK'S ANGELFISH
Genicanthus lamarck

Distribution: Central Indo-Pacific from Indonesia to Vanuatu, Southern Japan and the Great Barrier Reef in Australia.
Size: Up to 23 centimeters.
Habitat: Outer reefs, slopes and drop-offs in clear water from 10 to 50 meters deep.
Life Habits: Not very colorful but truly beautiful: body white with four black longitudinal stripes and a broad black trim on dorsal fin, yellow blotch on nape. Occasionally observed swimming well above the substrate, possibly feeding in the water column or checking range.

YELLOW-BAND ANGELFISH
Pomacanthus maculosus

Distribution: Red Sea, ranging to the Arabian Gulf, Somalia and Kenya.
Size: Up to 50 centimeters.
Habitat: Coastal and outer reefs, wrecks from 5 to 60 meters deep.
Life Habits: Large, impressive. Body from bright to powder blue but always with "Africa"-shaped yellow blotch on side. Dorsal and anal fin with long, thin, curved ends. Very territorial, constantly patrolling its range along the reefs, alone or in pairs. Feeds on sponges, algal growth and tunicates scraping them from rocks and live or dead coral.

EMPEROR ANGELFISH
Pomacanthus imperator

Distribution: Tropical Indo-Pacific from the Red Sea to French Polynesia, Southern Japan and Australia.
Size: Up to 40 centimeters.
Habitat: Coral-rich areas in coastal and outer reefs, slopes and drop-offs from 5 to 60 meters deep.
Life Habits: Unmistakable. Body alternating bright yellow and bright blue thin longitudinal stripes, white mouth, black, blue edged "mask" across eyes. Very territorial, usually encountered alone or in pairs. Feeds on sponges, algae and tunicates; makes clearly audible grunting or thumping sound when disturbed.

BLUE-GIRDLED ANGELFISH
Pomacanthus navarchus

Distribution: Central Indo-Pacific from Indonesia to the Solomons and the Great Barrier Reef.
Size: Up to 25 centimeters.
Habitat: Coral-rich areas on drop-offs and slopes along coastal and outer reefs from 3 to 40 meters deep.
Life Habits: Possibly the most beautiful angelfish species: body yellow with blue spots, dark blue areas on head and lower rear body with bright blue trim. Generally solitary, territorial; rather shy and not easily approached. Feeds on sponges, algae and tunicates.

SEMICIRCLE ANGELFISH
Pomacanthus semicirculatus

Distribution: Tropical Indo-Pacific from East Africa to Fiji, Southern Japan and Australia.
Size: Up to 35 centimeters.
Habitat: Coastal reefs on walls and drop-offs from 10 to 40 meters deep.
Life Habits: Body broad, laterally compressed, greenish or greenish-yellow with a multitude of blue spots. Rather uncommon, solitary, very territorial. Wary, not easily approached, always keeping its distance and ready to take shelter. Feeds on sponges and tunicates.

SIX-BANDED ANGELFISH
Pomacanthus sexstriatus

Distribution: Western Pacific from Indonesia to New Caledonia, Southern Japan and Australia.
Size: Up to 46 centimeters.
Habitat: Coastal and outer reefs on slopes and drop-offs from 3 to 60 meters.
Life Habits: Very large and thick set; body pale yellow with six blackish bars and a multitude of blue spots; head dark blue with sharp white bar behind eye. Solitary or in pairs, patrolling its range along the reef. Wary, not easily approached. Feeds mostly on sponges.

BLUE-RINGED ANGELFISH
Pomacanthus annularis

Distribution: Central Indo-Pacific from East Africa to the Solomons and Southern Japan.
Size: Up to 45 centimeters.
Habitat: Coastal reefs, wrecks from 5 to 60 meters deep.
Life Habits: Unmistakable: body large, roundish, orange-brown with several curved bright blue bands; tail white, clearly marked blue ring above pectoral fin.One of the few species of angelfish regularly observed in very turbid waters. Alone or in pairs, territorial: may make thumping sounds when disturbed.

BLUE-FACE ANGELFISH
Pomacanthus xanthometopon

Distribution: Tropical Indo-Pacific from the Maldives to Southern Japan, Vanuatu and the Great Barrier Reef in Australia.
Size: Up to 35 centimeters.
Habitat: Coral-rich areas on steep slopes and drop-offs on outer reefs from 5 to 30 meters deep.
Life Habits: Large, majestic: body yellow with bright blue reticulated pattern, face blue with fine yellow vermiculations and sharply marked bright yellow mask. Solitary, very territorial, usually observed patrolling its range. Feeds mostly on sponges and tunicates.

GRAY ANGELFISH
Pomacanthus arcuatus

Distribution: Tropical Western Atlantic from New York to Florida, Bermuda, the Caribbean and the Amazon estuary in Southern Brazil.
Size: Up to 50 centimeters.
Habitat: On coastal and outer reefs from 5 to 30 meters deep.
Life Habits: Large, majestic, slow-moving: body grey with darker spots and elongated dorsal and anal fins tips. Locally common, often observed alone or in pairs in shallow water. Feeds on sponges, soft corals, algae and tunicates.

FRENCH ANGELFISH
Pomacanthus paru

Distribution: Tropical Western Atlantic from Florida to Bermuda and Southern Brazil.
Size: Up to 40 centimeters.
Habitat: Coastal and outer reefs from 5 to 100 meters deep.
Life Habits: Very similar to the preceding species but a very dark grey, with a pale grey head and with posterior edge of scales a bright yellow. Eye and cheek spine are also yellow. Territorial, commonly observed alone or in pairs on shallow coral reefs, where it feeds on algae, sponges and tunicates.

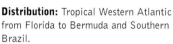

REGAL ANGELFISH
Pygoplites diacanthus

Distribution: Tropical Indo-Pacific from the Red Sea to Polynesia, New Caledonia, Southern Japan and Australia.
Size: Up to 25 centimeters.
Habitat: Coral-rich areas on coastal and outer reefs from 3 to 50 meters deep.
Life Habits: Striking, unmistakable livery: body bright yellow with several dark-edged blue-white vertical stripes, tail yellow, anal fin striped in bright blue and pink. Quite common but solitary and rather shy, not easily approached. Territorial, living in well-defined ranges. Feeds on sponges and tunicates.

KING ANGELFISH
Holacanthus passer

Distribution: Tropical Eastern Pacific from the Gulf of Mexico in Baja California to the Galapagos.
Size: Up to 25 centimeters.
Habitat: Rocky reefs and boulder-strewn slopes from 5 to 80 meters deep.
Life Habits: Body bluish with vertical white stripe and bright yellow tail. Often observed alone in oceanic locations, acting as a cleaner for other fish, including large scalloped hammerheads *Sphyrna lewini*. Able to tolerate very low water temperatures, down to 12° centigrades.

QUEEN ANGELFISH
Holacanthus ciliaris

Distribution: Tropical Western Atlantic from Florida to Southern Brazil.
Size: Up to 45 centimeters.
Habitat: Outer reefs and rubble slopes from 5 to 60 meters deep.
Life Habits: One of the most beautiful and striking fish of the Caribbean: body blue speckled in yellow, with elongated dorsal and anal fins and a conspicuous blue "crown" on nape. Generally observed in pairs in sponge-rich areas and rather easily approached. Feeds mostly on sponges, encrusting algae and tunicates.

ROCK BEAUTY
Holacanthus tricolor

Distribution: Tropical Western Atlantic from Georgia to Bermuda and Trinidad.
Size: Up to 30 centimeters.
Habitat: Coastal and outer reefs from 5 to 90 meters deep.
Life Habits: Easily identified: body black with the anterior third a bright yellow. Fins and tail are yellow, lips dark grey. Commonly observed in pairs or in small harems in well-defined ranges on shallow reefs. Usually unafraid and easily approached. Feeds mostly on encrusting sponges.

ANEMONEFISHES AND DAMSELFISHES
Pomacentridae

This is one of the largest and most important coral reef families, numbering a grand total of more than 300 different species. All these are small or very small, often extremely colorful, living in harems or aggregations and always close to shelter on healthy coral reefs. Anemonefishes or clownfishes in particular are very well known by most divers thanks to their peculiar commensalistic relationship with sea anemones, whose deadly sting they are capable of avoiding thanks to the mucus covering their body. In fact, clownfish cannot survive in the wild once separated from their host. ~ **U/W Photo Tips:** While the much-loved clownfishes are easily approached while sheltering in their anemones, damselfishes are more difficult subjects. Both given to rapid movements, they need patience and a macro lens doubling up as a telephoto in clear water, such as a 105mm. Sadly, it is almost impossible to capture correctly the dazzling electric blue shown underwater by many of the smaller species.

EASTERN SKUNK ANEMONEFISH
Amphiprion sandaracinos

Distribution: Central Indo-Pacific from Indonesia to the Solomons and Southern Japan. Replaced further West by the very similar Skunk Clownfish *A. akallopisos.*
Size: Up to 13 centimeters.
Habitat: On shallow, well-lit coastal and outer reefs from 3 to 20 meters deep.
Life Habits: Body orange with white longitudinal dorsal stripe. Commonly observed in pairs or small groups living in symbiotic relationship with large *Heteractis crispa* and *Stychodactyla mertensii* sea anemones .

PINK ANEMONEFISH
Amphiprion perideraion

Distribution: Western Pacific from Indonesia to New Caledonia, Southern Japan and Australia.
Size: Up to 10 centimeters.
Habitat: Shallow, well-lit coral reefs from 3 to 20 meters deep.
Life Habits: Body orange-pink with white dorsal stripe and diagnostic white vertical bar on head. Often observed in pairs living in symbiosis with several large sea anemones species. Strictly territorial like all clownfish species.

CLARK'S ANEMONEFISH
Amphiprion clarkii

Distribution: Tropical Indo-Pacific from the Arabian Sea to New Caledonia, Fiji, Southern Japan and Australia.
Size: Up to 12 centimeters.
Habitat: Shallow, well-lit coral reefs from 5 to 60 meters deep.
Life Habits: Body blackish with two white vertical bars, fins yellow. Associates with a large variety of different sea anemones species. Easily confused with two very similar-looking species, the Seba Anemonefish *A. sebae* and the Orange-fin Anemonefish *A. chrysopterus.*

BRIDLED ANEMONEFISH
Amphiprion frenatus

Distribution: Central Indo-Pacific from the South China Sea to Southern Japan.
Size: Up to 14 centimeters.
Habitat: Shallow, well-lit coral reefs from 2 to 12 meters deep.
Life Habits: Body deep red suffused with black, bright white vertical stripe across cheek. Restricted to a small distribution area but locally common and exclusively observed in association with Lightbulb anemone *Entacmaea quadricolor.*

PANDA ANEMONEFISH
Amphiprion polymnus

Distribution: Central Indo-Pacific from Indonesia to the Solomons.
Size: Up to 12 centimeters.
Habitat: Silty bottoms on coastal reefs from 3 to 35 meters.
Life Habits: Body black with yellow belly and white saddles of variable size and shape. Commonly observed on silty, muddy substrates well away from reefs in association with *Heteractis crispa* and *Stychodactyla haddoni* sea anemones. Very aggressive towards intruders, including divers, like most anemonefishes.

TOMATO ANEMONEFISH
Amphiprion ephippium

Distribution: Eastern Indian Ocean from the Andamans to Sumatra and Java.
Size: Up to 12 centimeters.
Habitat: Rocky reefs from 2 to 15 meters deep.
Life Habits: Reddish orange with diffused, variable amount of black on rear body. Distributed in a rather small geographical area but locally common, most often observed in rocky, boulder-strewn areas. Lives in association with *Entacmaea quadricolor* and *Heteractis crispa* sea anemones.

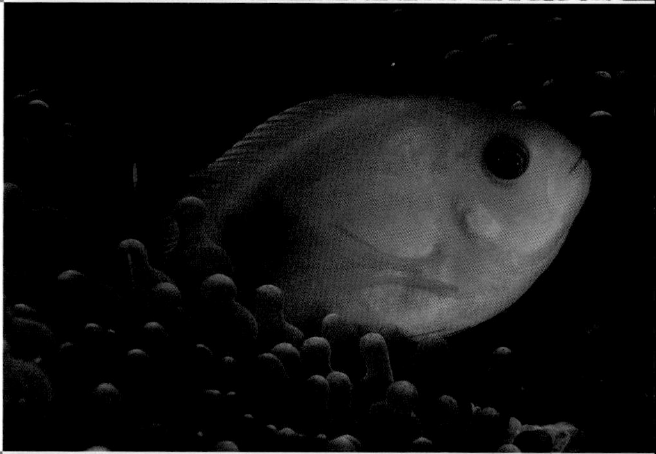

WESTERN CLOWN ANEMONEFISH
Amphiprion ocellaris

Distribution: Central Indo-Pacific from the Andamans to Australia. Replaced from Australia to New Guinea by the very similar Eastern Clown *A. percula*.
Size: Up to 9 centimeters.
Habitat: Coastal reefs from 1 to 15 meters deep.
Life Habits: Probably the best-known anemonefish: body bright orange with three white irregular bands. Often observed in association with its sea anemone hosts *Heteractis magnifica, Stichodactyla gigantea* and *S. mertensii*.

TWO-BANDED ANEMONEFISH
Amphiprion bicinctus

Distribution: Red Sea, Western Indian Ocean.
Size: Up to 12 centimeters.
Habitat: Shallow, well-lit coastal and outer reefs from 1 to 30 meters deep.
Life Habits: Body bright yellow with two white bars; the only anemonefish species in the Red Sea, living in association with *Entacmaea quadricolor*, *Heteractis aurora*, *H. crispa* and *Stichodactyla gigantea* sea anemones. Often observed in huge colonies with several hundred individuals sheltering on "living carpets" made up of closely-set sea anemones.

BLACK-FOOTED ANEMONEFISH
Amphiprion nigripes

Distribution: Indian Ocean.
Size: Up to 11 centimeters.
Habitat: Shallow, brightly-lit coral reefs from 2 to 25 meters deep.
Life Habits: The most commonly observed anemonefish species in the Lakshadweep and Maldives islands and in Sri Lanka. Body orange-pink with white vertical stripe across cheek and diagnostic black ventral fins. Often living in large aggregations in current-prone areas.

EASTERN CLOWN ANEMONEFISH
Amphiprion percula

Distribution: Western Pacific from Papua New Guinea to the Solomons and the Great Barrier Reef in Australia.
Size: Up to 9 centimeters.
Habitat: Shallow coastal reefs from 1 to 10 meters deep.
Life Habits: Body orange with three vertical, irregular white bands, often with highly variable amount of black trim. Associates with *Heteractis magnifica*, *Stichodactyla gigantea* and *S. mertensii* sea anemones. Replaced further West by the very similar *A. ocellaris*.

SPINE-CHEEK ANEMONEFISH
Premnas biaculeatus

Distribution: Central Indo-Pacific from Indonesia to the Great Barrier Reef.
Size: Up to 14 centimeters.
Habitat: Coastal coral reefs from 3 to 15 meters deep.
Life Habits: Deep red or maroon in older larger females (males are smaller), always with three thin red white stripes and a very large, easily seen cheek spine. Only observed in association with *Entacmaea quadricolor* sea anemones.

SERGEANT MAJOR
Abudefduf vaigiensis

Distribution: Tropical Indo-Pacific from the Red Sea to Southern Japan and the Great Barrier Reef in Australia.
Size: Up to 19 centimeters.
Habitat: Almost anywhere, usually in the water column on drop-offs and slopes from 1 to 12 meters.
Life Habits: Grey with five black or blue stripes and a yellow back. Often observed in a variety of environments and in large aggregations, feeding on drifting matter in the water column. Easily confused with several similarly striped species.

GOLDEN SERGEANT
Amblyglyphidodon aureus

Distribution: Central Indo-Pacific from the Andamans to Micronesia and from Southern Japan to New Caledonia.
Size: Up to 15 centimeters.
Habitat: Along drop-offs on coastal and outer reefs from 10 to 40 meters deep.
Life Habits: Body a luminous golden yellow with bright blue scribbled markings on the head and the eye. Solitary, often observed among gorgonians or sea whips. This species shares a typical body shape with all other large damselfishes.

WHITE-BELLY DAMSELFISH
Amblyglyphidodon leucogaster

Distribution: Western Pacific from Sumatra to Vanuatu and from Southern Japan to the Great Barrier Reef.
Size: Up to 13 centimeters.
Habitat: Coastal reefs and lagoons from 2 to 50 meters deep.
Life Habits: Body silver-grey with bright yellow ventral fins; black margin on dorsal, anal and caudal fin. Locally common and easily encountered feeding in the water column alone or in small groups but usually ignored by divers.

THREE-BAND DAMSELFISH
Amblyglyphidodon curacao

Distribution: Western Pacific from Singapore to the Great Barrier Reef.
Size: Up to 12 centimeters.
Habitat: Coastal reefs and lagoons from 1 to 15 meters deep.
Life Habits: Body greenish-silver with three wide darker stripes, midbody often with a yellow tinge. Commonly observed in small groups sheltering among *Acropora* branching coral colonies but usually ignored by divers.

YELLOWTAIL DAMSELFISH
Neoglyphidodon nigroris

Distribution: Central Indo-Pacific from the Andamans to Vanuatu and from Southern Japan to the Great Barrier Reef.
Size: Up to 11 centimeters.
Habitat: Coastal and outer reef slopes from 2 to 25 meters deep.
Life Habits: Body brownish fading to yellow on rear and dorsal and anal fins. Normally solitary or in small groups, often feeding in the water column in passes or channels but usually ignored by divers. For the juvenile form see page 219.

JAVANESE DAMSELFISH
Neoglyphidodon oxyodon

Distribution: Central Indo-Pacific from Indonesia to the Philippines.
Size: Up to 14 centimeters.
Habitat: Coastal reefs and lagoons in shallow water to 4 meters deep.
Life Habits: Body blackish or dark brown, lacking any specific markings. Normally observed alone or in small loose aggregations, feeding on algae off dead corals. Easily confused with at least four very similar species sharing the same distribution.

BARHEAD DAMSELFISH
Neoglyphidodon thoracotaeniatus

Distribution: Central Indo-Pacific from Indonesia to Papua New Guinea and the Solomons.
Size: Up to 10 centimeters.
Habitat: Coastal reefs, sheltered slopes and lagoons from 15 to 45 meters deep.
Life Habits: Body dark grey with three faded black bars on silvery head. Solitary or in small loose aggregations, feeding on plankton in the water column or algae growing on dead coral. Strongly territorial like most damselfishes.

JEWEL DAMSELFISH
Plectroglyphidodon lacrymatus

Distribution: Tropical Indo-Pacific from East Africa to French Polynesia and from Southern Japan to Australia.
Size: Up to 10 centimeters.
Habitat: Reef tops, rubble bottoms and lagoons from 2 to 12 meters deep.
Life Habits: Alone or in small groups often observed taking shelter among corals, easily identified by the brown body, the paler tail and the sprinkling of small bright blue spots on the back and head. Very territorial; feeds mostly on algae growing on dead corals.

TALBOT'S DAMSELFISH
Chrysiptera talboti

Distribution: Central Indo-Pacific from the Andamans to Fiji and the Coral Sea.
Size: Up to 6 centimeters.
Habitat: Coastal and outer reefs, lagoons, rubble bottoms from 6 to 30 meters deep.
Life Habits: Small, wary, jewel-like: body pinkish with blue edges on scales, head bright yellow, black spot on the middle of dorsal fin. Usually alone but often in small loose aggregations, tending to algal "farms" on dead coral rubble

BLEEKER'S DEMOISELLE
Chrysiptera bleekeri

Distribution: Localized Central Indo-Pacific, from Komodo Island to West Papua in Indonesia and the Philippines.
Size: Up to 8 centimeters.
Habitat: Coastal reefs in coral-rich areas from 3 to 12 meters deep.
Life Habits: Body bright blue or purple with bright yellow upper head, back and dorsal fin; replaced furthes East by almost identical Yellowfin Demoiselle *C. flavipinnis.* Alone or in small groups, always close to sand bottom at the feet of coral bommies and colonies.

BLUE DEVIL
Chrysiptera cyanea

Distribution: Western Pacific from Indonesia to Southern Japan and the Great Barrier Reef in Australia.
Size: Up to 8 centimeters.
Habitat: Coastal reefs and lagoons on rubble bottoms from 1 to 10 meters deep.
Life Habits: Body bright neon blue with black band from snout to eye; males have yellow tail (female illustrated). Very active but wary, often sheltering among branching corals. Several very similar species, all belonging to the *Chrysiptera* genus, share its general distribution area.

THREE-SPOT HUMBUG
Dascyllus trimaculatus

Distribution: Tropical Indo-Pacific from the Red Sea to French Polynesia.
Size: Up to 14 centimeters.
Habitat: Among corals on coastal and outer reefs from 2 to 50 meters deep.
Life Habits: Bright white spots on juveniles (illustrated) disappear in adults, which are a uniform dirty brown. Very territorial and easily observed, feeding on algae and living in groups; juveniles are often observed living symbiotically with sea anemones, mixing with clownfishes.

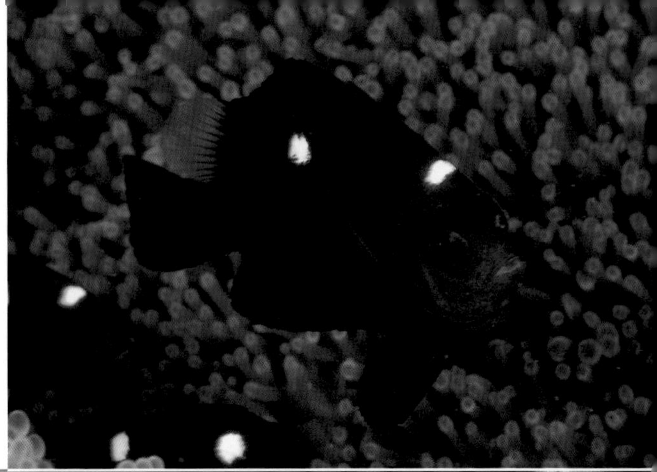

COMMON HUMBUG
Dascyllus aruanus

Distribution: Tropical Indo-Pacific from the Red Sea to French Polynesia and from Southern Japan to Australia.
Size: Up to 8 centimeters.
Habitat: Thick coral growth in sheltered reefs from 1 to 12 meters deep.
Life Habits: Unmistakable black and white striped livery; commonly observed in very active groups, sheltering rapidly among branching corals when approached too closely. The very similar *D. melanurus* has a black tail.

RETICULATE HUMBUG
Dascyllus reticulatus

Distribution: Central Indo-Pacific from Cocos-Keeling to Samoa and from Southern Japan to Australia.
Size: Up to 8 centimeters.
Habitat: Thick coral growth on coastal and outer reefs from 2 to 50 meters.
Life Habits: Body pale grey or tan with a faded black stripe behind head. Commonly observed in groups, always ready to take shelter among branching corals if disturbed.Feeds on algae it grows and tends to on dead coral like most damselfishes.

BLACKVENT DAMSELFISH
Dischistodus melanotus

Distribution: Central Indo-Pacific from Indonesia to Southern Japan and the Great Barrier Reef in Australia.
Size: Up to 15 centimeters.
Habitat: Coastal reefs and lagoons from 2 to 10 meters deep.
Life Habits: Body thick-set, robust, white, with slanting brown area on back and head and pale pink spots on yellow cheeks. Blackish spot on belly diagnostic. Larger than most other damselfishes and very territorial: usually encountered alone, feeding on algal matter.

HONEYHEAD DAMSELFISH
Dischistodus prosopotaenia

Distribution: Central Indo-Pacific from the Andamans to the Great Barrier Reef.
Size: Up to 18 centimeters.
Habitat: Coastal reefs and lagoons, often on silty bottoms, from 2 to 12 meters.
Life Habits: Very large and heavy-bodied for a damselfish: coloration rather variable but usually brownish body with a midway paler vertical stripe and a dark blotch at the base of the pectoral fin. Alone or in small loose groups, usually very territorial. Feeds on algae.

BLACK-AXIL CHROMIS
Chromis atripectoralis

Distribution: Tropical Indo-Pacific from Seychelles to French Polynesia and from Southern Japan to the Great Barrier Reef in Australia.
Size: Up to 10 centimeters.
Habitat: Coral-rich areas on coastal and outer reefs from 2 to 15 meters.
Life Habits: Body a dazzling fluorescent blue green, with black spot at the base of the pectoral fin. Commonly observed in large schools hovering above staghorn and branching corals. Feeds on plankton in the water column. The very similar Blue-green Chromis *C. viridis* lacks markings.

BLUE-GREEN CHROMIS
Chromis viridis

Distribution: Tropical Indo-Pacific from the Red Sea and East Africa to French Polynesia and from Southern Japan to Australia.
Size: Up to 8 centimeters.
Habitat: Coastal and outer reefs, lagoons from 2 to 20 meters deep.
Life Habits: Jewel-like body a luminous blue-green with no distinct markings: commonly observed in large, thich schools hovering above coral heads and taking refuge among the ramifications when disturbed. Very common all over its area.

WHITETAIL CHROMIS
Chromis xanthura

Distribution: Tropical Indo-Pacific from Cocos-Keeling to French Polynesia and from Southern Japan to New Caledonia.
Size: Up to 15 centimeters.
Habitat: Steep slopes and drop-offs on outer reefs from 3 to 40 meters.
Life Habits: Body greenish black with sharply marked white tail, large body scales. Commonly observed in large groups feeding in the water column along oceanic drop-offs, relatively distant from the reef itself.

LINED CHROMIS
Chromis lineata

Distribution: Central Indo-Pacific from Indonesia to the Solomons and the Great Barrier Reef in Australia.
Size: Up to 5 centimeters.
Habitat: Thick coral growth along drop-offs from 2 to 10 meters deep.
Life Habits: Small, very active, jewel-like: body yellowish with horizontal rows of bright neon blue spots. Occasionally observed in small loose aggregations hovering above branching coral "thickets" along drop-offs and steep slopes.

YELLOW CHROMIS
Chromis analis

Distribution: Western Pacific from Indonesia to New Caledonia.
Size: Up to 15 centimeters.
Habitat: Steep slopes or drop-offs on outer reefs from 10 to 70 meters.
Life Habits: Body and all fins bright yellow with bright blue ring around eye. Occasionally observed in small loose aggregations in deep water along drop-offs and steep slopes, often sheltering in crevices. Feeds on plankton in the water column. Possibly the most colorful among all large *Chromis* species.

BLUE CHROMIS
Chromis cyanea

Distribution: Tropical Western Atlantic from Florida to Brazil, also Caribbean and the Bahamas.
Size: Up to 10 centimeters.
Habitat: Outer and coastal coral reefs from 10 to 25 meters deep.
Life Habits: Body a brilliant metallic blue and a dark back, tail forked with black borders. Commonly observed hovering in large aggregations above reef formations, feeding on zooplankton. Very abundant all over its distribution range.

AMBON DAMSELFISH
Pomacentrus amboinensis

Distribution: Central Indo-Pacific from the Andamans to Micronesia and from Southern Japan to Australia.
Size: Up to 10 centimeters.
Habitat: Sand and coral rubble areas on coastal and outer reefs from 2 to 40 meters deep.
Life Habits: Body yellow with bright blue and pink markings on lower head. Commonly observed alone or in small loose aggregations on sandy bottoms, always close to branching coral heads. Can be occasionally confused underwater with the yellow phase of the Brown Damsel *P. opisthostigma*.

PRINCESS DAMSELFISH
Pomacentrus vaiuli

Distribution: Western Pacific from Bali in Indonesia to Micronesia and from Southern Japan to Australia.
Size: Up to 10 centimeters.
Habitat: Coral-rich areas in lagoons and outer reef slopes from 3 to 45 meters.
Life Habits: Small, active, jewel-like: body orange-yellow with bright blue scales and with orange-yellow area on head and back. Black ocellus at the base of rear dorsal fin. Common but usually very wary, alone or in small loose groups, always ready to shelter under corals.

SPECKLED DAMSELFISH
Pomacentrus bankanensis

Distribution: Central Indo-Pacific from the Andamans to Fiji and from Southern Japan to Australia.
Size: Up to 10 centimeters.
Habitat: Coral rubble areas on coastal and outer reefs from 2 to 12 meters.
Life Habits: Small, very active, jewel-like: body yellow-brown with thick rows and lines of bright blue spots, tail white, clearly visible black ocellus at the base of the rear dorsal fin. Wary, always ready to shelter among corals if threatened.

LEMON DAMSELFISH
Pomacentrus moluccensis

Distribution: Central Indo-Pacific from the Andamans to Fiji and from Southern Japan to Australia.
Size: Up to 8 centimeters.
Habitat: Coral-rich areas on coastal and outer reefs from 2 to 15 meters deep.
Life Habits: Body a uniform bright golden yellow, often with faint blue markings, thin black or blue margin on anal fin. Commonly observed in small loose aggregations around coral heads on sandy bottoms, always ready to hide among branches for protection.

GOLDBELLY DAMSEL
Pomacentrus auriventris

Distribution: Central Indo-Pacific from Bali in Indonesia to Micronesia.
Size: Up to 7 centimeters.
Habitat: Coral rubble reef tops and slopes from 1 to 15 meters deep.
Life Habits: Bright neon-blue head and upper body, bright yellow lower and rear body. Very active, alone or in small loose aggregations, easily confused underwater with several other similar neon-blue and yellow damselfishes in the area: precise distribution of color on the body is usually the best diagnostic key to identification.

GOLDBACK DAMSEL
Pomacentrus nigromanus

Distribution: Tropical Central Indo-Pacific from Indonesia to the Solomons.
Size: Up to 9 centimeters.
Habitat: Coastal and outer reefs, lagoons from 5 to 60 meters deep.
Life Habits: Body pale grey with yellow upper rear and black margin to anal fin, large black spot at the base of pectoral fin. Solitary or in small groups like most other damselfishes, commonly observed alone or in small groups above coral formations: unique color pattern is diagnostic for a correct identification.

NEON DAMSEL
Pomacentrus coelestis

Distribution: Tropical Indo-Pacific from Sri Lanka to French Polynesia and Southern Japan.
Size: Up to 7 centimeters.
Habitat: Coastal and outer reefs on rubble bottoms from 1 to 12 meters deep.
Life Habits: Another very abundant and commonly observed neon-blue damselfish, usually encountered by divers in very shallow water: bright luminous blue body, rounded head profile and yellow-transparent anal and caudal fins are diagnostic for correct identification.

Symbiotic Relationships

In the complex universe of tropical reefs all life is interconnected, and in the course of evolution several species have developed fascinating relationships of mutual interest with other ones. Without whom they now cannot survive

Many of the reef's countless species have developed fascinating relationships, usually based on mutual interest in a highly competitive universe. Generally known as symbiosis, this relationship is more specifically called mutualism if its advantages apply to both species involved and commensalism when only one partner benefits (it would be parasitism if the host is taken advantage of). We are still a long way, though, from being able to draw precise distinctions in most of the known cases. Perhaps the best known of these curious and fascinating "marriages of convenience" is the one that transpires between various species of *Amphiprion* clownfish and the large sea anemones of several different species. The young fish gradually develop total immunity to their hosts' poisonous nematocysts - the stinging tentacles proving fatal for other fish - and they never stray from the microhabitat offered by the anemone. Other visitors that also find anemones convenient are various species of crustaceans such as *Periclemenes* shrimp (commonly also found on nudibranchs, sea cucumbers, urchins and starfish) and *Neopetrolisthes* porcelain crabs.

In this case, however, commensalism seems to be the more accurate term since no obvious advantages are due to the host organism from the presence of the small crustaceans. On the other hand, a

Squat lobsters cannot survive if separated from their crinoid host.

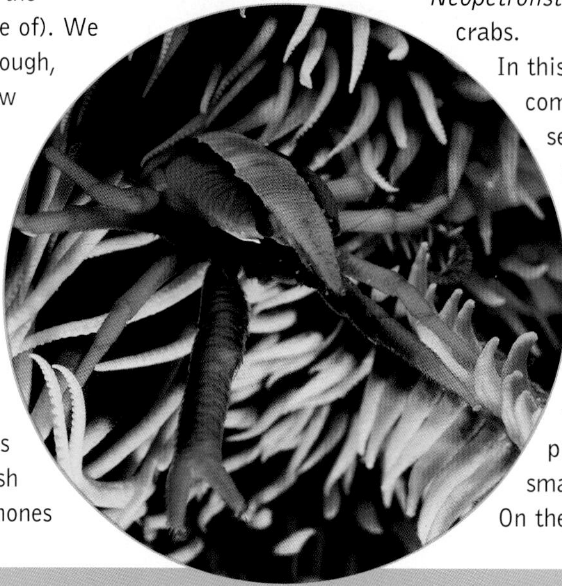

Clownfish and their anemone offer what is possibly the best known symbiotic relationship among those occurring in the reef environment.

clearly mutualistic relationship unites little alpheid shrimp to their gobies on muddy and sandy bottoms. These two species share a burrow - a tunnel dug into the soft substrate - which the almost blind shrimp keeps clean and orderly with the fish acting as a guardian. The two species communicate according to a precise language: oscillating antennas for the shrimp and tail-fin vibrations for the goby. Still other shrimp - *Periclemenes*, *Lysmata* and *Stenopus* species, not to mention fish (in this case wrasses or labrids in particular) - take the lead role in a complex symbiotic, mutualistic relationship that bonds the so-called "cleaners" to their "clients." Both partners adhere to a complex ritual that serves a precise function. The cleaners, with their unmistakable banded coloration, position themselves in open view on easily found locations in

Several small semitransparent goby species are exclusively found on soft corals.

the open; the clients come to these "cleaning stations" and display a total lack of aggression while the cleaners remove parasites and leftover food from their skin, gills and mouth. A field experiment artificially removed cleaners from a tract of coral reef and showed that its inhabitants quickly registered a significant increase in infections and parasitism. Species involved in this activity - mostly small labrids and shrimp, but several young angelfish and butterflyfish as well - essentially enjoy total immunity. They can visit the mouths of predators such as groupers and morays whenever they like with almost no risk of being swallowed. Less defined but similarly intriguing relationships finally occur between some pelagic species - like *Echeneis naucrates* suckerfish and *Naucrates ductor* pilotfish - and the big creatures - turtles, sharks and mantas above all - they attend, whose gain in this kind of relationship is still rather unclear. One thing is however clear: examples of more or less well defined symbiotic relationships among reef species are truly infinite.

One of the most fascinating examples of symbiosis is offered by the close relationship between several species of gobies and their attendant blind shrimps.

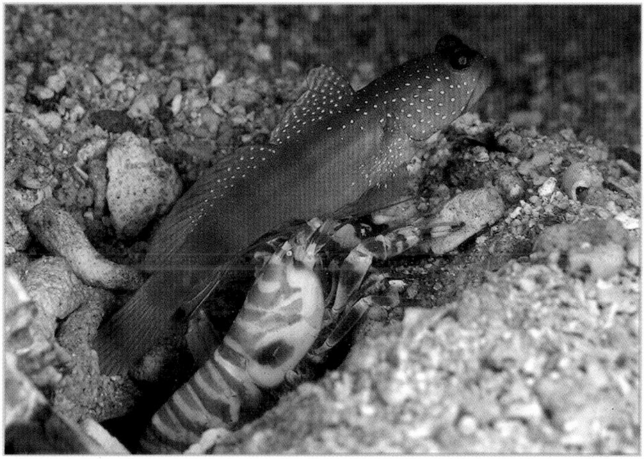

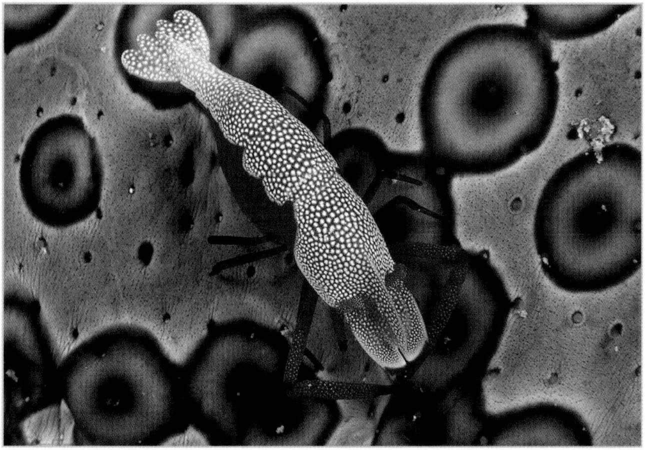

The Emperor shrimp *Periclemenes imperator* is commonly found on a variety of hosts.

Diver and Forster's Hawkfish *Parracirrhites forsteri*, Raja Ampat, West Papua, Indonesia

HAWKFISHES

Cirrhitidae

This well-known tropical family numbers 9 genera and about 35 species, mostly found in the Indo-Pacific. Hawkfish perch on the substrate or on gorgonians on their thickened pectoral fins, always ready to rapidly pounce on some unsuspecting prey in the water column or on corals nearby. They are normally very active, flitting to and fro among coral colonies: most are habitat-specific and are usually found in small loose aggregations on certain species of sponges or gorgonians. ~ **U/W Photo Tips:** Hawkfishes are a very much sought-after photographic subject, but they need a lot of patience and stealth as they usually are extremely skittish. Use a macro lens (105mm) and wait for them to return to their perch of choice if you have momentarily scared them away.

BLOTCHED HAWKFISH

Cirrhitichthys aprinus

Distribution: Central Indo-Pacific from Malaysia to Papua New Guinea and from Southern Japan to Australia.
Size: Up to 10 centimeters.
Habitat: Coastal reefs from 5 to 40 meters deep.
Life Habits: Body white with irregular or rounded reddish spots; unmarked tail and ocellated spot on cheek are diagnostic. Tufted dorsal fin ray tips. Usually observed on soft corals or black coral colonies. Territorial, alone or in small loose aggregations.

SPOTTED HAWKFISH

Cirrhitichthys oxycephalus

Distribution: Tropical Indo-Pacific from the Red Sea to Panama.
Size: Up to 10 centimeters.
Habitat: Coastal and rocky reefs from 3 to 40 meters deep.
Life Habits: Body white with many rounded bright red to brown blotches. Tail spotted, lacks ocellus on cheek. Usually solitary. Individuals living in deep water usually have a redder coloration.Feeds on small prey it catches with sudden bursts of speed, returning to its chosen perch.

CORAL HAWKFISH
Cirrhitichthys falco

Distribution: Central Indo-Pacific from the Maldives to Micronesia and from Southern Japan to Australia.
Size: Up to 10 centimeters.
Habitat: Coral-rich areas on outer reefs from 4 to 50 meters deep.
Life Habits: Body white with irregular reddish bars and saddles; red stripes below eye are diagnostic. Tufted dorsal fin rays tips, spotted tail. Solitary, feeding on small prey it catches with sudden bursts of speed, returning to its chosen perch.

LONGNOSE HAWKFISH
Oxycirrhites typus

Distribution: Tropical Indo-Pacific from the Red Sea to Panama and from Southern Japan to the Great Barrier Reef.
Size: Up to 13 centimeters.
Habitat: Exclusively found on gorgonians and black coral colonies on outer reefs from 12 to 100 meters deep.
Life Habits: Unmistakable "tartan"-like livery with white background and red intercrossing stripes; long pointed snout is also diagnostic. Tufted dorsal fin rays tips. Solitary or in small loose groups, usually very skittish, only found on large gorgonians and black coral colonies.

RING-EYE HAWKFISH
Paracirrhites arcatus

Distribution: Tropical Indo-Pacific from the Red Sea to French Polynesia and from Southern Japan to Australia.
Size: Up to 13 centimeters.
Habitat: Coral heads on coastal and outer reefs from 1 to 35 meters deep.
Life Habits: Yellowish, reddish or olive-brown with white horizontal stripe on body and sharply defined orange, red and blue markings behind eye and on gill cover. Usually alone or in small loose aggregations on nearby coral heads. Feeds on prey it catches with hawk-like sudden outbursts of speed.

FORSTER'S HAWKFISH
Paracirrhites forsteri

Distribution: Tropical Indo-Pacific from the Red Sea to French Polynesia and from Southern Japan to Australia.
Size: Up to 22 centimeters.
Habitat: Coral heads on coastal and outer reefs from 1 to 35 meters deep.
Life Habits: Very variable, usually with finely spotted head and striped body: may be brownish, yellowish or reddish. Stocky, heavy-bodied, usually alone or in small loose aggregations on nearby coral heads. Feeds on prey it catches with hawk-like sudden outbursts of speed, always returning to its chosen perch.

GIANT HAWKFISH
Cirrhitus rivulatus

Distribution: Eastern Pacific from California to Colombia.
Size: Up to 50 centimeters.
Habitat: Rocky coastal reefs and boulder-strewn areas from 5 to 25 meters.
Life Habits: Very large for a hawkfish, with a stocky body and a large head; livery is brownish or olive brown with several irregular yellowish, blue-bordered stripes and bands. Surprisingly well camouflaged despite its large size. Usually observed alone, waiting immobile in ambush among rocks and boulders.

LYRETAIL HAWKFISH
Cyprinocirrhites polyactis

Distribution: Tropical Indo-Pacific from East Africa to Australia and Southern Japan.
Size: Up to 15 centimeters.
Habitat: Coastal reefs and steep slopes from 10 to 130 meters deep.
Life Habits: Body orange-brown or pinkish with distinctly forked tail. The only hawkfish which feeds on plankton, hovering and schooling in midwater. Occasionally observed in turbid waters and mistaken by divers for a basslet (*Anthias* sp) due to its unusual behavior.

JAWFISHES

Opistognathidae

A small and not very well known family numbering about 3 genera and about 70 species, with several more yet undescribed but well known to divers and u/w photographers. All are typically tadpole-shaped, with a large frog-like head, a very broad mouth and bulging eyes. The body, in comparison, is surprisingly elongated and quite small. They all live in vertical burrows they dig in the substrate, often with several individuals close to each other, and feed on zooplankton floating by. ~ **U/W Photo Tips:** Jawfishes make very interesting subjects, particularly when brooding eggs in their mouth or when digging their hole in the substrate. Some patience and stealth are needed as they are quite shy and always ready to disappear inside their burrow. A macro lens (105mm) is a must.

GOLD-SPEC JAWFISH

Opistognathus sp.

Distribution: Central Indo-Pacific from Indonesia to Borneo and the Philippines.
Size: Up to 12 centimeters.
Habitat: Sand and rubble bottoms on coastal reefs from 5 to 30 meters deep.
Life Habits: Easily identified by bright golden marking above iris; body - seldom seen by divers - is white with 8-10 golden vertical bars. Commonly observed peeking out of its burrow, waiting for some food to drift by. Strictly territorial. The individual illustrated is brooding a clutch of almost ready to hatch eggs in its mouth.

GIANT JAWFISH

Opistognathus dendriticus

Distribution: Central Indo-Pacific, only known from the Sulu Sea between Sabah and the Philippines.
Size: Up to 25 centimeters.
Habitat: Sand or silt bottoms on coastal reefs from 1 to 40 meters deep.
Life Habits: Very localized in its distribution; large, yellowish, with dark brown "mask" across eyes. Solitary, often observed peeking out of its burrow keeping an eye of food passing by and possible intruders. The specimen in the photograph is brooding a clutch of almost ready to hatch eggs in its mouth.

UNDESCRIBED JAWFISH
Opistognathus sp.

Distribution: Presently unknown, observed in the Sulu and Sulawesi seas off Malaysian Borneo .
Size: Up to 15 centimeters.
Habitat: Coral rubble bottoms on coastal reefs from 10 to 30 meters deep.
Life Habits: Unknown but probably similar to most other jawfish species in the area. Body pale with red-brown blotches and a distinct brown ring surrounding the eye. Still undescribed.

UNDESCRIBED JAWFISH
Opistognathus sp.

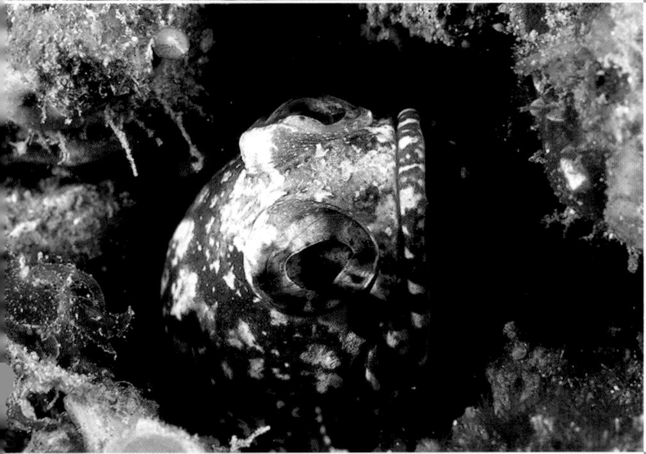

Distribution: Observed in the Lembeh Strait, Northern Sulawesi, Indonesia.
Size: Up to 15 centimeters.
Habitat: Coral rubble bottoms at a depth of 15 meters.
Life Habits: A still undescribed jawfish species. Body heavily marbled in white, deep brown and yellow. Documented from the Lembeh Strait in Northern Sulawesi, Indonesia, but possibly widespread elsewhere in the area.

UNDESCRIBED JAWFISH
Opistognatus sp.

Distribution: Observed in the Lembeh Strait, Northern Sulawesi, Indonesia and in the Sulu and Sulawesi Seas, Sabah, Malaysia.
Size: Up to 15 centimeters.
Habitat: Coral rubble bottoms at a depth of 18 meters.
Life Habits: A still undescribed jawfish species. Body a uniform bright yellow. Documented from the Lembeh Strait in Northern Sulawesi, Indonesia, and from several locations in Sabah in Malaysian Borneo but possibly widespread elsewhere in the general geographical area.

MULLETS
Mugilidae

This is a rather large family numbering about 13 genera and more than 70 species, many of which can be found in temperate and cold waters. Most mullets are also able to enter brackish and fresh water, being frequently observed in estuaries and around river mouths. They usually move in large, fast-moving schools which swim close to the sandy or muddy bottom, taking mouthfuls of sand which are sifted through the gills to extract food particles. Their head is generally broad and depressed with a terminal mouth; body is covered in large, chrome-like reflecting scales. ~ **U/W Photo Tips:** Mullets are rather indifferent photo subjects as they inhabit generally murky water, being also fast and erratic swimmers.

WARTY-LIP MULLET
Crenimugil crenilabrus

Distribution: Tropical Indo-Pacific from the Red Sea to French Polynesia and from Southern Japan to Australia.
Size: Up to 40 centimeters.
Habitat: Sand or silt bottoms at the base of coral reefs from 2 to 10 meters deep.
Life Habits: Body elongate, silvery, with horizontal dark stripe on each row of scales. Tail darker, lunate. Often observed in fast-moving schools swimming close to the substrate, raising clouds of sand and mud while taking mouthfuls of silt to be sifted by gills for food particles.

WRASSES
Labridae

This is one of the largest and most important coral reef fish families, counting more than 60 genera and about 400 known species, with many more still undescribed. Most are highly diverse, generally very colorful but also extremely variable, with juveniles looking completely different from adults. They usually live in harems with dominant males originating from females after a sex change. All species are diurnal, feeding off the bottom and sometimes acting as cleaners towards other, larger species. ~ **U/W Photo Tips:** Most wrasses are exceptionally beautiful and colorful, but they are a bane to most photographers due to their very fast, erratic movements. A good picture of a wrasse is a trophy to be treasured indeed! Fast reflexes and very clear water are needed: best chances are offered by individuals following goatfishes, opportunistically looking for scraps of food.

YELLOWTAIL CORIS
Coris gaimard

Distribution: Central Indo-Pacific from Indonesia to French Polynesia and from Southern Japan to the Great Barrier Reef.
Size: Up to 40 centimeters.
Habitat: Coral rubble ares on coastal and outer reefs from 3 to 50 meters deep.
Life Habits: Large, highly variable in respect to age (adult illustrated). Size, yellow tail and brilliant blue spots on rear body can help with identification underwater. Solitary, often observed turning over rocks or pieces of coral looking for small invertebrates. For juvenile color phase see page 220.

CLOWN CORIS
Coris aygula

Distribution: Tropical Indo-Pacific from East Africa to French Polynesia and from Southern Japan to Australia.
Size: Up to 40 centimeters.
Habitat: Coral rubble areas on coastal and outer reefs from 2 to 30 meters deep.
Life Habits: White head, spotted in black, and dark grey rear body in adults. Juveniles (illustrated) more brightly marked, featuring two orange saddles on back and two black ocelli on dorsal fin. Solitary, often observed turning over coral pieces looking for invertebrates.

BATU CORIS
Coris batuensis

Distribution: Western Pacific from East Africa to Micronesia and from Southern Japan to Australia.
Size: Up to 17 centimeters.
Habitat: Sand and coral rubble bottoms on reefs from 2 to 30 meters deep.
Life Habits: Whitish, with several faded brown bars on upper body and small ocellus on dorsal fin. Often observed following closely goatfishes foraging on the substrate, actively competing for food.

RAGGED-TAIL WRASSE
Cheilinus lunulatus

Distribution: Red Sea ranging to the Arabian Sea and the Gulf of Aden.
Size: Up to 45 centimeters.
Habitat: Lagoons, passes, coral rubble patches on coastal reefs from 2 to 30 meters deep.
Life Habits: Body shaded in green and blue, with numerous pink vermiculations on head and bright yellow spot on gill cover. Solitary and very shy, not easily approached: occasionally observed swimming just above the substrate, actively looking for food. The very similar Tripletail Wrasse *C. trilobatus* takes its place further East to Australia.

FLORAL WRASSE
Cheilinus chlorourus

Distribution: Tropical Indo-Pacific from East Africa to French Polynesia and from Southern Japan to Australia.
Size: Up to 36 centimeters.
Habitat: Sand and coral rubble patches on coastal reefs from 2 to 30 meters.
Life Habits: Brownish with whitish mottling, usually with rows of clearly visible coral-pink dots on the sides. Solitary, commonly observed resting on the bottom, leaning against rocks or coral heads.Feeds like most wrasses on benthic invertebrates, including shellfish.

REDBREASTED WRASSE
Cheilinus fasciatus

Distribution: Tropical Indo-Pacific from the Red Sea to New Caledonia and from Southern Japan to Australia.
Size: Up to 36 centimeters.
Habitat: Sand and coral rubble areas on coastal and outer reefs from 3 to 40 meters deep.
Life Habits: Body strongly banded in black and white, bright red area behind head, the latter greenish with orange stripes radiating from the eye. Solitary, often observed swimming slowly just above the substrate, looking for food. Feeds mostly on benthic invertebrates.

NAPOLEON WRASSE
Cheilinus undulatus

Distribution: Tropical Indo-Pacific from the Red Sea to French Polynesia and from Southern Japan to Australia.
Size: Up to 130 centimeters.
Habitat: Steep slopes and drop-offs from 5 to 60 meters deep.
Life Habits: Very well known, unmistakable: body very large, a bright blue-green, with typical hump above forehead and fine maze-like darker markings. Solitary or in pairs, occasionally very inquisitive and "friendly" but seriously endangered all over its distribution area due to unchecked fishing for Oriental market.

ANCHOR TUSKFISH
Choerodon anchorago

Distribution: Central Indo-Pacific from India to Papua New Guinea and from Southern Japan to Australia.
Size: Up to 40 centimeters.
Habitat: Coral rubble patches on coastal reefs and in lagoons from 2 to 25 meters.
Life Habits: Grey thick-set head with jutting teeth, white lower and rear body with black rectangular blotch on back. Able to fade or darken at will in a few seconds. A few similar species in the same area, but this is the most commonly observed and the most easily identified.

BLUESIDED WRASSE
Cirrhilabrus cyanopleura

Distribution: Central Indo-Pacific from the Andamans to Papua New Guinea and from Southern Japan to Australia.
Size: Up to 10 centimeters.
Habitat: Mixed coral and rubble areas in lagoons and slopes from 2 to 25 meters.
Life Habits: Striking blue head and forebody with orange-brown rear. Rarely solitary, most often in large loose aggregations hovering and swimming above the substrate. Variations in coloration due to sex and age are well documented.

YELLOWBACK WRASSE
Cirrhilabrus lubbocki

Distribution: Central Indo-Pacific from Indonesia to the Philippines.
Size: Up to 8 centimeters.
Habitat: Above rubble bottoms on seaward coral reefs from 4 to 45 meters.
Life Habits: Bright yellow-orange head and back, body with purple spots or bands. Several other species looking very similar underwater. Observed in small groups, swimming fast to and fro above the coral rubble substrate and feeding on plankton in the water column.

ORANGEBACK WRASSE
Cirrhilabrus aurantidorsalis

Distribution: Central Indo-Pacific in Central Sulawesi, Indonesia.
Size: Up to 10 centimeters.
Habitat: Above coral rubble bottoms on coastal reefs and slopes from 10 to 30 meters deep.
Life Habits: Bright orange back, purple to violet body, very similar to terminal phase of following species. Very restricted distribution; usually observed in loosely organized harems swimming fast to and fro above the substrate, feeding on plankton in the water column.

SOLOR WRASSE
Cirrhilabrus solorensis

Distribution: Central Indo-Pacific, in Northern and Central Sulawesi, Indonesia.
Size: Up to 12 centimeters.
Habitat: Coral rubble bottoms on coastal reefs from 5 to 35 meters deep.
Life Habits: Normally almost identical to preceding species; specimen illustrated is in nuptial color phase, occasionally displayed all the time. Commonly observed in harems with one male and several females, all swimming to and fro above the substrate.Difficult to identify correctly underwater.

FILAMENTED FLASHER WRASSE
Paracheilinus filamentosus

Distribution: Central Indo-Pacific from Bali in Indonesia to Papua New Guinea and the Solomons.
Size: Up to 8 centimeters.
Habitat: Above coral rubble areas on slopes and coastal reefs from 10 to 40 meters deep.
Life Habits: Orange-red with bright violet stripes, deeply lunate tail, spectacular erected dorsal fin with filamented tips in displaying and courting males. In harems, often in large aggregations, with one dominant male and several females swimming very rapidly to and fro above the substrate.

BLUE FLASHER WRASSE
Paracheilinus cyaneus

Distribution: Central Indo-Pacific from Borneo to Western Papua.
Size: Up to 7 centimeters.
Habitat: Above coral rubble bottoms on coastal reefs from 6 to 20 meters deep.
Life Habits: Very similar to preceding species but with bright blue markings on nape. Distribution very restricted and localized. Commonly observed in harems swimming very rapidly above the substrate: one dominant male and two females illustrated.

LEOPARD WRASSE
Macropharyngodon meleagris

Distribution: Tropical Indo-Pacific from Cocos-Keeling to Micronesia and from Southern Japan to Australia.
Size: Up to 15 centimeters.
Habitat: Coral and rubble bottoms on coastal and outer reefs from 2 to 30 meters deep.
Life Habits: White with leopard-like pattern of black spots on juveniles (illustrated) becoming pale orange with blue-green spots in terminal-phase adults.Solitary or in small groups, often observed foraging on the substrate.

ORNATE WRASSE
Macropharyngodon ornatus

Distribution: Central Indo-Pacific from the Andamans to Samoa and from Southern Japan to Australia.
Size: Up to 12 centimeters.
Habitat: Coral rubble and sand bottoms on coral reefs from 3 to 30 meters.
Life Habits: Spectacularly marked: body is blackish with a bright blue-green spot on each scale; head reddish in juveniles. Fast-swimming and always on the move like most wrasses, often encountered just above the substrate, foraging for food.

YELLOWTAIL WRASSE
Anampses meleagrides

Distribution: Tropical Indo-Pacific from the Red Sea to French Polynesia and from Southern Japan to Australia.
Size: Up to 22 centimeters.
Habitat: Coral rubble and sand areas on coastal reefs from 2 to 60 meters deep.
Life Habits: Terminal adults are brownish with blue-edged scales; juveniles (illustrated) are a striking black with rows of bright white spots and yellow tail. Often observed swimming erratically close to the bottom, looking for food.

BLUE-SPOTTED WRASSE
Anampses caeruleopunctatus

Distribution: Tropical Indo-Pacific from the Red Sea to Easter Island.
Size: Up to 42 centimeters.
Habitat: Coral or rocky reefs in shallow water from 1 to 30 meters deep.
Life Habits: Body fusiform, deep to brownish green with a light blue-green streak on each scale, blue lips and a lime-green or yellow bar behind the pectoral fin. Solitary or in harems, usually swimming swiftly above corals; like most wrasses sleeps buried under the sand.

YELLOW-BREASTED WRASSE
Anampses twistii

Distribution: Tropical Indo-Pacific from the Red Sea to French Polynesia and from Southern Japan to Australia.
Size: Up to 18 centimeters.
Habitat: Coral rubble patches on outer reefs and lagoons from 3 to 30 meters.
Life Habits: Purplish brown with bright yellow breast; juveniles (illustrated) with clearly visible ocelli at the rear margin of the dorsal and anal fins, a trait shared with several other *Anampses* species. Usually solitary or occasionally in pairs.

SLINGJAW WRASSE
Epibulus insidiator

Distribution: Tropical Indo-Pacific from the Red Sea to French Polynesia and Hawai'i and from Southern Japan to Australia.
Size: Up to 35 centimeters.
Habitat: Coral-rich areas in lagoons, coastal and outer reefs from 3 to 40 meters deep.
Life Habits: Coloration extremely variable, from bright yellow to olive to black and orange. Solitary and stealthy; a cunning predator which is able to suddenly swallow unexpectedly large prey thanks to its underslung and greatly extensible large jaw.

BLACKEYE THICKLIP
Hemigymnus melapterus

Distribution: Tropical Indo-Pacific from the Red Sea to French Polynesia and from Southern Japan to Australia.
Size: Up to 60 centimeters.
Habitat: Sand, coral and rubble patches on coastal and outer reefs from 2 to 30 meters deep.
Life Habits: Body robust, thick-set, with typically fleshy lips and a blue-green spot on each greyish scale. A solitary and active swimmer, often observed moving over rocks and pieces of dead coral and messily feeding on benthic invertebrates.

BANDED THICKLIP
Hemigymnus fasciatus

Distribution: Tropical Indo-Pacific from the Red Sea to French Polynesia and from Southern Japan to Australia.
Size: Up to 50 centimeters.
Habitat: Sheltered coral-rich areas in sand channels and lagoons from 2 to 25 meters deep.
Life Habits: Black body with five narrow white bars, bright light green head with showy blue and pink irregular stripes, typically fleshy lips. Locally common, often encountered alone or in small loose groups swimming close to the substrate, foraging for food.

BIRD WRASSE
Gomphosus varius

Distribution: Tropical Pacific from Indonesia to French Polynesia and from Southern Japan to Australia.
Size: Up to 30 centimeters.
Habitat: Coastal and outer reefs, lagoons from 5 to 40 meters deep.
Life Habits: Comical, unmistakable appearance with greatly elongated snout and body; body blue-green in terminal-phase adults with a bright yellow-green streak behind the pectoral fin. Juveniles are grey with orange snout. A fast and active swimmer, replaced further West by the almost identical Indian Ocean Bird Wrasse *G. caeruleus.*

CIGAR WRASSE
Cheilio inermis

Distribution: Tropical Indo-Pacific from the Red Sea to Hawai'i and from Southern Japan to Australia.
Size: Up to 50 centimeters.
Habitat: Seaweed areas on lagoons and coastal reefs from 2 to 30 meters deep.
Life Habits: Body very elongate, cigar-shaped, with long snout, greenish or yellow. A stealthy predator, usually encountered alone - occasionally one male with several attendant females - in seagrass patches along reef flats.

RING WRASSE
Hologymnosus annulatus

Distribution: Tropical Indo-Pacific from the Red Sea to French Polynesia and from Southern Japan to Australia.
Size: Up to 40 centimeters.
Habitat: Coral-rich coastal and outer reef slopes from 5 to 40 meters deep.
Life Habits: Body very elongate, dark green or bluish-green with several thin vertical purplish stripes. Solitary, hunting stealthily among the corals. The specimen illustrated is being cleaned by a Cleaner Wrasse *Labroides dimidiatus*.

PASTEL RING WRASSE
Hologymnosus doliatus

Distribution: Tropical Indo-Pacific from the Red Sea to Micronesia and from Southern Japan to Australia.
Size: Up to 40 centimeters.
Habitat: Sand, coral and rubble areas on coastal and outer reefs from 3 to 30 meters deep.
Life Habits: Body elongate, a pale blue-green, with many thin vertical bluish stripes. Adults (juvenile illustrated) with a wide pale area with blue borders on forebody. Solitary and diurnal like most wrasses, feeds on benthic invertebrates.

CANARY WRASSE
Halichoeres chrysus

Distribution: Central Indo-Pacific from Indonesia to Micronesia and from Southern Japan to Australia.
Size: Up to 12 centimeters.
Habitat: Sand, coral and rubble patches on reef edges from 2 to 60 meters deep.
Life Habits: Bright golden yellow with two ocelli on dorsal fin. Very small juveniles often observed in sea anemones, mixing with other species. Adults in small groups, actively swimming among the corals and close to the bottom.

PINSTRIPED WRASSE
Halichoeres melanurus

Distribution: Western Pacific from Indonesia to Samoa and from Southern Japan to the Great Barrier Reef.
Size: Up to 12 centimeters.
Habitat: Coral-rich sheltered areas on reefs from 2 to 15 meters deep.
Life Habits: Spectacularly marked in blue-green, green and orange; large yellow spot on cheek, tail electric blue with black margin. Often observed actively swimming alone, moving over pieces of dead coral and bits of debris while looking for food on the bottom.

TAILSPOT WRASSE
Halichoeres richmondi

Distribution: Central Indo-Pacific from Indonesia to Papua New Guinea and from Southern Japan to the Marshalls.
Size: Up to 19 centimeters.
Habitat: Coral-rich areas on sheltered coastal reefs from 2 to 15 meters deep.
Life Habits: Body rather elongate, yellow-green with blue stripes on head and bright blue margins on fins. A fast and erratic swimmer, solitary or in small loose groups, often observed feeding on benthic invertebrates near the bottom.

YELLOW-FACE WRASSE
Halichoeres solorensis

Distribution: Tropical Central Indo-Pacific from Indonesia to West Papua and the Philippines.
Size: Up to 18 centimeters.
Habitat: Coastal and outer reefs in coral-rich areas from 10 to 40 meters deep.
Life Habits: Body very variable from green to pink to mauve, but red dorsal fin and yellow head with bright pink bands are diagnostic. Usually observed swimming gracefully and rapidly above or among corals, occasionally stopping to feed on benthic invertebrates.

CHECKERBOARD WRASSE
Halichoeres hortulanus

Distribution: Tropical Indo-Pacific from the Red Sea to French Polynesia and from Southern Japan to Australia.
Size: Up to 30 centimeters.
Habitat: Coral, sand and rubble patches in lagoons and on coastal reefs from 2 to 35 meters deep.
Life Habits: Body pale with blue bar on each scale, head pink with green stripes, yellow tail and spot before dorsal fin. Solitary, commonly observed swimming rapidly and erratically close to the substrate, moving fragments of dead coral looking for benthic invertebrates.

GOLDSTRIPE WRASSE
Halichoeres zeylonicus

Distribution: Indian Ocean and Western Pacific from the Red Sea to Samoa and from Southern Japan to Australia.
Size: Up to 15 centimeters.
Habitat: Sand and rubble bottoms on coastal reefs from 2 to 40 meters deep.
Life Habits: Body pink in juveniles (illustrated) and green in adults with bright pink-violet horizontal stripe from eye to tail. Often observed in small groups close to sea anemones on sand and silt channels among coral heads.

ZIGZAG WRASSE
Halichoeres scapularis

Distribution: Central Indo-Pacific from the Red Sea to Papua New Guinea and from Southern Japan to Australia.
Size: Up to 25 centimeters.
Habitat: Sand and rubble patches, often on silty bottoms, on coastal reefs from 2 to 20 meters deep.
Life Habits: Pale green with blue scale edges, green markings on pink head, bright red eye and diffuse black spot near gill cover. Solitary or in small loose aggregations, always swimming rapidly and erratically close to the substrate.

TORPEDO WRASSE
Pseudocoris heteroptera

Distribution: Tropical Indo-Pacific from Chagos to Papua New Guinea and Japan.
Size: Up to 20 centimeters.
Habitat: Sand, rubble or coral reef top flats from 10 to 25 meters deep.
Life Habits: Livery can be rapidly varied, but usually bluish in the front with yellow and black bars on the rear; tail with thin thread-like tips. Rather uncommon; large adult males occasionally observed swimming fast and erratically well above the substrate, feeding on zooplankton in the water column.

CELEBES WRASSE
Oxycheilinus celebicus

Distribution: Central Indo-Pacific from Borneo to the Solomons.
Size: Up to 25 centimeters.
Habitat: Coral-rich areas on coastal reefs from 3 to 30 meters deep.
Life Habits: Body brownish with intricate red and purple markings, elongate snout with pink, red or orange lines radiating from the eye. Can fade or darken dramatically in a very short time. Solitary, slow-moving, often seen resting against corals or rocks.

TWOSPOT WRASSE
Oxycheilinus bimaculatus

Distribution: Tropical Indo-Pacific from East Africa to French Polynesia and from Southern Japan to Australia.
Size: Up to 15 centimeters.
Habitat: Rubble patches and seagrass areas on coastal sheltered reefs from 2 to 100 meters.
Life Habits: Body mottled in red, brown and green, tail clearly rhomboidal, small bright red and blue spot on tip of dorsal fin. Slow-moving and always close to the substrate, commonly sheltering in debris, often encountered in small groups .

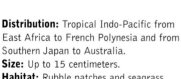

LINEDCHEEKED WRASSE
Oxycheilinus digrammus

Distribution: Tropical Indo-Pacific from the Red Sea to Micronesia and from Southern Japan to Australia.
Size: Up to 30 centimeters.
Habitat: Coral-rich areas in lagoons and outer reefs from 3 to 60 meters deep.
Life Habits: Coloration very variable, usually reddish, bluish or green with pale green head; oblique violet lines on head and gill cover. Occasionally very colorful (see accompanying photo). Solitary or in broadly spread loose aggregations, swimming deliberately above the coral colonies.

RINGTAIL WRASSE
Oxycheilinus unifasciatus

Distribution: Central Indo-Pacific from Indonesia to Hawai'i and from Southern Japan to Australia.
Size: Up to 45 centimeters.
Habitat: Coral-rich areas in lagoons and outer reefs from 3 to 60 meters deep.
Life Habits: Coloration very variable, may darken or pale at will in a very short time: usually purplish, with broad white, red-bordered band on cheek and white ring around tail base. A cunning and stealthy predator, often observed while swimming deliberately above corals, occasionally stopping in mid-water.

KLUNZINGER'S WRASSE
Thalassoma klunzingeri

Distribution: Red Sea and Western Indian Ocean.
Size: Up to 20 centimeters.
Habitat: Coral-rich areas on outer reefs from 1 to 15 meters deep.
Life Habits: Bright green body with violet bands on head and blue stripes on sides; very similar to Fivestripe Wrasse *T. quinquevittatum* which replaces it further east from East Africa to French Polynesia. A very fast and active swimmer, often encountered in small harems flitting above coral heads.

SIXBAR WRASSE
Thalassoma hardwicke

Distribution: Tropical Indo-Pacific from East Africa to French Polynesia and from Southern Japan to Australia.
Size: Up to 20 centimeters.
Habitat: Coastal and outer reefs in shallow water from 1 to 15 meters deep.
Life Habits: Body pale green to white with six black saddles fading on sides, lime-green head with bright pink stripes. Commonly observed in very active, fast-swimming harems darting erratically above coral formations. Beautiful and abundant but very shy and not easily approached, like most tropical wrasses.

CRESCENT WRASSE
Thalassoma lunare

Distribution: Tropical Indo-Pacific from the Red Sea to Southern Japan, Australia and Northern New Zealand.
Size: Up to 25 centimeters.
Habitat: Coastal and outer reefs from 2 to 20 meters deep.
Life Habits: Body elongate, blue and green; head green with lavender to blue bands, tail deeply lunate with bright yellow center. A very common, fast and active swimmer, usually observed in small harems, moving rapidly in the water column above the coral colonies.The Yellow Moon-Wrasse *T. lutescens* is similar but with pink accents.

TWO-TONE WRASSE
Thalassoma amblycephalum

Distribution: Central Indo-Pacific from Chagos to French Polynesia and from Southern Japan to Australia and Northern New Zealand.
Size: Up to 14 centimeters.
Habitat: Coral-rich areas on reef edges from 2 to 15 meters deep.
Life Habits: Blue-green head with two pink lines under the eye, yellow-green "collar", bluish-red body with many thin vertical blue stripes. Extremely colorful but very active and a fast swimmer, always darting erratically - alone or in small groups - above the coral colonies.

REDSPOT WRASSE
Pseudocoris yamashiroi

Distribution: Tropical Indo-Pacific from East Africa to Samoa and from Southern Japan to Australia.
Size: Up to 15 centimeters.
Habitat: Coastal and outer reef edges from 5 to 30 meters.
Life Habits: Body green with paler belly and black spots on scales, dark forked tail. Uncommon and unconspicuous, a fast swimmer often overlooked by divers and not easily identified underwater.

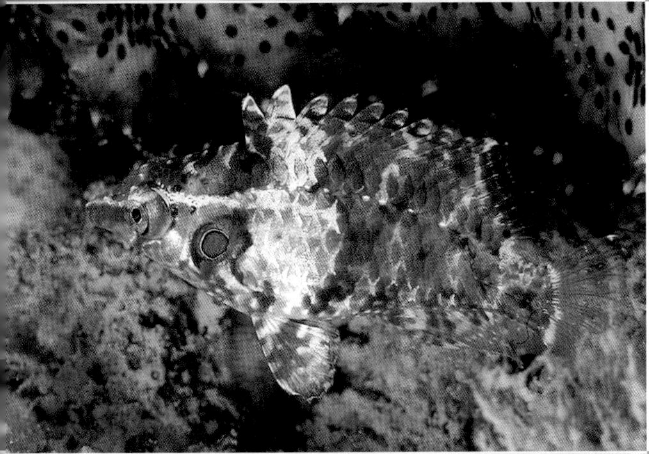

CRYPTIC WRASSE
Pteragogus cryptus

Distribution: Tropical Indo-Pacific from the Red Sea to Micronesia and Australia.
Size: Up to 10 centimeters.
Habitat: Coral-rich areas on coastal reefs from 5 to 60 meters deep.
Life Habits: Very cryptic and slow-moving: body mottled in red and brown with diagnostic white stripe above eye going to base of pectoral fin. Occasionally observed sheltering among branching corals, soft corals and gorgonians but usually overlooked by most divers.

COCKEREL WRASSE
Pteragogus enneacanthus

Distribution: Central Indo-Pacific from Indonesia to Micronesia and Australia.
Size: Up to 12 centimeters.
Habitat: Coastal reefs from 3 to 30 meters deep.
Life Habits: Cryptic, slow-moving, very well camouflaged; body mottled in red and brown, with clearly visible ocellus on gill cover. Solitary, occasionally observed among soft corals and branching corals, but usually unnoticed by most divers.

MEXICAN HOGFISH
Bodianus diplotaenia

Distribution: Eastern Pacific from the Gulf of California to Chile.
Size: Up to 80 centimeters.
Habitat: Rocky reefs and boulder-strewn slopes from 2 to 70 meters deep.
Life Habits: Stocky, with grey-green body and red head separated by a bright yellow stripe. Often observed swimming in typical irregular Labrid fashion, using only pectoral fins. Juveniles often observed cleaning larger fish and even sharks as it often happens with Labrids.

BLACKBELT HOGFISH
Bodianus mesothorax

Distribution: Central Indo-Pacific from Indonesia to Papua New Guinea and from Southern Japan to Australia.
Size: Up to 20 centimeters.
Habitat: Coral-rich areas on drop-offs and steep walls from 5 to 30 meters.
Life Habits: Purple-brown head with bright white rear body separated by a diagonal black band at midbody. An active hunter, often observed swimming in mid-water in typical "wrasse fashion", using only the pectorals for propulsion.

DIANA'S HOGFISH
Bodianus diana

Distribution: Tropical Indo-Pacific from the Red Sea to New Caledonia and from Southern Japan to Australia.
Size: Up to 25 centimeters.
Habitat: Coral-rich steep slopes and walls from 6 to 25 meters deep.
Life Habits: Body golden with purple back ; bright yellow-white spots on back and black ones on ventral and anal fins are diagnostic. Commonly observed alone or in pairs, swimming with unmistakable "fluttering" motion typical of wrasses .

ROCKMOVER WRASSE
Novaculichthys taeniourus

Distribution: Tropical Indo-Pacific from the Red Sea to Panama and from Southern Japan to Australia.
Size: Up to 30 centimeters.
Habitat: Sand and coral rubble patches on reef tops from 1 to 20 meters deep.
Life Habits: Unmistakable: pale grey head with radiating black lines from the eye, body dark, elongate, with pale spots on each scale.Commonly observed moving over rocks and pieces of dead coral looking for benthic invertebrates. For the juvenile phase see page 220.

KNIFE RAZORFISH
Cymolutes praetextatus

Distribution: Tropical Indo-Pacific from East Africa to French Polynesia.
Size: Up to 20 centimeters.
Habitat: Sand and silt bottoms in lagoons from 2 to 10 meters deep.
Life Habits: Pale body, rounded snout; solitary, normally observed hovering close to bottom, ready to disappear under the sand if threatened like all razorfish.Very shy, not easily approached.

WHITEPATCH RAZORFISH
Iniistius aneitensis

Distribution: Tropical Indo-Pacific from Chagos to Hawai'i and from Southern Japan to Australia.
Size: Up to 24 centimeters.
Habitat: Sand or silt bottoms close to reefs from 10 to 90 meters deep.
Life Habits: Body thick-set, with rounded blunt snout; coloration very pale, with white patch behind pectoral fin. Solitary, wary, occasionally observed hovering close to the substrate, always ready to disappear in a flash under the sand if approached too closely.

PEACOCK RAZORFISH
Iniistius pavo

Distribution: Tropical Indo-Pacific from the Red Sea to Central America and from Southern Japan to Australia.
Size: Up to 35 centimeters.
Habitat: Sand and silt areas close to reefs from 20 to 100 meters deep.
Life Habits: Pale body with very blunt profile (juvenile illustrated, mimicking dead leaf); solitary, wary, occasionally seen hovering close to the bottom but always ready to disappear under the sand.

BLACKBARRED RAZORFISH
Iniistius tetrazona

Distribution: Central Indo-Pacific from Indonesia to the Philippines.
Size: Up to 25 centimeters.
Habitat: Sand areas close to coastal reefs from 1 to 20 meters deep.
Life Habits: Body white with 4-5 brown bars, banner-like first dorsal fin. Solitary, occasionally observed hovering close to the substrate. Very wary, will disappear under the sand if approached closely.

IMMACULATE RAZORFISH
Xyrichtys dea

Distribution: Tropical Indo-Pacific from India to Southern Japan and Australia.
Size: Up to 30 centimeters.
Habitat: Sand and silt areas close to reefs from 20 to 100 meters deep.
Life Habits: Pale body with very blunt profile (juvenile illustrated); solitary, wary, occasionally seen hovering close to the bottom but always ready to disappear under the sand.Uncommon and when encountered usually overlooked or ignored by divers like most razorfish species.

CHISELTOOTH WRASSE
Pseudodax mollucanus

Distribution: Tropical Indo-Pacific from the Red Sea to French Polynesia and from Southern Japan to Australia.
Size: Up to 25 centimeters.
Habitat: Coral-rich areas on slopes from 3 to 40 meters deep.
Life Habits: Body blue-green with rusty tinge, head with clearly visible bright yellow upper lip and protruding chisel-like teeth. Occasionally encountered on coral-rich slopes, swimming in unmistakable undulating Labrid fashion, foraging for benthic invertebrates close to the substrate.

TUBELIP WRASSE
Labrichthys unilineatus

Distribution: Tropical Indo-Pacific from East Africa to Southern Japan and Australia.
Size: Up to 16 centimeters.
Habitat: Healthy, sheltered coral reefs from 2 to 20 meters deep.
Life Habits: Body elongate, dark green, with several thin blue longitudinal lines and a pale green or pale yellow bar behind head. Swims erratically in typical Labrid mode, sometimes observed in small groups feeding on coral polyps and small benthic invertebrates.

CLEANER WRASSE
Labroides dimidiatus

Distribution: Tropical Indo-Pacific from the Red Sea to Australia, Southern Japan and French Polynesia.
Size: Up to 11 centimeters.
Habitat: In well-defined "cleaning stations" on coral reefs from 2 to 40 meters deep.
Life Habits: The most commonly observed cleaner wrasse, often encountered in pairs while cleaning "clients" along the reef. Feeds on ectoparasites and bits of dead skin: the two specimens in the photograph are cleaning the gill opening of a batfish.

Giant Bumphead Parrotfish *Bolbometopon muricatus*,
Layang Layang, South China Sea, Malaysia

PARROTFISHES

Scaridae

Very common, often easily observed circumtropical reef fishes grouped in a very important family, counting 9 genera and at least 80 different species. Most feed on algal growth off dead coral or rocks, crushing and scraping it with their beak-like fused teeth. The result is a large amount of white sand, regularly excreted in mid-water after digestion and ending up on beaches. Parrotfishes are very conspicuous and extremely colorful, but they also are rather difficult to identify underwater as livery greatly varies depending on age and sex. ~ **U/W Photo Tips:** Parrotfish make great subjects, but most of them are extremely wary and prone to an erratic, fast, bird-like way of swimming, very similar to that of wrasses. Best chances for well-posed shots are at night, when they can be closely approached while sleeping tucked among close-fitting corals and rocks.

BLEEKER'S PARROTFISH

Chlorurus bleekeri

Distribution: Tropical Western Pacific from Indonesia to Fiji and Australia.
Size: Up to 50 centimeters.
Habitat: Healthy coral reefs and slopes from 3 to 35 meters deep.
Life Habits: Blue-green with lavender-edged body scales; best identified by large, pale yellow or pale green cheek patch, easily noticed at a distance. Usually solitary, locally common.

BULLETHEAD PARROTFISH

Chlorurus sordidus

Distribution: Tropical Indo-Pacific from the Red Sea to French Polynesia and from Southern Japan to Australia.
Size: Up to 40 centimeters.
Habitat: Healthy coral reefs and slopes from 2 to 30 meters deep.
Life Habits: Very colorful and quite variable, usually with apricot or orangish cheeks, blue-green body with lavender-edged scales and pale green patch at the base of the tail. Usually solitary.

BLUNTHEAD PARROTFISH
Chlorurus gibbus

Distribution: Red Sea.
Size: Up to 80 centimeters.
Habitat: Helthy coral reefs and slopes from 2 to 50 meters deep.
Life Habits: Body massive, blunt-headed, a bright blue-green with lavender-edged scales and blue head. Solitary or in small groups along the outer reef. The species complex comprises the almost identical Roundhead Parrotfish *C. strongylocephalus* found in the Indian Ocean and the Stephead Parrotfish *C. microrhinos* found in the Western and Central Pacific.

STEEPHEAD PARROTFISH
Chlorurus microrhinos

Distribution: Tropical Western and Central Indo-Pacific from Indonesia to French Polynesia and from Southern Japan to Australia.
Size: Up to 80 centimeters.
Habitat: Outer coral reefs from 2 to 50 meters deep.
Life Habits: Body a bright blue-green with lavender-edged scales, blunt, steep forehead on pale blue head. For more details on this interesting species complex see the preceding species.

JAPANESE PARROTFISH
Chlorurus japanensis

Distribution: Tropical Western Pacific from Indonesia to Micronesia and from Southern Japan to Australia.
Size: Up to 30 centimeters.
Habitat: Healthy outer coral reefs and slopes from 5 to 20 meters deep.
Life Habits: Body light yellow to green with bright blue tail and unmistakable diagnostic diagonal purple band at mid-body from head to belly. Usually observed alone and not easily approached.

BICOLOR PARROTFISH
Cetoscarus bicolor

Distribution: Tropical Indo-Pacific from the Red Sea to French Polynesia and from Southern Japan to Australia.
Size: Up to 80 centimeters.
Habitat: Healthy, sheltered coral reefs and lagoons from 2 to 30 meters deep.
Life Habits: Spectacular and exceptionally colorful: body green with pink-edged scales and pink spots and lines on head. Usually in small groups with one mature male and two or three yellow-brown females. Very wary and quite difficult to approach closely.
For the juvenile stage see page 221.

LONGNOSE PARROTFISH
Hipposcarus harid

Distribution: Red Sea and Indian Ocean from East Africa to Indonesia.
Size: Up to 75 centimeters.
Habitat: Sheltered coral reefs with sandy bottoms and lagoons from 2 to 25 meters.
Life Habits: Pale yellow or pale green (specimen illustrated wears mottled nocturnal livery, quite different from diurnal one as it often happens with many fish species); one of the less colorful parrotfishes, easily recognized by its elongate snout. Often encountered in aggregations inside lagoons.

RUSTY PARROTFISH
Scarus ferrugineus

Distribution: Western Indian Ocean from the Red Sea to the Gulf of Aden.
Size: Up to 40 centimeters.
Habitat: Sheltered coral reefs, lagoons and slopes from 5 to 60 meters deep.
Life Habits: Body a pale green with pink-edged scales, bright blue-green band around mouth. Solitary or in small aggregations. Replaced further East - from Indonesia to the Great Barrier Reef in Australia - by the almost identical Bluepatch Parrotfish *S. forsteni.*

BLUE-BARRED PARROTFISH
Scarus ghobban

Distribution: Tropical Indo-Pacific from the Red Sea to the Gulf of California and from Southern Japan to Australia.
Size: Up to 75 centimeters.
Habitat: Sheltered reefs, lagoons and rubble slopes from 2 to 30 meters deep.
Life Habits: Exceptionally widespread all over the tropical Indo-Pacific range, easily identified: body a dirty yellow with several broken blue bands. Terminal phase males yellow with blue-edged scales. Usually solitary, locally common.

RED-LIP PARROTFISH
Scarus rubroviolaceus

Distribution: Tropical Indo-Pacific from East Africa to Panama and from Southern Japan to Australia.
Size: Up to 70 centimeters.
Habitat: Outer coral reef slopes from 5 to 30 meters deep.
Life Habits: Widely distributed all over the Indo-Pacific. Body blue-green, often darker in front, with blunt rounded forehead and blue double "chinstrap". Solitary or in pairs, usually very wary.

DUSKY PARROTFISH
Scarus niger

Distribution: Tropical Indo-Pacific from the Red Sea to French Polynesia and from Southern Japan to Australia.
Size: Up to 35 centimeters.
Habitat: Healthy coral reefs and sheltered lagoons from 2 to 20 meters.
Life Habits: The only purplish parrotfish, easily identified by the dark streak behind the red eye and the bright orange lips. Generally encountered alone.The individual illustrated at right wears a typically mottled nocturnal livery.

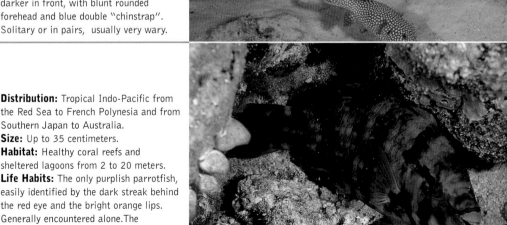

GREENTHROAT PARROTFISH
Scarus prasognathos

Distribution: Tropical Indo-Pacific from the Seychelles to Papua New Guinea and Southern Japan.
Size: Up to 70 centimeters.
Habitat: Healthy coral reefs and slopes from 3 to 25 meters deep.
Life Habits: Body dark green with yellowish head and turquoise-green throat. Often observed in large groups roving on reef flats, busily feeding on algal growth on corals.

BRIDLED PARROTFISH
Scarus frenatus

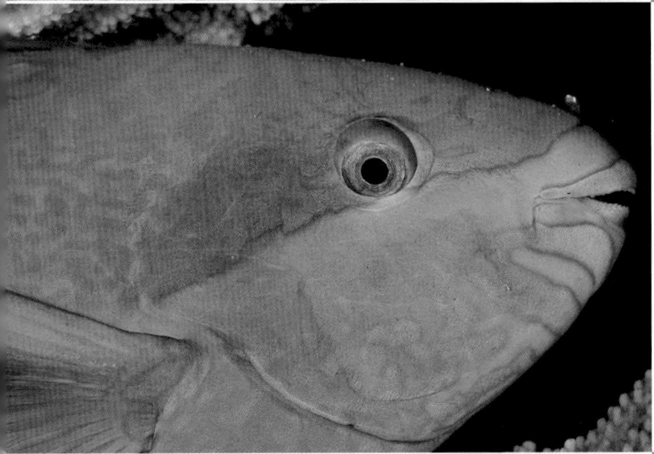

Distribution: Tropical Indo-Pacific from the Red Sea to French Polynesia and from Southern Japan to Australia.
Size: Up to 50 centimeters.
Habitat: Outer coral reef slopes and reef crests from 2 to 25 meters deep.
Life Habits: Body in several bright shades of green, abruptly becoming much paler on the rear; pale luminous green and bright pink bands around mouth. Very wary and fast swimming, usually encountered alone feeding on algal growth along reef crests.

YELLOW-TAIL PARROTFISH
Scarus hypselopterus

Distribution: Tropical Asian Pacific from Indonesia to Japan and Vanuatu.
Size: Up to 30 centimeters.
Habitat: Coral reefs and outer slopes from 10 to 30 meters deep.
Life Habits: Coloration very variable, usually darker - occasionally brownish - at midbody with blue tail and diagnostic reddish markings radiating from the eye. Also bright blue-green stripe going from the eye to the base of the pectoral fin. Occasionally observed in silty habitats but not particularly common anywhere.

YELLOW-FIN PARROTFISH
Scarus flavipectoralis

Distribution: Tropical Central Indo-Pacific from the Andamans to Micronesia and the Great Barrier Reef.
Size: Up to 40 centimeters.
Habitat: Lagoons and coastal sheltered reefs from 10 to 40 meters deep.
Life Habits: Body bicolored in shades of green, with a pale yellow patch at the base of the tail and a bright blue-green stripe running from the mouth across the eye to the base of the pectoral fin.Females are a uniform yellow-green.

QUOY'S PARROTFISH
Scarus quoyi

Distribution: Tropical Indo-Pacific from India to Micronesia and from Japan to New Caledonia.
Size: Up to 20 centimeters.
Habitat: Sheltered coral reefs and outer slopes from 2 to 20 meters deep.
Life Habits: Very small, the "lorikeet" of parrotfish. Body green and violet with bright lime green saddle at the base of the tail and green band above the mouth. Solitary or in small groups, very shy and usually unnoticed by divers.

TRICOLOR PARROTFISH
Scarus tricolor

Distribution: Tropical Indo-Pacific from East Africa to Papua New Guinea.
Size: Up to 55 centimeters.
Habitat: Outer coral reef slopes from 10 to 40 meters deep.
Life Habits: Body green, often with a pinkinsh tinge on the sides; tail lunate, brightly marked in pink and green; green bands clearly visible around mouth. Usually observed alone, often among coral bommies on reef crests.

GIANT BUMPHEAD PARROTFISH
Bolbometopon muricatus

Distribution: Tropical Indo-Pacific from the Red Sea to French Polynesia and from Southern Japan to Australia.
Size: Up to 130 centimeters.
Habitat: Lagoons and outer reefs and drop-offs from 2 to 40 meters deep.
Life Habits: Huge, extremely impressive: one of the most spectacular creatures of the coral reef. Body massive, pale green, with large hump on forehead. Often observed in "herds", smashing corals to pieces and munching noisily on fragments. Powerful and with no natural enemies but absolutely harmless to humans.

SAND DIVERS
Trichonotidae

Restricted to the Indo-Pacific, a very small family numbering just one genus and about 4 described species. Usually unnoticed by divers, these fish spend most of their time hidden under the sand with only their snout and eyes exposed, but when the current is right they will hover above the substrate, waiting for some zooplankton to drift by and always ready to dive in a flash under the sand, only to reappear several meters away after the danger has passed. Males are quite colorful and often sport elegant, elongate dorsal fin rays. ~ **U/W Photo Tips:** Sand divers are not easy subjects. They have to be spotted first, which is not always easy on the sandy or silty bottoms they prefer, and then they have to be approached very slowly and with great care. There's no use in waiting for them without moving if they disappear under the sand however, as they will "swim" under the substrate and reappear somewhere else.

BLUE-SPOTTED SAND DIVER
Trichonotus setigerus

Distribution: Tropical Indo-Pacific from the Persian Gulf to New Caledonia.
Size: Up to 25 centimeters.
Habitat: Sand and very fine rubble bottoms from 1 to 20 meters deep.
Life Habits: Body thin, elongate, pale tan with several translucent, pearly white spots. Snout spotted in iridescent blue and orange. Often observed in spread, loose aggregations on very shallow sand bottoms; difficult to approach closely, always ready to disappear under the sand in a flash.

The Grass-Eaters of the Reef

Peacefully grazing off seagrasses and algae growing on live and dead corals, reef herbivores such as surgeonfish and parrotfish occupy a very specialized ecological niche. Constantly modifying their environment

The unmistakable bite marks left by parrotfish on coral.

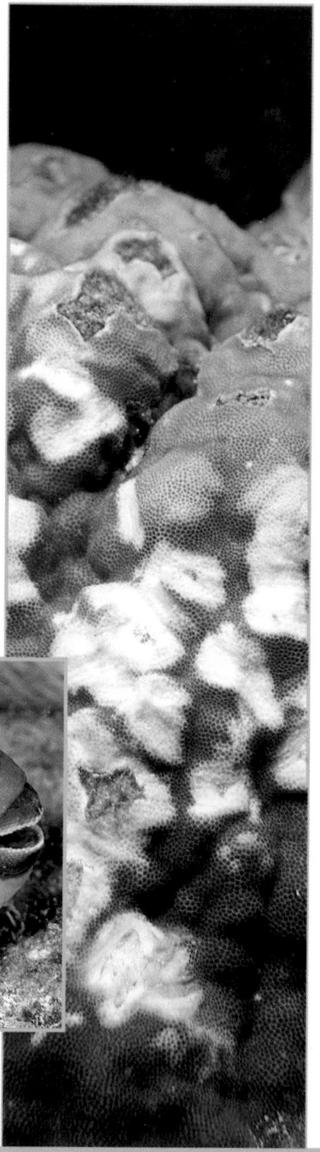

Strange as it may sound, several among the reef's inhabitants are herbivores or plant-eaters. In fact, several species have strongly evolved in this direction, having developed sophisticated adaptations of their teeth along with special behaviors to better exploit their unique ecological niche. Just like many plant-eaters on land (one only has to think of antelopes, zebras or elephants), reef herbivores tend to gather in herds, and just like their land-dwelling equivalents they end up modifying the very structure of territory they cross through their feeding behavior. Beware, however: not all "grazers" are true herbivores, even if their way of behaving looks the same. Although they are easily observed as they continuously "graze" coral summits, butterflyfish are essentially carnivores, despite appearances. Using teeth composed of rigid bristles and a tweezer-like mouth apparatus, they can pluck

Parrotfish are able to bite through live hard coral.

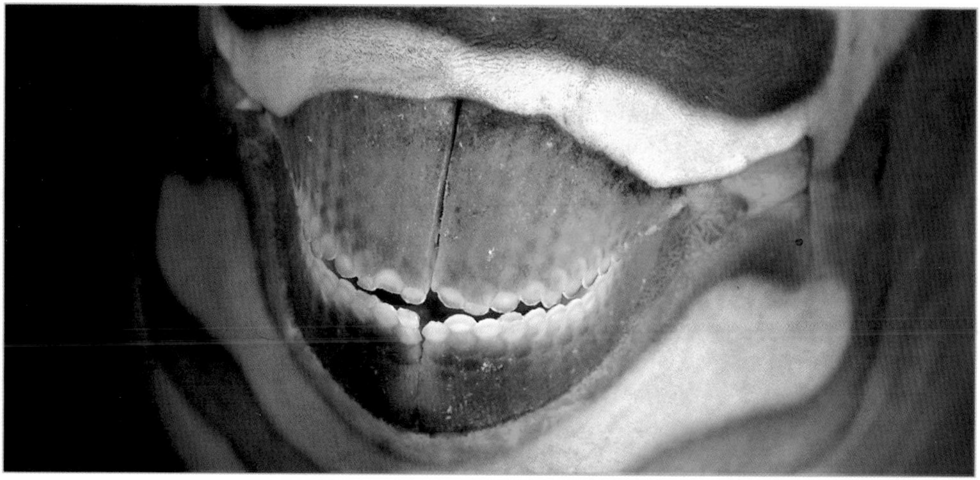

The typical fused dention of parrotfishes is incredibly strong.

Surgeonfish move and feed in fast-moving schools.

soft polyps out of impregnable stony coral colonies without too much trouble. Angelfish - quite more robust - do more or less the same to sponges and coelenterates, scraping them to pieces with their stiff, bristly teeth. Surgeonfish instead are proper and true vegetarians, using very similar teeth - which look a bit like toothbrushes - to efficiently scrape large quantities of encrusting green algae off living or dead coral formations, thereby competing with much smaller and less efficient herbivores, such as several species of gobies and blennies. Their common name derives from the sharp horizontal blades on their caudal peduncle: in at least one species these dangerous scalpels are also connected to a venom gland. Damselfish or pomacentrids are instead small, sedentary fish that actively cultivate and defend their own personal "orchard" of algae, usually on broken coral rubble patches. However, despite being quite fearless, they are powerless to resist the surgeonfish that attack in overwhelming, fast-swimming schools numbering hundreds. Damselfish show aggression toward other herbivorous species, but on such

A mixed school of Powderblue and Ringtail Surgeonfishes, Indian Ocean, Maldives.

occasions are defeated by sheer numbers. Different but just as fascinating are finally the well-known and very colorful parrotfish, whose teeth are fused into a very strong "beak" composed of two upper and two lower plates. Thanks to their highly evolved dental apparatus - integrated with powerful and bony pharyngeal plaques - parrotfish are quite capable of crunching whole chunks of live coral. Once the symbiotic algae within the coral scraps are digested,

Giant bumphead parrotfish *Bolbometopon muricatus*, Sulawesi Sea, Malaysia.

everything else is expelled from the intestine in the form of very fine sand. That is mostly what sunbathers lie on - parrotfish excreta! In fact, it has been calculated that a healthy population of parrotfish can produce up to a ton of coral sand for every hectare per year, which probably makes them - along with the unsung sea urchins, which are also intensely efficient algae scrapers - the chief modifiers of the reef landscape. The sudden changes in parrotfish coloration generate wild confusion about their classification: it is believed, however, that the Indo-Pacific alone hosts at least fifty different species of this family, all characterized by a blunt, rounded muzzle, a fused dentition, and big, flinty scales. Parrotfish are often consumed for food by local fishermen even though their meat is very flabby and the taste is said to be quite bland.

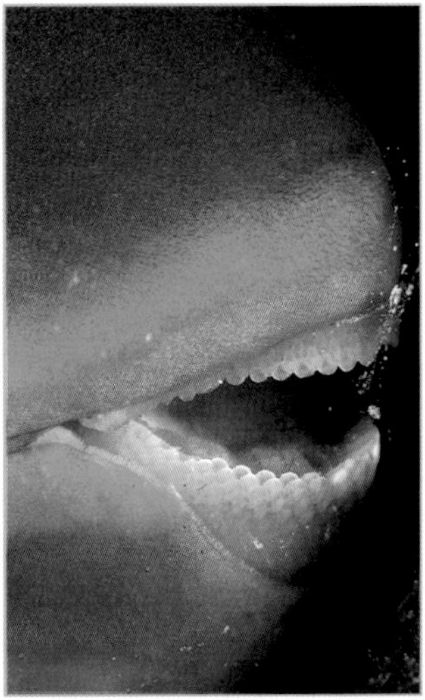

Parrotfish teeth are subject to an enormous amount of wear.

SANDPERCHES
Pinguipedidiae

Sandperches - also known as grubfishes or smelts - are grouped in a medium-sized family numbering about 4 genera and about 60 species. There is a lot of confusion however as these fish are little researched and often very similar to each other, being regularly ignored by most divers. All share a torpedo-shaped body, large antero-dorsal and very mobile eyes and the habit of perching on the substrate using their pectoral and ventral fins. Most are rather drably colored showing similar chequered patterns and are often observed in pairs. ~ **U/W Photo Tips:** Grubfishes are extremely common but due to their rather drab liveries and their quiet benthic habits are usually ignored by divers and photographers. Always ready to speedily dash away if approached too closely, they request a macro lens (60mm or 105mm) to be framed successfully.

FALSE-EYE SANDPERCH
Parapercis clathrata

Distribution: Tropical Central Indo-Pacific from the Andamans to Samoa and from Southern Japan to Australia.
Size: Up to 18 centimeters.
Habitat: Sand and coral rubble bottoms in lagoons and outer reef flats from 3 to 50 meters deep.
Life Habits: Pale tan with draker mottled pattern, row of black-centered orangish spots on lower body and dark ocellus above gill cover are diagnostic. Commonly encountered alone or in pairs. Feeds on small benthic invertebrates.

SPECKLED SANDPERCH
Parapercis hexophthalma

Distribution: Tropical Indo-West Pacific from the Red Sea to Micronesia and from Southern Japan to the Great Barrier Reef in Australia.
Size: Up to 28 centimeters.
Habitat: Sand and coral rubble bottoms in lagoons and on outer reef slopes from 5 to 25 meters deep.
Life Habits: White with numerous small black spots; large black blotch at base of the tail is diagnostic. Commonly observed resting on the substrate, alone or in pairs. Feeds on small benthic invertebrates.

NOSESTRIPE SANDPERCH
Parapercis lineopunctata

Distribution: Tropical Central Indo-Pacific from Indonesia to Papua New Guinea.
Size: Up to 12 centimeters.
Habitat: Sand bottoms close to coral reefs from 5 to 40 meters deep.
Life Habits: Whitish with darker saddles and stripes; dark line on snout is diagnostic. Easily confused with several other similar looking species, commonly observed resting on the substrate alone or in pairs. Feeds on small benthic invertebrates.

BLACKFIN SANDPERCH
Parapercis snyderi

Distribution: Central Tropical Indo-Pacific from Indonesia to the Great Barrier Reef in Australia and Korea.
Size: Up to 12 centimeters.
Habitat: Sand and coral rubble bottoms in lagoons and outer reef slopes from 10 to 40 meters deep.
Life Habits: Pinkish with dark brown saddles and spots; black first dorsal fin is diagnostic. Commonly observed resting on the bottom, perching on ventral fins. Feeds on small benthic invertebrates.

WHITESTRIPE SANDPERCH
Parapercis sp.

Distribution: Central Tropical Indo-Pacific from Singapore to Micronesia.
Size: Up to 23 centimeters.
Habitat: Sand, silty or coral rubble bottoms in lagoons and reef slopes from 10 to 30 meters deep.
Life Habits: One of several yet undescribed sandperches. Body is whitish, showing six u-shaped brown saddles on back and ten darker bars on lower side. Commonly observed alone or in pairs resting on the substrate, locally common. Feeds on small benthic invertebrates.

TRIPLEFINS
Tripterygiidae

These extremely small but exceedingly colorful fishes are grouped in a very large family numbering more than 20 genera and about 200 species, many of which are apparently undescribed yet. Usually less than five centimeters long, sporting bright iridescent liveries, they can usually be admired perching in the open on flat corals and sponges. Strictly territorial, they are related to blennies and feed on small invertebrates. Most species however are very cryptic and are rarely observed by divers. ~ **U/W Photo Tips:** The few species of triplefins regularly observed by divers are truly beautiful and make wonderful subjects for the photographer. Being quite territorial, they are not difficult to approach, but their diminutive size makes the use a 105mm macro lens imperative to avoid disturbing them.

STRIPED TRIPLEFIN
Helcogramma striata

Distribution: Tropical Indo-Pacific from the Andamans to Micronesia, Southern Japan and Australia.
Size: Up to 5 centimeters.
Habitat: Coastal and outer reefs in clear water 2 to 20 meters deep.
Life Habits: Iridescent red with three luminous white longitudinal stripes and bright yellow eye, often observed alone or in small loose aggregations perching on specialized narrow ventral fins on large brain corals.Very territorial and rather easily approached by divers.

YELLOW-LIP TRIPLEFIN
Helcogramma gymnauchen

Distribution: Central Tropical Indo-Pacific from Indonesia to Papua New Guinea and Australia.
Size: Up to 5 centimeters.
Habitat: Coastal and outer reefs in clear water from 2 to 10 meters deep.
Life Habits: Variable livery, most often translucent with red bands; large protruding lower lip. Very colorful and easily approached, often observbed perchin in the open on large sponges. A few very similar species in the area.

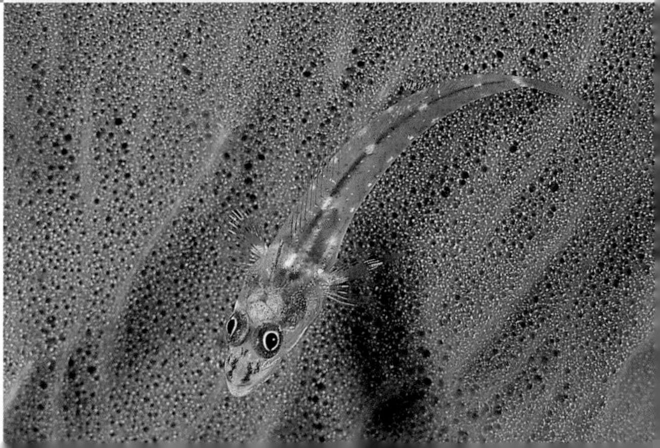

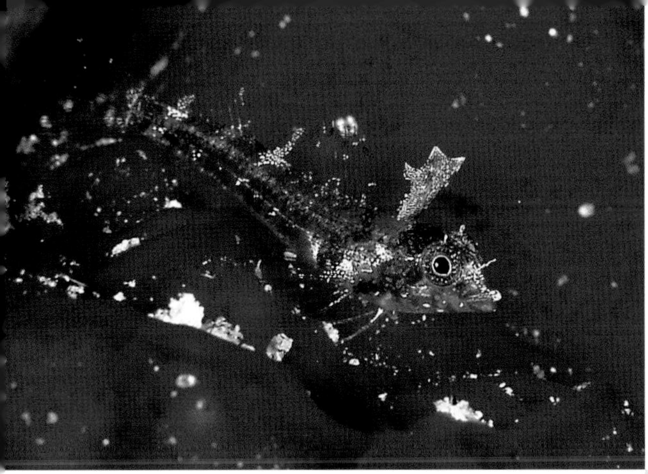

CROWNED TRIPLEFIN
Enneapterygius pusillus

Distribution: Tropical Indo-Pacific from the Andamans to Southern Japan and Australia.
Size: Up to 2,5 centimeters.
Habitat: Surge areas on outer reef flats and drop-offs from 1 to 5 meters deep.
Life Habits: Extremely small and very well camouflaged, rarely observed by very attentive divers in shallow surge areas, occasionally perching on large sponges. Usually noticed by rythmic raising and lowering of bright white first dorsal fin, marking its territory to intruders.

CONVICT BLENNIES
Pholidichthyidae

A single monospecific family found only in the Western Pacific, these strange little fish are commonly mistaken for gobies or eel-tail catfishes by divers, but in fact are more closely related to blennies. Juvenile convict blennies are occasionally observed in large schools hovering about gorgonians or close to coral outcrops on outer reefs, usually rapidly closing up to each other when approached. These fish lack scales like blennies but have a set of teeth like gobies. Striped, larger adults are almost never observed by divers. ~ **U/W Photo Tips:** Given their free-swimming habits, juvenile convict blennies are almost impossible to photograph properly with a macro set-up. They offer however spectacular opportunities for wide-angle shots which can show them in the surrounding reef environment.

CONVICT BLENNIES
Pholidichthys leucotaenia

Distribution: Tropical Indo-Pacific from the Red Sea to French Polynesia and from Southern Japan to the Great Barrier Reef.
Size: Up to 10 centimeters.
Habitat: Coastal and outer reefs from 3 to 30 meters deep.
Life Habits: Body eel-like, black with whitish longitudinal stripe. A mimic of Eel-tail Catfish *Plotosus lineatus* when immature, often observed in large, spread out schools close to gorgonian fans and black coral colonies on coastal reefs.

BLENNIES
Blenniidae

More than 50 genera and over 300 different species are grouped into this large and rather confusing family. Most are extremely small fish, covered with a slimy skin (rather than scales) and with very small teeth arranged in a comb-like structure, evolved to cleanly scrape algae off dead corals. Most are very territorial, with strictly benthic habits and very well defined ranges with carefully chosen lairs (old shells, holes in the coral and most often empty worm tubes). They are usually observed in the open, sometimes swimming for very short distances, but are always ready to hide into their refuge if carelessly approached. ~ **U/W Photo Tips:** Some blennies are extremely colorful and most make great subjects for the macro photographer due to their cartoonish appearance. In fact most are difficult to approach and all require a good macro lens.

TUBE-WORM BLENNY
Plagiotremus rhinorynchos

Distribution: Tropical Indo-Pacific from East Africa to French Polynesia and from Southern Japan to Australia.
Size: Up to 12 centimeters.
Habitat: Coastal and outer reefs from 3 to 40 meters deep.
Life Habits: Ribbon-like orange body with two neon-blue longitudinal stripes: often observed peeking from lair or free swimming in mid-water with undulating movements. Feeds biting off little bits of fins and skin from other fishes, pretending to be a cleaner wrasse.

LANCE BLENNY
Aspidontus dussumieri

Distribution: Tropical Indo-Pacific from East Africa to French Polynesia and from Southern Japan to Australia.
Size: Up to 12 centimeters.
Habitat: Coastal and outer reefs from 2 to 20 meters deep.
Life Habits: Whitish or tan with a dark longitudinal stripe, often observed swimming in the water column with undulating movements. Feeds off bits of fins and skin from other fishes; very shy, always ready to retreat to its lair.

SHORTHEAD SABRETOOTH BLENNY
Petroscirtes breviceps

Distribution: Tropical Indo-Pacific from East Africa to Papua New Guinea and from Southern Japan to New Caledonia.
Size: Up to 13 centimeters.
Habitat: Coastal reefs and lagoons, often in silty and weedy habitats, from 2 to 20 meters deep.
Life Habits: White or yellow with three black longitudinal stripes, very similar to Striped Fangblenny *Meiacanthus grammistes* which it closely mimics. Often observed taking refuge or nesting in small discarded bottles, abandoned tube worm holes and dead shells.

CRESTED SABRETOOTH BLENNY
Petroscirtes mitratus

Distribution: Tropical Indo-Pacific from East Africa to New Caledonia.
Size: Up to 15 centimeters.
Habitat: Coastal reefs and lagoons, often in silty or weedy habitats, from 1 to 5 meters deep.
Life Habits: Body pale, in rare occasions pure white, more often mottled in brown and olive: easily identified by very high first dorsal fin. Commonly encountered on old buoy ropes during safety stops, on old discarded nets, on jetty pylons and on sargassum beds.

BICOLOR BLENNY
Ecsenius bicolor

Distribution: Tropical Indo-Pacific from the Maldives to Micronesia and from Southern Japan to the Great Barrier Reef in Australia.
Size: Up to 10 centimeters.
Habitat: Coastal and outer reefs from 2 to 25 meters deep.
Life Habits: Very variable, usually with dark grey front and bright orange rear body as illustrated. Usually observed alone, perching in the open, always ready to dash to its tube worm hole lair. Feeds on algae and small benthic invertebrates.

WHITE-LINED BLENNY
Ecsenius pictus

Distribution: Central Tropical Indo-Pacific from Indonesia to the Solomons.
Size: Up to 5 centimeters.
Habitat: Coastal and outer reefs from 10 to 40 meters deep.
Life Habits: Head pale brown, body dark grey with numerous finely dotted longitudinal white stripes, bright yellow area at the base of the tail. Commonly observed alone or in small loose aggregations on reef flats, usually in deeper water than other similar species.

BATH'S BLENNY
Ecsenius bathi

Distribution: Central Tropical Indo-Pacific, from Malaysian Borneo to Indonesia and West Papua.
Size: Up to 4 centimeters.
Habitat: Coastal and outer reefs from 3 to 30 meters deep.
Life Habits: Locally common, usually observed in a striped phase (yellow head, grey body, black stripes) and in a very different orangish chequered one (illustrated). Often seen perching in the open on sponges or among tunicates on coral bommies and along walls. Replaced further East by the very similar Philippines Blenny *E. dilemma*.

CLOWN BLENNY
Ecsenius axelrodi

Distribution: Tropical Central Indo-Pacific from Sulawesi in Indonesia to West Papua and the Solomons.
Size: Up to 5 centimeters.
Habitat: Outer reefs and slopes from 5 to 30 meters deep.
Life Habits: Bright orange with black "tiger stripes" on body and darker head; ocellated spot above pectoral fin base diagnostic. Beautiful and very distinctive but with a very restricted, localized distribution. Usually observed alone or in pairs, perching in the open on large sponges and among tunicates.

EYESPOT BLENNY
Ecsenius ops

Distribution: Tropical Central Indo-Pacific from Java to Northern Sulawesi.
Size: Up to 5 centimeters.
Habitat: Sheltered coastal reefs and lagoons from 2 to 15 meters deep.
Life Habits: Beautiful and very distinctive but with a very restricted and localized distribution. Body a rich brown, head blue-grey with bright yellow eye and a small, distinct spot behind it. Commonly observed perching in the open among sponges and tunicates, alone or in pairs.

TRICOLOR BLENNY
Ecsenius tricolor

Distribution: Central Tropical Indo-Pacific from Malaysian Borneo to the Philippines.
Size: Up to 5 centimeters.
Habitat: Sheltered coastal reefs from 5 to 30 meters deep.
Life Habits: Body blue-grey in the front and bright yellow or orange in the rear, with bright white longitudinal stripe, edged with orange and blue in the front. Commonly observed perching in the open among sponges and tunicates, alone or in small loose aggregations. Locally common but with a very localized distribuition.

MONOCLE BLENNY
Ecsenius monoculus

Distribution: Tropical Asian Pacific from Indonesia to the South China Sea.
Size: Up to 6 centimeters.
Habitat: Coastal reefs from 2 to 10 meters deep, often in silty environments.
Life Habits: Body a pale brown, finely spotted with bright pale yellow or white dots; a darker saddle clearly visible at the base of the tail. Commonly observed alone or in small groups, perching in the open, often in dead or damaged coral areas.

TWINSPOT BLENNY
Ecsenius bimaculatus

Distribution: Central Tropical Indo-Pacific from Malaysian Borneo to the Philippines.
Size: Up to 4 centimeters.
Habitat: Coastal and outer reefs slopes from 1 to 15 meters deep.
Life Habits: Brown back with bright white belly; pair of dark elongate spots on side are diagnostic. Locally common - especially in Sabah, Malaysia - but with a very restricted distribution. Commonly observed alone or in small aggregations, perching in the open among sponges.

TAILSPOT BLENNY
Ecsenius stigmatura

Distribution: Very localized, Central Indo-Pacific from the Moluccas to Raja Ampat in Indonesia and the Philippines.
Size: Up to 5.5 centimeters.
Habitat: Coral-rich areas on outer reefs and lagoons from 2 to 30 meters deep.
Life Habits: Very localized but locally common and truly beautiful: body a rich orange fading to green in the front with bright blue head; a dark edged line under the eye, which is surrounded by a bright orange ring. White-edged black spot at the base of the tail. Solitary or in pairs.

YAEYAMA BLENNY
Ecsenius yaeyamaensis

Distribution: Tropical Indo-Pacific from Sri Lanka to Western Australia and from Southern Japan to Micronesia.
Size: Up to 6 centimeters.
Habitat: Coastal rocky reefs from 2 to 15 meters deep.
Life Habits: Body pale grey to pale brown with rows of whitish spots and two darker lines behind the eye. Easily confused with several almost identical species in the same distribution range; usually observed alone or in small loose groups perched on exposed spots.

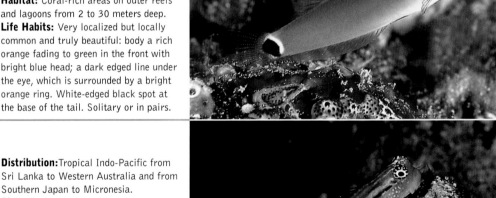

ORANGE-SPOTTED BLENNY
Blenniella chrysospilos

Distribution: Tropical Indo-Pacific from the Red Sea and East Africa to Australia and Southern Japan.
Size: Up to 14 centimeters.
Habitat: Surge areas and wave-swept intertidal flats in very shallow water.
Life Habits: Pale tan with bright red spots on head: beautiful and easily identified but very rarely observed due to its shyness and its choice of habitats. Solitary or in small groups, usually with only the head protruding from its hole.

LEOPARD BLENNY
Exallias brevis

Distribution: Tropical Indo-Pacific from the Red Sea to Hawai'i and from Southern Japan to Australia.
Size: Up to 15 centimeters.
Habitat: Coastal and outer reefs in clear water from 3 to 20 meters deep.
Life Habits: Body pale with numerous leopard-like brown to red spots; usually observed among *Pocillopora* coral colonies branches.Specimen illustrated is a color variation from black volcanic sand habitats. Very shy, not easily approached.

STARRY BLENNY
Salarias ramosus

Distribution: Tropical Asian Pacific from Malaysian Borneo and Indonesia to the Philippines and Australia.
Size: Up to 6 centimeters.
Habitat: Sheltered coral reefs and mixed coastal sand-seagrass habitats from 1 to 6 meters deep.
Life Habits: Yellow brown body with numerous small bright white spots; highly branched cirrhi above the eyes. Often observed alone, sitting in the open on coral heads, but usually very wary and difficult to approach closely.

DRAGONETS

Callionymidae

Dragonets number about 9 genera and more than 125 species, all grouped in a quite large tropical family which comprises mostly small or very small benthic fishes, covered with a slimy (and sometimes quite smelly) skin instead of scales and with a more or less spiny, broad head. Dragonets tend to move around on the bottom, rarely if ever leaving the substrate (except when mating), hopping on their ventral fins or even burying themselves in the sand. All have a rather small, protrusible mouth which gives them a typical "puckered" look and some are extraordinarily colorful. ~ **U/W Photo Tips:** Most dragonets are not difficult subjects and are often found hopping around on the substrate: despite sporting very cryptic liveries, some are quite colorful. Mandarinfish are exceptionally so, and make wonderful subjects: taking good shots of a mating pair requires a lot of patience and a good macro (105mm) lens.

FINGERED DRAGONET

Dactylopus dactylopus

Distribution: Tropical Asian Pacific from the Andamans to Taiwan and from Southern Japan to Australia.
Size: Up to 20 centimeters.
Habitat: Sand and silt bottoms in sheltered areas from 3 to 60 meters deep.
Life Habits: Body elegantly mottled in green and brown with small blue and orange dots: finger-like separate rays of ventral fins used to walk on the substrate. Often observed in pairs, foraging in the open for small benthic invertebrates. The specimen illustrated is displaying in response to a perceived threat.
For the juvenile form see page 221.

KUITER'S DRAGONET

Dactylopus kuiteri

Distribution: Central Tropical Indo-Pacific from Flores to North Sulawesi.
Size: Up to 15 centimeters.
Habitat: Sand or silt bottoms in lagoons and sheltered coastal reefs from 5 to 40 meters deep.
Life Habits: Body elegantly mottled in brown with several very small orange and bright blue spots; first finger-like free rays of ventral fins used for walking on substrate; first dorsal fin very long with clearly visible ocellus at the base. The specimen illustrated is displaying in response to a perceived threat.
For the juvenile form see page 221.

SUPERB DRAGONET
Callionymus superbus

Distribution: Indonesia.
Size: Up to 12 centimeters.
Habitat: Sand and coral rubble bottoms from 1 to 15 meters deep.
Life Habits: Body dark brown or black with several lunate gray or white spots; male sports greatly elongate first dorsal fin. Uncommon and exquisitely camouflaged, occasionally observed on black volcanic sand shallow bottoms. The specimen illustrated was photographed in the Lembeh Strait of Northern Sulawesi.

MANDARIN FISH
Synchiropus splendidus

Distribution: Tropical Asian Pacific from Indonesia to Micronesia and from Southern Japan to New Caledonia.
Size: Up to 6 centimeters.
Habitat: Coral rubble bottoms of sheltered coastal reefs and lagoons from 1 to 18 meters deep.
Life Habits: Unmistakable: spectacular, "psychedelic" livery with fluorescent green and blue meandering dark-edged blotches and stripes on bright orange background. Very shy, but commonly observed at dusk when it comes out in the open in small groups and for a short time during mating rituals.

PICTURE DRAGONET
Synchiropus picturatus

Distribution: Tropical Asian Pacific from Indonesia to Australia.
Size: Up to 6 centimeters.
Habitat: Coral rubble bottoms in lagoons and on sheltered coastal reefs from 2 to 10 meters deep.
Life Habits: Less commonly observed and less well known than the preceding species: body is light green or tan with numerous fluorescent green- and orange-edged black spots. Occasionally observed in small, loose aggregations at dusk.

CIRCLED DRAGONET
Synchiropus circularis

Distribution: Unknown: observed in a few Central Indo-Pacific localities.
Size: Up to 6 centimeters.
Habitat: Thick coral growth and coral rubble areas in very shallow and clear water.
Life Habits: Exceptionally uncommon and very rarely observed but strictly related to *S. splendidus* and *S. picturatus*. Body is a rich brown with several tan spots edged in fluorescent white. Specimens illustrated have been photographed while mating at dusk.

BARTEL'S DRAGONET
Neosynchiropus bartelsi

Distribution: Tropical Asian Pacific from Indonesia to the Philippines and Papua New Guinea.
Size: Up to 5 centimeters.
Habitat: Coral rubble in lagoons and outer reefs from 3 to 35 meters deep.
Life Habits: Commonly observed in a brown or bright red phase, always however with small ocellated blue spots on back and sides. Occasionally observed alone or in pairs, hopping around on bottom among coral rubble in secluded reef areas, usually in the late afternoon. Replaced further East by the very similar Morrison's Dragonet *S. morrisoni.*

MOYER'S DRAGONET
Neosynchiropus moyeri

Distribution: Tropical Asian Pacific from Indonesia to Southern Japan and the Great Barrier Reef in Australia.
Size: Up to 7 centimeters.
Habitat: Coral rubble areas in sunlit patches with rich algal growth on coastal reefs from 3 to 30 meters deep.
Life Habits: White with brown or bright red irregular spots. Occasionally observed in small loose aggregations, hopping around warily in the late afternoon. Large dominant males sport a fan-shaped, finely ornamented dorsal fin.

MARBLED DRAGONET
Neosynchiropus ocellatus

Distribution: Central Tropical Indo-Pacific from Malaysia to French Polynesia and from Southern Japan to the Great Barrier Reef.
Size: Up to 7 centimeters.
Habitat: Coral rubble areas on coastal reefs from 1 to 50 meters deep.
Life Habits: Olive to yellow-brown with several irregular white spots, blotches and saddles: easily confused with several similar species. Occasionally observed hopping on the substrate, searching for small benthic invertebrates.

SAND DRAGONET
Diplogrammus goramensis

Distribution: Central Tropical Indo-Pacific from Malaysia to Micronesia and from China to the Great Barrier Reef.
Size: Up to 8 centimeters.
Habitat: Coarse sand patches in sunlit areas from 2 to 15 meters deep.
Life Habits: Body flattened, with distinct horizontal ridge on lower side; pale brown with innumerable white or pale grey irregular spots and pale blue striopes below the eye. Very cryptic, but quite active in daylight and easily approached.

FILAMENTED DRAGONET
Callionymus keeleyi

Distribution: Tropical Indo-Pacific from Indonesia to Papua New Guinea.
Size: Up to 6 centimeters.
Habitat: Coral rubble and coarse sand bottoms in sheltered areas on coastal reefs from 5 to 60 meters deep.
Life Habits: Body liberally mottled in shades of brown, wavy blue and brown bands on dorsal fin, blue spots and lines on snout. Correct identification of several less common dragonet species is still very difficult as the genus is at the moment under revision.

GOBIES
Gobiidae

Despite their generally small size and their usually rather shy habits, gobies belong to the largest family of marine fishes, numbering more than 200 genera and a staggering total of over 1.500 species. The great majority are benthic, rarely if ever leaving the substrate, sometimes just hovering above it, and intimately linked to the reef ecosystem, often associating to soft corals and gorgonians. Many species live in burrows dug in the soft substrate, sharing symbiotic relationships with several different organisms like alpheid shrimps. ~ **U/W Photo Tips:** Unnoticed by most, ignored by many, most gobies - even the smallest ones - make in fact spectacular photographic subjects. Offering a wide range of behavioral opportunities, most can be closely approached with lots of patience, excellent buoyancy control and of course a good macro lens (60 or 105mm).

PINK-LINED GOBY
Amblygobius decussatus

Distribution: Tropical Indo-Pacific from Cocos-Keeling to New Caledonia and from Southern Japan to Australia.
Size: Up to 12 centimeters.
Habitat: Silty, sandy bottoms in lagoons and coastal reefs from 3 to 30 meters.
Life Habits: Body pale gray, with several regularly intersecting orange lines and bars, which become darker and very clearly visible on head; round bright orange spot at the base of the tail. Commonly observed in pairs on silty bottoms, not easily approached.

SPHYNX GOBY
Amblygobius sphynx

Distribution: Tropical Indo-Pacific from East Africa to Papua New Guinea and from Southern Japan to Australia.
Size: Up to 12 centimeters.
Habitat: Sand and coral rubble bottoms in sheltered lagoons and seagrass areas from 1 to 20 meters deep.
Life Habits: Pale with four or five dark olive bands: rather colorful but very well camouflaged and usually ignored by divers. Occasionally observed while swimming above the substrate, "hopping" in mid-water with spread-out fins.

WHITE-BARRED REEF GOBY
Amblygobius phalaena

Distribution: Tropical Indo-Pacific from Cocos-Keeling to French Polynesia and from Southern Japan to Australia.
Size: Up to 15 centimeters.
Habitat: Sand and silt bottoms in lagoons and on sheltered coastal reefs from 2 to 20 meters deep.
Life Habits: Common, usually encountered in large, spread-out aggregations. Often observed in a pale color phase, especially on white sand bottoms and in seagrass areas. Replaced in the Indian Ocean by the very similar Half-Banded Goby *A. semicinctus*.

HECTOR'S REEF GOBY
Amblygobius hectori

Distribution: Tropical Indo-Pacific from the Red Sea to Micronesia and Australia.
Size: Up to 8.5 centimeters.
Habitat: Coral-rich areas on slopes and shallow drop-offs from 3 to 30 meters.
Life Habits: Dark brown with four bright yellow stripes and a large, yellow-edged elongate spot on second dorsal fin. Beautiful but rather small and often mistaken by divers for a wrasse, which in fact it possibly mimics. Solitary, always observed swimming in midwater and among corals, never seen perching or in burrows like most other reef gobies.

RAINFORD'S REEF GOBY
Amblygobius rainfordi

Distribution: Tropical Central Indo-Pacific from Indonesia to Micronesia and Australia.
Size: Up to 5.5 centimeters.
Habitat: Coral-rich areas on coastal and outer reefs from 3 to 30 meters deep.
Life Habits: Body green-grey with five bright orange longitudinal stripes and a row of white spots on upper back. Beautiful, fast-moving, mimicking a wrasse and commonly observed swimming in "bounces" close to the substrate, usually among rich coral growth.

BLUE-SPECKLED RUBBLE GOBY
Asterropteryx ensifera

Distribution: Tropical Indo-Pacific from the Red Sea to French Polynesia and from Southern Japan to Australia.
Size: Up to 3.5 centimeters.
Habitat: Coral rubble bottoms in lagoons and sheltered reefs from 5 to 40 meters.
Life Habits: Body dark brown with several rows of very small iridescent blue spots: appears black at a distance. Often in large aggregations hovering over rubble slopes, but generally ignored by divers.

DOUBLE-SPOTTED RUBBLE GOBY
Asterropteryx bipunctatus

Distribution: Tropical Central Indo-Pacific from Chagos to Samoa and Japan.
Size: Up to 10 centimeters.
Habitat: Inside caves and crevices and on sandy ledges on drop-offs on outer reefs from 5 to 40 meters deep.
Life Habits: Bluish with bright orange spots; pale-edged round spot on first dorsal fin. Very beautiful but rarely observed as it is very shy. Occasionally observed inside caves or under deep overhangs, immediately retreating to darker recesses if approached by divers.

ORANGE-SPOTTED SHRIMP GOBY
Amblyeleotris guttata

Distribution: Tropical West Pacific from Malaysia and Indonesia to Samoa and from Southern Japan to Australia.
Size: Up to 8 centimeters.
Habitat: Sand and rubble ledges on outer reefs from 4 to 40 meters deep.
Life Habits: Body a luminous white with several bright gold-orange spots, two dark bands on front belly and many fluorescent blue spots on fins. Lives in burrows with symbiont alpheid shrimp. Locally common and very beautiful but rather shy and not easily approached.

SAILFIN SHRIMP GOBY
Amblyeleotris randalli

Distribution: Tropical Central Indo-Pacific from Malaysia and Indonesia to Fiji and Southern Japan.
Size: Up to 12 centimeters.
Habitat: Sand ledges on slopes and drop-offs on outer reefs from 10 to 50 meters.
Life Habits: Body bright white with 6-7 bright orange bars, first dorsal fin round with many white spots and a white-edged black spot at the base. Commonly observed while rythmically flicking dorsal fin open for territorial purposes; lives in burrows with symbiont alpheid shrimp.

STEINITZ'S SHRIMP GOBY
Amblyeleotris steinitzi

Distribution: Tropical Indo-Pacific from the Red Sea to Micronesia and from Southern Japan to the Great Barrier Reef.
Size: Up to 12 centimeters.
Habitat: Sandy areas on slopes in lagoons and along sheltered reefs from 5 to 35 meters deep.
Life Habits: Body white with five red-brown bars, many fine blue spots all over; easily confused underwater with several similar-looking species. Very common on sand and fine rubble substrates in lagoons and sheltered areas. Lives in burrows with symbiont blind alpheid shrimp.

METALLIC SHRIMP GOBY
Amblyeleotris latifasciata

Distribution: Tropical Central Indo-Pacific from Malaysia and Indonesia to the Philippines.
Size: Up to 14 centimeters.
Habitat: Clear sand and fine rubble bottoms in lagoons and sheltered coastal reefs from 10 to 40 meters deep.
Life Habits: Body greenish-brown, heavily speckled with iridescent blue and orange flecks; pale-edged orange spots on first dorsal fin. Beautiful and unmistakable. Lives in burrows with symbiont blind alpheid shrimp.

GORGEOUS SHRIMP GOBY
Amblyeleotris wheeleri

Distribution: Tropical Indo-Pacific from the Red Sea and East Africa to the Marshalls and from Southern Japan to Australia.
Size: Up to 10 centimeters.
Habitat: Sand and rubble ledges and gutters on outer reef slopes from 2 to 40 meters deep.
Life Habits: Body yellow with six burgundy wide bars, heavily flecked in gold and iridescent blue: many local variations in color intensity. Usually very shy and not easily approached. Shares burrow with symbiont alpheid shrimp.

BROAD-BANDED SHRIMP GOBY
Amblyeleotris periophtalma

Distribution: Tropical Indo-Pacific from the Red Sea to Papua New Guinea and from Southern Japan to Australia.
Size: Up to 11 centimeters.
Habitat: Sand and coral rubble patches on coastal and outer reef slopes from 5 to 20 meters deep.
Life Habits: Body pale pink or white with six deep pink or brownish bars: easily confused with many other similarly barred goby species. Very common but with many local color variations. Shares burrow with symbiont alpheid shrimp.

DIAGONAL SHRIMP GOBY
Amblyeleotris diagonalis

Distribution: Tropical Indo-Pacific from East Africa to the Solomons and from Southern Japan to the Great Barrier Reef.
Size: Up to 10 centimeters.
Habitat: Sand and fine rubble patches on reef slopes from 8 to 15 meters deep.
Life Habits: White with five red-brown bands; two narrow dark bands on head are diagnostic. Heavily speckled with golden and iridescent flecks; easily confused with several other similarly barred species. Shares burrow with blind symbiont alpheid shrimp.

RED-MARGIN SHRIMP GOBY
Amblyeleotris gymnocephala

Distribution: Tropical Central Indo-Pacific from Malaysia and Indonesia to Micronesia and Australia.
Size: Up to 12 centimeters.
Habitat: Sand patches on reef slopes, in lagoons and bays from 6 to 40 meters.
Life Habits: Body white or pale tan with five orange bars; dark flecks on back and red margin of dorsal fin are diagnostic. Many iridescent blue and gold spots all over, but local color variations are common. Shares burrow with blind symbiont alpheid shrimp.

FLAG-TAIL SHRIMP GOBY
Amblyeleotris yanoi

Distribution: Tropical Central Indo-Pacific from Bali in Indonesia to Papua New Guinea and Southern Japan.
Size: Up to 13 centimeters.
Habitat: Sand and fine rubble bottoms on slopes and in lagoons and sheltered bays from 3 to 40 meters deep.
Life Habits: Body white with five diffuse orange bars and spectacular, red and yellow flag-like tail. Replaced further West in the Indian Ocean by the very similar Sunrise Goby *A. aurora*. Shares burrow with symbiont alpheid shrimp *Alpheus randalli*.

SINGAPORE SHRIMP GOBY
Cryptocentrus singapurensis

Distribution: Tropical Asian Pacific from Malaysia and Indonesia to Australia and Southern Japan.
Size: Up to 12 centimeters.
Habitat: Silty bottoms in bays and sheltered areas from 1 to 10 meters deep.
Life Habits: Body pale tan, with several diffuse oblique darker bars and heavily marked with fluorescent green-edged, bright pink spots and stripes. Heavy-bodied, often near mangroves, always sharing burrow with commensal shrimp. Occasionally classified as *C. leptocephalus*.

YELLOW SHRIMP GOBY
Cryptocentrus cinctus

Distribution: Tropical Central Indo-Pacific from the Andamans to Micronesia and from Southern Japan to Australia.
Size: Up to 6 centimeters.
Habitat: Sand and silt bottoms in coastal reefs and lagoons from 2 to 15 meters.
Life Habits: Commonly observed in two color phases, a bright golden one with several small fluorescent blue spots (illustrated) and a dark brown one, spotted in white and fluorescent blue. Locally very common and often observed in loose aggregations, it shares its burrow with one or more alpheid shrimps.

BLACK SHRIMP GOBY
Cryptocentrus fasciatus

Distribution: Tropical Indo-Pacific from the Red Sea to the Solomons and the Great Barrier Reef in Australia.
Size: Up to 10 centimeters.
Habitat: Sand and silt bottoms in sheltered areas on coastal reefs and lagoons from 2 to 15 meters deep.
Life Habits: Generally pale with four brown irregular bars but locally variable: head often scribbled in orange or pale blue. Rather nondescript, often observed in pairs sharing their burrow with one or more commensal alpheid shrimps.

MAROON SHRIMP GOBY
Cryptocentrus inexplicatus

Distribution: Tropical Central Indo-Pacific from Malaysia and Indonesia to Micronesia and Southern Japan.
Size: Up to 7 centimeters.
Habitat: Coarse sand and rubble bottoms in sheltered reefs from 1 to 5 meters.
Life Habits: Body pale grey or whitish with undefined darker saddles and bars, face mostly white: rather drab and nondescript. Often observed in pairs, sharing burrow with one or two commensal alpheid shrimps.

DANCING SHRIMP GOBY
Lotilia graciliosa

Distribution: Tropical Indo-Pacific from the Red Sea to Fiji and from Southern Japan to Australia.
Size: Up to 4 centimeters.
Habitat: Fine sand or silty bottoms, often on reef faces, from 5 to 40 meters deep.
Life Habits: Very unusual, commonly misidentified shrimp goby: undulating movements and sharply disruptive coloration (white back, black or dark brown body, spotted fins) easily confuse the observer. Usually found alone, sharing its burrow with blind commensal shrimp.

CRAB-EYE GOBY
Signigobius biocellatus

Distribution: Tropical Central Indo-Pacific from Malaysia and Indonesia to Micronesia and the Great Barrier Reef.
Size: Up to 11 centimeters.
Habitat: Coral rubble or fine silt bottoms, often along the base of sheltered coastal reefs, from 2 to 30 meters deep.
Life Habits: Body pale tan with brown mottling, two black and yellow "eyes" on dorsal fins, ventral and anal fins black with blue spots. Mimics a crab "hopping" sideways. Commonly observed in pairs, often sharing burrow dug in substrate. A fascinating and not uncommon species.

BLACK-RAY SHRIMP GOBY
Stonogobiops nematodes

Distribution: Tropical Western Indo-Pacific from Indonesia to Samoa and from Southern Japan to Australia.
Size: Up to 6 centimeters.
Habitat: Coral rubble and sand bottoms in current-swept areas on outer reef flats from 10 to 40 meters deep.
Life Habits: White with bright yellow head and four broad dark brown to black bars; very long black-edged first ray of dorsal fin. Usually observed in pairs, hovering on top of burrow they share with blind commensal shrimp *Alpheus randalli*.

BLACK-RAY FIN GOBY
Stonogobiops xanthorhinica

Distribution: Tropical Central Indo-Pacific from Malaysia and Indonesia to Southern Japan and Australia.
Size: Up to 6 centimeters.
Habitat: Coral rubble flats in current-swept areas on outer reefs from 10 to 50 meters deep.
Life Habits: Very similar to preceding species but with hooked - not filamented - tip of first dorsal fin. Replaced further West in the Indian Ocean by the almost identical Dracula Shrimp Goby *S. dracula*. Very shy like all its conspecifics.

SMILING SHRIMP GOBY
Mahidolia mystacina

Distribution: Tropical Indo-Pacific from East Africa to French Polynesia and from Southern Japan to Australia.
Size: Up to 10 centimeters.
Habitat: Coral rubble, sand and mud bottoms in lagoons and sheltered reefs from 5 to 25 meters deep.
Life Habits: Commonly observed in two distinct color phases, grey with brown bands or, more often, golden yellow with darker bands. In both cases large flag-like striped first dorsal fin is diagnostic. Shares burrow with commensal blind alpheid shrimp.

BLACK SAILFIN GOBY
Flabelligobius sp.

Distribution: Unknown, at the moment documented from Indonesia and Malaysia to Southern Japan.
Size: Up to 10 centimeters.
Habitat: Coral rubble or fine sand bottoms in current-prone areas on coastal reef flats from 15 to 60 meters deep.
Life Habits: Spectacular but still undescribed shrimp goby, sporting an enormous dorsal fin mottled in browns and golden yellows on a dark brown, white-speckled body. Tube nostrils and bright electric blue lines on ventral, anal and caudal fins are noteworthy too.

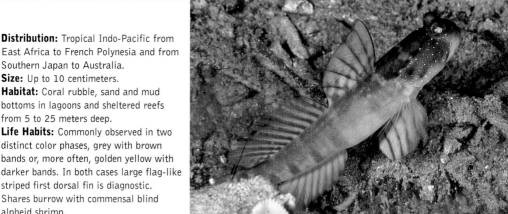

FAN SHRIMP GOBY
Tomiyamichthys oni

Distribution: Tropical Central Indo-Pacific from the Andamans to Micronesia and Southern Japan.
Size: Up to 10 centimeters.
Habitat: Rubble, sand and silt slopes on coastal reefs from 10 to 30 meters deep.
Life Habits: Generally mottled in drab, brownish colors but with large, spotted first dorsal fin usually kept erect. Often observed alone in current-prone areas, sharing its burrow with commensal shrimp. Replaced further West - from the Red Sea to the Western Indian Ocean - by the almost identical *Flabelligobius latruncularius*.

RAY-FIN GOBY
Tomiyamichthys sp.

Distribution: Unknown but documented from Kalimantan in Indonesia and Sabah in Malaysian Borneo.
Size: Up to 7 centimeters.
Habitat: Coral rubble bottoms on sheltered coastal reefs from 5 to 40 meters deep.
Life Habits: Body dark brown frontally and white with darker mottles on the rear; spectacular, filamented first dorsal fin showing bright blue spot on the rear. Extremely well camouflaged, occasionally observed in pairs hovering above burrow shared with blind commensal shrimp. Still scientifically undescribed.

FULL-MOON REEF GOBY
Priolepis nocturna

Distribution: Tropical Indo-Pacific from East Africa to Papua New Guinea and French Polynesia.
Size: Up to 4.5 centimeters.
Habitat: Under coral heads on sand bottoms and ledges on outer and coastal reefs from 5 to 30 meters deep .
Life Habits: Bright white or grey with black or dark brown banding. Solitary, very cryptic and always well hidden under coral heads and inside small crevices, probably not uncommon in the area but rarely observed and even less photographed by divers.

BANDED REEF GOBY
Priolepis cincta

Distribution: Tropical Indo-Pacific from East Africa to Micronesia and Hawai'i.
Size: Up to 7 centimeters.
Habitat: Under ledges and overhangs on coastal and outer reefs from 2 to 70 meters deep.
Life Habits: Body greenish gold with pale thin bars. Occasionally observed hanging on the roof of overhangs and ledges or inside large barrel sponges. Several very similar species, all banded and all belonging to the same Genus.

ORANGE REEF GOBY
Priolepis sp.

Distribution: Northern Sulawesi in Indonesia.
Size: Up to 4 centimeters.
Habitat: Inside sponges or under overhangs in silty coastal habitats from 2 to 30 meters deep.
Life Habits: Body bright orange with darker banding on the front. Apparently undescribed, often observed in pairs inside old discarded coconut husks. Distribution very localized: the specimen illustrated was photographed in the Lembeh Strait of Northern Sulawesi, Indonesia.

RED-LINED PYGMY GOBY
Trimma striatum

Distribution: Tropical Indo-Pacific from the Maldives to Papua New Guinea.
Size: Up to 3.5 centimeters.
Habitat: Inside caves or under overhangs in lagoons and coastal reefs from 10 to 30 meters deep.
Life Habits: Body purplish with clearly visible red stripes on head; often observed hanging upside down on the reef of caves or inside large barrel sponges. Usually encountered in small loose aggregations. Feeds on small benthic invertebrates.

RED PYGMY GOBY
Trimma naudei

Distribution: Tropical Indo-West Pacific from the Seychelles to New Caledonia and Southern Japan.
Size: Up to 3.5 centimeters.
Habitat: Inside caves, under ledges or overhangs on coastal reefs from 5 to 30 meters deep.
Life Habits: Body white or yellow almost completely covered in large, irregular, bright red spots. Commonly observed perching in the open, resting upside down on the roof of caves or under overhangs. Feeds on small benthic invertebrates like all pygmy gobies.

ORANGE-SPOTTED PYGMY GOBY
Trimma flammeum

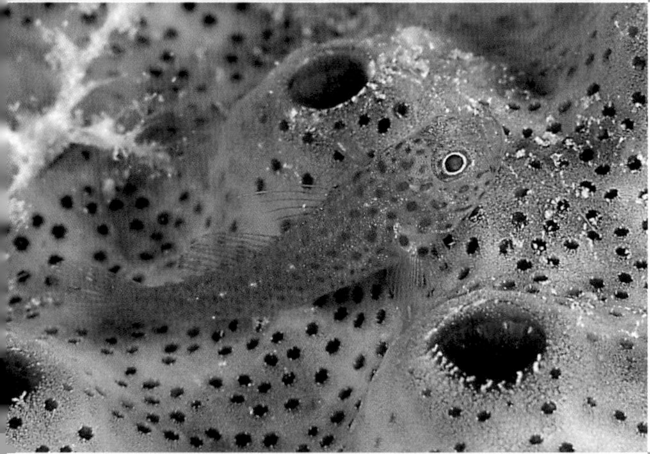

Distribution: Tropical Central Indo-Pacific from Malaysia and Indonesia to Papua New Guinea.
Size: Up to 3 centimeters.
Habitat: On or inside sponges in coral rich environments on coastal and outer reefs from 10 to 30 meters deep.
Life Habits: Body semi-transparent beautifully spotted in bright red or orange; several similar species with overlapping ranges still waiting to be described. Usually perched inside sponges, waiting for food (mostly benthic invertebrates and zooplankton) to drift by.

CAVE PYGMY GOBY
Trimma caudomaculatum

Distribution: Tropical Indo-Pacific from the Red Sea to Micronesia, Southern Japan and Australia.
Size: Up to 3 centimeters.
Habitat: Inside caves and deep dark crevices on coastal and outer reefs from 10 to 50 meters deep.
Life Habits: Body golden orange with a bright white longitudinal stripe; deep purple band preceded by a white one on caudal peduncle. Commonly encountered in loose aggregations inside caves, normally hovering upside down in mid-water. Extremely wary.

RED-BLOTCHED PYGMY GOBY
Eviota melasma

Distribution: Tropical Central Indo-Pacific from Cocos-Keeling to Samoa, Southern Japan and Australia.
Size: Up to 2 centimeters.
Habitat: Coastal and outer coral reefs from 5 to 15 meters deep.
Life Habits: Body semi-transparent spotted in red, eyes bright yellow. Easily confused with many other similar species in the general distribution area. Commonly observed perching in the open on sponges or coral heads, waiting for zooplankton or tiny benthic invertebrates to drift by and surveying its territory.

SEBREE'S PYGMY GOBY
Eviota seebrei

Distribution: Tropical Indo-Pacific from the Red Sea to Micronesia and from Southern Japan to Australia.
Size: Up to 2 centimeters.
Habitat: Coastal and outer reefs from 1 to 15 meters deep.
Life Habits: Body translucent/brown with string-of-pearls golden spots on the sides. Very common, usually observed in small loose aggregations perching on large *Porites* coral heads in sunlit areas. Several adults and small juveniles often encountered on the same coral head.

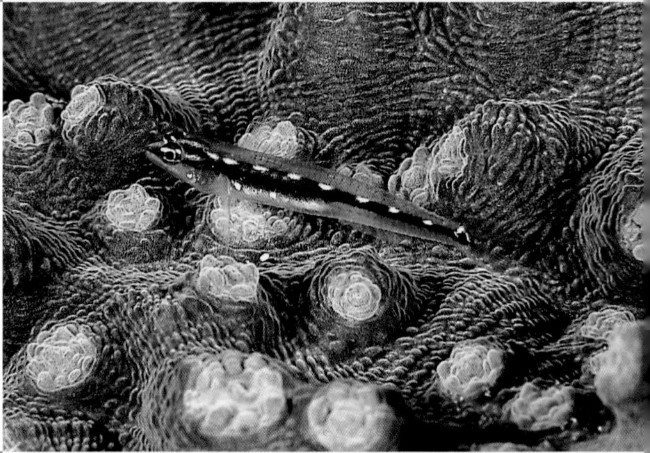

WHITE-SPOTTED PYGMY GOBY
Eviota zebrina

Distribution: Tropical Central Indo-Pacific from Indonesia to New Caledonia and from Southern Japan to Australia.
Size: Up to 2 centimeters.
Habitat: Sheltered rubble areas in coastal reefs from 10 to 50 meters deep.
Life Habits: White and wine-red spots on a generally translucent body; many similar species in the same area. Locally common, usually perching in the open and surveying its clarly defined territory. Sometimes described as *E. prasites*.

PINK-LINED REEF GOBY
Bryaninops erythrops

Distribution: Tropical Indo-Pacific from the Red Sea to Southern Japan and the Great Barrier Reef in Australia.
Size: Up to 1.5 centimeters.
Habitat: Rich coral growth in coastal and outer reefs from 5 to 15 meters deep.
Life Habits: Very small, best identified by the bright red or pink longitudinal stripe running on the sides of its transparent body. Commonly observed in small loose aggregations, perching in the open on large coral heads and waiting for some zooplankton to drift by.

PURPLE-EYED GOBY
Bryaninops natans

Distribution: Tropical Indo-Pacific from the Red Sea to Micronesia and from Southern Japan to Australia.
Size: Up to 2 centimeters.
Habitat: Rich coral growth in clear water from 5 to 20 meters deep.
Life Habits: Transparent body with bright golden belly and unmistakable, brilliant fuchsia eyes. Occasionally observed in small loose groups hovering a short distance above branching *Acropora* coral colonies, but due to its small size most often ignored by divers.

SEA-WHIP GOBY
Bryaninops yongei

Distribution: Tropical Indo-Pacific from the Red Sea to French Polynesia and from Southern Japan to Australia.
Size: Up to 4 centimeters.
Habitat: In association with *Cirrhipates* wire coral exclusively, in current-prone areas from 3 to 40 meters deep.
Life Habits: Body translucent with several darker saddles: one of a complex of several similar species, all living in a symbiotic association on wire, whip and black coral exclusively , usually in fairly deep water and in current-prone areas.

PEPPERMINT GOBY
Coryphopterus lipernes

Distribution: Western Atlantic Ocean in Florida and the Caribbean.
Size: Up to 2.5 centimeters.
Habitat: Rich coral areas on coastal and outer reefs from 10 to 40 meters deep.
Life Habits: Body yellow or golden, semi-transparent, faintly lined; head delicately lined in electric blue.Possibly the most colorful of Western Atlantic pygmy gobies, often observed in the Caribbean perching in the open on large coral heads, surveying its territory and waiting for some zooplankton to drift by.

SLENDER SPONGE GOBY
Pleurosicya elongata

Distribution: Tropical Central Indo-Pacific from Indonesia and Malaysia to Papua New Guinea and Australia.
Size: Up to 4 centimeters.
Habitat: Under floppy, leaf-like large sponges on sheltered coastal reefs from 2 to 10 meters deep.
Life Habits: Body large, flattened, semi-transparent but usually tinged in the same coloration of the leaf-like sponge the fish lives on. Often several individuals observed living together on the same host. Presumably feeds on zooplankton and small benthic invertebrates.

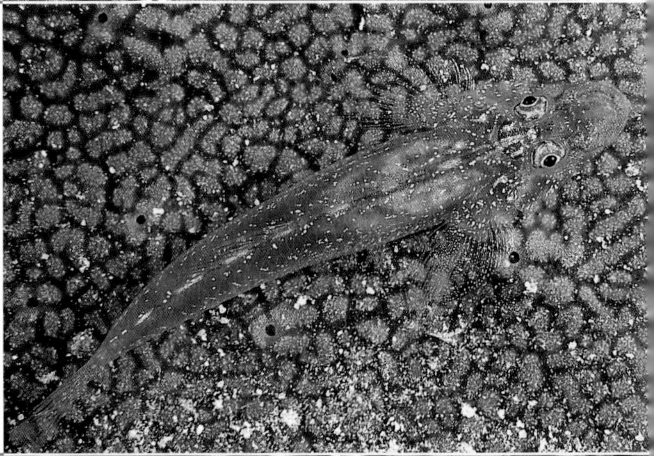

MANY-HOST GOBY
Pleurosicya mossambica

Distribution: Tropical Indo-Pacific from the Red Sea to French Polynesia and from Southern Japan to Australia.
Size: Up to 3 centimeters.
Habitat: In association with a variety of hosts on coastal and outer reefs from 3 to 30 meters deep.
Life Habits: The most commonly observed commensal goby species, easily found on soft corals, ascidians, sponges and gorgonians. Generally red or purple, with red eyes and white spots all over the body, but many local color variations.

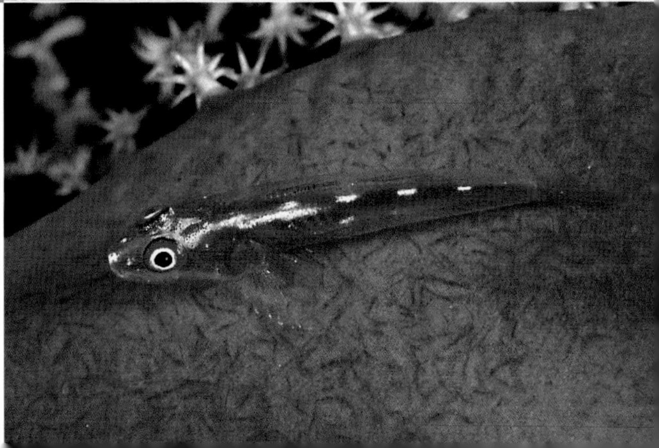

WHITE-SPOTTED SAND GOBY
Fusigobius neophytus

Distribution: Tropical Indo-Pacific from East Africa to French Polynesia and from Southern Japan to Australia.
Size: Up to 5.5 centimeters.
Habitat: Sand and rubble ledges inside caves or ledges from 5 to 50 meters deep.
Life Habits: One of the *Fusigobius* complex of species, described by some as *Coryphopterus*. All are benthic fish with a semi transparent body dotted in gold or brown, commonly observed in caves or under ledges, often displaying a more or less strongly marked first dorsal fin which is rythmically flicked up and down to mark their territory and attract females.

MUD REEF GOBY
Exyrias bellissimus

Distribution: Tropical Indo-Pacific from East Africa to Micronesia and from Southern Japan to Australia.
Size: Up to 20 centimeters.
Habitat: Silty or muddy bottoms in sheltered coastal reefs, mangrove forests and lagoons from 2 to 30 meters deep.
Life Habits: Large, usually observed while taking big mouthfuls of sand or silt to sift out particles of food. Body is greenish-brown with diffuse darker spots. Several similar species, all with large flag-like dorsal fins, mostly ignored by divers due to their choice of habitat.

BLACK-LINED MUD GOBY
Myersina nigrivirgata

Distribution: Tropical Central Indo-Pacific from Malaysia and Indonesia to the Philippines and Papua New Guinea.
Size: Up to 10 centimeters.
Habitat: Silty or muddy soft slopes in coastal waters from 10 to 30 meters.
Life Habits: Commonly observed in two sharply different color phases, pale tan or golden yellow, both however always with a darker longitudinal stripe. Often encountered in pairs or in loose aggregations but murky, rarely dived habitats make identification difficult.

PRETTY LAGOON GOBY
Oplopomus oplopomus

Distribution: Tropical Indo-Pacific from the Red Sea to French Polynesia and from Southern Japan to Australia.
Size: Up to 12 centimeters.
Habitat: Silty or sandy bottoms in sheltered bays and lagoons from 2 to 12 meters deep.
Life Habits: Thick-bodied, whitish with many small pearlescent blue, black and golden-yellow flecks all over, blue-edged black spot on first dorsal fin. Commonly encountered on fine sand or silt bottoms, often close to mangroves: lives alone or in pairs in burrows dug in the soft substrate.

WIDE-BARRED GOBY
Valenciennea wardii

Distribution: Tropical Indo-Pacific from the Red Sea and East Africa to Southern Japan and Australia.
Size: Up to 12 centimeters.
Habitat: On silt or mud bottoms in sheltered lagoons and coastal reefs from 10 to 35 meters deep.
Life Habits: Body whitish with three wide brown bars on sides and conspicuous pale-edged black spot on first dorsal fin; pearlescent blue streak on cheek. Rather uncommon, occasionally encountered in pairs on silty bottoms in fairly deep water. Very wary and not easily approached.

SIX-SPOT SLEEPER GOBY
Valenciennea sexguttata

Distribution: Tropical Indo-Pacific from the Red Sea to Micronesia and from Southern Japan to Australia.
Size: Up to 16 centimeters.
Habitat: Sand and silt bottoms at the base of coral bommies from 1 to 30 meters deep.
Life Habits: Body white or light grey with six pearlescent blue spots on cheek and a black spot on first dorsal fin. Locally common and easily approached, benthic like all conspecifics, often encountered in pairs or small loose aggregations.Lives in burrows.

GOLDEN-HEAD SLEEPER GOBY
Valenciennea strigata

Distribution: Tropical Indo-Pacific from East Africa to French Polynesia and from Southern Japan to Australia.
Size: Up to 20 centimeters.
Habitat: Reef crests and rubble bottoms from 6 to 30 meters deep.
Life Habits: Body white or very pale grey with bright yellow snout and fluorescent blue streak under eye. Commonly observed in close pairs sharing burrows, often hovering just above the substrate. Feeds taking mouthfuls of substrate and sifting food particles.

SMALL SLEEPER GOBY
Valenciennea parva

Distribution: Tropical Indo-Pacific from the Seychelles to Southern Japan and Australia.
Size: Up to 10 centimeters.
Habitat: Sand, silt and coral rubble bottoms from 5 to 25 meters deep.
Life Habits: White or pale grey with two longitudinal orange stripes on the sides: one of the least colorful species of its genus. Commonly observed in pairs, feeding on benthic organisms sifting mouthfuls of sand. Found in pairs or small groups, sharing burrows in the substrate.

YELLOWLIP SLEEPER GOBY
Valenciennea muralis

Distribution: Tropical Central Indo-Pacific from the Andamans to the Great Barrier Reef in Australia.
Size: Up to 15 centimeters.
Habitat: Coarse sand and silt bottoms in sheltered bays and lagoons on coastal reefs from 10 to 30 meters deep.
Life Habits: Pale grey with pink-orange longitudinal stripes on sides; yellow lip and black spot on first dorsal fin are diagnostic. Usually observed in pairs, sharing burrow dug in the soft substrate and methodically feeding on benthic organisms sifting mouthfuls of sand.

BLACK-LINED SLEEPER GOBY
Valenciennea helsdingeni

Distribution: Tropical Indo-Pacific from the Red Sea and East Africa to French Polynesia, Southern Japan and Australia.
Size: Up to 25 centimeters.
Habitat: Sand and coral rubble bottoms, often close to rich algal growth, from 10 to 40 meters deep.
Life Habits: Pale grey or white body with two well-defined red-brown longitudinal stripes; pale-edged black spot on first dorsal fin diagnostic. Usually encountered in pairs, sharing burrow dug in the soft substrate and sifting food particles from mouthfuls of sand.

GREEN-BAND SLEEPER GOBY
Valenciennea randalli

Distribution: Tropical Asian Pacific from Singapore to French Polynesia and Southern Japan.
Size: Up to 20 centimeters.
Habitat: Sand, silt or coral rubble flat bottoms from 10 to 30 meters, rarely deeper.
Life Habits: Body pale grey to mauve, diagnostic blue-green, orange-edged stripe on cheek. Occasionally observed in pairs, sifting mouthfuls of sand for particles of food and small benthic invertebrates. Lives in burrows dug in the soft substrate.

ORANGE-SPOTTED SLEEPER GOBY
Valenciennea puellaris

Distribution: Tropical Indo-Pacific from the Red Sea and East Africa to Micronesia, Southern Japan and Australia.
Size: Up to 15 centimeters.
Habitat: Silt and coral rubble bottoms from 3 to 30 meters deep.
Life Habits: Body white or very pale grey with double row of bright, well-defined orange spots on sides; pearlescent blue spots and stripes on cheeks. Commonly observed in pairs, sharing a burrow dug in the soft substrate.

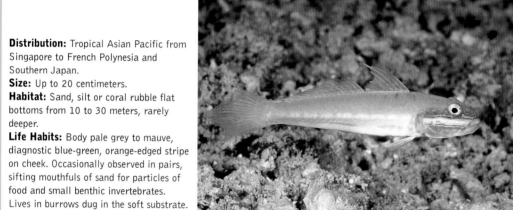

SPOTTED SHRIMP GOBY
Vanderhorstia ambanoro

Distribution: Tropical Indo-Pacific from East Africa to Southern Japan and Great Barrier Reef in Australia.
Size: Up to 12 centimeters.
Habitat: Silt or mud slopes in lagoons and bays from 10 to 40 meters deep.
Life Habits: Body pale, with dark blotches; many similar species sharing the same environment and habits. Usually encountered on soft silty bottoms, hovering about the entrance to its burrow, but generally ignored or unnoticed by divers. Pearlescent markings common to all murky habitat species are used for intraspecific communication.

ORNATE SHRIMP GOBY
Vanderhorstia ornatissima

Distribution: Tropical Indo-Pacific from East Africa to Southern Japan and Australia.
Size: Up to 9 centimeters.
Habitat: Mud and fine silt slopes in sheltered bays and lagoons on coastal reefs from 15 to 40 meters deep.
Life Habits: Pale body with numerous scattered blue-edged golden spots and streaks, long filamented first dorsal fin rays in males. Several undescribed very similar species in the same region, sharing similar habitats and life habits, all belonging to the same genus.

UNDESCRIBED SHRIMP GOBY
Vanderhorstia sp.

Distribution: Presently unknown but observed by the authors on several occasions in the Sulu Sea between Sabah and the Philippines.
Size: Up to 12 centimeters.
Habitat: Silt and mud slopes in coastal channels from 15 to 40 meters deep.
Life Habits: A very beautiful but still undescribed shrimp goby, clearly belonging to the *Vanderhorstia* genus. Muddy coastal habitats host many interesting and remarkably beautiful species which are still new to science.

YELLOW CORAL GOBY
Gobiodon okinawae

Distribution: Tropical Indo-Pacific from Cocos-Keeling to Micronesia, Southern Japan and the Great Barrier Reef.
Size: Up to 3 centimeters.
Habitat: Thickly branching corals on sheltered reefs from 1 to 15 meters.
Life Habits: Body thick-set and bright yellow; many similar species - generally yellow or red, often thinly banded - sharing the same habitat. Very secretive but often observed by attentive divers, living in colonies among branching or tabletop corals in shallow water.

MUDSKIPPER
Periophthalmus argentilineatus

Distribution: Tropical Indo-West Pacific from the Andamans to Micronesia.
Size: Up to 27 centimeters.
Habitat: Mangrove forests and mudflats.
Life Habits: The most commonly observed of several mudskipper species, often encountered on muddy banks of brackish mangrove estuaries. Able to survive for long periods out of water and in fact most often seen on shore, climbing on mangrove aerial roots; best identified by protruding frog-like eyes and sail-like dorsal fin. Very territorial, feeds on small littoral crustaceans and mollusks.

DART GOBIES
Microdesmidae

Very closely related to true gobies, this family numbers about 12 different genera grouping more than 45 species further divided in two subfamilies. Worm- or torpedo-shaped, these fish are usually very colorful and are often observed by divers hovering in pairs in the water column just above the entrance to their burrow. Most feed on zooplankton drifting by and are extremely shy, bolting down their burrow at the slightest sign of perceived danger. ~ **U/W Photo Tips:** Dart gobies are well known for their photogenic qualities and are not too difficult to get very close to if one has the necessary patience. A good idea with these - as with all very shy fishes like gobies in general - is to approach the chosen subjects in deeper waters, as the markedly lower temperature apparently makes them less responsive to approaching photographers and observers.

RED FIRE GOBY
Nemateleotris magnifica

Distribution: Tropical Indo-Pacific from East Africa to French Polynesia, Southern Japan and New Caledonia.
Size: Up to 7.5 centimeters.
Habitat: Sand or coral rubble bottoms on ledges in current-prone areas on outer and coastal reefs from 10 to 60 meters.
Life Habits: Yellow head, white front body fading to bright red on the rear, and long filamented first dorsal fin are diagnostic. Commonly observed alone or in pairs - sometimes in loose aggregations - hovering just above the substrate and its burrow entrance. Very shy: feeds on zooplankton in the water column.

PURPLE FIRE GOBY
Nemateleotris decora

Distribution: Tropical Indo-Pacific from East Africa to Micronesia, Southern Japan and New Caledonia.
Size: Up to 7.5 centimeters.
Habitat: Sand or coral rubble bottoms on ledges in clear water on outer reefs from 10 to 50 meters deep.
Life Habits: Body pale yellow with purple snout and red, blue-edged fins. Shares the same habitat of the preceding species but is usually encountered at greater depths. Usually observed alone or in pairs hovering in the water column just above the substrate. Very wary.

ARROW DART GOBY
Ptereleotris evides

Distribution: Tropical Indo-Pacific from Red Sea and East Africa to French Polynesia, Southern Japan and Australia.
Size: Up to 12 centimeters.
Habitat: Coral rubble bottoms in current-prone areas on outer reefs from 3 to 50 meters deep.
Life Habits: Body pearly grey in the front fading to blue-black on the rear; large median fins kept erect, forked tail diagnostic. Usually observed in pairs, hovering just above the substrate, always ready to bolt down their burrow if approached too rapidly or too closely.

SPLENDID DART GOBY
Ptereleotris grammica

Distribution: Tropical Central Indo-Pacific from Indonesia to Papua New Guinea, Southern Japan and Australia.
Size: Up to 10 centimeters.
Habitat: Sand or coral rubble bottoms in current-prone areas and deep water, usually from 40 to 60 meters.
Life Habits: Body pale grey or white with longitudinal metallic blue and yellow stripes; first dorsal fin large, usually kept erect, strongly marked in blue and gold. Beautifully marked but rarely observed by divers due to its deep-water habits.

TAIL-SPOT DART GOBY
Ptereleotris heteroptera

Distribution: Tropical Indo-Pacific from the Red Sea to French Polynesia, Southern Japan and Australia.
Size: Up to 10 centimeters.
Habitat: Sand and coral rubble flat bottoms from 5 to 50 meters deep.
Life Habits: Body pale or bright blue, tail yellow with black spot. Usually in pairs hovering above the substrate, juveniles sometimes in small loose aggregations. Several similar species belonging to the same genus widespread in the central Indo-Pacific area.

NEON WORM GOBY
Gunnellichthys curiosus

Distribution: Tropical Indo-Pacific from East Africa to French Polynesia, Hawai'i and the Great Barrier Reef in Australia.
Size: Up to 10 centimeters.
Habitat: Sand bottoms on outer reefs from 10 to 50 meters deep.
Life Habits: Body worm-like, blue-white with bright orange longitudinal stripe on side; black spot at the base of tail is diagnostic. At least three very similar species in the area: all are active, sinuous swimmers, often observed hovering in mid-water waiting for some zooplankton.

Rabbitfishes are grouped in a family numbering one single genus and about 30 species, all very similar in their habits. All have rather rounded bodies with a slightly protruding small snout and all feature very sharp and venomous spines in their pectoral fins. Rabbitfishes are phytophages, ie herbivorous, and - being rather common - are often encountered in large shoals close to seagrass areas. ~ **U/W Photo Tips:** Rabbitfishes are rather shy and will not let interested divers approach them too closely by day; at night however, when sleeping among the corals, their colors change or even fade completely. To get reasonably good shots one will have to be very patient and possibly use a medium focal length lens.

RABBITFISHES

Siganidae

SPOTTED RABBITFISH

Siganus punctatus

Distribution: Tropical Indo-West Pacific from Cocos-Keeling to New Caledonia.
Size: Up to 30 centimeters.
Habitat: Coastal and outer coral reefs from 1 to 40 meters deep.
Life Habits: Body pale brown or light blue with many very small, close-set brassy or orange spots. Often observed in large schools, feeding on algal growth in coastal and occasionally silty waters.

STARRY RABBITFISH

Siganus stellatus

Distribution: Indian Ocean from the Red Sea to the Andamans and Indonesia.
Size: Up to 35 centimeters.
Habitat: Coastal and outer reefs from 1 to 30 meters deep.
Life Habits: Very similar to preceding species - also intergrading with it in overlapping distribution areas - but with diagnostic white edging on caudal fin. The Red Sea population is recorded as having a yellow tail. Often encountered in pairs or in schools feeding on algal growth.

JAVA RABBITFISH
Siganus javus

Distribution: Tropical Indo-Pacific from the Arabian Gulf to Micronesia, Southern Japan and Australia.
Size: Up to 53 centimeters.
Habitat: Coastal reefs and brackish mangrove forests from 1 to 15 meters.
Life Habits: Body silvery with numerous bluish and dark grey scribbles and spots; yellow snout and median fins. Often observed in large schools in the water column, feeding on zooplankton and algal matter suspended in mid-water.

DOUBLE-BARRED RABBITFISH
Siganus virgatus

Distribution: Tropical Indo-Pacific from India to West Papua, Southern Japan and Australia.
Size: Up to 30 centimeters.
Habitat: Coastal reefs from 1 to 12 meters deep.
Life Habits: Body yellow above and white below with two faded blackish bars on head and numerous blue scribbles and spots all over. Often encountered in small schools in inshore, murky waters, feeding on algal matter and zooplankton suspended in the water column. Barred Rabbitfish *S. doliatus* is very similar..

MASKED RABBITFISH
Siganus puellus

Distribution: Tropical Indo-Pacific from Cocos-Keeling to New Caledonia.
Size: Up to 16 centimeters.
Habitat: Coastal and outer reefs with rich coral growth from 3 to 12 meters.
Life Habits: A true coral reef dweller, easily identified by the bright yellow body finely lined with pale blue vertical and horizontal lines; single black bar across eye is diagnostic. Feeds on sponges, tunicates and encrusting algal growth.

GOLDEN RABBITFISH
Siganus guttatus

Distribution: Tropical Indo-Pacific from the Andamans to West Papua and Southern Japan.
Size: Up to 35 centimeters.
Habitat: Coastal rocky reefs and mangroves from 1 to 25 meters deep.
Life Habits: Body pale grey with numerous round brassy-orange dots and a clarly visible, diagnostic bright yellow saddle at the base of the tail.Often encountered in stationary schools sheltering among corals. Lined Rabbitfish *S. lineatus* is very similar (but scribbled and not spotted) and is found from the Maldives to New Caledonia.

CORAL RABBITFISH
Siganus corallinus

Distribution: Tropical Indo-Pacific from the Seychelles to New Caledonia, Southern Japan and Australia.
Size: Up to 25 centimeters.
Habitat: Coral-rich coastal and outer reefs from 1 to 20 meters deep.
Life Habits: A truly reef-dwelling rabbitfish species, easily identified by the finely blue-spotted bright yellow or orange livery. Often observed in pairs, sheltering among *Acropora* table corals. Distribution area overlaps West with that of the very similar Blackeye Rabbitfish *S. puelloides*.

FOXFACE RABBITFISH
Siganus vulpinus

Distribution: Tropical Central Indo-Pacific from Indonesia to New Caledonia.
Size: Up to 24 centimeters.
Habitat: Coral-rich coastal and outer reefs from 1 to 30 meters deep.
Life Habits: Easily identified by the very long and protruding snout, the bright yellow body and the black and white, sharply defined "mask" on head. The similar Onespot Rabbitfish *S. unimaculatus* sports a black blotch on the side. Often observed in healthy coral reefs, commonly sheltering in pairs or small groups among staghorn colonies.

MOORISH IDOLS
Zanclidae

Often confused by novice divers with a butterflyfish, the Moorish Idol *Zanclus cornutus* belongs in fact to the monotypic family of *Zanclidae*, being more closely related to Rabbitfishes (*Siganidae*) and to Surgeonfishes (*Acanthuridae*) in general. However, this beautiful species lacks the venomous spines of the Rabbitfishes and the caudal "scalpels" of Surgeonfishes: it can be easily identified by the disc-shaped, compressed body, the protruding mouth, the barred livery and the greatly elongate dorsal fin ray. ~ **U/W Photo Tips:** Moorish Idols make spectacular subjects, both alone or in groups. They can be easily approached with the usual amount of caution and good sense, and will give their best if fully framed from the side. Excellent macro details are offered by the eyes and forehead also.

MOORISH IDOL
Zanclus cornutus

Distribution: Tropical Indo-Pacific from East Africa to the Galapagos and Mexico and from Southern Japan to Australia.
Size: Up to 16 centimeters.
Habitat: Walls, lagoons, slopes and drop-offs on coastal and outer reefs from 5 to 180 meters deep.
Life Habits: Easily identified by black, white and yellow broadly barred livery, long protruding snout and long, thin, trailing dorsal fin filament. Alone or more often in small and large aggregations, feeding on sponges and bryozoans.

SURGEONFISHES
Acanthuridae

A very important, conspicuous and large family, numbering more than 6 genera and about 70 species spreading from tropical to temperate seas. Most are distinguished by a laterally compressed, oval body and by the presence of two or more forward-facing, sometimes venomous sharp spines or "scalpels" (hence their common name) on the caudal peduncle, used in defense or intraspecific fighting. Most are gregarious herbivores, often integrating their diet with zooplankton, and regularly observed in large schools raiding the reef to graze on algae growing on dead coral. ~ **U/W Photo Tips:** Many surgeonfish are quite colorful and make very interesting subjects, especially when schooling. Most, however, are rather shy and will not allow a close approach except when being cleaned by wrasses.

BLUE TANG
Acanthurus coeruleus

Distribution: Western Atlantic Ocean from New York to Florida, the Caribbean, Bermuda and Brazil.
Size: Up to 20 centimeters.
Habitat: Shallow reef flats and crests from 3 to 18 meters deep.
Life Habits: Body blue overall, with yellow spine at the base of the tail; can darken or lighten up dramatically. Juveniles bright yellow. Often observed grazing on algae in thick schools, occasionally mixing with other species. The most commonly observed surgeonfish in Western Atlantic tropical waters.

ORANGEBAND SURGEONFISH
Acanthurus olivaceus

Distribution: Tropical Indo-Pacific from Cocos-Keeling to French Polynesia and from Southern Japan to Australia.
Size: Up to 35 centimeters.
Habitat: Sand botoms on coastal and outer reefs from 3 to 45 meters deep.
Life Habits: Extremely variable, can switch background body color from dark olive to tan to dark blue in a few seconds; blue-edged elliptical orange blotch behind eye is however always present and diagnostic. Commonly observed alone or in schools grazing on algae growing on sand bottoms among coral heads.

MIMIC SURGEONFISH
Acanthurus pyroferus

Distribution: Tropical Pacific from Indonesia and the Philippines to New Caledonia and from Southern Japan to the Great Barrier Reef in Australia.
Size: Up to 25 centimeters.
Habitat: Coastal reefs and lagoons from 4 to 60 meters deep.
Life Habits: Very variable, able to switch from olive to brown to yellow in a few seconds; yellow-edged tail and bright orange blotch at the base of the pectoral fin are diagnostic. Locally common, usually solitary or in very spread-out groups grazing on algae on sand or rocks.

WHITECHEEK SURGEONFISH
Acanthurus nigricans

Distribution: Tropical Indo-Pacific from Indonesia to Hawai'i and from Southern Japan to the Great Barrier Reef.
Size: Up to 21 centimeters.
Habitat: In surge areas, gutters and channels or coastal or outer reefs from 1 to 40 meters deep.
Life Habits: Body ranging from dark brown to velvety deep blue to black with yellow-striped white tail, yellow-based median fins, yellow tail spine and diagnostic white patch below eye. Often observed in schools, grazing on bottom-growing algae in surge areas and exposed parts of the reef like gutters or channels.

POWDERBLUE SURGEONFISH
Acanthurus leucosternon

Distribution: Indian Ocean from East Africa to Sumatra and Bali in Indonesia.
Size: Up to 38 centimeters.
Habitat: Outer reef flats and crests from 1 to 25 meters deep.
Life Habits: Unmistakable: body bright blue with black face, white throat, tail and ventral fin, and bright yellow dorsal fin. Commonly encountered - especially in the Maldives - in shallow water and in very large schools, often mixing with other surgeonfish species. Replaced further East by the very similar Japanese Surgeonfish *A. japonicus* (see below).

JAPANESE SURGEONFISH
Acanthurus japonicus

Distribution: Tropical Asian Pacific from Indonesia to Southern Japan.
Size: Up to 21 centimeters.
Habitat: Lagoons and outer reef crests in clear water from 2 to 12 meters deep.
Life Habits: Very similar to the preceding species but suffused with yellow on rear body and with orange stripe on black median fins. Snout is also white rather than black. Occasionally observed in large schools, grazing on algae and raiding damselfishes' algal "orchards".

YELLOWMASK SURGEONFISH

Acanthurus mata

Distribution: Tropical Indo-Pacific from the Red Sea to French Polynesia and from Southern Japan to the Great Barrier Reef.
Size: Up to 50 centimeters.
Habitat: Coastal and outer reefs, often in turbid waters, from 5 to 30 meters deep.
Life Habits: Large, slender: body pale blue with many thin darker blue to yellow longitudinal stripes and a clearly visible yellow "mask" on the eye. Often ecountered in large schools feeding on zooplankton in the water column on coastal reefs and around estuaries.

BLACKSTREAK SURGEONFISH

Acanthurus nigricauda

Distribution: Tropical Indo-Pacific from East Africa to French Polynesia and from Southern Japan to Australia.
Size: Up to 40 centimeters.
Habitat: On sand bottoms in coastal and outer reefs or lagoons from 3 to 30 meters deep.
Life Habits: Body pale grey or brown, caudal fin strongly lunate, black elongated patch behing eye always present and diagnostic; another dark streak marking position of caudal spine. Solitary or in small aggregations, often encountered grazing algae on sand bottoms among rocky outcrops or coral heads.

YELLOWFIN SURGEONFISH

Acanthurus xanthopterus

Distribution: Tropical Indo-Pacific from East Africa to Mexico and from Southern Japan to Australia and New Caledonia.
Size: Up to 56 centimeters.
Habitat: Coastal and outer reefs and drop-offs from 10 to 100 meters deep.
Life Habits: The largest surgeonfish. Body pale blue, pale yellow or pale brown with yellowish pectoral fins and yellow patch through eye; white band on tail base. Solitary or in small groups, occasionally observed feeding on the bottom, grazing on algal matter.

WHITETAIL SURGEONFISH
Acanthurus thompsonii

Distribution: Tropical Indo-Pacific from East Africa to Hawai'i and from Southern Japan to Australia.
Size: Up to 27 centimeters.
Habitat: Outer reefs and drop-offs from 5 to 75 meters deep.
Life Habits: White tail, body from black-brown to pale grey in a matter of seconds. Generally observed in large spread-out schools, feeding on zooplankton suspended in the water column, in front of steep slopes and drop-offs on outer reefs.

STRIPED SURGEONFISH
Acanthurus lineatus

Distribution: Tropical Indo-Pacific from East Africa to French Polynesia and from Southern Japan to New Caledonia.
Size: Up to 38 centimeters.
Habitat: Reef tops and crests on outer and coastal reefs from 1 to 5 meters.
Life Habits: Unmistakable and truly beautiful: body yellow, longitudinally striped in black-edged bright blue stripes, white belly. Territorial, solitary and very aggressive towards other surgeonfishes and occasionally even trespassing divers. Commonly observed in surge areas and on very shallow reef crests and flat tops.

PALETTE SURGEONFISH
Paracanthurus hepatus

Distribution: Tropical Indo-Pacific from East Africa to Micronesia and from Southern Japan to Australia.
Size: Up to 30 centimeters.
Habitat: Current-swept crests on outer reefs from 2 to 25 meters deep.
Life Habits: Unmistakable: body bright blue with diagnostic pincer-like sweeping black marking, tail bright yellow. One of the most beautiful of all surgeonfishes, occasionally observed alone or in spread-out small groups in current-prone areas and shallow water on flat reef crests.

BRUSHTAIL TANG
Zebrasoma scopas

Distribution: Tropical Indo-Pacific from East Africa to French Polynesia and from Southern Japan to the Great Barrier Reef.
Size: Up to 20 centimeters.
Habitat: Coastal and outer reefs, lagoons from 5 to 50 meters deep.
Life Habits: Body pale brown fading into black towards rear. Juvenile (illustrated) golden brown with several bright blue dots and stripes all over. Alone or in small loose aggregations, often observed feeding on algal growth on reef tops.

PACIFIC SAILFIN TANG
Zebrasoma veliferum

Distribution: Tropical Pacific from Indonesia to French Polynesia and from Southern Japan to Australia.
Size: Up to 40 centimeters.
Habitat: Lagoons, coastal and outer reefs among corals from 2 to 45 meters deep.
Life Habits: Spectacular, apparently oval shaped thanks to more or less permanently spread-out median fins; body with brown and grey bands finely striped in yellow and blue. Head finely spotted in yellow. Often observed feeding on algae among corals. Can be distinguished by the sibling following species - replacing it in the Indian Ocean - by the unmarked tail.

INDIAN SAILFIN TANG
Zebrasoma desjardinii

Distribution: Indian Ocean from the Red Sea and East Africa to the Andamans and Sumatra in Indonesia.
Size: Up to 40 centimeters.
Habitat: Coral-rich areas on coastal and outer reefs from 3 to 30 meters deep.
Life Habits: Almost identical - and similarly beautiful - to the preceding species, from which it can be separated by the range of its geographical distribution and by the blue-spotted tail. Occasionally observed alone or in small groups feeding on algal matter among coral growth.

LINED BRISTLETOOTH
Ctenochaetus striatus

Distribution: Tropical Indo-Pacific from East Africa to French Polynesia and from Southern Japan to Australia.
Size: Up to 26 centimeters.
Habitat: Lagoons, coastal and outer reefs from 2 to 35 meters deep.
Life Habits: Body olive or brown with several fine longitudinal blue stripes. Solitary or in loose aggregations but usually extremely common everywhere and almost always visible on any coral reef. Feeds on algae it scrapes off rocks and dead coral thanks to its bristle-like teeth, common to all surgeonfishes.

BLUESPOTTED BRISTLETOOTH
Ctenochaetus marginatus

Distribution: Central and Eastern Pacific from Micronesia to French Polynesia and Central America.
Size: Up to 25 centimeters.
Habitat: Surge zone and current-prone areas in shallow water on exposed reefs from 2 to 10 meters deep.
Life Habits: Body bluish-brown finely dotted in luminous white, steeply sloping forehead, thick fleshy lips. Occasionally observed in pairs or in small groups in surge areas, scraping off algal growth from rocks and dead corals.

ORANGETIP BRISTLETOOTH
Ctenochaetus tominiensis

Distribution: Tropical Central Indo-Pacific from Indonesia to Micronesia.
Size: Up to 15 centimeters.
Habitat: Lagoons and outer reef slopes from 5 to 40 meters deep.
Life Habits: Unmistakable: body pale brown with clearly visible orange-yellow outer edge of dorsal and anal fins and bright white tail. Occasionally observed alone or in small loose aggregations in coral-rich areas, feeding on algal matter it scapes off dead corals and rocks.

BARRED UNICORNFISH
Naso thynnoides

Distribution: Tropical Indo-Pacific from East Africa to Australia and Japan.
Size: Up to 30 centimeters.
Habitat: Outer reefs and lagoons from 3 to 30 meters deep.
Life Habits: Body a pale pearly gray, very "fish-like" in shape, with several vertical short blue-gray bars and a faint yellow stripe on the sides; eyes large and rather dark. Juveniles and sub-adults often observed in large, fast-swimming schools, feeding in the water column in close proximity to deep drop-offs.

BLUESPINE UNICORNFISH
Naso unicornis

Distribution: Tropical Indo-Pacific from the Red Sea and East Africa to Hawai'i and from Southern Japan to Australia.
Size: Up to 70 centimeters.
Habitat: Outer reefs and drop-offs from 1 to 80 meters deep.
Life Habits: Large, impressive unicornfish: body light olive (occasionally faintly striped) with blue, clearly visible tail spines; short horn on forehead does not overlap mouth. Tail with long filaments. Often observed in large, thick schools in front of slopes and drop-offs.

HUMPBACK UNICORNFISH
Naso brachycentron

Distribution: Tropical Indo-Pacific from East Africa to French Polynesia and from Southern Japan to Australia.
Size: Up to 60 centimeters.
Habitat: Outer reef slopes and drop-offs from 5 to 30 meters deep.
Life Habits: Blue-grey back, sharply separated pale belly, with clearly defined, strange-looking hump on back (which gives it a deformed look) and long, pointed horn projecting well over mouth in males; long filaments on caudal fin. Occasionally observed in small groups in front of slopes and drop-offs.

SPOTTED UNICORNFISH
Naso brevirostris

Distribution: Tropical Indo-Pacific from the Red Sea and East Africa to the Galapagos and from Southern Japan to the Great Barrier Reef in Australia.
Size: Up to 50 centimeters.
Habitat: Lagoons, coastal and outer reefs from 5 to 45 meters deep.
Life Habits: Body blue-grey or pale brown with several fine darker lines and scribbles; well-developed, broad-based horn projecting well over mouth. Commonly observed in small groups on drop-offs, feeding on zooplankton.

SLEEK UNICORNFISH
Naso hexacanthus

Distribution: Tropical Indo-Pacific from the Red Sea and East Africa to Hawai'i and from Southern Japan to Australia.
Size: Up to 75 centimeters.
Habitat: Drop-offs on outer reefs from 10 to 135 meters deep.
Life Habits: Body large, elongate, dark blue-grey on back and pale yellow on belly, but very variable and often entirely a pale powder blue; best identified by diagnostic dark diagonal stripe on gill cover. Commonly observed in very large schools, feeding on zooplankton in front of drop-offs and steep slopes.

HUMPNOSE UNICORNFISH
Naso tuberosus

Distribution: Tropical Indo-Pacific from East Africa to Micronesia and from Southern Japan to New Caledonia.
Size: Up to 60 centimeters.
Habitat: Outer reefs slopes and seamounts from 3 to 20 meters deep.
Life Habits: Strange-looking and peculiar body shape, with rounded bulbous snout and hump on mid-back. Body pale grey to yellowish; commonly observed in small groups, occasionally mixing with other unicornfish species. Rather uncommon anywhere in its range.

BIGNOSE UNICORNFISH
Naso vlamingii

Distribution: Tropical Indo-Pacific from East Africa to Galapagos and from Southern Japan to New Caledonia.
Size: Up to 50 centimeters.
Habitat: Outer reefs slopes and drop-offs from 4 to 50 meters deep.
Life Habits: A spectacular and unmistakable unicornfish species: body pale grey or blue with yellow head and anal fin, blue lines and spots all over, blue blotch in front of eyes. Tail very lunate and filamented. Can darken or lighten dramatically in a matter of seconds. Usually encountered alone on drop-offs, feeding on zooplankton in mid-water.

ORANGESPINE UNICORNFISH
Naso lituratus

Distribution: Tropical Indo-Pacific from the Red Sea and East Africa to Hawai'i and from Southern Japan to Australia.
Size: Up to 30 centimeters.
Habitat: Lagoons, coastal and outer reefs from 2 to 70 meters deep.
Life Habits: Body pale velvety grey with yellow anal fin, bright orange spots on tail spines, pale grey or white tail and complex black and yellow markings on snout. Commonly observed alone or more rarely in small groups feeding on algal matter in coral-rich areas and channels.

YELLOWTAIL SURGEONFISH
Prionurus punctatus

Distribution: Eastern Pacific.
Size: Up to 60 centimeters.
Habitat: Boulder-strewn slopes in surge areas on coastal and outer reefs from 1 to 30 meters deep.
Life Habits: Body blue-grey with clearly visible bright yellow tail and two blackish bars on paler snout. Often encountered in very thick schools in surge and current-prone areas in shallow water, feeding on algal matter it scrapes away from rocks and dead coral using its bristly teeth.

BARRACUDAS
Sphyraenidae

Barracudas are very powerful, streamlined predators grouped in a family comprising only one genus and about 20 species. Most are very difficult to differentiate underwater as the majority of species shares the same attributes of the family: a long streamlined silvery body with small median fins and a pike-like mouth with fearsome teeth. Often encountered in large schools, most barracudas are not dangerous to divers; the Great Barracuda *S. barracuda* however has been responsible of several documented, often deadly attacks on waders and snorkelers. ~ **U/W Photo Tips:** Barracudas are in general rather easily approached underwater. Some species - like the Great Barracuda - have in fact the rather disconcerting habit of swimming up close to divers and shadowing them during the dive. They are very reflective however, and this has to be taken into account when shooting. Caution! Never wear reflective objects whem swimming with barracudas, as this might provoke an attack.

GREAT BARRACUDA
Sphyraena barracuda

Distribution: Circumtropical.
Size: Up to 200 centimeters.
Habitat: Coral reefs and drop-offs from 1 to 15 meters deep.
Life Habits: Very large and impressive silvery torpedo-like body with large eyes and fanged jutting jaw; often scattered dark spots or faint bars on sides. Powerful, lightning-fast predator with a fearsome, very dangerous bite: will attack shiny reflective objects (jewels, bracelets) mistaking them for fish prey. Very inquisitive, will occasionally allow divers a close, cautious approach.

BIGEYE BARRACUDA
Sphyraena forsteri

Distribution: Tropical Indo-Pacific from East Africa to French Polynesia, Southern Japan and Australia.
Size: Up to 70 centimeters.
Habitat: Coastal and outer reefs from 10 to 300 meters deep.
Life Habits: Body silvery, elongated; head with large round eye and fanged protruding jaw. White-tipped darker rear dorsal fin is diagnostic. Usually encountered in stationary or drifting schools along drop-offs in daytime.

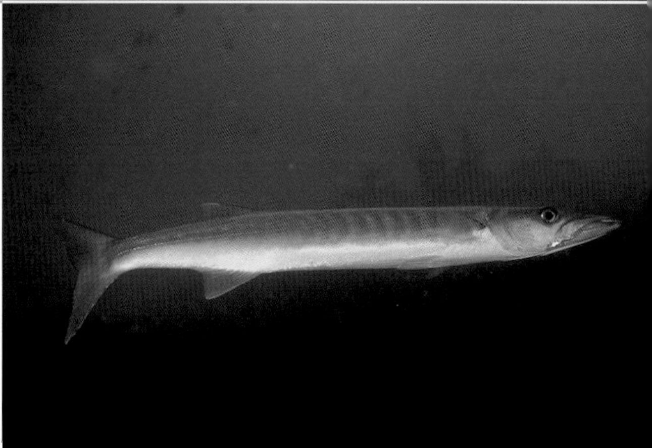

PICKHANDLE BARRACUDA
Sphyraena jello

Distribution: Tropical Indo-Pacific from East Africa to Fiji, Southern Japan and Australia.
Size: Up to 150 centimeters.
Habitat: Coastal and outer reefs from 1 to 60 meters deep.
Life Habits: Large, cylindrical silvery body with dusky fins, pointed head with large round eye and jutting jaw with pointed, sharp teeth. A row of about twenty bars often visible on upper side. Commonly encountered in large, tight-swimming schools drifting along drop-offs durinmg daytime. Locally very common.

BLACKFIN BARRACUDA
Sphyraena qenie

Distribution: Tropical Indo-Pacific from the Red Sea to Panama, Southern Japan and Australia.
Size: Up to 100 centimeters.
Habitat: Along slopes and drop-offs on outer reefs from 1 to 50 meters deep.
Life Habits: Elongated, powerful silvery body with about twenty darker chevrons on sides; long pointed head with large round eye and jutting jaw. Commonly observed in daytime schooling in large packs along seaward reefs drop-offs, presumably dispersing at night.

STRIPED BARRACUDA
Sphyraena helleri

Distribution: Tropical Indo-Pacific from East Africa to Hawai'i and from Southern Japan to Australia.
Size: Up to 90 centimeters.
Habitat: Lagoons, coastal and outer reefs from 1 to 60 meters deep.
Life Habits: Silvery, elongated body with a smoother "finish" compared to previous species; two brassy longitudinal stripes on side, long pointed head with large round eye and protruding jaw. Several very similar species in the same range. Commonly observed in large schools during daytime, dispersing at night.

TUNAS AND MACKERELS
Scombridae

A large family of great commercial interest to the fishing and canning industry, numbering about 15 genera and more than 50 species. These are the "roadsters" of the sea, with immensely strong bodies, powerful muscles, a very smooth, naked or finely scaled silvery skin and perfectly streamlined, pointed heads. Powerful, aggressive and exceptionally fast predators, several members of this family can in fact boast a body temperature several degrees higher than that of the surrounding water, ie they are "warm blooded" like mammals and a few sharks. Several species worldwide are severely threatened with extinction due to overfishing by commercial fleets. ~ **U/W Photo Tips:** Tunas and mackerels occasionally make fast, sweeping appearances along reefs, offering great opportunities for dramatic, ambient-light shots. Fast reflexes and a wide aperture are needed to obtain good photos - always keep an eye towards the open sea!

DOGTOOTH TUNA
Gymnosarda unicolor

Distribution: Tropical Indo-Pacific from the Red Sea and East Africa to French Polynesia, Southern Japan and Australia.
Size: Up to 180 centimeters.
Habitat: Drop-offs and slopes on outer reefs from 5 to 60 meters deep.
Life Habits: Genuinely impressive, occasionally terrifying large tuna: body steely-silvery, darker above, with great falcate tail and large mouth with clearly visible pointed teeth. Often encountered alone or in pairs raiding the reef from the blue, looking for trevallies. The most commonly observed tuna on tropical reefs.

SPANISH MACKEREL
Scomberomorus commerson

Distribution: Tropical Indo-Pacific from the Red Sea and East Africa to Southern Japan and Australia.
Size: Up to 230 centimeters.
Habitat: Pelagic, occasionally along slopes and drop-offs on outer reefs from 1 to 60 meters deep.
Life Habits: Very impressive, torpedo-shaped predator. Silvery-steely body marked with several wavy darker bars; pointed head, large round eye, great falcate tail. Usually alone, occasionally in small (3-12 individuals) roving schools coming from the blue and raiding the reef.

FLOUNDERS

Bothidae

Flounders belong to a very large family numbering about 15 genera and more than 100 species. These are very well camouflaged, rather oblong and exceptionally laterally compressed fishes, with their eyes positioned on the left side of their head. The upper side is very cryptic while the lower (right) is normally unpigmented. They are born as "normal" fishes but at a certain age the eyes move to the left side and they adopt a sideways way of life.Flounders are strictly benthic, living and feeding on small fishes and invertebrates without ever leaving the sea floor. They usually can be observed lying in the open on the bottom or hiding, half- or fully submerged in the soft substrate with only their eyes showing. ~ **U/W Photo Tips:** Flounders are very easy subjects once they've been sighted, and despite being generally ignored by divers and photographers alike they offer very interesting opportunities for macro.

PEACOCK FLOUNDER

Bothus mancus

Distribution: Tropical Indo-Pacific from the Red Sea and East Africa to Hawai'i, Southern Japan and Australia.
Size: Up to 45 centimeters.
Habitat: Sandy or rocky bottoms from 1 to 80 meters deep.
Life Habits: Pale green-grey with many blue spots and circles; males sport greatly elongate pectoral fin rays. Commonly observed lying in the open on sand or on bare rocks, confiding in its disruptive camouflage to avoid predation.

LEOPARD FLOUNDER

Bothus pantherinus

Distribution: Tropical Indo-Pacific from the Red Sea and East Africa to French Polynesia, Southern Japan and Australia.
Size: Up to 40 centimeters.
Habitat: Sand or silt bottoms from 2 to 250 meters deep.
Life Habits: Pale grey with many lighter, dark-edged spots and circles, often darker spot on the side towards the rear; male has elongate pectoral fin rays. Commonly observed on soft substrates, often half dug-in with only the eyes showing.

ANGLER FLATFISH
Asterorhombus fijiensis

Distribution: Tropical Indo-Pacific from East Africa to Southern Japan and the Great Barrier Reef in Australia.
Size: Up to 20 centimeters.
Habitat: Sand or silt bottoms near coral reefs from 1 to 30 meters deep.
Life Habits: Mottled in grey and brown, very well camouflaged; dark spots with pale reticulations on ocular side. This species sports a peculiar lure above the mouth, probably used to attract small unwary prey. Occasionally observed on sandy or silty bottoms near coral reefs.

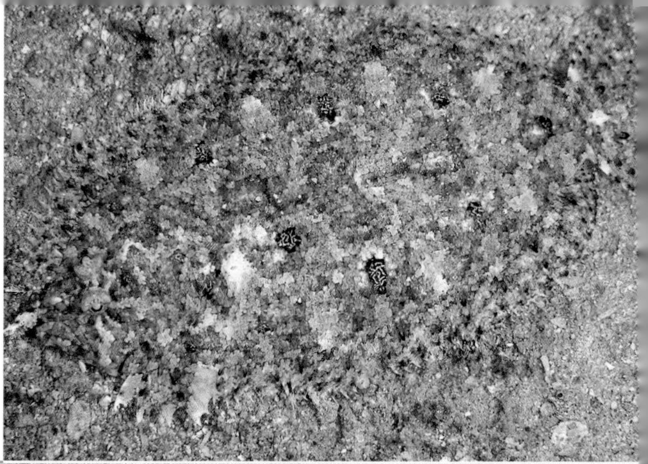

COCKATOO FLOUNDER
Samaris cristatus

Distribution: Tropical Central Indo-Pacific from Thailand to the Great Barrier Reef in Australia.
Size: Up to 23 centimeters.
Habitat: Sandy and silty bottoms on sheltered reefs from 5 to 70 meters deep.
Life Habits: Ocular side mottled in various shades of brown, apparently mimicking a large cuttlefish resting on sea bottom; suddenly spreads greatly elongate white dorsal fin rays in front of head when in danger, possibly mimicking sticky white cuverian tubules excreted in defense by holoturians when handled.

OCELLATED FLOUNDER
Pseudorhombus dupliciocellatus

Distribution: Tropical Central Indo-Pacific from the Andamans to Australia and Southern Japan.
Size: Up to 40 centimeters.
Habitat: Sandy and silty bottoms on coastal reefs from 5 to 150 meters deep.
Life Habits: Pale grey with brown spots, circles and mottling; dark brown eyes and paired dark spots inscripted in lighter circles on ocular side are diagnostic. Encountered on silty or sandy substrates on coastal reefs; feeds on small fish and benthic invertebrates like all flounders.

Soles can be quite easily distinguished by flounders as in these fishes the eyes are found on the right side of the body and not on the left. They are grouped in a large family numbering about 30 genera and more than 100 species, generally smaller than left-eyed flounders but equally well camouflaged and equipped for survival. Like flounders, soles are benthic fishes, feeding on small prey and generally spending most of their daily time half-submerged in the sandy or silty substrate with only their eyes showing. ~ **U/W Photo Tips:** As in the case of flounders, soles are generally ignored by divers and photographers, often escaping detection thanks to their exceptionally cryptic coloration. In fact, these are very interesting and easily approachable subjects, offering remarkable opportunities to macro.

SOLES
Soleidae

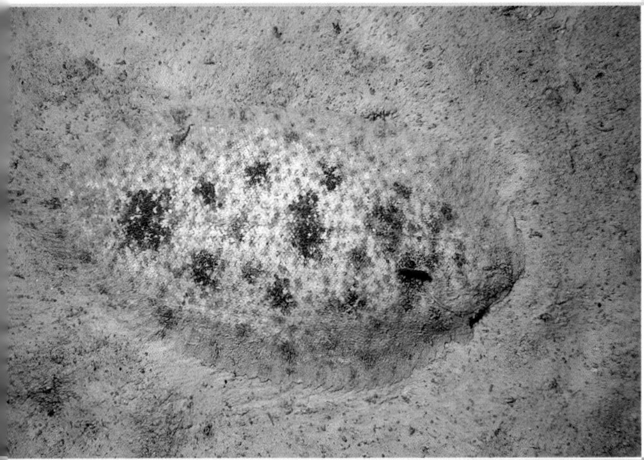

MARGINED SOLE
Synaptura marginata

Distribution: Tropical Indo-Pacific from East Africa to Indonesia and Japan.
Size: Up to 40 centimeters.
Habitat: Sand and silt bottoms in coastal waters from 2 to 50 meters deep.
Life Habits: Body large, pale grey or brownish with irregular darker blotches and white dusting all over. Occasionally observed on during daytime silty substrates, often semi-submerged in the sand with only the eyes emerging: feeds on small fish and benthic invertebrates, hunting in the open at dawn and dusk.

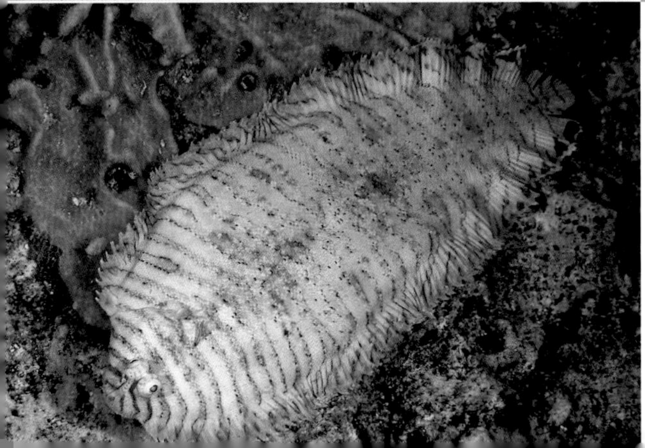

BANDED SOLE
Soleichthys heterorhinos

Distribution: Tropical Indo-Pacific from the Red Sea and East Africa to Micronesia and Southern Japan.
Size: Up to 15 centimeters.
Habitat: Sand and coral rubble bottoms from 1 to 20 meters deep.
Life Habits: Body elongate, pale, with several thin darker bands and sharp black margins on rear median and tail fins: glides on the substrate and occasionally swims in open water with an undulating motion reminiscent of a flatworm. Occasionally encountered at night.

PEACOCK SOLE
Pardachirus pavoninus

Distribution: Tropical Indo-Pacific from the Maldives to Micronesia, Southern Japan and Australia.
Size: Up to 22 centimeters.
Habitat: Sandy or silty bottoms on coastal reefs from 3 to 40 meters deep.
Life Habits: Body brown or reddish with many dark-edged yellowish or tan round spots, some with a darker centre. Like several other species of Soleidae, it can excrete a milky toxic secretion from specially evolved glands found at the base of the median fins to avoid predation.

TRIGGERFISHES
Balistidae

Triggerfishes are very conspicuous reef denizens, grouped in a large family numbering 12 genera and about 40 species. All are unmistakable large-headed, laterally-compressed fishes, featuring a two-part lockable fist dorsal fin and very strong teeth. Most are very colorful and distinctly patterned, being some of the most easily recognizable inhabitants of the reef; some species are quite territorial and will not hesitate in attacking divers, often pursuing them for relatively long distances and occasionally inflicting painful bites with their very strong jaws, which they normally use to feed on crustaceans, shellfish and sea urchins. ~ **U/W Photo Tips:** Triggerfishes are extremely interesting fishes, often showing a distinct personality and fascinating behavior. Rather unpredictable, they are usually rather wary, but can be closely approached when feeding or nesting. Beware of large marauding Titan Triggerfish males guarding their territory, as they can inflict painful bites.

QUEEN TRIGGERFISH
Balistes vetula

Distribution: Tropical Western Atlantic from Massachusetts to Bermuda, Florida, Caribbean, Gulf of Mexico and Brazil; also Eastern Atlantic.
Size: Up to 60 centimeters.
Habitat: Coral reef tops and slopes in clear water from 3 to 15 meters deep.
Life Habits: Large, in various shades of blue, turquoise and yellow; dark lines radiating from the eye and bright blue stripes across the snout. Beautiful but very shy, will not usually allow a close approach; feeds on sea urchins.

CLOWN TRIGGERFISH
Balistoides conspicillum

Distribution: Tropical Indo-Pacific from East Africa to Micronesia, Southern Japan and Australia.
Size: Up to 50 centimeters.
Habitat: Coral-rich coastal and outer reefs in clear water from 5 to 75 meters.
Life Habits: Spectacular and unmistakable, even at a distance: pale reticulated area on back, white-spotted black belly, yellow stripe across snout, orange-lipped mouth.Large and solitary, often observed among thick corals on healthy reefs. Rather common; possibly the most beautiful of all triggerfishes.

TITAN TRIGGERFISH
Balistoides viridescens

Distribution: Tropical Indo-Pacific from the Red Sea and East Africa to French Polynesia, Southern Japan and Australia.
Size: Up to 75 centimeters.
Habitat: Lagoons, coastal and outer reefs from 3 to 50 meters deep.
Life Habits: Large, impressive: body in shades of yellow-green with darker reticulations, pale throat, clearly visible very strong canine-like teeth. Very territorial, often extremely aggressive and absolutely fearless: will not hesitate in attacking divers entering its territory, Feeds on sea urchins and other hard-bodied benthic invertebrates.

BLUE TRIGGERFISH
Pseudobalistes fuscus

Distribution: Tropical Indo-Pacific from the Red Sea and East Africa to Micronesia, Southern Japan and the Great Barrier Reef in Australia.
Size: Up to 55 centimeters.
Habitat: Sand bottoms on coastal and outer reefs from 5 to 50 meters deep.
Life Habits: Large, blue to blue-grey, often with fine yellow vermiculations. Solitary, occasionally very aggressive, especially when nesting like preceding species. Feeds on sea urchins and other hard-shelled benthic invertebrates.
For the jouvenile form see page 218.

YELLOW-MARGIN TRIGGERFISH
Pseudobalistes flavimarginatus

Distribution: Tropical Indo-Pacific from the Red Sea and East Africa to French Polynesia, Southern Japan and Australia.
Size: Up to 60 centimeters.
Habitat: Coral rubble bottoms on coastal and outer reefs from 2 to 50 meters deep.
Life Habits: Body tan with darker crosshatches, rounded pinkish snout, orange tail. Solitary, locally common, occasionally observed nesting on coral rubble bottoms. Feeds on hard-bodied benthic invertebrates like sea urchins, shellfish and crustaceans.

STARRY TRIGGERFISH
Abalistes stellatus

Distribution: Tropical Indo-Pacific from the Red Sea and East Africa to Fiji, Southern Japan and Australia.
Size: Up to 60 centimeters.
Habitat: Silt, sand or coral rubble slopes on sheltered coastal reefs from 4 to 120 meters deep.
Life Habits: Body pale grey with yellow network, darker back with three or four white saddles. Solitary, occasionally observed in aggregations near reefs, especially in mating and courting season. Feeds on hard-bodied benthic invertebrates like sea urchins and crabs.

HALF-MOON TRIGGERFISH
Sufflamen chrysopterus

Distribution: Tropical Indo-Pacific from East Africa to Micronesia, Southern Japan and Australia.
Size: Up to 22 centimeters.
Habitat: Coastal and sheltered outer coral reefs from 2 to 30 meters deep.
Life Habits: Very variable, able to switch from dark brown to pale yellow in a few seconds; blue throat and yellow narrow vertical stripe below eye are diagnostic.Usually alone but often with several individuals in the vicinity, always close to the substrate. Feeds on small hard-bodied benthic invertebrates.

BOOMERANG TRIGGERFISH
Sufflamen bursa

Distribution: Tropical Indo-Pacific from East Africa to Hawai'i, Southern Japan and the Great Barrier Reef in Australia.
Size: Up to 24 centimeters.
Habitat: Sand or coral rubble bottoms on coastal and outer reefs from 3 to 90 meters deep.
Life Habits: Very variable, from pale grey to brown but always with variable boomerang-shaped marking below the eye going from dark brown to bright yellow-orange. Solitary but often with several individuals living on well-marked territories on the same patch of reef.

BROWN TRIGGERFISH
Sufflamen fraenatus

Distribution: Tropical Indo-Pacific from East Africa to Hawai'i, Southern Japan and Australia.
Size: Up to 35 centimeters.
Habitat: Sand and coral rubble bottoms on outer reefs from 8 to 180 meters deep.
Life Habits: Light to dark brown with no distinctive markings except faintly visible pale stripe on corner of the mouth. Extremely wary, will always keep a safe distance when approached by divers; probably the less commonly observed among reef triggerfishes.

STRIPED TRIGGERFISH
Balistapus undulatus

Distribution: Tropical Indo-Pacific from the Red Sea and East Africa to Hawai'i, Southern Japan and Australia.
Size: Up to 30 centimeters.
Habitat: Coral-rich areas on coastal and outer reefs from 2 to 50 meters deep.
Life Habits: Unmistakable: body green with many diagonal orange-yellow stripes. Solitary, rather common. Feeds on worms and benthic invertebrates like sea urchins, shellfish and crustaceans, but will take small fishes when the opportunity arises like all other triggerfishes. Males lack orange-yellow stripes on snout.

PICASSO TRIGGERFISH
Rhinecanthus aculeatus

Distribution: Tropical Indo-Pacific from East Africa to French Polynesia, Southern Japan and Australia.
Size: Up to 25 centimeters.
Habitat: Sheltered lagoons in shallow water from 1 to 4 meters deep.
Life Habits: Unmistakable, easily identified by combination of pale body and intersecting pale blue and dark red-brown diagonal stripes; sharp orange line on snout and blue bands over the eyes. Beautiful but rarely observed by divers as restricted to very shallow water on reef flats. Wary, will not allow close approach.

BLACKPATCH TRIGGERFISH
Rhinecanthus verrucosus

Distribution: Tropical Indo-Pacific from the Seychelles to Micronesia, Southern Japan and the Great Barrier Reef.
Size: Up to 23 centimeters.
Habitat: Shallow reef flats in sand and seagrass habitats from 1 to 20 meters.
Life Habits: Pale tan back, white belly, large round dark brown or black blotch on sides, red line on snout. Generally solitary and very territorial like most triggerfishes but rarely observed by divers as usually restricted to very shallow water in lagoons and on bare reef flats.

GILDED TRIGGERFISH
Xanthichthys auromarginatus

Distribution: Tropical Indo-Pacific from Mauritius to Hawai'i and Southern Japan.
Size: Up to 22 centimeters.
Habitat: Outer reef walls and drop-offs from 15 to 140 meters deep.
Life Habits: Body blue-grey with white-spotted scales, yellow margins on median and caudal fins and bright blue-violet patch on chin (in males only). Often observed in loose aggregations feeding on zooplankton in the water column along oceanic drop-offs, usually rather deep.

PADDLEFIN TRIGGERFISH
Melichthys vidua

Distribution: Tropical Indo-Pacific from East Africa to Galapagos and from Southern Japan to Australia.
Size: Up to 30 centimeters.
Habitat: Outer reefs in clear water from 4 to 60 meters deep.
Life Habits: Body from pale to very dark brown with white tail and black-edged white dorsal and anal fins; snout, eye and pectoral fin yellowish. Often observed in loose aggregations in the water column along slopes and drop-offs. Feeds on zooplankton, drifting algal matter and small benthic invertebrates.

EBONY TRIGGERFISH
Melichthys niger

Distribution: Circumtropical.
Size: Up to 35 centimeters.
Habitat: Outer reefs in clear water from 2 to 70 meters deep.
Life Habits: Body black to very dark blue with yellowish cheeks and a white stripe at the base of the dorsal and the anal fins. Solitary or in loose aggregations swimming in the water column; in the Red Sea and the Indian Ocean can be easily confused with the very similar Indian Triggerfish *M. indicus*. Feeds on zooplankton, drifting algal matter and small benthic invertebrates.

REDTOOTH TRIGGERFISH
Odonus niger

Distribution: Tropical Indo-Pacific from the Red Sea and East Africa to French Polynesia, Southern Japan and Australia.
Size: Up to 30 centimeters.
Habitat: Outer reefs slopes in clear water from 5 to 40 meters deep.
Life Habits: Body purple-blue with pale blue chin, red protruding teeth and deeply lunate tail. Often observed in enormous schools feeding on zooplankton in the water column along slopes on outer reefs. Very shy, will rapidly tuck inside tight-fitting holes when approached, leaving tail lobes sticking out. Extremely common.

FILEFISHES
Monacanthidae

Superficially similar to triggerfishes and also known in Australia as leatherjackets, these fish are grouped in a rather large family numbering about 30 genera and more than 100 species. Distinctly colored and shaped, filefishes are often very cryptic and slow-moving; their skin has no visible scales, rather resembling leather. Most can be easily identified by the long first ray of the dorsal fin, which is commonly kept erect and which can be locked in position. Filefishes are commonly observed near the substrate, where they generally feed on algal matter and small benthic invertebrates. ~ **U/W Photo Tips:** Easily approached (but some species are frustratingly shy, avoiding a close approach in any circumstance), filefishes are very interesting and generally amenable subjects.They give their best when squarely framed from the side, showing their peculiar liveries.

WEEDY FILEFISH
Chaetoderma penicilligera

Distribution: Central Tropical Indo-Pacific from Malaysia and Indonesia to Southern Japan and the Great Barrier Reef in Australia.
Size: Up to 30 centimeters.
Habitat: Sand and seagrass bottoms on sheltered coastal reefs from 2 to 30 meters deep.
Life Habits: Pale yellow-green with two or more dark blotches on the sides and an abundance of skin flaps resembling algae; slow-moving, very deliberate, always presenting side to the observer. Showy but also extremely well camouflaged.

LONGNOSE FILEFISH
Oxymonacanthus longirostris

Distribution: Tropical Indo-Pacific from East Africa to Micronesia, Southern Japan and Australia.
Size: Up to 10 centimeters.
Habitat: Coastal and outer reef tops in clear water from 1 to 35 meters deep.
Life Habits: Exceptionally colorful: body blue-green with many orange dots, elongated snout with small mouth. Often observed in pairs or in small close groups flitting around *Acropora* table corals, sometimes head-down, feeding on polyps and small invertebrates. Very wary, will not allow a close approach.

MIMIC FILEFISH
Paraluteres prionurus

Distribution: Tropical Indo-Pacific from East Africa to Micronesia, Southern Japan and Australia.
Size: Up to 10 centimeters.
Habitat: Among corals on outer reefs and walls from 2 to 25 meters deep.
Life Habits: Body white with brown or black saddles and fine scribbling on the sides: closely mimics the poisonous pufferfish *Canthigaster valentini*, with which it is easily confused. Commonly observed alone or in pairs among thick coral growth on reef tops and along walls.

BRISTLE-TAIL FILEFISH
Acreichthys tomentosum

Distribution: Tropical Indo-Pacific from East Africa to Fiji, Southern Japan and Australia.
Size: Up to 10 centimeters.
Habitat: Sand and seaweed bottoms on sheltered reefs from 1 to 15 meters deep.
Life Habits: Rhomboidal body mottled in brown, green and white; first ray of dorsal fin usually kept erect. Very cryptic, occasionally observed close to submerged artifacts like discarded nets or jetty pylons; completely green individuals are not uncommon on thick seagrass beds.

SPECTACLED FILEFISH
Cantherhines fronticinctus

Distribution: Tropical Indo-Pacific from East Africa to Micronesia, Papua New Guinea and Southern Japan.
Size: Up to 23 centimeters.
Habitat: Thick coral growth on outer reefs from 15 to 40 meters deep.
Life Habits: Body brownish or yellowish mottled in black, darker area around eye and diagnostic white band at the base of the tail. Solitary and rather wary, occasionally observed feeding among coral colonies but not easily approached.

WIRENET FILEFISH
Cantherines pardalis

Distribution: Tropical Indo-Pacific from the Red Sea to French Polynesia, Southern Japan and Australia.
Size: Up to 25 centimeters.
Habitat: Thick coral growth on outer reefs from 2 to 20 meters deep.
Life Habits: Body brownish or yellowish with pale blue netting and blue striping on snout; first ray of dorsal fin usually kept erect. Solitary, not easily approached; occasionally observed feeding among thick coral growth on seaward reef slopes.

WHITE-SPOTTED FILEFISH
Cantherhines macrocerus

Distribution: Tropical Western Atlantic from Florida to Bahamas, the Caribbean, Bermuda and Brazil.
Size: Up to 40 centimeters.
Habitat: On coastal and outer reef tops from 6 to 20 meters deep.
Life Habits: Body olive or grey on top and yellow to orange on sides and belly; tail dark, fins transparent with a yellowish tinge. Belly flap usually broadly extended; occasionally sports faded white spots all over. Large, not shy: often observed in pairs, will usually allow a fairly close approach. Feeds on benthic invertebrates.

BLACK-HEAD FILEFISH
Pervagor melanocephalus

Distribution: Central Tropical Indo-Pacific from Indonesia to Micronesia, Southern Japan and Australia.
Size: Up to 10 centimeters.
Habitat: Thick coral growth on coastal and outer reefs from 2 to 40 meters.
Life Habits: Head dark, often with a bluish tinge, body red or bright orange, red or orange tail. Very secretive and wary, occasionally observed among thick coral growth, often close to shelter. Orangetail Filefish *P. aspricaudus* in the same general area, very similar but with small black spots on head and front body.

BLACK-LINED FILEFISH
Pervagor nigrolineatus

Distribution: Central Tropical Indo-Pacific from Malaysia and Indonesia to Australia and the Solomons.
Size: Up to 10 centimeters.
Habitat: Thick coral growth on outer reefs and lagoons from 3 to 25 meters.
Life Habits: Body brown with diagnostic bright white stripe from snout to dorsal fin base; irregular thin white stripe often present across side. Secretive, very wary; occasionally observed alone or in pairs feeding on small benthic invertebrates and coral polyps among thick coral growth.

STRAPWEED FILEFISH
Pseudomonacanthus macrurus

Distribution: Central Tropical Indo-Pacific from Malaysia to the Philippines and Papua New Guinea.
Size: Up to 45 centimeters.
Habitat: Sand and seaweed bottoms on coastal reefs from 1 to 15 meters deep.
Life Habits: Body large, pale, mottled in greens and browns, with many small skin flaps; locally rather common but very cryptic, blending well with its chosen habitat. Feeds on benthic invertebrates. Solitary or in pairs, slow-moving, usually easily approached by divers.

SCRIBBLED FILEFISH
Aluterus scriptus

Distribution: Circumtropical.
Size: Up to 75 centimeters.
Habitat: Pelagic, often on coastal and outer reefs from 2 to 80 meters deep.
Life Habits: Body tan or grey with many black spots and several bright blue scribbles; becomes heavily mottled when resting or sleeping among corals. Usually solitary but also encountered in small groups along reef tops and slopes.Feeds on algal matter and invertebrates; long first dorsal fin ray often kept erect. Easily the most commonly observed filefish but usually wary and not easily approached.

BOXFISHES
Ostraciidae

These are very unusual and interesting fishes, grouped in a family which numbers about 6 genera and about 20 species. They can be easily identified underwater by their rigid body, made up of semi-fused but well defined hexagonal bony plates: a truly armored box-like strong casing with holes through which emerge the eyes, the mouth, the gills, the fins and the caudal peduncle. Despite an understandable lack of flexibility, boxfishes are surprisingly agile and can be quite fast swimmers; several species feature sharp horns above the eyes and at the corners of their "box". ~ **U/W Photo Tips:** Fascinating, often very colorful and strangely shaped subjects, boxfishes are usually quite difficult to get close to: always avoid a direct approach and trust their curiosity to let them get close to you. Never try chasing them, as they can be very fast and agile swimmers.

LONG-HORN COWFISH
Lactoria cornuta

Distribution: Tropical Indo-Pacific from the Red Sea to French Polynesia, Southern Japan and Australia.
Size: Up to 50 centimeters.
Habitat: Sand and seagrass bottoms on coastal reefs from 1 to 50 meters deep.
Life Habits: Body grey, olive or yellowish with several blue spots; long broom-like tail; a pair of long sharp horns above the eyes and another pair of shorter ones at the lower rear. Solitary, often observed blowing water on sand to uncover the small benthic prey it feeds on.

THORN-BACK COWFISH
Lactoria fornasini

Distribution: Tropical Indo-Pacific from East Africa to French Polynesia, Southern Japan and Australia.
Size: Up to 20 centimeters.
Habitat: Sand, silt, seaweed and rubble bottoms on sheltered coastal reefs and lagoons from 1 to 30 meters deep.
Life Habits: Body tan or yellowish with bright blue sribbles; paired short horns above the eyes and on rear lower end, one single diagnostic hooked thorn in the middle of the back. Solitary, often observed blowing water on substrate to uncover small benthic invertebrates.

BLACK BOXFISH
Ostracion meleagris

Distribution: Tropical Indo-Pacific from East Africa to Baja California and from Southern Japan to Australia.
Size: Up to 20 centimeters.
Habitat: Coastal and outer reefs from 2 to 30 meters deep.
Life Habits: Very colorful, unmistakable: back black with white spots, sides blue with yellow-orange dots. Commonly observed alone or in pairs: not rare but very wary. Often encountered among thick coral growth: will flee if approached but out of curiosity will often stop, turn and come back to take a peek if not harassed.

CUBE BOXFISH
Ostracion cubicus

Distribution: Tropical Indo-Pacific from the Red Sea and East Africa to French Polynesia, Southern Japan and New Zealand.
Size: Up to 45 centimeters.
Habitat: Coastal and outer reefs from 5 to 40 meters deep.
Life Habits: Large, brownish or purple with many faint darker spots; yellow crack-like lines are best for identification. Solitary, locally common; jewel-like beautiful juveniles (see page 217) are bright yellow with black spots. Like all boxfishes, this species may secrete a very toxic mucus from the skin if harassed.

SHORT-NOSE BOXFISH
Ostracion nasus

Distribution: Tropical Indo-Pacific from East Africa to Micronesia, Southern Japan and Australia.
Size: Up to 30 centimeters.
Habitat: Sand or rock bottoms on coastal reefs from 2 to 80 meters deep.
Life Habits: Body grey or greenish with many small black spots in clusters. Identification is difficult as this species is very similar to the Rhino Boxfish *Ostracion rhinorhynchus*, usually encountered in deeper water from 15 to 50 plus meters. May secrete a toxic mucus from the skin if harassed.

SOLOR BOXFISH
Ostracion solorensis

Distribution: Central Tropical Indo-Pacific from Indonesia to Papua New Guinea and from Southern Japan to the Great Barrier Reef in Australia.
Size: Up to 10 centimeters.
Habitat: Coral-rich areas on coastal and outer reef crests from 2 to 20 meters.
Life Habits: Back black with labyrinth-like light blue pattern, head and sides blue with black-edged white dots and scribbles. Solitary or in pairs, quite wary and not easily approached, usually observed close to some sort of shelter among the corals.

PUFFERFISHES
Tetraodontidae

So-called because of their ability to inflate themselves to deter predators, these curious fishes belong to a large family which numbers about 20 genera and more than 100 species divided in many groups and sub-families. Most are poisonous either externally (skin) or internally (body organs) and their consumption may prove fatal to fish and to man alike: some harmless species (ie Filefishes) take advantage of these properties mimicking at least one pufferfish to avoid predation. They are quite common and easily approachable, but should never be harassed just for the kick of seeing them inflate themselves, as this process puts a great strain on them. ~ **U/W Photo Tips:** Very easily approachable even if quite agile, pufferfishes are often quite colorful and make great subjects, especially at night when sleeping hidden among the corals. Resist the temptation to pet them however, as their teeth, fused in a sharp and exceptionally strong beak, are quite capable of severing a human finger.

SPOTTED PUFFERFISH
Arothron hispidus

Distribution: Tropical Indo-Pacific from the Red Sea and East Africa to Panama and from Southern Japan to Australia.
Size: Up to 50 centimeters.
Habitat: Coastal and outer reef crests and slopes from 1 to 50 meters deep.
Life Habits: Large, grey with bright white round spots and large black blotch at the base of the pectoral fin; yellow-orange eye. Teeth fused in sharp beak protruding and clearly visible: feeds on benthic invertebrates such as crustaceans and shellfish. Solitary and common.

RETICULATED PUFFERFISH
Arothron reticularis

Distribution: Tropical Central Indo-Pacific from India to Fiji and from Southern Japan to Australia.
Size: Up to 30 centimeters.
Habitat: Sand and silt bottoms in lagoons, mangroves and estuaries from 1 to 20 meters deep.
Life Habits: Brownish with white spots on rear body and white lines around eye and pectoral fin base in the front. Solitary, feeds on benthic hard-shelled invertebrates such as crustaceans and shellfish. Often observed on silty bottoms.

STARRY PUFFERFISH
Arothron stellatus

Distribution: Tropical Indo-Pacific from the Red Sea and East Africa to French Polynesia and from Southern Japan to New Zealand.
Size: Up to 90 centimeters.
Habitat: Coastal and outer reefs from 3 to 60 meters deep.
Life Habits: Large, very impressive: body pale grey with many tiny black spots often forming maze-like pattern. Strong teeth fused in sharp beak clearly visible. Solitary, locally common, often observed resting motionless under table corals or on the floor of small caves.

MANILA PUFFERFISH
Arothron manilensis

Distribution: Central Tropical Indo-Pacific from Borneo to Micronesia, Southern Japan and Australia.
Size: Up to 30 centimeters.
Habitat: Sand and silt bottoms, mangroves and seagrass beds in sheltered bays from 2 to 20 meters deep.
Life Habits: Body tan or pale brown with longitudinal brown stripes and large dark blotch at the base of the pectoral fin; golden-green eye. Commonly encountered alone or in small loose aggregations, resting motionless on the substrate.

MAPPA PUFFERFISH
Arothron mappa

Distribution: Tropical Indo-Pacific from East Africa to New Caledonia, Southern Japan and the Great Barrier Reef.
Size: Up to 70 centimeters.
Habitat: Coastal and outer reefs from 4 to 30 meters deep.
Life Habits: Very variable: body pale grey with dark dots, lines or scribbles or tan with white dots and scribbles; lines radiating from the eye are usually diagnostic. Large, with a peculiar "bloated" appearance; solitary, often observed resting motionless under large table corals or inside small caves. Feeds on hard-shelled benthic invertebrates.

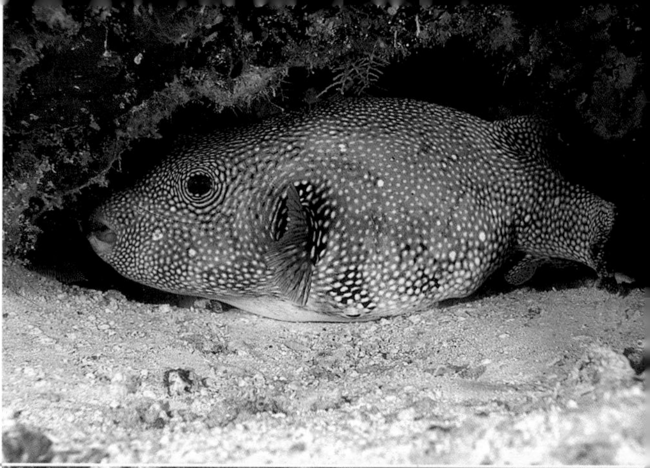

WHITE-SPOTTED PUFFERFISH
Arothron meleagris

Distribution: Tropical Indo-Pacific from East Africa to Baja California and from Southern Japan to Australia.
Size: Up to 50 centimeters.
Habitat: Coastal and outer reefs from 1 to 20 meters deep.
Life Habits: Body black with many bright white spots. Often observed in coral-rich areas: feeds mostly on live corals and benthic invertebrates, but like most pufferfishes will accept almost every kind of food, dead or alive. Occasionally encountered in a rather uncommon xanthic (all yellow) color variation.

BLACK-SPOTTED PUFFERFISH
Arothron nigropunctatus

Distribution: Tropical Indo-Pacific from the Red Sea and East Africa to New Caledonia, Southern Japan and Australia.
Size: Up to 35 centimeters.
Habitat: Coastal and outer reefs from 3 to 25 meters deep.
Life Habits: Extremely variable, from white to yellow to pale tan to blue and in a combinations of these colors, but always with scattered black spots, black lips and a white area above the lips. Solitary, often observed in thick coral growth: an opportunistic feeder which eats mostly live corals but will accept almost any prey.

WHITEBELLY TOBY
Canthigaster bennetti

Distribution: Tropical Indo-Pacific from East Africa to Galapagos and from Southern Japan to Australia.
Size: Up to 10 centimeters.
Habitat: Sand and silt bottoms on sheltered coastal reefs and lagoons from 2 to 15 meters deep.
Life Habits: Olive back, whitish belly, blue and orange lines radiating from eye and around mouth, blue-edged black spot at the base of dorsal fin. Peppered all over with violet and orange spots, more intense during courtship (illustrated). Solitary or in small loose aggregations.

SPOTTED TOBY
Canthigaster solandri

Distribution: Tropical Indo-Pacific from East Africa to French Polynesia, Southern Japan and Australia.
Size: Up to 10 centimeters.
Habitat: Coral-rich areas on coastal and outer reefs from 1 to 35 meters deep.
Life Habits: Body brown with many light blue-green spots and lines; blue-edged black spot at the base of the dorsal fin, orange eye. Solitary or in pairs, commonly observed feeding on algae, coral polyps and benthic invertebrates: easily confused with the following species.

FALSE-EYE TOBY
Canthigaster papua

Distribution: Central Tropical Indo-Pacific from Indonesia to Australia.
Size: Up to 9 centimeters.
Habitat: Coral-rich areas on coastal and outer reefs from 1 to 35 meters deep.
Life Habits: Body orangish or red brown with many small bright blue-green spots on the sides and lines on the back and snout; dark spot at the base of the dorsal fin; bright green eye and orange mouth. Occasionally observed alone or in pairs among rich coral growth, feeding on polyps and small benthic invertebrates.

FINGERPRINT TOBY
Canthigaster compressa

Distribution: Central Tropical Indo-Pacific from Indonesia and Malaysia to Micronesia and Southern Japan.
Size: Up to 10 centimeters.
Habitat: Sand and silt bottoms often in turbid water from 2 to 25 meters deep.
Life Habits: Body brownish with a paler belly, several fine bright blue-green lines and/or small dots all over, light blue-edged dark ocellus at the base of the dorsal fin. Easily confused with the two preceding species but commonly observed in siltier habitats, often under piers.

SPLENDID TOBY
Canthigaster janthinoptera

Distribution: Tropical Indo-Pacific from the Red Sea and East Africa to French Polynesia, Southern Japan and Australia.
Size: Up to 10 centimeters.
Habitat: Coral-rich areas on coastal and outer reefs from 1 to 30 meters deep.
Life Habits: Body brown with many pale green or white spots. Very secretive and rarely observed, occasionally encountered very close to shelters among rich coral growth and easily confused with the preceding species: lack of ocellus at the base of the dorsal fin may be helpful in identification underwater.

CROWN TOBY
Canthigaster coronata

Distribution: Tropical Indo-Pacific from the Red Sea and East Africa to Hawai'i, Southern Japan and Australia.
Size: Up to 14 centimeters.
Habitat: Sand, silt and rubble bottoms on outer reefs from 10 to 80 meters.
Life Habits: Similar to the following species - white body with darker saddles - but more colorful, as saddles are outlined in orange; blue and orange lines radiating from the eye. Solitary or in small loose aggregations, occasionally observed in deeper water than most pufferfishes.

Distribution: Tropical Indo-Pacific from the Red Sea and East Africa to French Polynesia, Southern Japan and Australia.
Size: Up to 9 centimeters.
Habitat: Coastal and outer reefs from 1 to 50 meters deep.
Life Habits: Body white with dark brown or black saddles and light brown spots on the sides. Possibly the most commonly observed toby, mimicked by the Mimic Filefish *Paraluteres prionurus*, with which it is easily confused underwater. Toxic like all other pufferfishes if harassed or eaten.

Distribution: Central Tropical Indo-Pacific from Indonesia to Japan and New Caledonia.
Size: Up to 20 centimeters.
Habitat: Sand and silt bottoms and seagrass beds in sheltered bays and estuaries from 2 to 100 meters deep.
Life Habits: Back flattened, brown with many white spots, belly white, yellow stripe on side. Occasionally encountered in small loose aggregations lying on the substrate, very frequently half-submerged in it: more active at night, when it hunts for hard-shelled benthic invertebrates.

PORCUPINEFISHES
Diodontidae

Porcupinefishes are very similar to pufferfishes in the general shape and in the fact that they are also able to inflate themselves, but in addition they feature large hard spines which point outward when they are inflated, transforming them into bristling, thorny "balloons" which are very hard to swallow even for a shark. Their strong, sharp front teeth are fused into a powerful beak which they use to good effect to break open the shell of the hard-bodied benthic invertebrates - like crustaceans and shellfish - on which they feed, mostly at night. They should never be harassed or handled. ~ **U/W Photo Tips:** Porcupinefishes are clumsy, ungraceful swimmers, and are usually found sleeping during the day. Their shimmering eyes make great macro subjects, but please avoid handling them to make them inflate themselves as this is very stressful to the fish. They can also inflict very damaging bites, easily cutting off a human finger.

BLACK-BLOTCHED PORCUPINEFISH
Diodon liturosus

Distribution: Tropical Indo-Pacific from the Red Sea and East Africa to French Polynesia, Southern Japan and Australia.
Size: Up to 50 centimeters.
Habitat: Coastal and outer coral reefs from 1 to 90 meters deep.
Life Habits: Large, pale tan body with brown or black, white-edged large blotches: the backward-pointing moveable spines are rather short. Solitary, usually observed during the day resting under large table corals. Feeds mostly at night on crustaceans and shellfish.

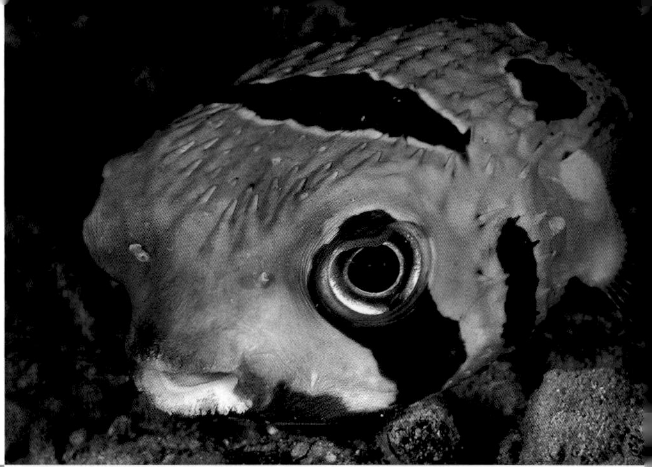

PORCUPINEFISH
Diodon hystrix

Distribution: Circumglobal in tropical, subtropical and temperate seas.
Size: Up to 70 centimeters.
Habitat: Coastal and outer coral and rocky reefs from 1 to 50 meters deep.
Life Habits: Body large, pale tan, yellowish or grey with white belly and many small black spots all over; moveable spines are rather short. Solitary and nocturnal, often observed during the day resting or sleeping un large *Acropora* table corals or under overhangs. Can be approached with slow, non-threatening movements like most porcupinefishes.

ORBICULAR BURRFISH
Cyclichthys orbicularis

Distribution: Tropical Indo-Pacific from the Red Sea and East Africa to Southern Japan and the Great Barrier Reef.
Size: Up to 20 centimeters.
Habitat: Sand and silt bottoms in bays and lagoons from 5 to 30 meters deep.
Life Habits: Body reddish brown with white belly, mottled in darker tones; spines are short, often yellowish, more or less fixed. Solitary but occasionally observed resting on the bottom in the open in small loose aggregations. Commonly observed sheltering inside sponges or submerged objects like tires.

BRIDLED BURRFISH
Chilomycterus antennatus

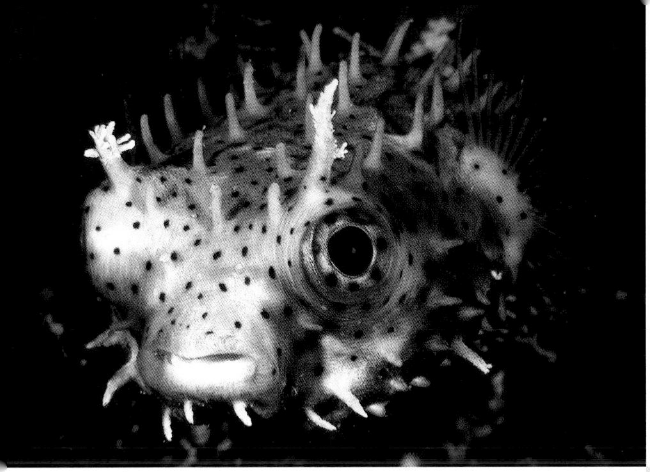

Distribution: Tropical Western Atlantic from Florida to the Bahamas and Caribbean.
Size: Up to 30 centimeters.
Habitat: Seagrass beds and coral reefs from 2 to 12 meters deep.
Life Habits: Body tan with darker mottles, occasionally blotched; spines short, always erect. Several very similar species worldwide in tropical waters, often with a very localized distribution. The large eye shows at close inspection many beautiful iridescent blue-green specks as in most pufferfishes.

SUNFISHES
Molidae

Three distinct species of Oceanic Sunfish are presently recognized within the family *Molidae*, including the Oceanic Sunfish proper *Mola mola*, the Sharp-tailed Sunfish *Masturus lanceolatus*, and the Slender Sunfish *Ranzania laevis*. All belong to the Order Tetraodontiformes, the same of Triggerfishes, Boxfishes, Pufferfishes and Porcupinefishes. Females produce up to 300 million eggs in a single ovary: this to date remains the largest number of eggs ever recorded in a single vertebrate. Oceanic Sunfish can reach a weight of more than two tons despite feeding almost exclusively on gelatinous zooplankton. ~ **U/W Photo Tips:** Meeting an Oceanic Sunfish would be a rare and precious occasion indeed, so no chances should be missed: given their great size, a good wide-angle would be the best choice, using ambient light and possibly keeping other divers in the shot to add perspective to the image.

OCEAN SUNFISH
Mola mola

Distribution: Worldwide in tropical, subtropical and temperate seas.
Size: Up to 300 centimeters.
Habitat: Pelagic, from the surface to 600 meters deep, occasionally visiting outer reefs to be cleaned from parasites.
Life Habits: Gigantic, unmistakable and very queer disk-shaped fish, with long dorsal and anal fins but without a tail. Mostly opalescent silvery grey or whitish, harmless: usually pelagic but occasionally and seasonally (for example in Bali) observed near coastal reefs in areas of cool upswellings, often in small groups.

CRUSTACEANS

Shrimps, crabs and lobsters

Crustaceans feature an external, armor-like skeleton based on calcium carbonate, a rigid carapace to protect the head and the sense organs, two sets of antennae, compound eyes and jointed legs. All periodically outgrow the jointed sections of their rigid skeleton and regularly shed it ("moulting"). Most crustaceans found on reefs - their Class, belonging to the Phylum Arthropoda together with land-based insects, spiders, scorpions, millipedes and centipedes, numbers about 45.000 species over a total of more than three quarters of a million - are decapods (with ten legs) and are nocturnal. They feed on living or dead organisms and are heavily predated on by their own kin, cephalopods and fish. Despite their generally inconspicuous habits, many species have evolved colorful liveries and interesting shapes, particularly when interacting with other species. In fact, the symbiotic associations between many shrimps and their hosts are some of the reef's most fascinating phenomena. ~ **U/W Photo Tips:** Most crustaceans make exceptional macro subjects. Look especially for commensal species interacting with their host or for interesting, very cryptic species.

BANDED BOXER SHRIMP
Stenopus hispidus

Distribution: Circumtropical.
Size: Up to 5 centimeters.
Habitat: Coral reefs, jetty pylons, caves and generally where suitable shelter is available from 1 to 40 meters deep.
Life Habits: Red and white banded body and legs with very long white antennae. Very common and easily observed, waving pincers and antennae in front of its shelter, offering its services to passing fish, which it will carefully clean from bits of dead skin, pieces of food between teeth and external parasites. Usually safe from predation thanks to its habits, it will often try to clean patient divers.

BLUE BOXER SHRIMP
Stenopus tenuirostris

Distribution: Central Tropical Indo-Pacific from South Africa to Indonesia.
Size: Up to 2 centimeters.
Habitat: On coral reef faces and under overhangs from 1 to 15 meters deep.
Life Habits: Body blue and purple, tail and pincers with unmistakable alternating white, red and yellow bands. Extremely colorful and often observed in pairs, offering its services to passing fish (including predators) from the shelter of its "cleaning station". Less commonly observed than other "cleaner" species.

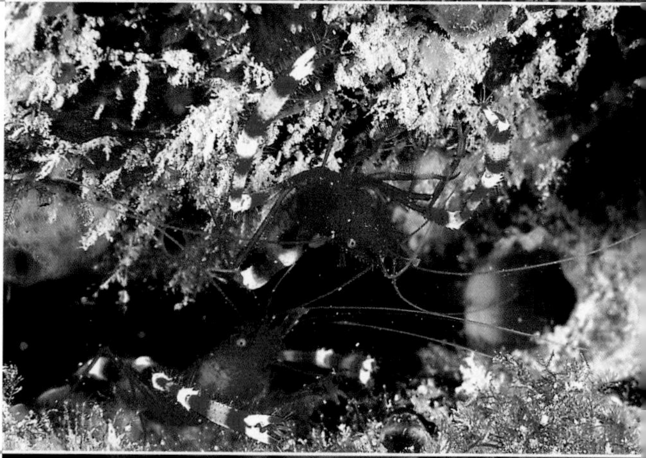

WHITE-BANDED CLEANER SHRIMP
Lysmata amboinensis

Distribution: Tropical Indo-Pacific from the Red Sea to Hawai'i; the almost identical *L. grabhami* in the Tropical Western Atlantic.
Size: Up to 6 centimeters.
Habitat: Coral reef caves, holes, crevices and ledges from 1 to 10 meters deep.
Life Habits: Easily identified: yellow body, red back, white longitudinal stripe on back from head to telson (tail). Often observed picking at large fishes - in particular groupers and moray eels - in the open in front of its "cleaning station".

SQUAT SHRIMP
Thor amboinensis

Distribution: Circumtropical.
Size: Up to 2 centimeters.
Habitat: Commensal on anemones, corals and *Cerianthus* mucus tubes from 3 to 20 meters deep.
Life Habits: Small but quite colorful, unmistakable: body yellow-green with pearlescent white saddles ringed in purple or blue. Females are twice the size of the male. Commonly observed with the head pointing down and the tail pointing up, flexing mechanically its legs. Usually observed in groups: despite appearances this species is not a cleaner.

MARBLED SHRIMP
Saron marmoratus

Distribution: Tropical Indo-Pacific.
Size: Up to 4 centimeters.
Habitat: Coral rubble bottoms in sheltered areas from 1 to 10 meters deep.
Life Habits: Spectacularly marked with mottling, spots and rosettes but surprisingly cryptic. Strictly nocturnal and very wary, immediately retreating among corals when lit. Several similar and equally beautiful species, most with a fine row of bristles ("cirrhi") on the rostrum and the back, many still undescribed. Seldom observed by the average diver due to its secretive habits.

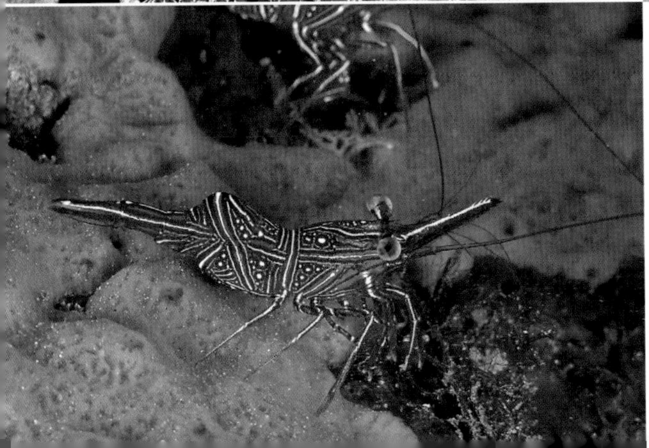

HINGE-BEAK SHRIMP
Rhyncocinetes sp.

Distribution: Circumtropical.
Size: Up to 4 centimeters.
Habitat: Inside caves, crevices, cracks or under overhangs from 6 to 15 meters.
Life Habits: Several very similar species, all tropical and here treated under the collective Genus grouping them all: all are bright red with a variable amount of white striping and fine spotting, and are commonly observed in large groups deep inside caves or in any other suitable dark place, often sharing it with large morays. Quite active during daytime in shady spots, will rapidly retreat if approached.

SAW-BLADE SHRIMP
Tozeuma armatum

Distribution: Tropical Indo-Pacific from the Red Sea and East Africa to Southern Japan and New Caledonia.
Size: Up to 5 centimeters.
Habitat: Exclusively on black coral colonies on coastal and outer reefs from 15 to 40 meters deep.
Life Habits: Very beautiful and exceptionally cryptic, with a very elongated, colorfully banded and semi-transparent body which camouflages it to perfection among black coral colonies. The long serrated rostrum is almost one third of the total length of the animal. *T. carolinense* replaces it in the Atlantic.

PLUMED SHRIMP
Leander plumosus

Distribution: Central Tropical Indo-Pacific from the Maldives to Australia.
Size: Up to 4 centimeters.
Habitat: Under overhangs and ledges or close to sponges on coastal and outer reefs from 3 to 15 meters deep.
Life Habits: Slow-moving, cryptic, with a reddish light brown body, transparent legs and a very elongated, flattened rostrum covered in tufts of bristles. Usually solitary but occasionally in pairs or threesomes. Locally common but usually unnoticed by divers.

COMMENSAL SHRIMP
Periclemenes tosaensis

Distribution: Widespread Tropical Indo-Pacific sharing distribution area with several similar-looking species.
Size: Up to 2.5 centimeters.
Habitat: In association with a great variety of hosts from sea anemones to mushroom and bubble corals.
Life Habits: Body transparent with white, pink and purple saddles, chelipeds barred in white, deep purple or bright blue. Easily confused with at least one very similar species, *P. holthuisi*; commonly observed in large groups sharing sea anemones with clownfish.

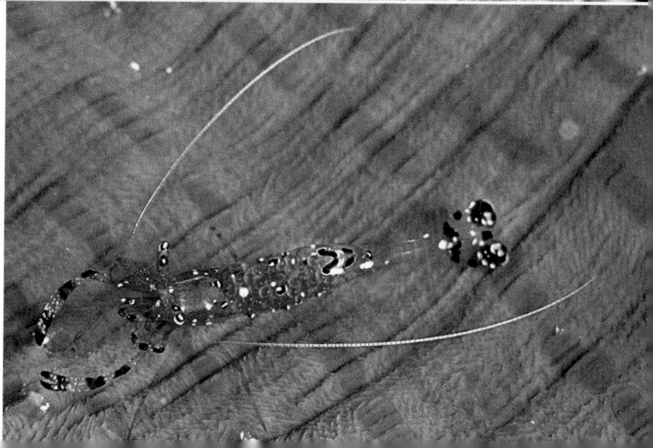

COMMENSAL SHRIMP
Periclemenes pedersoni

Distribution: Tropical Western Atlantic from Florida to the Bahamas and the Caribbean.
Size: Up to 2 centimeters.
Habitat: On a variety of sea anemones from 3 to 18 meters deep.
Life Habits: Transparent body with many purple, blue or lavender spots, long white antennae. Commonly observed on many sea anemones species, openly advertising its services as a cleaner by waving its very visible antennae. Can be easily approached like most cleaner shrimps.

COMMENSAL SHRIMP
Periclemenes venustus

Distribution: Tropical Central Indo-Pacific from Malaysia and Indonesia to Southern Japan and Australia.
Size: Up to 2.5 centimeters.
Habitat: On mushroom corals and sea anemones from 1 to 5 meters deep.
Life Habits: Body transparent with a variable amount of white and blue spots but always with a diagnostic large white round saddle with a bright pink center on the abdominal hump. A true cleaner shrimp, commonly observed on a multitude of sea anemones and other hosts in very shallow and often silty water.

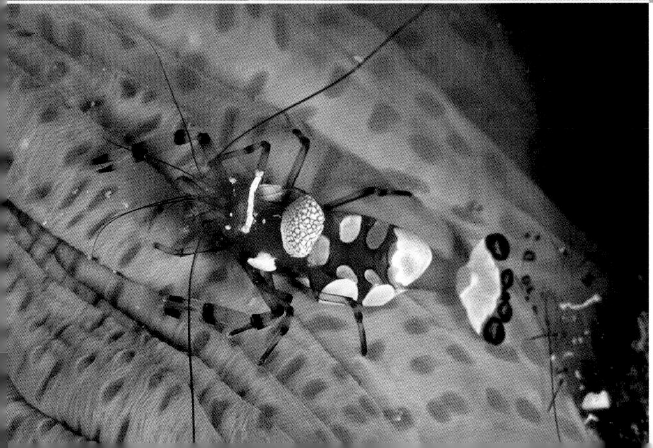

COMMENSAL SHRIMP
Periclemenes brevicarpalis

Distribution: Tropical Indo-Pacific from the Red Sea and East Africa to Australia.
Size: Up to 4 centimeters.
Habitat: On coral reefs and exclusively on large sea anemones.
Life Habits: Large, beautiful, often observed alone or in pairs on sea anemones: body is transparent with several bright white spots, tail is bright white with five black-rimmed orange ocelli. Large chelipeds and legs are transparent with blue or purple bands. Quite common and easily approached.

COMMENSAL SHRIMP
Periclemenes kororensis

Distribution: Tropical Central Indo-Pacific from Malaysia and Indonesia to the Marshalls.
Size: Up to 4 centimeters.
Habitat: On coral reefs in association with sea anemones and mushroom corals.
Life Habits: Strange-looking and often overlooked by divers: chelipeds are very long and transparent, body is bright red and head is white and spiny. Since the abdomen is transparent and usually kept hidden the general appearance is that of a tiny crab and not that of a shrimp.

PARTNER SHRIMP
Periclemenes soror

Distribution: Tropical Indo-Pacific from the Red Sea and East Africa to Hawai'i and the Gulf of California.
Size: Up to 1.3 centimeters.
Habitat: Exclusively in association with several sea stars species.
Life Habits: Very small, with a large, duck-billed rostrum: commonly observed in association with several sea stars belonging to the *Linckia, Mithrodia, Acanthaster, Choriaster* and especially *Culcita* genera.Coloration usually dependent on that of the host, but generally red, purple, yellow, orange or blue. Common on pincushion *Culcita*.

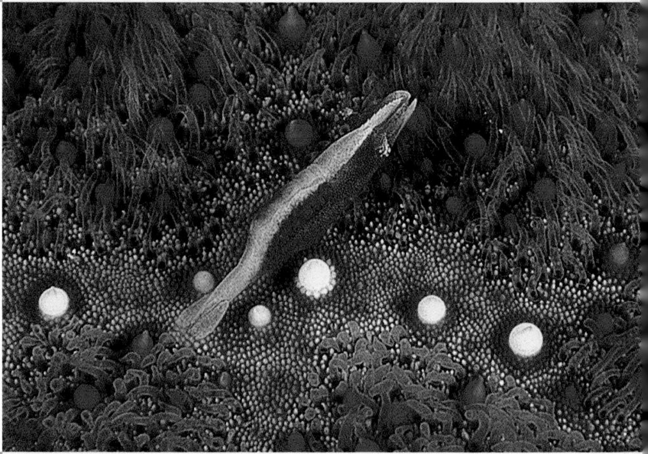

EMPEROR PARTNER SHRIMP
Periclemenes imperator

Distribution: Tropical Indo-Pacific from the Red Sea and East Africa to Southern Japan and Hawai'i.
Size: Up to 2 centimeters.
Habitat: In association with holothurians, sea stars and nudibranchs.
Life Habits: Spectacular, unmistakable: quite variable but usually bright orange or red with white saddles and purple accents. The rostrum is wide and duck-billed. Commonly observed in pairs in association with several holothurians species but also on large nudibranchs or sea stars.

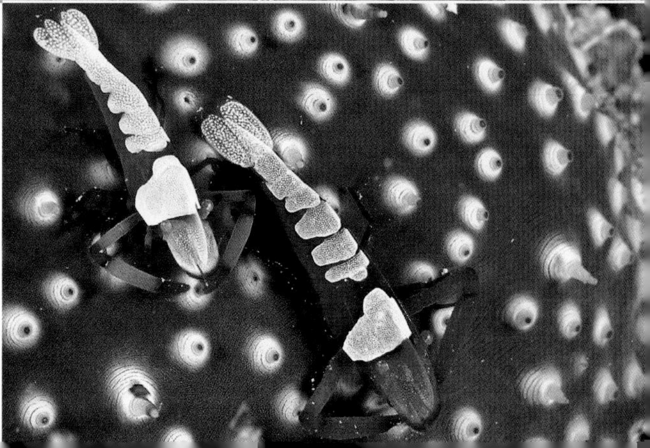

COLEMAN'S SHRIMP
Periclemenes colemani

Distribution: Tropical Central Indo-Pacific from Malaysia to Australia.
Size: Up to 2 centimeters.
Habitat: Exclusively in association with *Asthenosoma varium* fire urchins.
Life Habits: Spectacularly marked: bright white or pale yellow with large white-edged purple spots and purple-banded legs and chelipeds. Uncommon and with a localized distribution. Rarely observed by divers, usually in pairs (the female is the largest of the two) and exclusively on venomous *Asthenosoma varium* fire urchins. Often shows lateral bloating due to internal parasites.

CRINOID SHRIMP
Periclemenes sp.

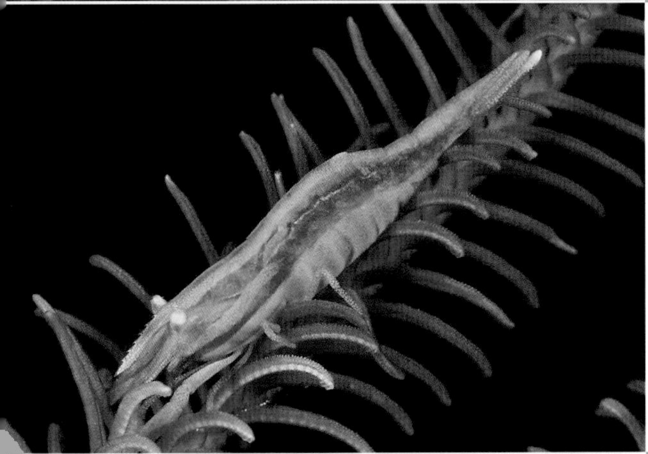

Distribution: Widespread Tropical Indo-Pacific from the Red Sea to Australia.
Size: Up to 1.5 centimeters.
Habitat: On coral reefs exclusively in association with crinoids.
Life Habits: Common but very cryptic, exclusively observed in association with crinoids. Several very similar species (*cornutus, commensalis, amboinensis, ceratophthalmus*) which are not easy to correctly differentiate from each other underwater. The coloration - monochromatic, spotted or banded but frequently very bright - always matches that of the featherstar hosting it.

BUBBLE CORAL SHRIMP
Vir philippinensis

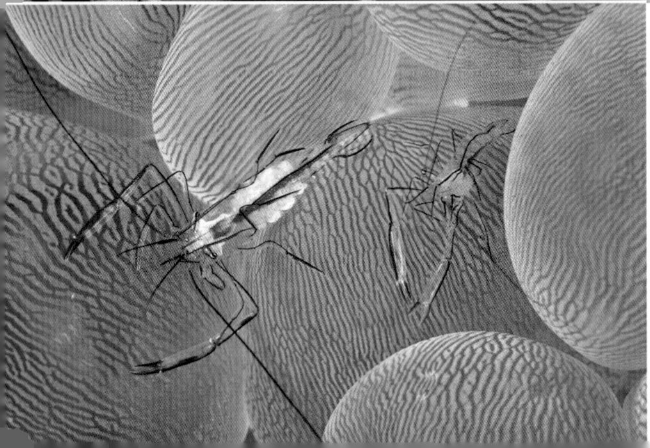

Distribution: Tropical Central Indo-Pacific from Myanmar to Southern Japan and Australia.
Size: Up to 2 centimeters.
Habitat: On coral reefs in association with bubble coral *Pleurogyra sinuosa*.
Life Habits: Body completely transparent with very thin purple lines on body, legs and chelipeds. Antennae are also purple. Rather common and often encountered in pairs but always exclusively associated to the bubble or grape coral *Pleurogyra sinuosa*.

HARLEQUIN SHRIMP
Hymenocera elegans

Distribution: Tropical Indo-Pacific from the Red Sea to Southern Japan and Australia. Replaced in the Eastern Pacific by the almost identical *H. picta*.
Size: Up to 5 centimeters.
Habitat: Shallow intertidal coral reefs.
Life Habits: Spectacularly marked, with large paddle-like chelipeds: body is bright white with large blue-rimmed brown spots (in *H. picta* the spots are red with a yellow edge instead). Very rarely observed by divers: almost always in pairs, feeding exclusively on sea stars in shallow water.

GORGONIAN HORNED SHRIMP
Miropandalus hardingi

Distribution: Tropical Central Indo-Pacific from Malaysia to Southern Japan.
Size: Up to 2 centimeters.
Habitat: Exclusively observed on wire and black coral colonies on coastal and outer coral reefs from 15 to 40 meters.
Life Habits: Slow-moving, rather uncommon and spectacularly well-camouflaged shrimp occasionally observed in deep water, exclusively in association with antipatharian colonies such as wire or black coral. Rarely observed: very little is known of its life habits.

GHOST SHRIMP
Pliopontonia furtiva

Distribution: Tropical Indo-Pacific from East Africa to Australia.
Size: Up to 2 centimeters.
Habitat: Coastal coral reefs, only in association with corallimorpharians.
Life Habits: Queer, slow-moving, spider-like shrimp with a transparent body beautifully marked with white bands and white and yellow spots. Exclusively observed in association with corallimorpharians *Discosoma* spp. and *Rhodactis* spp., the only species belonging to its genus. Not really uncommon but rarely observed by divers.

STIMPSON'S SNAPPING SHRIMP
Synalpheus stimpsoni

Distribution: Tropical Indo-Pacific from East Africa to Japan and Australia.
Size: Up to 3,5 centimeters.
Habitat: Coral reefs, exclusively as a commensal on several different crinoid species, from 10 to 40 meters deep.
Life Habits: Highly variable but usually quite colorful and related to that of the host, commonly observed in pairs (the female is always the largest of the two) as a commensal on several crinoid species, especially *Comanthina*, *Comanthus* and *Comatula*. The greatly enlarged "snapping" claw is usually quite visible.

CRINOID SQUAT LOBSTER
Allogalathea elegans

Distribution: Tropical Indo-Pacific from the Red Sea to Micronesia.
Size: Up to 2 centimeters.
Habitat: On coral reefs, exclusively in association with a featherstar host.
Life Habits: Tick-like appearance with a flattened oval body and a long pointed rostrum: coloration very variable but often showy and with a longitudinal band, always matching that of the crinoid host. Alone or more often in pairs with the larger of the two being the female, but exclusively as a commensal of crinoids. Easily observed gently tickling the underside of the crinoid to make it open.

HAIRY SQUAT LOBSTER
Lauriea siagiani

Distribution: Central Tropical Indo-Pacific from Malaysia to West Papua.
Size: Up to 1,4 centimeters.
Habitat: Usually inside large barrel sponges from 10 to 40 meters deep.
Life Habits: Spectacular squat lobster with a bright neon pink body striped in fluorescent purple and covered with long white and pink bristles. Commonly observed in deeper water - alone or in pairs - on the surface of large barrel sponges belonging to the genus *Xestospongia*. Due to light absorption at depth it looks a drab brown underwater.

ARROW CRAB
Stenorhynchus seticornis

Distribution: Tropical Western Atlantic from Florida to the Bahamas and the Caribbean.
Size: Up to 5 centimeters.
Habitat: Coastal and outer coral reefs from 3 to 40 meters deep.
Life Habits: Body triangular, yellow-brown, with long pointed rostrum and many thin dark lines; chelipeds often with bright purple tips; slender legs give it a spider-like appearance. Very common, with a few very similar species replacing it in the Indo-Pacific. Found in a great variety of habitats and easily approached.

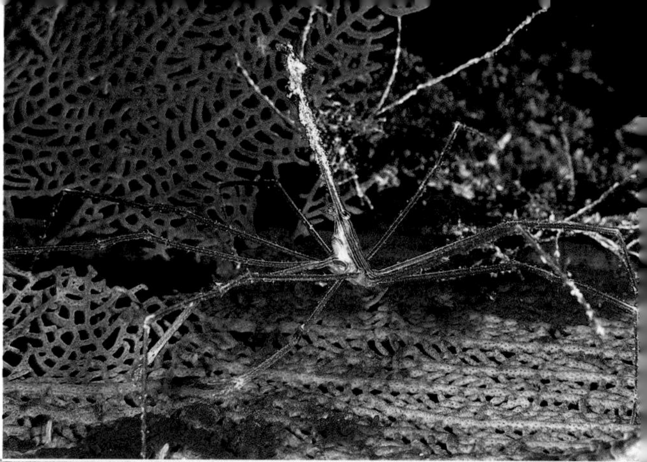

PORCELAIN CRAB
Neopetrolisthes oshimai

Distribution: Tropical Central Indo-Pacific from the Maldives to Australia.
Size: Up to 2.5 centimeters.
Habitat: On coral reefs in association with sea anemones from 1 to 15 meters.
Life Habits: Body pale tan or white with several large red spots; the very similar *N. maculatus* (on the right of the photo) can be differentiated by the much smaller and more numerous red spots. Both species are commonly found in pairs and in shallow waters living as commensals in association with large sea anemones belonging to the genera *Stichodactyla*, *Cryptodendrum* and *Heteractis*.

BOXER CRAB
Lybia tessellata

Distribution: Tropical Indo-Pacific from East Africa to the Marshall Islands.
Size: Up to 1.5 centimeters.
Habitat: On rubble bottoms and under blocks of dead coral from 1 to 5 meters.
Life Habits: Very small but quite beautiful: body unmistakably checkered in brown and cream, legs finely spotted in white. Extremely wary and cryptic, rarely observed by divers: carries small sea anemones belonging to the genus *Bunodeopsis* in its claws, waving them in a boxer-like stance at would-be predators.

ORANG-UTAN CRAB
Achaeus japonicus

Distribution: Tropical Central Indo-Pacific from Malaysia and Indonesia to Southern Japan and the Solomons.
Size: Up to 1,2 centimeters.
Habitat: On coral reefs in association with several sea anemones species.
Life Habits: Unmistakable and queer-looking: body and legs are covered with long flowing red hairs, often covered in small bits of debris. Commonly observed perching on several sea anemone species with bright red eyes clearly visible: when "hairless" whitish with brown bands but in fact completely unrecognizable.

RED-SPOTTED CORAL CRAB
Trapezia rufopunctata

Distribution: Widespread Tropical Indo-Pacific but absent from the Red Sea.
Size: Up to 1,5 centimeters.
Habitat: On outer reefs, inside hard coral branching colonies from 1 to 5 meters.
Life Habits: A small but truly beautiful species, easily identified by its bright yellow-green eyes and the white body finely spotted in deep red. Often found with several similar species and many commensal gobies among branching colonies of *Pocillopora* and *Stylopora* hard coral, which it will not leave even if the coral is taken out of the water.

ZEBRA CRAB
Zebrida adamsii

Distribution: Tropical Indo-West Pacific from Malaysia to Southern Japan.
Size: Up to 2,5 centimeters.
Habitat: Coastal reefs on sand bottoms, usually in association with fire urchins.
Life Habits: Very uncommon but extremely beautiful commensal crab: body is white with purple-brown bands and with specially adapted hooked rear legs to keep its grip on fire urchin hosts such as *Asthenosoma varium* and *ijimai*. Often observed in pairs, sheltering among the urchin's dangerously venomous spines.

ROUND-BACK CORAL CRAB
Carpilius convexus

Distribution: Widespread Tropical Indo-Pacific from the Red Sea to Japan.
Size: Up to 10 centimeters.
Habitat: Coastal and outer coral reefs from 2 to 20 meters deep.
Life Habits: Large and very colorful, with smooth carapace and legs and a typical "orange peel" surface texture. Easily identified by the bright orange-red color and the single wine-red spot with two small white dots inside. A strictly nocturnal and rather mobile species which commonly feeds on shelled mollusks.

SPOT-BACK CORAL CRAB
Carpilius maculatus

Distribution: Widespread Tropical Indo-Pacific from the Red Sea to Japan.
Size: Up to 10 centimeters.
Habitat: Coastal and outer coral and rocky reefs from 3 to 35 meters deep.
Life Habits: A slow-moving and strictly nocturnal species, easily identified by the warm caramel body color and its seven brown spots. Carapace is smooth, with four blunt interorbital spines. Commonly observed, it feeds on shelled mollusks like most other *Carpilius* species. Usually ignored by most divers but a beautiful and easy photographic subject.

SOFT CORAL CRAB
Hoplophrys oatesii

Distribution: Widespread Tropical Indo-Pacific from the Red Sea to Japan.
Size: Up to 1,5 centimeters.
Habitat: Coastal and outer coral reefs, exclusively observed in association with *Dendronephtya* soft corals.
Life Habits: Very small but exceptionally beautiful and incredibly well camouflaged, this small crab can only be found on *Dendonephtya* soft coral colonies, which it mimics to perfection. Body is translucent and covered with spines, with many red and white stripes. Also known as "candy crab" among Asian divers.

COMMENSAL CRAB
Lissocarcinus laevis

Distribution: Widespread Tropical Indo-Pacific from the Red Sea to Australia.
Size: Up to 3 centimeters.
Habitat: Coral reefs and sand or rubble bottoms, usually associated with sea anemones and soft corals.
Life Habits: Common but usually ignored, usually found in association with soft corals or sea anemones. Many local color variations but body usually brightly marked in white and mahogany brown or dark wine-red with translucent legs. Four weak interorbital spines present.

COMMENSAL CRAB
Lissocarcinus orbicularis

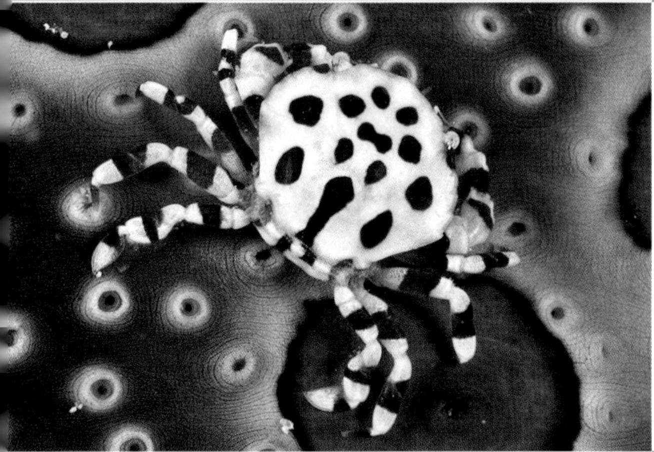

Distribution: Widespread Tropical Indo-Pacific from the Red Sea to Hawai'i.
Size: Up to 4 centimeters.
Habitat: Sand or silt bottoms, only found in association with large sea cucumbers and more rarely sea anemones.
Life Habits: Small and rather common commensal of large holothurians with a smooth interorbital space devoid of spines. Usually white with a pattern of brown spots but reverse pattern instances are known. Usually observed clinging to the sea cucumber's bottom side, feeding of its waste products .

GHOST SHRIMP
Caprellid sp.

Distribution: Pan-tropical with several different species from the Atlantic to the Indo-Pacific.
Size: Up to 2 centimeters.
Habitat: Commonly observed perching on feather-like hydrozoans.
Life Habits: Very strange, insect-looking amphipods with an elongated transparent body held upright and a large pair of hooked, raptorial claws held in praying mantis-like fashion. Seasonally observed in very large aggregations on urticating, feather-like hydroid colonies.

PEACOCK MANTIS SHRIMP
Odontodactylus scyllarus

Distribution: Tropical Indo-Pacific from East Africa to Southern Japan, Australia and Hawai'i.
Size: Up to 18 centimeters.
Habitat: Coral rubble and coarse sand bottoms from 1 to 70 meters deep.
Life Habits: Body is bright green and blue with blue head, yellow and red thoracic limbs and red-edged blue telson. The most colorful of several tropical mantis shrimps, represented by several species worldwide. Lives in burrows from which it rapidly emerges to powerfully smash at crustacean or fish prey with modified front raptorial claws.

GIANT MANTIS SHRIMP
Lysiosquillina lisa

Distribution: Central Tropical Indo-Pacific from the Maldives to Papua.
Size: Up to 30 centimeters.
Habitat: Coral rubble bottoms on coastal reefs from 8 to 35 meters deep.
Life Habits: Very large and unmistakable spearing species, easily identified by its large size, white and rust-red banded body and bright pink knuckles on large raptorial claws. Commonly observed peeking out of its deep, vertical, mucus-lined burrow in the substrate, ready to impale passing prey with a lightning-fast three-millisecond strike.

ORANGE MANTIS SHRIMP
Lysiosquilloides mapia

Distribution: Central Tropical Indo-Pacific from Malaysia to Fiji.
Size: Up to 25 centimeters.
Habitat: Coral rubble and coarse sand bottoms on coastal reefs from 2 to 30 meters deep.
Life Habits: Only recently described, a beautiful, unmistakable, bright orange spearing species, rarely observed while attentively peeking out of its vertical burrow on Malaysian and Indonesian reefs. Bright color and distinctly triangular stalked eyes are diagnostic.

PAINTED SPINY LOBSTER
Panulirus versicolor

Distribution: Tropical Indo-Pacific from the Red Sea and East Africa to Southern Japan and Micronesia.
Size: Up to 40 centimeters.
Habitat: Inside crevices and holes on coastal and outer reef slopes and walls.
Life Habits: Commonly observed on undisturbed reefs where it has not been fished to extinction for human consumption; nocturnal, hiding in shelters during the day. Body is light green with black and white bands, legs have white and blue stripes, antennae are very long, white, with a bright coral-pink base.

COMMON SPINY LOBSTER
Panulirus penicillatus

Distribution: Tropical Indo-Pacific from the Red Sea and East Africa to Mexico.
Size: Up to 35 centimeters.
Habitat: Coastal and outer coral reefs in holes and crevices.
Life Habits: The most common Indo-Pacific spiny lobster. Rather variable, with many local subspecies: dark antennae with a bright blue base and white striped legs are diagnostic. Usually nocturnal like all lobsters, normally hiding during the day in holes and crevices but occasionally out in the open in remote, undisturbed locations.

ORNATE SPINY LOBSTER
Panulirus ornatus

Distribution: Tropical Indo-West Pacific from the Red Sea to Malaysia.
Size: Up to 50 centimeters.
Habitat: Sand, coral or rubble bottoms from 5 to 50 meters deep.
Life Habits: Very colorful: carapace is blue-green, antennae are orange-red with a light blue base, legs are white with black bands.Commonly observed hiding in holes or under overhangs during the day but actively feeding in the open at night. Mature specimens can reach a great size and are extremely impressive animals.

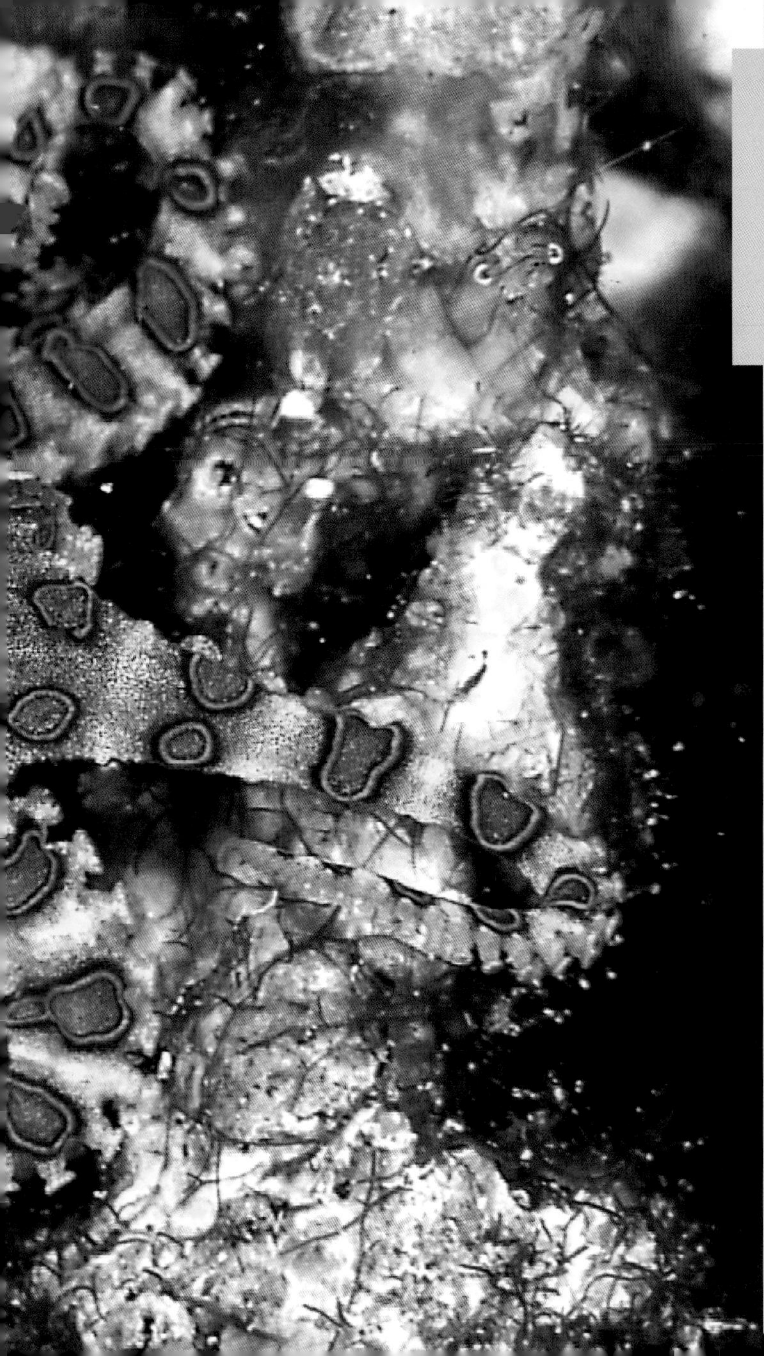

CEPHALOPODS

Octopi, squid and cuttlefish

Cephalopods (meaning "footed head" in Latin) are the most advanced of mollusks. This Class numbers more than 700 strictly marine species worldwide. All of them share a soft body lacking an internal skeleton, strong and incredibly flexible, muscular arms studded with horn-rimmed suckers and a central, horny, parrot beak-like mouth. Most of them also have a defense mechanism, the ink sac, which allows them to spurt a black jet of liquid towards the aggressor, creating a confusing "phantom image" of themselves and a smoke screen at the same time. All cephalopods are very active, voracious predators, often showing a strong degree of intelligence, human-like organs of sight and the capability of changing color, pattern, skin texture and even general body shape at will. Displaying a wonderful variety in colors, life habits and shapes, they are some of the coral reef's most amazing inhabitants. ~ **U/W Photo Tips:** Octopi, squid and cuttlefish are spectacular, ever-changing subjects. Use macro lenses and be very patient: it is not uncommon to catch them feeding, mating and laying eggs.

EMPEROR NAUTILUS
Nautilus pompilius

Distribution: Tropical Central Indo-Pacific from the Andamans to Southern Japan and Australia.
Size: Up to 17 centimeters in diameter.
Habitat: Very deep water (300-400 meters) but occasionally ascending to 200 meters after sunset.
Life Habits: Six very similar species which live far beyond the limits of sport diving but which are occasionally captured and shown to tourists. All have a chambered, gas-filled external shell, simple eyes without a lens, 90 ridged small tentacles and a fleshy wedge-shaped hood used to seal their shell when threatened.

BROADCLUB CUTTLEFISH
Sepia latimanus

Distribution: Tropical Central Indo-Pacific from the Andamans to Southern Japan and Australia.
Size: Up to 50 centimeters.
Habitat: Coastal and outer coral reefs from 2 to 30 meters deep.
Life Habits: Large and impressive, locally common and easily approached by careful divers: livery is exceedingly variable but usually pale with darker stripes and mottles when unafraid. Will often interact with observers showing unmistakable signs of "emotions", curiosity and speculative intelligence.

FLAMBOYANT CUTTLEFISH
Metasepia pfefferi

Distribution: Tropical Central Indo-Pacific from Malaysia to Australia.
Size: Up to 8 centimeters.
Habitat: Sand and silt bottoms from 1 to 10 meters deep, often close to coral heads.
Life Habits: Spectacularly colorful, with broad brown and purple bands flashing rythmically on white background; skin flaps edged in yellow, tentacles purple-red and kept erect. Usually observed ambling on the substrate using modified skin flaps as posterior legs. Uncommon but unmistakable: bright coloration possibly aposematic advertising venomous bite.

BIG-FIN REEF SQUID
Sepioteuthis lessoniana

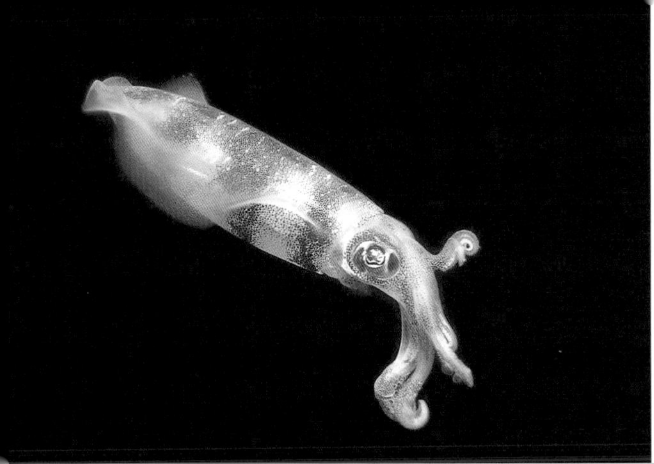

Distribution: Tropical Indo-Pacific.
Size: Up to 36 centimeters.
Habitat: Coastal reefs from 1 to 100 meters deep.
Life Habits: Several rather similar species distributed worldwide, all sharing elongated flattened body and large round eyes. Often encountered in schools, more active at sunset or at night when it displays fluorescent spots and stripes. Wary but also curious, it will readily interact with cautious divers if not harassed. Feeds on fish and crustaceans but it also is heavily harvested by man.

BLUE-RING OCTOPUS
Hapalochlaena lunulata

Distribution: Tropical Central Indo-Pacific from Malaysia to Micronesia.
Size: Up to 7 centimeters.
Habitat: Thick coral growth and coral rubble bottoms from 1 to 15 meters deep.
Life Habits: Rarely observed but very beautiful and quite unmistakable: body and arms pale tan or yellow-brown with several diagnostic fluorescent blue rings. Bright aposematic coloration warns of venomous bite, which has proven deadly to humans in several instances. At least five different but very similar species belong to the blue-ring octopus complex.

DAY OCTOPUS
Octopus cyanea

Distribution: Tropical Indo-Pacific.
Size: Up to 80 centimeters.
Habitat: Coastal and outer coral reefs from 1 to 30 meters deep.
Life Habits: A large number of very similar species distributed worldwide, all sharing a common appearance. Sac-like body, protruding eyes and long arms can switch from smooth to wrinkled and from monochromatic to heavily spotted, ringed or mottled in a matter of seconds. Common but very cryptic and heavily predated on by moray eels and groupers: feeds at night on shellfish and crustaceans.

PYGMY OCTOPUS
Octopus sp.

Distribution: Widespread Tropical Central Indo-Pacific from Malaysia and the Philippines to Fiji.
Size: Up to 8 centimeters.
Habitat: Coastal coral reefs on rubble bottoms from 2 to 20 meters deep.
Life Habits: Several similar species are commonly grouped under the umbrella name of "pygmy octopi", including Bock's Pygmy Octopus *O. bocki* and the Fiji Pygmy Octopus *O. fijiensis*. All are little known and of very small size, usually with tentacles less than 8 centimeters long. They spend the daylight hours well hidden among the corals and hunt at night.

VEINED OCTOPUS
Amphioctopus marginatus

Distribution: Tropical Indo-Pacific.
Size: Up to 15 centimeters.
Habitat: Sand and silt bottoms in coastal waters from 3 to 15 meters deep.
Life Habits: Also known as "coconut octopus" among divers or "sand bird" in Chinese fish markets, a small and quite common species found on sand and mud bottoms at shallow depth, often inside discarded coconut husks and old bottles. Body pale with purplish veined pattern and white suckers sharply contrasting with dark purple leading edge of arms; white spots occasionally under eyes.

MIMIC OCTOPUS
Thaumoctopus mimicus

Distribution: Tropical Indo-Pacific from the Red Sea to New Caledonia.
Size: Up to 30 centimeters.
Habitat: Mud and silt bottoms in sheltered bays from 3 to 30 meters deep.
Life Habits: Body and arms white with purplish brown bands, small head sac and stalked eyes. Probably not uncommon but very rarely observed due to its very cryptic habits: often hiding under the substrate with only the eyes showing. Will spectacularly and quite faithfully mimic several sea organisms (flounders, lionfish, sea kraits) trying to confuse predators.

WONDER OCTOPUS
Octopus sp.

Distribution: Tropical Central Indo-Pacific from Malaysia and Indonesia to Papua New Guinea.
Size: Up to 20 centimeters.
Habitat: Sand, silt and coral rubble bottoms from 3 to 25 meters deep.
Life Habits: Similar to the preceding species but still undescribed, much more colorful - white body with orange or rich brown bands - and rather less prone to mimicking other creatures. Head sac is small (up to 3 centimeters) and eyes are stalked. Will rapidly disappear under the substrate if harassed: aposematic coloration may advertise venomous bite.

HAIRY OCTOPUS
Octopus sp.

Distribution: Unknown, but probably extremely localized. Currently documented from the Central Indo-Pacific in Northern Sulawesi only.
Size: Up to 20 centimeters.
Habitat: Coral rubble bottoms in sheltered bays from 15 to 30 meters.
Life Habits: Rarely observed and exceptionally cryptic, with variable amount of hair-like growth on body and arms. One of many yet scientifically undescribed species of tropical octopi occasionally documented by divers, possibly belonging to the *horridus* complex.

LONG-ARMED OCTOPUS
Octopus sp.

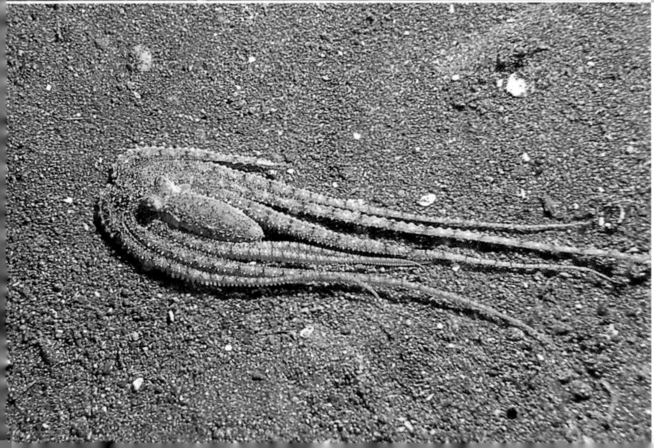

Distribution: Unknown. Currently documented from the Central Indo-Pacific in Sabah and Northern Sulawesi only.
Size: Up to 15 centimeters.
Habitat: Sand and silt bottoms in sheltered bays from 10 to 20 meters deep.
Life Habits: Body pale brown with very long, thin arms held in a flounder- or comet-like shape when swimming above the substrate. Occasionally observed during the day, moving out in the open but ready to rapidly disappear under the soft substrate if disturbed. Several very similar species worldwide, many still undescribed and of unknown habits.

Sea Shells

Quite mobile and nocturnal, sea snails belong to the gastropod ("feet on the belly" in Latin) class. The largest is *Syrinx aruanus*, an Indonesian snail that reaches lengths of 90 centimeters, but most are much smaller. They are extremely sophisticated predators whose principal trait is the *radula*, a semi-rigid tongue covered with teeth (up to 750,000) used to capture and swallow prey. Some are quite dangerous creatures, like those belonging to the *Conus* genus: these gastropods have a proboscis they use to shoot poisonous darts into their prey, and their venom can also be often lethal to humans. Bivalves are instead filtering animals that aspirate water through one siphon and expel it through another, having first extracted suspended nutrients and the oxygen needed to breathe. *Tridacna* species also avail themselves of symbiotic single-celled algae (zooxanthellae) in their tissues to increase the availability of energy, in the same way that corals do: zooxanthellae are also responsible for the spectacular colors of their mantle. Other bivalves capture their prey by rapidly contracting a modified gill.

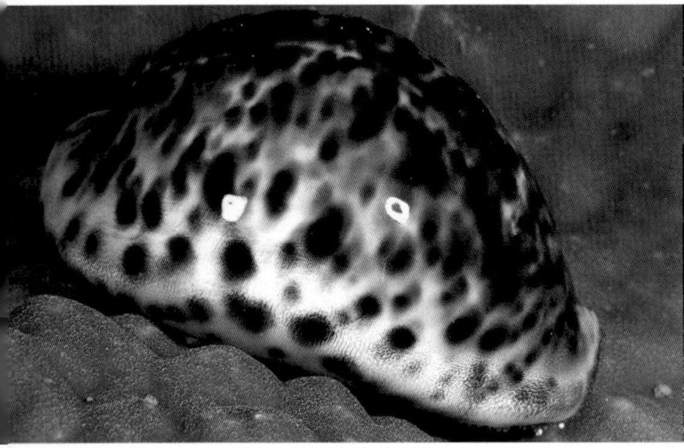

Tiger or Common Cowrie, *Cypraea tigris.*

Tiger Cowrie *Cypraea tigris* with extended mantle.

Zigzag Cowrie, *Cypraea ziczac.*

Pacific Deer Cowrie, *Cypraea vitellus.*

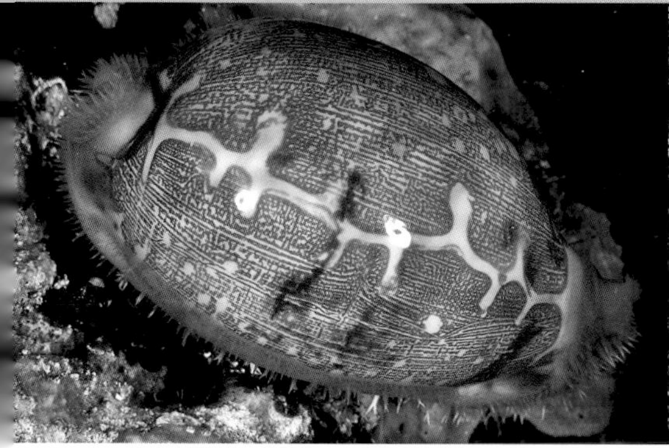

Map Cowrie, *Cypraea mappa.*

Mile Cowrie, *Cypraea miliaris.*

Unidentified Cowrie, *Cypraea* sp.

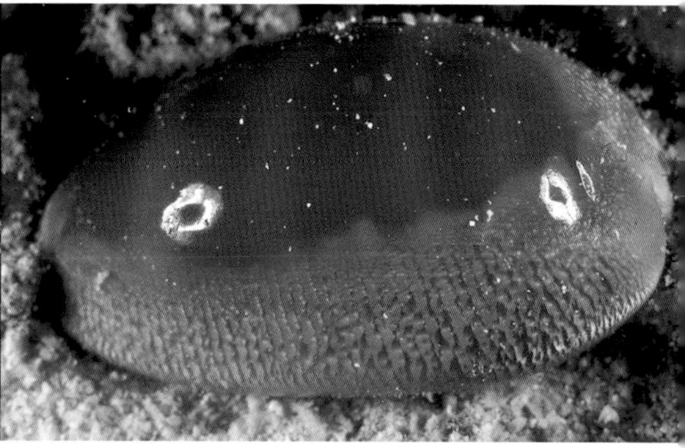

Carnelian Cowrie, *Cypraea carneola.*

Ivory Cone, *Conus eburneus.*

Onyx Cowrie, *Cypraea onyx.*

Honey Cowrie, *Cypraea helvola.*

Harp Snail, *Harpa articularis.*

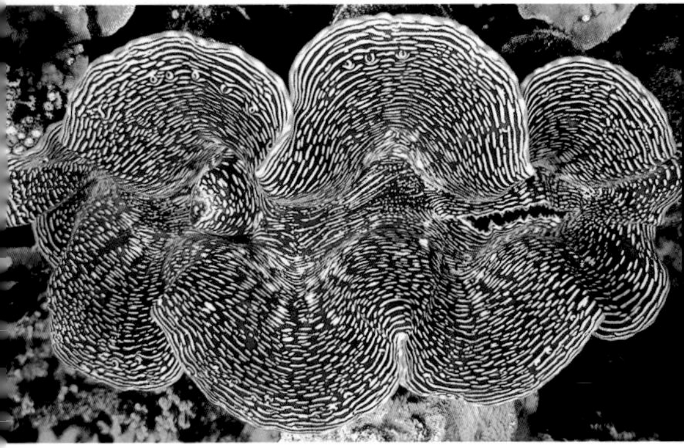

Giant clam, *Tridacna maxima.*

Giant Clam, *Tridacna gigas.*

Giant Clam, *Tridacna crocea.*

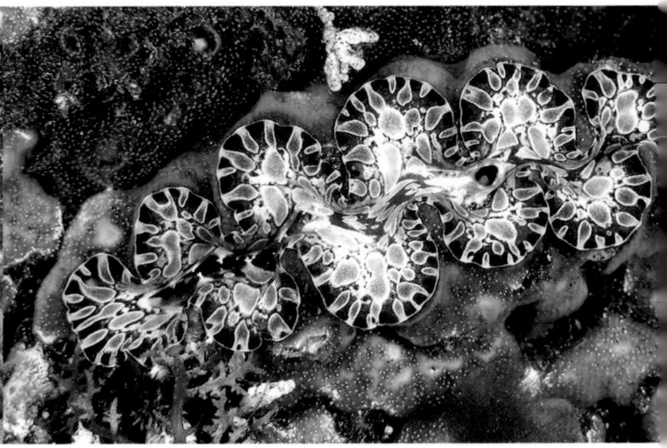

Giant Clam, *Tridacna squamosa.*

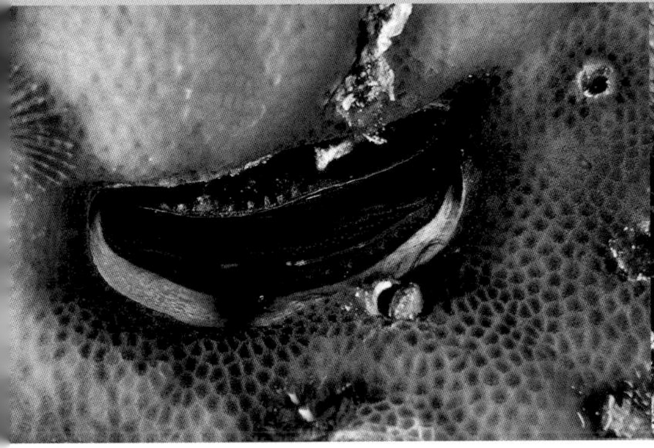

Coral Clam, *Pedum spondyloidum.*

Thorny Oyster, *Spondylus varius.*

Cock's comb Oyster, *Lopha cristagalli.*

Triton's Trumpet, *Charonia tritonis.*

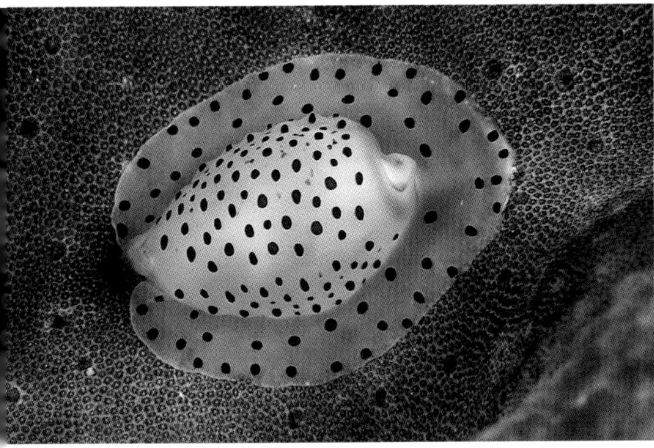

Spotted Egg Cowrie, *Calpurnus verrucosus.*

Egg Cowrie, *Ovula ovum.*

Bat Volute, *Cymbiola vespertilio.*

Geography Cone, *Conus geographus.* Deadly to humans.

Pearl Oyster, *Pinctada margaritifera.*

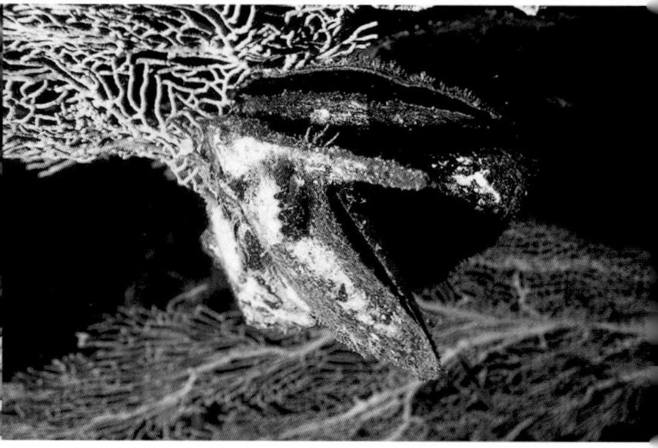

Pearl Oyster, *Pteria penguin.*

Murex Shell, *Murex* sp.

Sundial, *Architectonica perspectiva.*

Spider Shell, *Lambis lambis.*

Horned Helmet, *Cassis cornuta.*

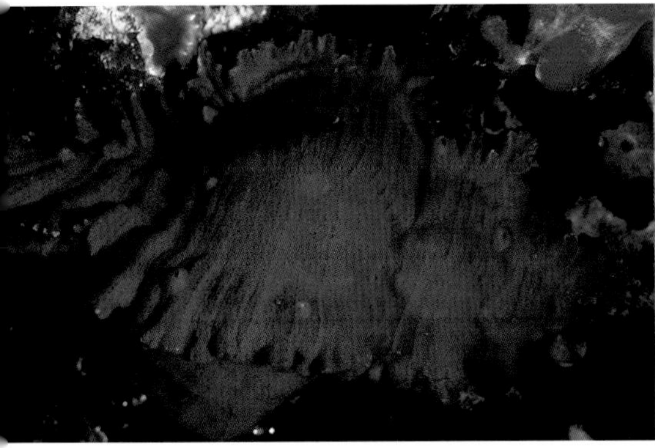

Murex Shell, *Chicoreus ramosus.*

File Shell, *Limaria* sp.

Thorny Oyster, *Spondylus* sp.

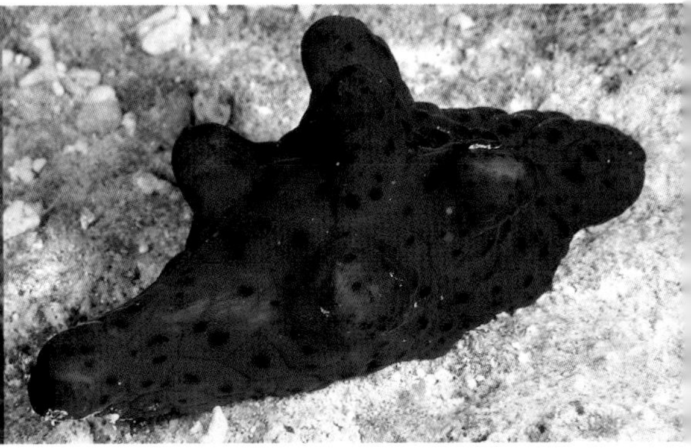

Velvet Snail, *Coriocella nigra.*

Allied Cowry, *Crenavolva rosewateri.*

Slender Allied Cowry, *Phenacovolva tokioi.*

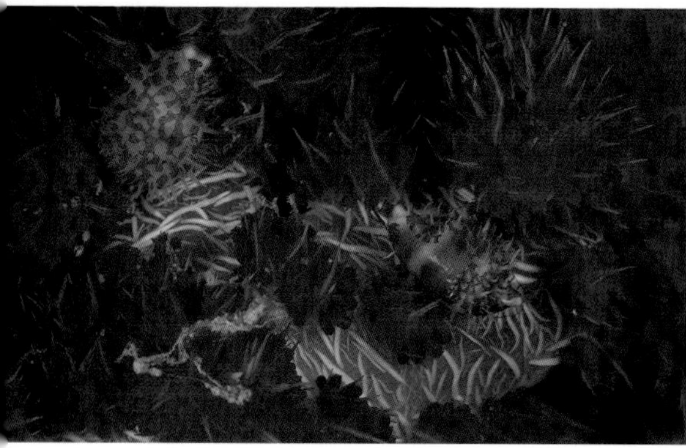

Allied Cowry, *Pseudosimnia punctata.*

Allied Cowry, *Dentiovula dorsuosa.*

Flamingo Tongue, *Cyphoma gibbosum.*

Allied Cowry, *Phenacovolva gracilis.*

Diver and Giant Clam *Tridacna gigas*,
Layang Layang, South China Sea, Malaysia

Sea Urchins

Belonging to the phylum Echinodermata (meaning "spiny- skinned" in Latin) like sea stars, feather stars and sea cucumbers, sea urchins are slow-moving bottom dwellers which feed on algal mats and detritus. Their movement on the substrate is achieved by a very complex hydrovascular system, in which water is pumped to hundreds of tiny tube-like feet equipped with small suckers. Sea urchins are quite common on sand, silt and rocky bottoms on coral reefs, and often among hard corals themselves, and despite being generally ignored by most divers - who think only of avoiding their sharp spines - they do deserve a close look underwater as they often host a variety of most interesting commensals, mainly shrimps and occasionally small fish. Generally nocturnal, sea urchins pose however a real danger to careless divers, as bumping into one at night - especially if it belongs to the long-spined *Diadema* genus - can result in a large number of quite painful and potentially infected wounds, since the long barbed spines break at predetermined pressure points and become embedded in the skin.

Fire Urchin *Asthenosoma ijimai*, Indo-Pacific.

Fire Urchin *Asthenosoma varium*, Indo-Pacific.

Long-spined Sea Urchin *Astropyga radiata*, Indo-Pacific.

Long-spined Sea Urchin *Diadema* sp., circumtropical.

Banded Sea Urchin *Echinothrix calamaris*, Indo-Pacific.

Slate pencil Urchin *Heterocentrotus mammillatus*, Indo-Pacific.

Jewelbox Sea Urchin *Mespilia globulus*, Indo-Pacific.

Imperial Sea Urchin *Phyllacanthus imperialis*, Indo-Pacific.

Thorn-spined Sea Urchin *Prionocidaris verticillata*, Indo- Pacific.

Flower Urchin *Toxopneustes pileolus*, Indo-Pacific. Very dangerous, occasionally deadly.

Sea Stars

Belonging together with sea urchins, featherstars or crinoids and sea cucumbers or holothurians to the phylum Echinodermata (meaning "spiny-skinned" in Latin), sea stars (Class Asteroidea) and brittle stars (Class Ophiuroidea) clearly show at first sight a characteristic radial symmetry with five or more arms radiating from a central body. Sea stars and brittle stars are benthic animals which are covered with a great number of calcareous plates of varying size and which surprisingly feel quite brittle to the touch of a bare hand. They commonly feed on dead or living prey, including many sea shells or living corals, and are in turn predated by harlequin shrimps and occasionally triggerfish. Virtually static when sighted underwater, sea stars and especially brittle stars are quite capable of comparatively rapid movement, which is achieved by a very complex hydrovascular system in which the surrounding water is pumped to hundreds of tiny tube-like feet equipped with small suckers. Such power is produced in this way that a sea star is even able to pull open a strongly muscular bivalve.

Crown-of-thorns Sea Star *Acanthaster planci*, Indo-Pacific.

Comb Sea Star *Astropecten polyacanthus*, Indo-Pacific.

Granulated Sea Star *Choriaster granulatus*, Indo-Pacific.

Pincushion Sea Star *Culcita novaeguineae*, Indo-Pacific.

Tuberculated Sea Star *Echinaster callosus*, Indo-Pacific.

Indian Sea Star *Fromia indica*, Indo-Pacific.

Necklace Sea Star *Fromia monilis*, Indo-Pacific.

Noduled Sea Star *Fromia nodosa*, Indo-Pacific.

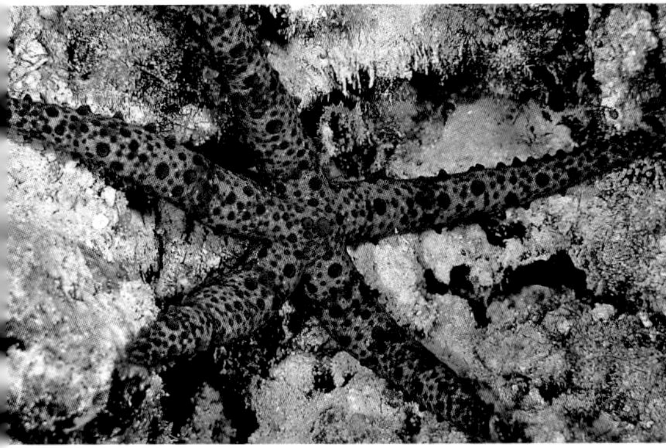

Egyptian Sea Star *Gomophia egyptiaca*, Indo-Pacific.

Smooth Sea Star *Leiaster speciosus*, Indo-Pacific.

Blue Sea Star *Linckia laevigata*, Indo-Pacific.

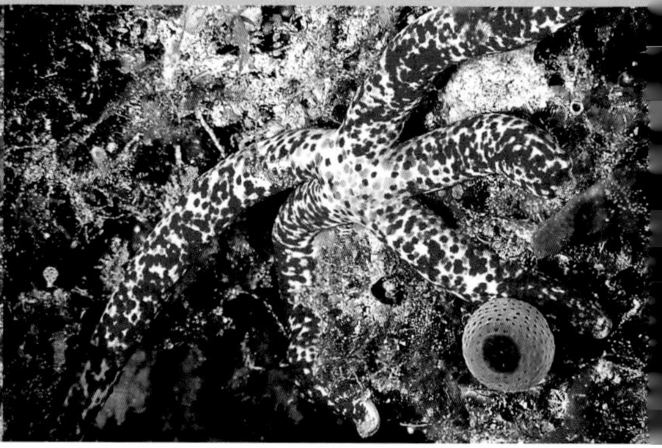

Multi-pore Sea Star *Linckia multifora*, Indo-Pacific.

Nail-armed Sea Star *Mithrodia clavigera*, circumtropical.

Warty Sea Star *Nardoa frianti*, Indo-Pacific.

Cuming's Sea Star *Neoferdina cumingi*, Indo-Pacific.

Jewel Sea Star *Neoferdina insolita*, Indo-Pacific.

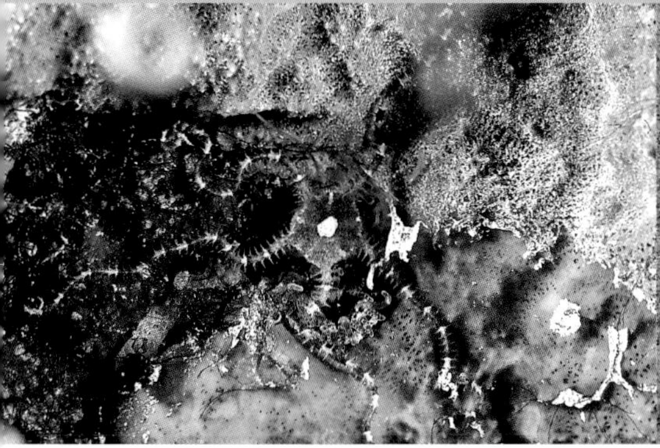

Savigny's Brittle Star *Ophiactis savignyi*, circumtropical.

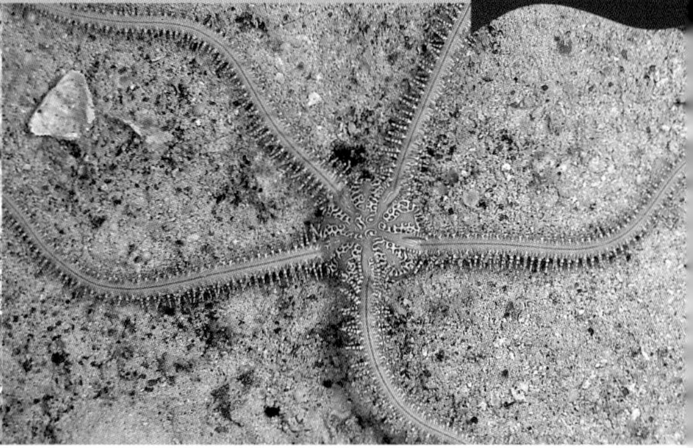

Spider Brittle Star *Ophiarachna affinis*, Indo-Pacific.

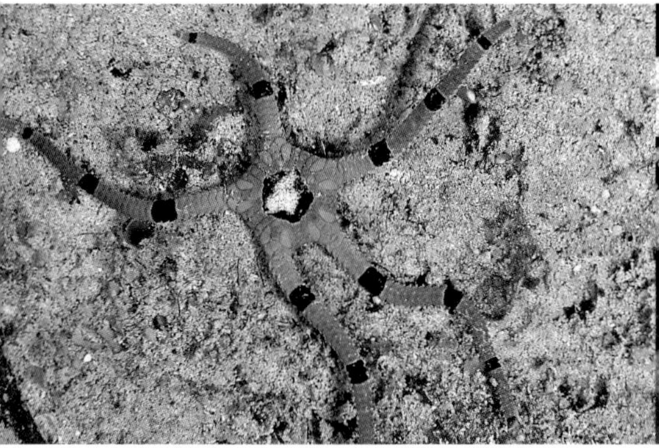

Superb Brittle Star *Ophiolepis superba*, Indo-Pacific.

Elegant Brittle Star *Ophiomastix variabilis*, Indo-Pacific.

Cushion Sea Star *Pentaceraster* sp., Indo-Pacific.

Knobbly Sea Star *Protoreaster nodosus*, Indo-Pacific.

Holothurians or Sea Cucumbers

Closely related to starfish and sea urchins, these echinoderms have developed an elongated and almost cylindrical shape while keeping their typical pentagonal symmetry in section. Unlike other echinoderms, they actually have a "head" and a "tail", and they normally lie on the substrate with one side of their body facing down. Generally diurnal, holothurians feed on benthic detritus which they pick up together with large quantities of sand using the sticky tentacles rimming the oral aperture. Quite common on many Indo-Pacific reefs, they are fished in enormous quantities to be used - after having been sun-dried - as an ingredient of Chinese cuisine called *trepang* or *beche-de-mer*. This practice has wiped out entire populations, severely endangering the survival of these harmless and useful creatures in many areas. Ironically, holothurians have almost no natural enemies in their habitat: beyond producing more or less toxic substances, they can also excrete large quantities of sticky, noxious white threads which glue themselves to the aggressor, severely impeding its movements.

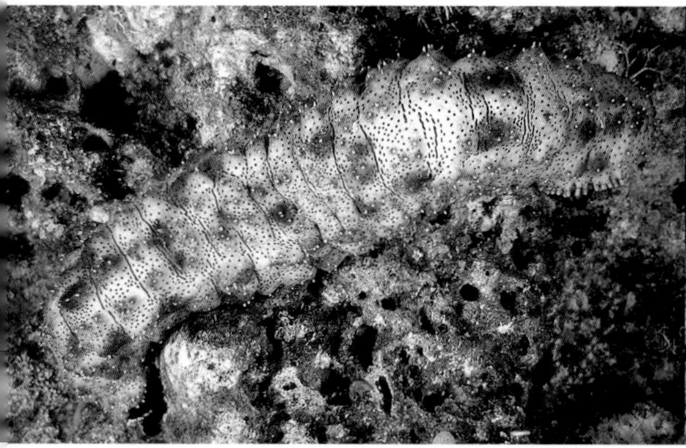

Bohadschia graeffei, 60 centimeters, Indo-Pacific.

Stichopus horrens, 35 centimeters, Indo-Pacific.

Actinopyga lecanora, 30 centimeters, Indo-Pacific.

Thelenota anax, 60 centimeters, Indo-Pacific.

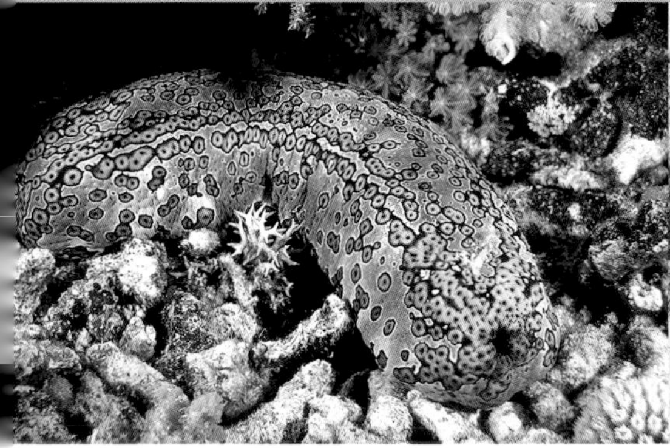

Bohadschia argus, 40 centimeters, Indo-Pacific.

Stichopus chloronotus, 40 centimeters, Indo-Pacific.

Thelenota ananas, 50 centimeters, Indo-Pacific.

Thelenota rubralineata, 40 centimeters, Indo-Pacific.

Colochirus robustus, 6 centimeters, Indo-Pacific.

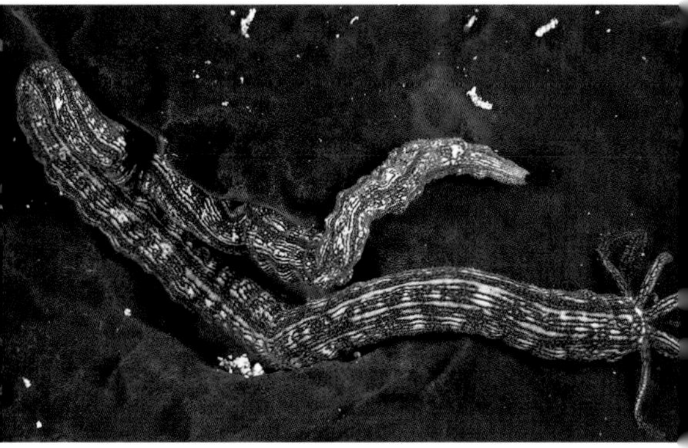

Synaptula sp., 10 centimeters, Indo-Pacific.

Gallery

Sticky, toxic *Cuverian tubules* are expelled by holothurians in defense from predators.

The adhesive feeding apparatus of *Bohadschia graeffei* picking up food particles from the substrate.

The Emperor partner shrimp *Periclemenes imperator* is a commonly observed commensal of several holothurians.

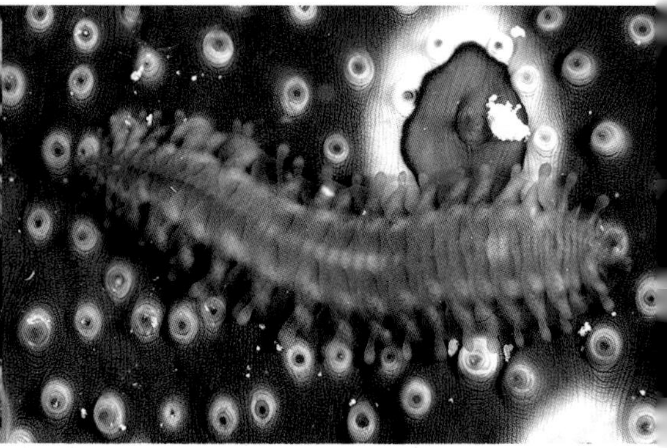

Scale worms *Gastrolepidia clavigera* are often found on the soft underside of large sea cucumbers.

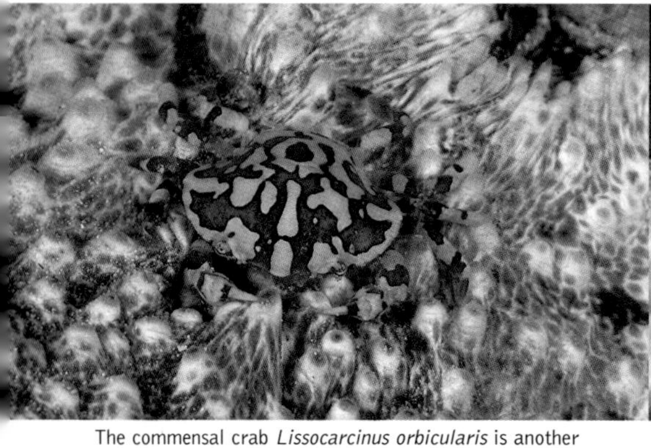

The commensal crab *Lissocarcinus orbicularis* is another frequent commensal of holothurians.

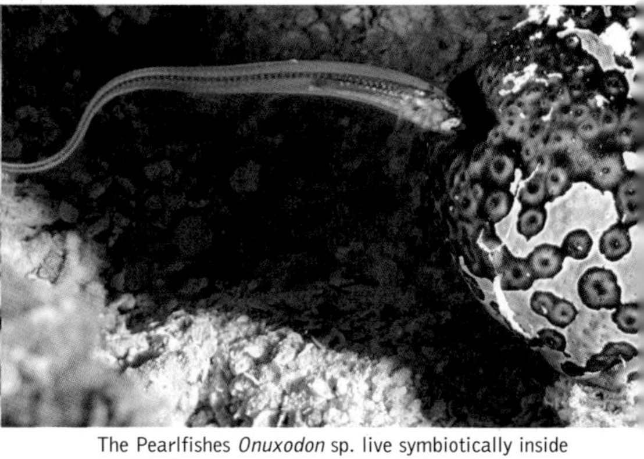

The Pearlfishes *Onuxodon* sp. live symbiotically inside several holothurians, entering their host through the anus.

Diver and *Thelenota rubralineata*, Kapalai, Sulawesi Sea, Malaysian Borneo

Flatworms

Looking exactly like tiny "living carpets", marine Flatworms belong to the Class Turbellaria, which accounts for a large number of species, many still undescribed. They are often easily mistaken for nudibranchs, but while size and coloration are in several instances quite similar (some are actually mimics), flatworms have an oval, wafer-thin body with no external gills. Color patterns are most often quite dazzling, being probably aposematic (ie warning of a danger), gaudily advertising the toxic properties of the animal to potential predators (the same, in fact, applies to most nudibranchs). Flatworms have no external gills, are hermaphrodites with male and female organs (but can also regenerate an entire individual from a fragment) and are carnivorous predators, mostly feeding on colonial ascidians. Their movement - a very elegant and surprisingly fast gliding on the substrate - is obtained by sliding on a self-secreted layer of mucus with the use of several microscopic ventral bristles. They usually shelter under slabs of coral and when disturbed they will rapidly swim away with undulating motions.

Maiazoon orsaki, Indo-Pacific. 3,5 centimeters.

Pseudobiceros bedfordi, Indo-Pacific. 8 centimeters.

Pseudobiceros ferrugineus, Indo-Pacific. 9 centimeters.

Pseudobiceros flowersi, Indo-Pacific. 6 centimeters.

Pseudobiceros fulgor, Indo-Pacific. 10 centimeters.

Pseudobiceros gloriosus, Indo-Pacific. 9 centimeters.

Pseudobiceros hancockanus, Indo-Pacific. 7 centimeters.

Pseudobiceros lindae, Indo-Pacific. 5 centimeters.

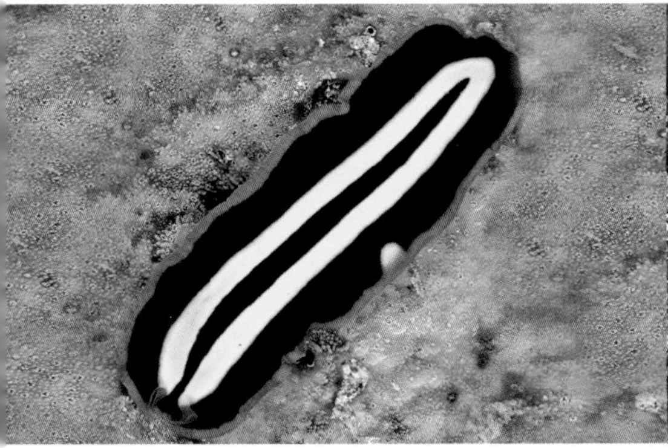

Pseudoceros dimidiatus, Indo-Pacific. 8 centimeters.

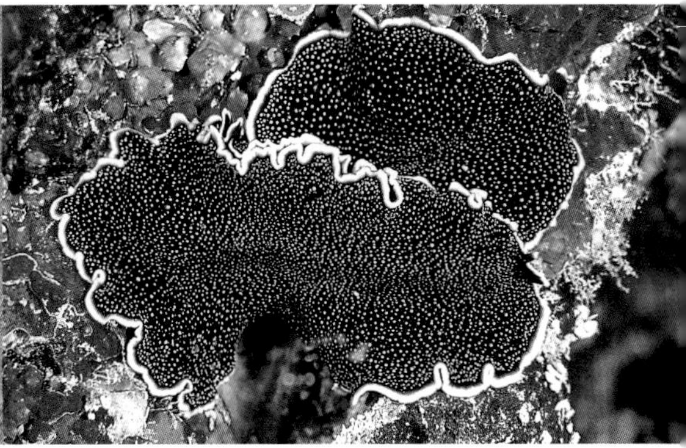

Thysanozoan nigropapillosum, Indo-Pacific. 9 centimeters.

Nudibranchs or Sea Slugs

Despite their generally small size, nudibranchs are among the showiest and most interesting creatures of the reef. These mollusks belong to the Order Nudibranchia, subclass Opistobranchia, numbering more than 3.000 species worldwide, with new ones being discovered and described on an almost daily basis. Nudibranchs are basically sea snails (or "slugs") with no internal or external shell, a pair of tentacle-like protrusions on top of the head acting as sense organs (called "rhinophores") and a more or less evident tuft of gills on the dorsal surface (which is however absent in some groups). Most are quite active, rather fast-moving (for their size, going from a few to 300 millimeters) and often exceptionally colorful, gaudily advertising their toxic properties to potential predators. Nudibranchs are able to absorbe and store noxious chemicals from their preys (mostly hydroids, sponges, ascidians and other small benthic organisms). All are predators, often cannibalistic, and hermaphrodites, meaning that a single individual possesses both male and female sexual organs at the same time.

Chelidonura amoena, Indo-Pacific.

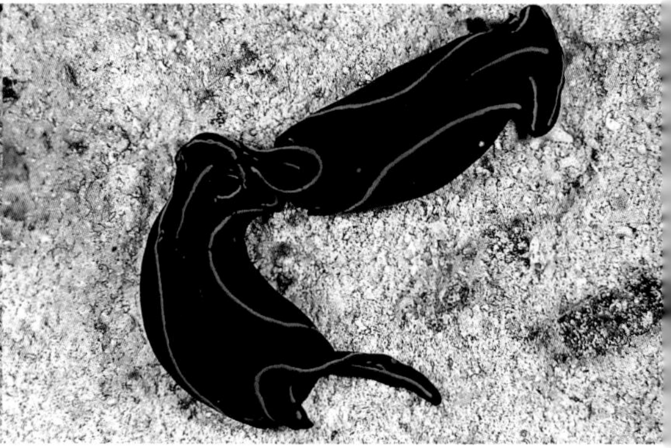

Chelidonura varians, Indo-Pacific.

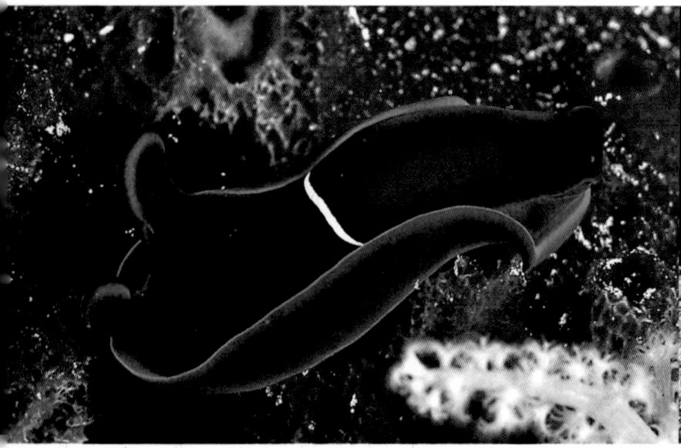

Philinopsis gardineri, Indo-Pacific.

Stylocheilus longicauda, Indo-Pacific.

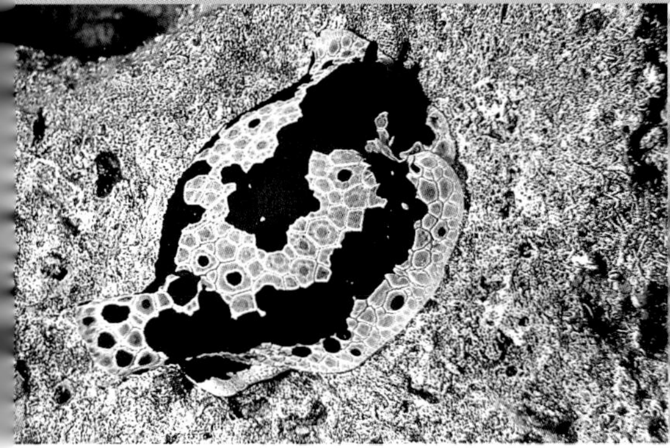

Pleurobranchus grandis, Indo-Pacific.

Berthella martensi, Indo-Pacific.

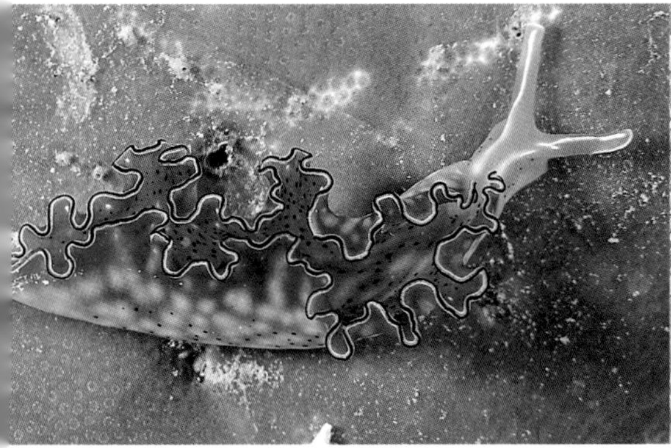

Elysia ornata, Indo-Pacific.

Elysia verrucosa, Indo-Pacific.

Thuridilla bayeri, Indo-Pacific.

Plakobranchus ocellatus, Indo-Pacific.

Nembrotha cristata, Indo-Pacific.

Nembrotha guttata, Indo-Pacific.

Nembrotha kubaryana, Indo-Pacific.

Nembrotha kubaryana 2, Indo-Pacific.

Nembrotha lineolata, Indo-Pacific.

Nembrotha milleri, Indo-Pacific.

Nembrotha purpureolineata, Indo-Pacific.

Nembrotha sp., Indo-Pacific.

Nembrotha sp. 2, Indo-Pacific.

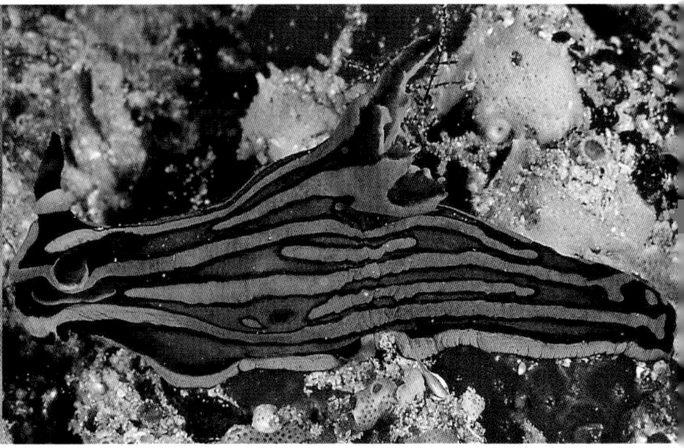

Roboastra arika, Indo-Pacific.

Roboastra gracilis, Indo-Pacific.

Tambja morosa, Indo-Pacific.

Tambja sagamiana, Indo-Pacific.

Thecacera picta, Indo-Pacific.

Notodoris minor, Indo-Pacific.

Notodoris serenae, Indo-Pacific.

Aphelodoris berghi, Indo-Pacific.

Dendrodoris denisoni, Indo-Pacific.

Dendrodoris tuberculosa, Indo-Pacific.

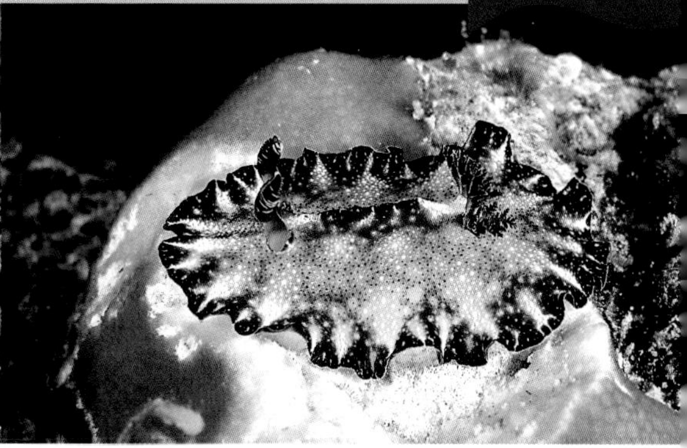

Discodoris boholiensis, Indo-Pacific.

Halgerda "Okinawa", Indo-Pacific.

Halgerda batangas, Indo-Pacific.

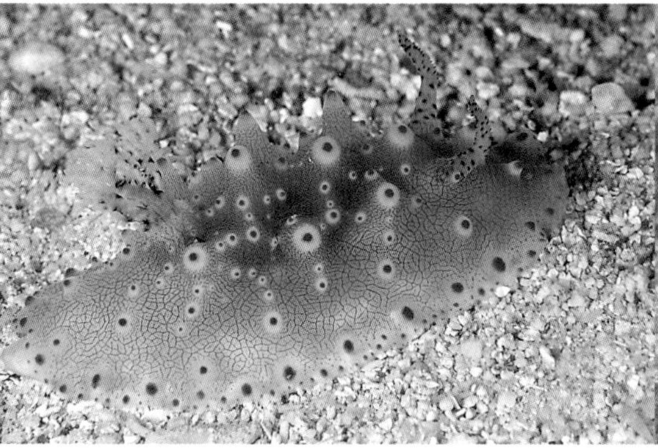

Halgerda malesso, Indo-Pacific.

Halgerda tessellata, Indo-Pacific.

Halgerda willeyi, Indo-Pacific.

Jorunna funebris, Indo-Pacific.

Jorunna rubrescens, Indo-Pacific.

Armina sp., Indo-Pacific.

Chromodoris lineolata, Indo-Pacific.

Chromodoris albopunctata, Indo-Pacific.

Chromodoris alius, Indo-Pacific.

Chromodoris annae, Indo-Pacific.

Chromodoris coi, Indo-Pacific.

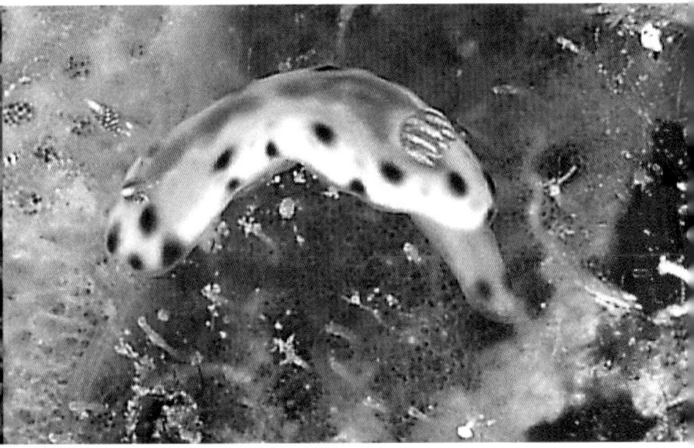

Chromodoris collingwoodi, Indo-Pacific.

Chromodoris dianae, Indo-Pacific.

Chromodoris fidelis, Indo-Pacific.

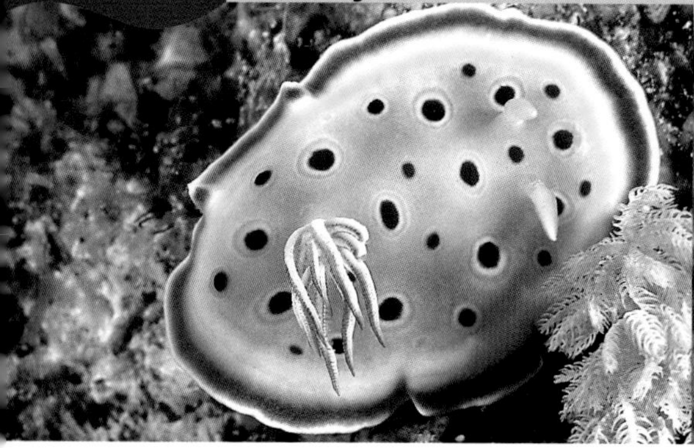

Chromodoris geminus, Indo-Pacific.

Chromodoris geometrica, Indo-Pacific.

Chromodoris hintuanensis, Indo-Pacific.

Chromodoris kuniei, Indo-Pacific.

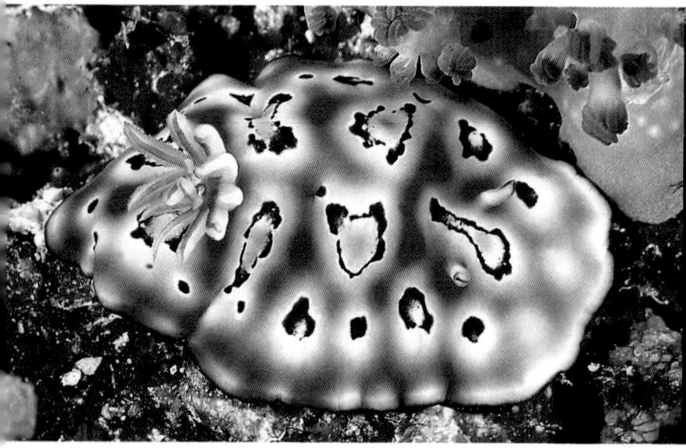

Chromodoris leopardus, Indo-Pacific.

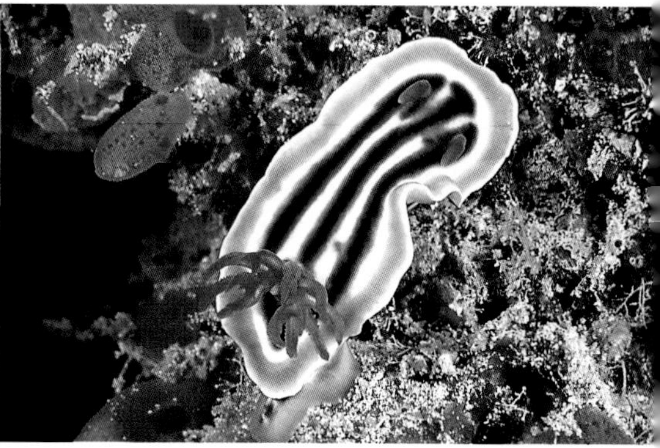

Chromodoris magnifica, Indo-Pacific.

Chromodoris michaeli, Indo-Pacific.

Chromodoris reticulata, Indo-Pacific.

Chromodoris splendida, Indo-Pacific.

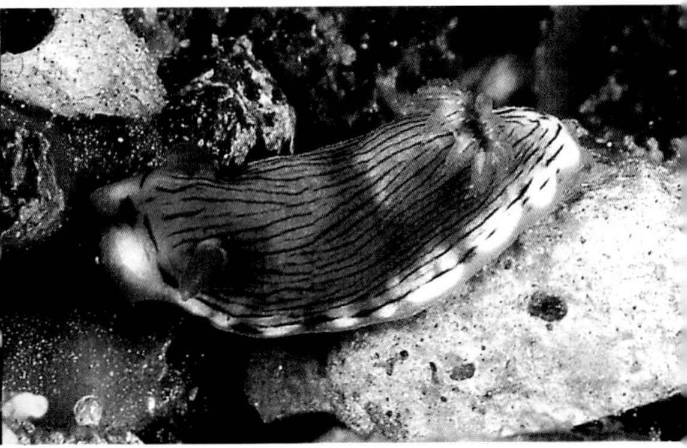

Chromodoris striatella, Indo-Pacific.

Chromodoris strigata, Indo-Pacific.

Chromodoris tinctoria, Indo-Pacific.

Chromodoris tritos, Indo-Pacific.

Chromodoris willani, Indo-Pacific.

Cadlinella ornatissima, Indo-Pacific.

Ardeadoris egretta, Indo-Pacific.

Glossodoris atromarginata, Indo-Pacific.

Glossodoris cincta, Indo-Pacific.

Glossodoris hikuerensis, Indo-Pacific.

Glossodoris pallida, Indo-Pacific.

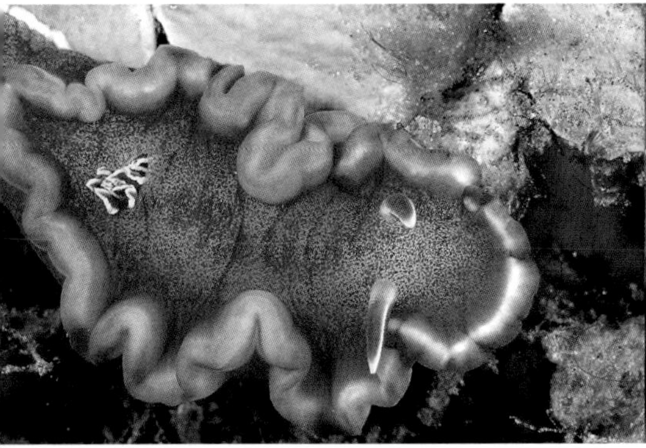

Glossodoris rufromarginata, Indo-Pacific.

Glossodoris stellata, Indo-Pacific.

Risbecia pulchella, Indo-Pacific.

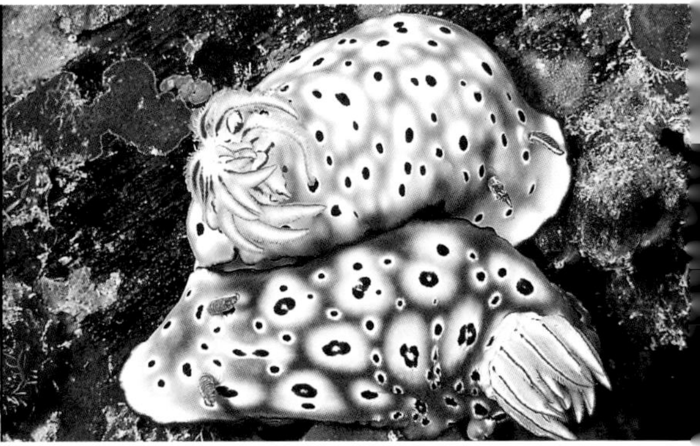

Risbecia tryoni, Indo-Pacific.

Ceratosoma gracillimum, Indo-Pacific.

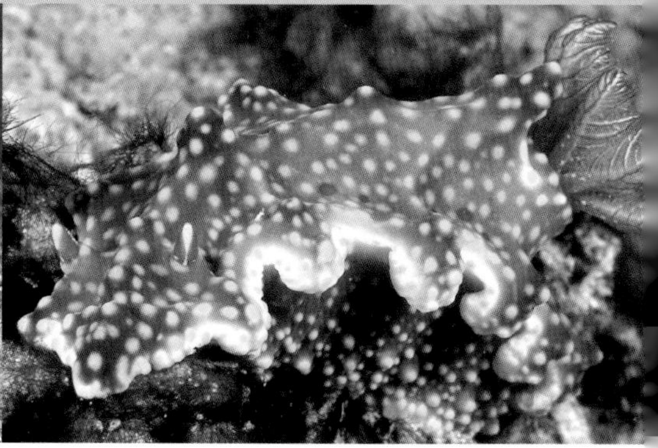

Ceratosoma sinuatum, Indo-Pacific.

Ceratosoma tenue, Indo-Pacific.

Ceratosoma trilobatum, Indo-Pacific.

Hypselodoris apolegma, Indo-Pacific.

Hypselodoris bullockii, Indo-Pacific.

Hypselodoris bullockii, Indo-Pacific.

Hypselodoris bullockii, Indo-Pacific.

Hypselodoris emmae, Indo-Pacific.

Hypselodoris infucata, Indo-Pacific.

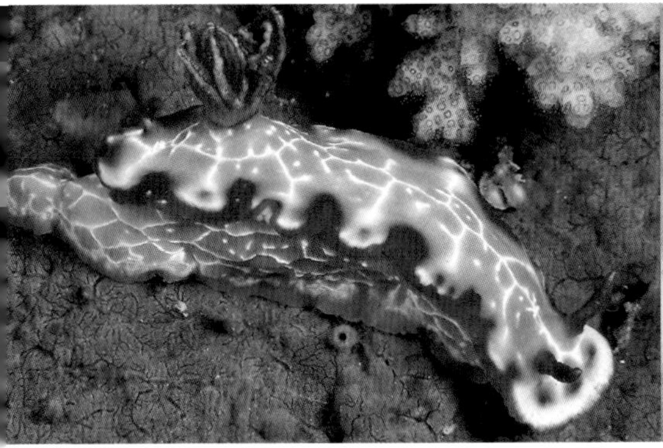

Hypselodoris jacula, Indo-Pacific.

Hypselodoris maculosa, Indo-Pacific.

Hypselodoris nigrostriata, Indo-Pacific.

Hypselodoris reidi, Indo-Pacific.

Hypselodoris whitei, Indo-Pacific.

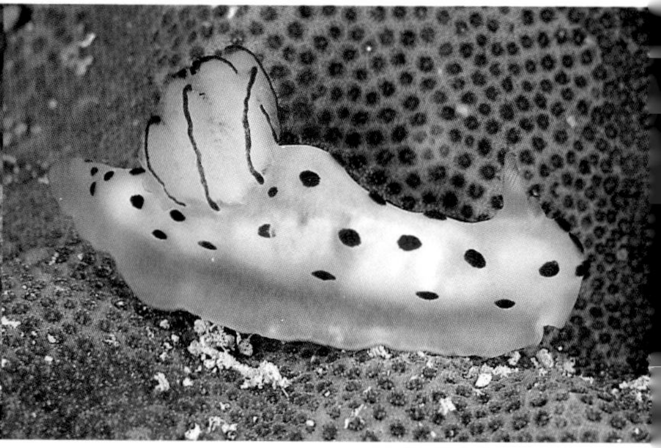

Gymnodoris ceylonica, Indo-Pacific.

Gymnodoris rubropapillosa, Indo-Pacific.

Mexichromis mariei, Indo-Pacific.

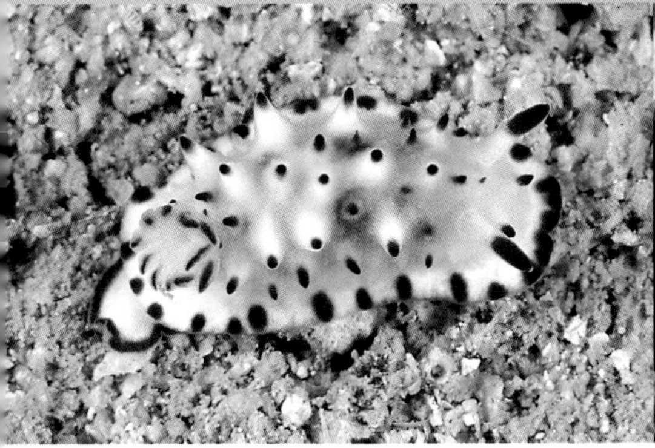

Mexichromis multituberculatus, Indo-Pacific.

Phyllidia babai, Indo-Pacific.

Phyllidia coelestis, Indo-Pacific.

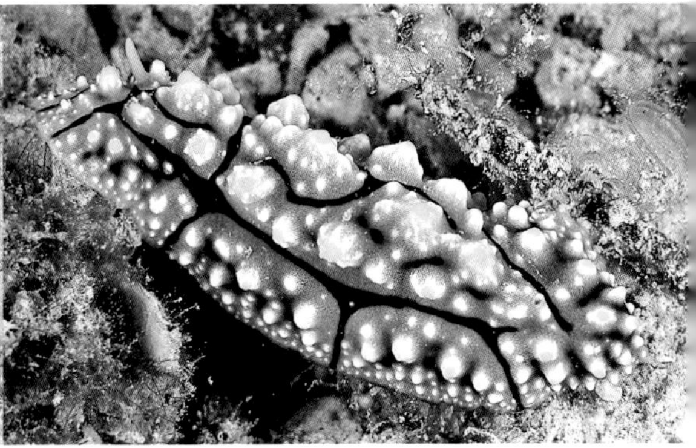

Phyllidia elegans, Indo-Pacific.

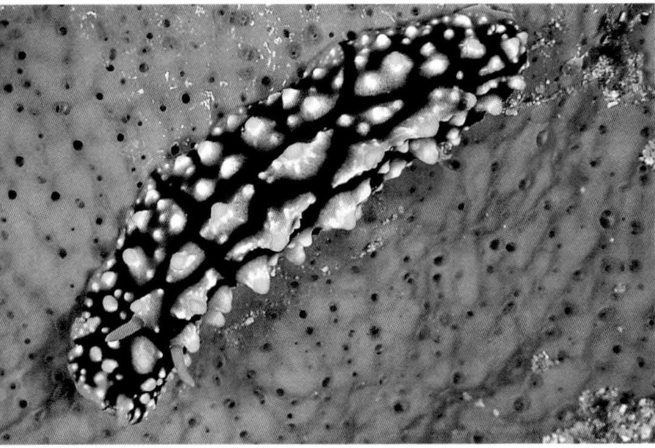

Phyllidia exquisita, Indo-Pacific.

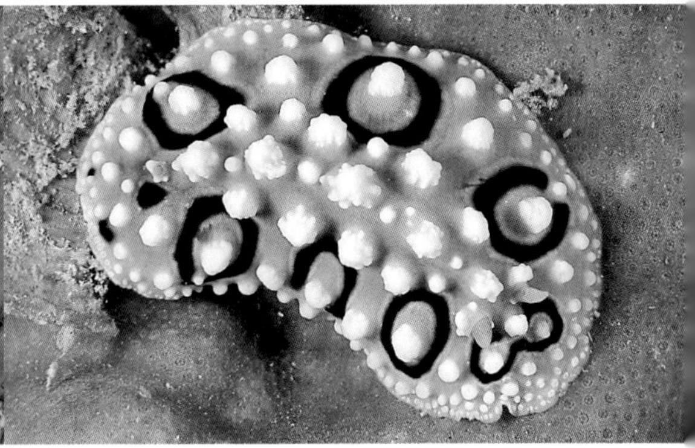

Phyllidia ocellata, Indo-Pacific.

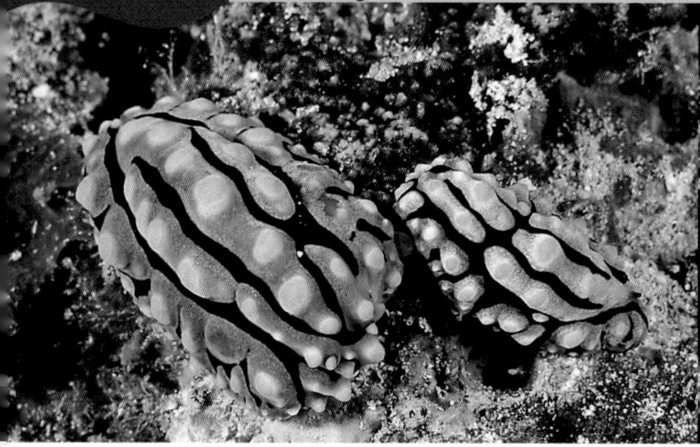

Phyllidia varicosa, Indo-Pacific.

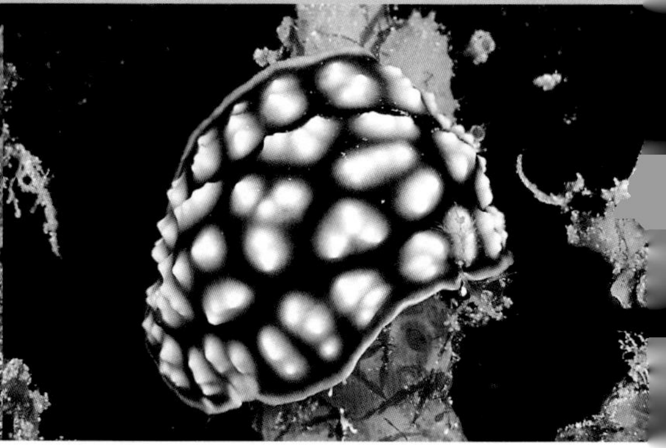

Phyllidiella pustulosa, Indo-Pacific.

Phyllidiella rosans, Indo-Pacific.

Phyllidiopsis fissuratus, Indo-Pacific.

Phyllidiopsis pipeki, Indo-Pacific.

Phyllidiopsis shireenae, Indo-Pacific.

Reticulidia fungia, Indo-Pacific.

Reticulidia halgerda, Indo-Pacific.

Crimora lutea, Indo-Pacific.

Marionia sp., Indo-Pacific.

Marionia sp., Indo-Pacific.

Melibe sp., Indo-Pacific.

Flabellina exoptata, Indo-Pacific.

Flabellina rubrolineata, Indo-Pacific.

Hexabranchus sanguineus, Indo-Pacific.

Phidiana indica, Indo-Pacific.

Pteraeolidia ianthina, Indo-Pacific.

Phyllodesmium briareum, Indo-Pacific.

Phyllodesmium longicirrum, Indo-Pacific.

Phyllodesmium magnum, Indo-Pacific.

Cuthona kanga, Indo-Pacific.

Godiva quadricolor, Indo-Pacific.

Janolus sp., Indo-Pacific.

Umbraculum umbraculum, circumtropical.

Strange Reef Creatures

Some of the creatures inhabiting coral reefs are so strange - some would even say weird - to defy description, and will leave even the most biased of divers puzzled. Even experienced researchers and photographers will occasionally still be perplexed facing uncommon creatures which at first sight cannot even be clearly defined as vegetable or animal. Fresh divers find themselves in this position even more often and in our experience will not ask their buddies or dive guides for fear of appearing ignorant or inexperienced. In fact, there's nothing wrong in asking when the reef environment is involved, since even most experts will have no definite answers regarding some subjects! In these pages some species which may look puzzling at first sight are more or less identified: some are very common and can be easily encountered, others less so. All require a degree of curiosity to be observed in the wild, since several are quite cryptic, others are nocturnal and some more are ironically taken for granted and commonly misidentified. They are just a few of the many we have often seen people wondering about.

Condylactis sp., a flower-like sea anemone commonly observed on sand bottoms.

Cerianthus sp., an anemone-like animal living in a mud-and-mucus flexible tube.

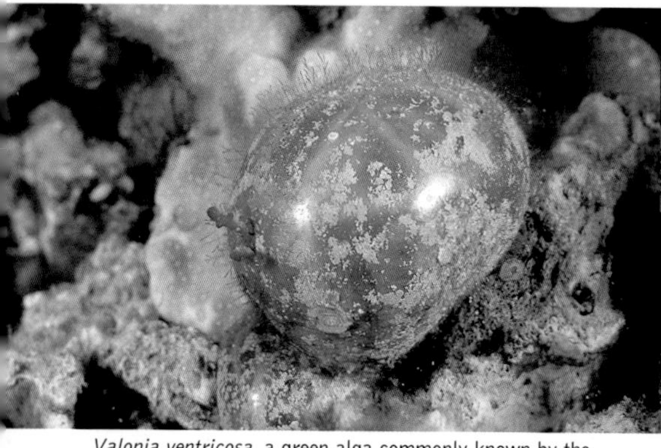

Valonia ventricosa, a green alga commonly known by the unsavoury name of Sailor's Eyeball.

Filogranella elatensis, a tube worm living in colonies.

Cynarina lacrimalis, a hard coral.This is an uncommon fuchsia color variation.

Possibly *Discosoma* sp., a corallimorpharian (intermediate between sea anemones and hard corals).

Minabea aldersladei, an alcyonarian or soft coral.

Neothyonidium magnum, a sea cucumber - usually buried in sand - which looks like an anemone.

Protopalythoa sp., a zoanthid. These are small colonial anemone-like animals.

Sabellid tube worms, unidentified species.

Gallery

Amplexidiscus fenestrafer, a corallimorpharian, fully contracted.

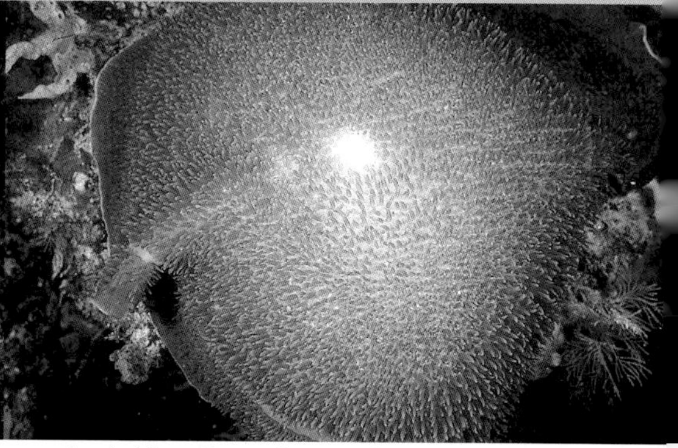

Amplexidiscus fenestrafer, a corallimorpharian, fully expanded.

Contracted Basket star *Astroboa nuda* during daytime.

Goniopora sp., a hard coral starting to form a small colony.

Sarcophyton sp., commonly known as Mushroom leather coral, is a soft coral (Alcyonacea).

Pseudocorynactis sp., an uncommon corallimorpharian looking like an anemone.

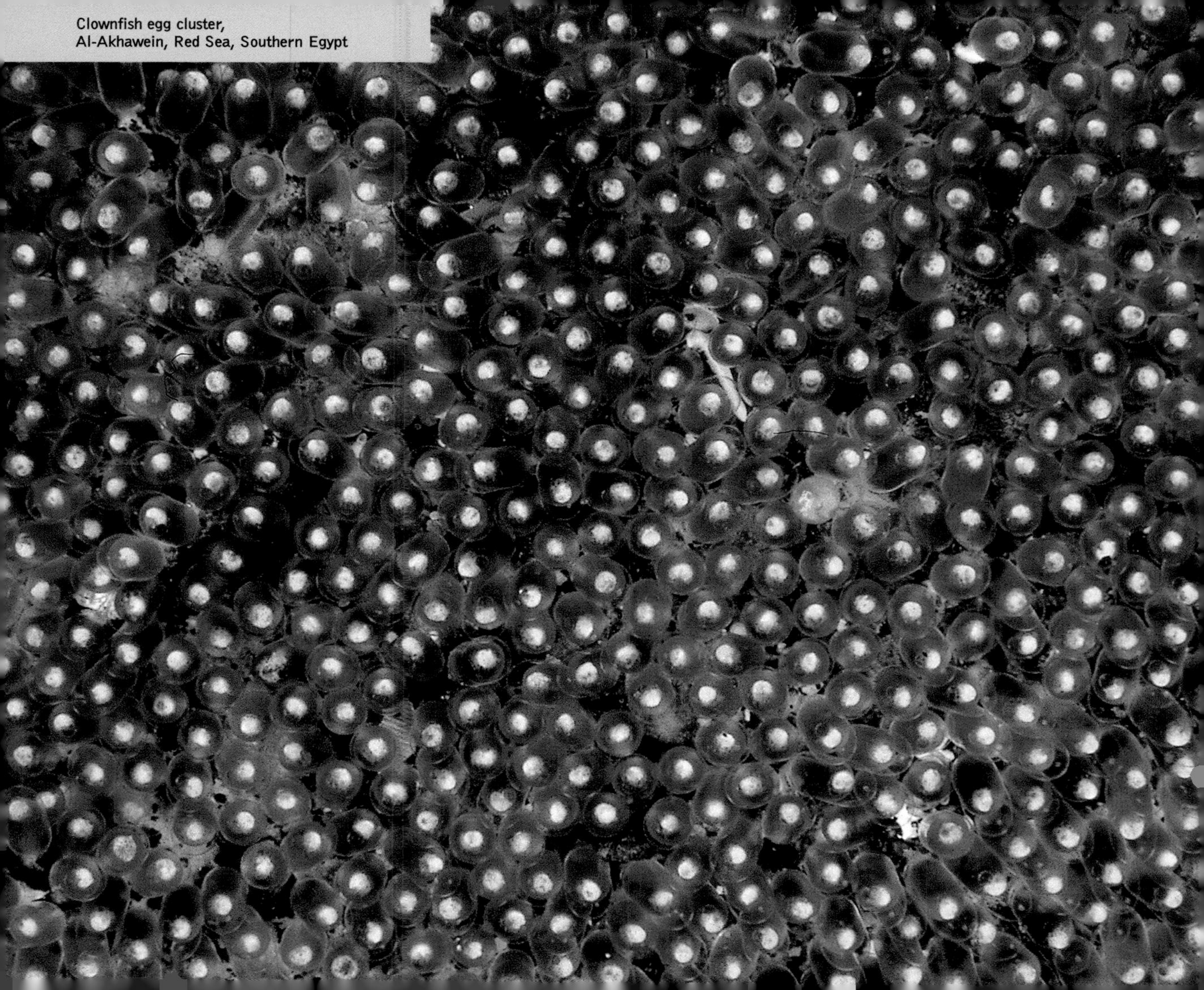

Clownfish egg cluster,
Al-Akhawein, Red Sea, Southern Egypt

REPTILES

Turtles, snakes and crocodiles

Reptiles count among their vast numbers a relatively small contingent of species which however represent a superb example of evolutionary adaptation to a sea-going existence. Most marine turtles and all sea snake species lead a strictly pelagic life, occasionally coming close to shore only to feed and mate and setting belly or flipper on land only to lay their eggs on deserted beaches, while the much feared saltwater crocodile will find itself equally at home in fresh, brackish or saltwater. All reptiles are air breathers and need to surface to fill their lungs, even if most are quite capable of spending a remarkable amount of time - up to two hours when not moving - underwater. Despite dating back to the age of dinosaurs, most marine reptiles are today severely endangered by human activities, particularly hunting and habitat destruction.~ **U/W Photo Tips:** While saltwater crocodiles and deadly venomous sea snakes are best left undisturbed for obvious reasons, the peaceful and gentle turtles can be easily approached. Try framing them from below with the sun in the background while they are swimming, taking care however never to harass them.

GREEN TURTLE
Chelonia mydas

Distribution: Circum- and subtropical.
Size: Up to 140 centimeters.
Habitat: Pelagic and coastal waters from 1 to 40 meters deep.
Life Habits: A superb swimmer: large rounded head, blunt beak and prefrontal scales between the eyes are diagnostic. Shell is brownish-olive, gracefully mottled in darker yellowish tones. Green turtles live their whole life at sea, feeding on seagrasses and mating in the ocean, coming to shore only to lay their eggs on undisturbed beaches. Despite being locally common this elegant and harmless species is severely threatened with extinction.

HAWKSBILL TURTLE
Eretmochelys imbricata

Distribution: Circum- and subtropical.
Size: Up to 90 centimeters.
Habitat: Pelagic and coastal waters from 1 to 40 meters deep.
Life Habits: Can be easily separated from the preceding species by the smaller size, the embricate shell plates and above all by the clearly distinguishable, sharp, hooked beak. The dazzlingly beautiful shell is softly mottled in black, brown and yellow. Lives its whole life in the ocean, coming to shore only to lay its eggs on undisturbed beaches. Feeds on sponges and soft corals. Seriously endangered by human activities like most marine turtles.

LEATHERBACK TURTLE
Dermochelys coriacea

Distribution: Circumglobal in tropical, temperate and seasonally in artic seas.
Size: Up to 180 centimeters.
Habitat: Pelagic.
Life Habits: The largest living turtle in the world, with an adult weight of almost 600 kgs. The shell is covered by a smooth, leathery skin which is slate black, bluish black, or black, with scattered small white to yellowish blotches. The skin of the head, neck, and limbs is black, brown, or dark green with scattered pale blotches. Feeds mostly on jellyfish, diving to over 1,000 meters. Severely endangered.

RINGED SEA SNAKE
Laticauda colubrina

Distribution: Tropical Central Indo-Pacific from Bangladesh to Australia.
Size: Up to 150 centimeters.
Habitat: Coastal and outer reef waters from 1 to 15 meters deep.
Life Habits: Body is slender, blue-grey with evenly-spaced black bands, head black with pale yellow lips. Tail is distinctly paddle-shaped. Normally not aggressive but extremely venomous and potentially deadly, belonging to the same family of land cobras. Locally common, often observed in large aggregations in shallow water and on beaches at night. Feeds on small eels, gobies and fish eggs.

OLIVE SEA SNAKE
Aipysurus laevis

Distribution: Tropical Central Indo-Pacific from Papua New Guinea to Australia and the Coral Sea.
Size: Up to 180 centimeters.
Habitat: Coastal and outer reefs from 1 to 40 meters deep, often in turbid waters.
Life Habits: Large, heavy-bodied, small-headed, olive or golden sea snake with a paddle-like tail and a very venomous bite. Several very similar species: about 60 sea snake species are known, all in the Indo-Pacific and mostly in Australian waters. All are air breathers: one single gulp will last them from 30 minutes to two hours.

SALTWATER CROCODILE
Crocodylus porosus

Distribution: Tropical Central Indo-Pacific from India to Papua New Guinea and Northern Australia.
Size: Up to 700 centimeters.
Habitat: Mangroves, brackish estuaries, tidal section of rivers, outer reefs.
Life Habits: Severely endangered and today rare everywhere but still locally common in Papua New Guinea and Northern Australia, this occasionally large and very aggressive crocodilian poses a real threat to waders, swimmers and snorkelers, with several humans killed every year. Divers may occasionally encounter juveniles or subadults.

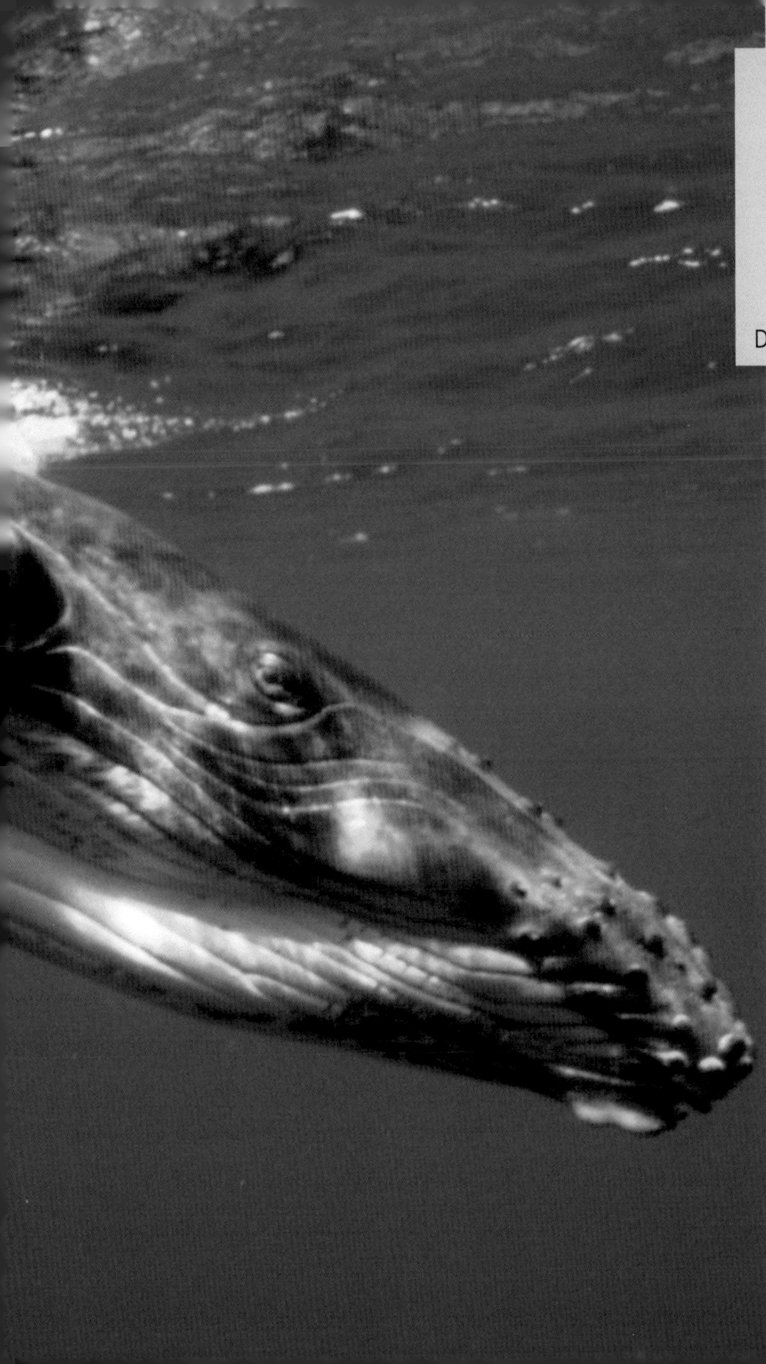

MAMMALS

Dugongs, dolphins and whales

Like sea-going reptiles, the more than 80 species of cetaceans presently classified have spectacularly and successfully adapted to a pelagic life. They too are obviously air breathers and need to periodically surface to breath fresh air, and yet several are quite more successful at surviving in the ocean than most fish. Superb swimmers, fantastic divers and clinical hunters, dolphins and whales in particular show a vast degree of intelligence, the capability of communicating with each other and a complex social structure. Like many other inhabitants of the deep, marine mammals too are today greatly suffering from man's activities, as underwater noise pollution in particular severely interferes with their sophisticated ecolocation systems, causing disorientation, deadly alterations of behavior and suicidal mass strandings. ~ **U/W Photo Tips:** Loved and admired by all, marine mammals are without doubt the most difficult subjects for underwater photographers. Curious but very cautious when present, they will often keep a safe distance from divers. Some individuals will however get used to humans, and these obviously offer the best chances for medium or wide angle shots.

DUGONG
Dugong dugon

Distribution: Tropical Indo-Pacific from the Red Sea and East Africa to Micronesia.
Size: Up to 400 centimeters.
Habitat: Seagrass beds and lagoons in shallow, sheltered coastal waters.
Life Habits: Harmless, gentle giants belonging to the Order Sirenia together with the Manatee *Trichechus manatus*. Feeds on seagrass, and as a mammal breathes air and gives birth to live young. Body of adults is slate grey, with smooth tough skin and sparse bristles on the muzzle. Relentlessly hunted and harassed throughout its distribution area, it is now exceedingly rare and severely endangered.

BOTTLENOSE DOLPHIN
Tursiops truncatus

Distribution: Circumtropical, subtropical and temperate seas.
Size: Up to 400 centimeters.
Habitat: Coastal and pelagic.
Life Habits: Body robust, in subtle shades of grey: possibly several very similar species which might be part of a complex. Often observed riding boats bow-waves and wakes, occasionally fully jumping out of the water: in general very wary of divers underwater, occasionally observed swimming in small pods together with sharks and turtles. Often interacting with humans: there is evidence of this species working together with fishermen.

SPINNER DOLPHIN
Stenella longirostris

Distribution: Circumtropical and subtropical worldwide.
Size: Up to 210 centimeters.
Habitat: Coastal and pelagic.
Life Habits: Several subspecies, all sharing a long beak and a straight dorsal fin. Body is usually in soft shades of grey but three-tone examples are known. Often encountered in large pods, loves to give acrobatic displays jumping high in the air and rolling up to seven times along its axis. Slaughtered in hundreds of thousands by drift net industrial tuna fishing boats, now endangered.

ATLANTIC SPOTTED DOLPHIN
Stenella frontalis

Distribution: Temperate, subtropical and tropical Atlantic.
Size: Up to 230 centimeters.
Habitat: Coastal and pelagic.
Life Habits: Dark purple-grey back, very pale belly, tall hooked dorsal fin; older individuals show a typical dark spotting on the underside which gets progressively thicker with age. Several local variations. Loves to swim on the surface in smallish (5-15) groups, often approaching boats: several wild pods in the Bahamas seem to enjoy the company of snorkellers, occasionally allowing close interaction.

SPERM WHALE
Physeter macrocephalus

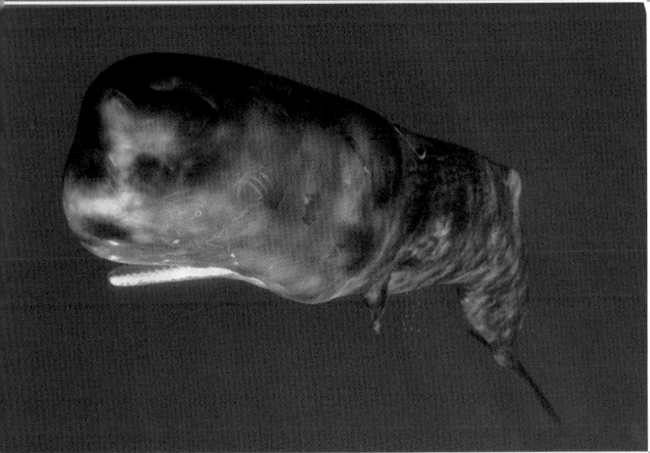

Distribution: Circumglobal.
Size: Up to 18 meters.
Habitat: Deep coastal and pelagic waters from 1 to at least 200 meters deep.
Life Habits: Spectacular, gigantic cetacean hunted in great numbers in the past but still relatively numerous: strongly angled surface blow and huge squarish head are unmistakable and diagnostic. Body is dark grey with typically wrinkled skin. May dive for more than two hours, feeding on deep water cephalopods. Occasionally observed on the surface in small family groups (10-20 sub-adults and females); old bulls are solitary..

HUMPBACK WHALE
Megaptera novaeanglíae

Distribution: Circumglobal from the Poles to the Equator.
Size: Up to 15 meters.
Habitat: Coastal and pelagic.
Life Habits: Unmistakable enormous, wing-like, knobbly front flippers with knobbly jaw and deeply arched head. Dorsal fin small, tail flukes very wide and with ragged edge. Body dark grey or blue grey with occasional white streaking and white underside. Often curious, will rarely allow close interaction: more than 250.000 have been slaughtered by whalers and less than 18.000 survive.

The Topside Reef

The exposed part of the reef includes stretches periodically uncovered by tides, beaches, mud flats and mangrove forests. These environments - and the nutrients they provide - attract many mammals, reptiles, birds and crustaceans. Mammals include wild boars and various monkeys such as the proboscis monkey *Nasalis larvatus*, and members of the sirenian family such as dugongs and manatees in water. Monitor lizards, several semi-aquatic snakes and the saltwater crocodile *Crocodylus porosus* are among the many reptiles associated with the brackish environment. Mangrove forests also host the mudskippers belonging to the *Periophtalmus* genus, fish up to 20 cm (8 in) long that can survive at length out of water. A large and endangered Indo-Pacific crustacean, the coconut crab *Birgus latro* is strictly nocturnal and can grow to more than 40 cm (16 in) in diameter. Depending upon the geographic zone, various species of pelicans, seagulls, herons, flamingoes and boobies can be observed. Other birds such as the frigatebird, *Fregata magnificens*, are dispersed circumtropically.

Very resistant to salt, the Screwpine *Pandanus* sp. is able to colonize many remote oceanic locations .

Nipa *Nipa* sp. palms form thick impenetrable forests in undisturbed Asian brackish estuarine environments.

Spread by man, the coconut palm *Cocos nucifera* is now commonly found along many tropical beaches worldwide.

Most large beach and mangrove crabs can be observed only at night, when they forage for food.

The spectacular coconut crab *Birgus latro* is today severely endangered throughout its range.

The mangrove snake *Boiga dendrophila* can be commonly observed in thick SE Asian mangrove forests.

Yellow-lipped sea kraits *Laticauda colubrina* are often encountered on Indo-Pacific reef beaches at night.

The estuarine or saltwater crocodile *Crocodylus porosus* is nowadays severely endangered over most of its range.

The water monitor *Varanus salvator* is commonly found on Asian reef beaches, hunting for crabs and turtle eggs.

Mudskippers *Periophtalmus* spp. live in thick mangrove forests and can survive for several minutes out of water.

Gallery

Undisturbed, deserted reef beachfronts are commonly used as nesting sites by green turtles *Chelonia mydas*.

Black-headed gulls *Larus atricilla* are common scavengers on Western Atlantic tropical beaches and reefs.

White-breasted boobies *Sula leucogaster* commonly nest in large, noisy colonies on deserted reef islets and atolls.

The large brown pelican *Pelecanus occidentalis* is a common sight on many Western Atlantic beaches.

The grey heron *Ardea cinerea* is one of several heron species occasionally associated with coral reefs.

Great frigatebirds *Fregata magnificens* are circumtropical and can often be observed soaring above coral reefs.

Proboscis Monkey *Nasalis larvatus*, Kinabatangan River, Sukau, Malaysian Borneo

In our search for unusual tropical marine species we have dived some of the most remote corners of the globe. Smooth and safe diving services in these locations are a must, especially considering the time and cost needed to reach them. For this very practical reason we believe readers might find the following dive resort and liveaboard listing of interest. Many others have been successfully operating worldwide for a long time, but we can personally vouch for these having tried and tested them over a number of years. All these operators have consistently proved highly reliable with regard to comfort, safety, low environmental impact and diving quality. They are highly committed to reef habitat conservation and diving with them usually brings impressive opportunities and excellent results.

Pulau Lankayan

Private island resort in the Sulu Sea, Malaysia. Visibility occasionally mediocre but many rare or undescribed macro species. Now a Marine Conservation Area.

www.dive-malaysia.com

Sipadan-Kapalai Dive Resort

Water village-styled resort in the Sulawesi Sea, Malaysia. One of the best destinations in the world for macro diving and the most comfortable to dive legendary Sipadan.

www.dive-malaysia.com

Layang Layang

Remote atoll in the South China Sea, Malaysia. Spectacular visibility, excellent opportunities for large pelagics and hammerheads.

www.layanglayang.com

Walea Dive Resort

Spectacular setting and excellent diving on untouched coral reefs in the Tomini Gulf, Central Sulawesi, Indonesia. Now a Marine Reserve.

www.walea.com

Sorido Eco Resort

Remote upper-class resort in amazing, untouched Raja Ampat, West Papua, Indonesia. Some of the world's most spectacular and pristine diving.

www.papua-diving.com

Tasik Ria

Comfortable mainland base close to Manado, Northern Sulawesi, Indonesia, to dive Bunaken National Park's colorful walls and coral gardens.

www.eco-divers.com

Kungkungan Bay Resort

Exceptional muck and macro diving in the Lembeh Strait, Northern Sulawesi, Indonesia. Many rare, strange and undescribed species.

www.kungkungan.com

M/Y Ocean Rover

Very stable and comfortable liveaboard from Phuket, Thailand. One of the best options for exploring the Andaman Sea and Myanmar.

www.ocean-rover.com

M/Y Okeanos Aggressor

Large oceanic vessel based in Puntarenas, Costa Rica. One of the best liveaboards to dive the remote Isla del Coco National Park.

www.aggressor.com

M/Y Majesty

Large, stable, upper-class liveaboard based in Marsa Alam, Egypt. One of the best options to dive the incredibly colorful Southern Egyptian Red Sea.

www.emperordivers.com

Posada Caracol

Small, pleasant resort in the Los Roques National Park, Venezuela. One of the best options to dive some of the most remote and still virgin sites of the Caribbean.

www.posadacaracol.com

Index

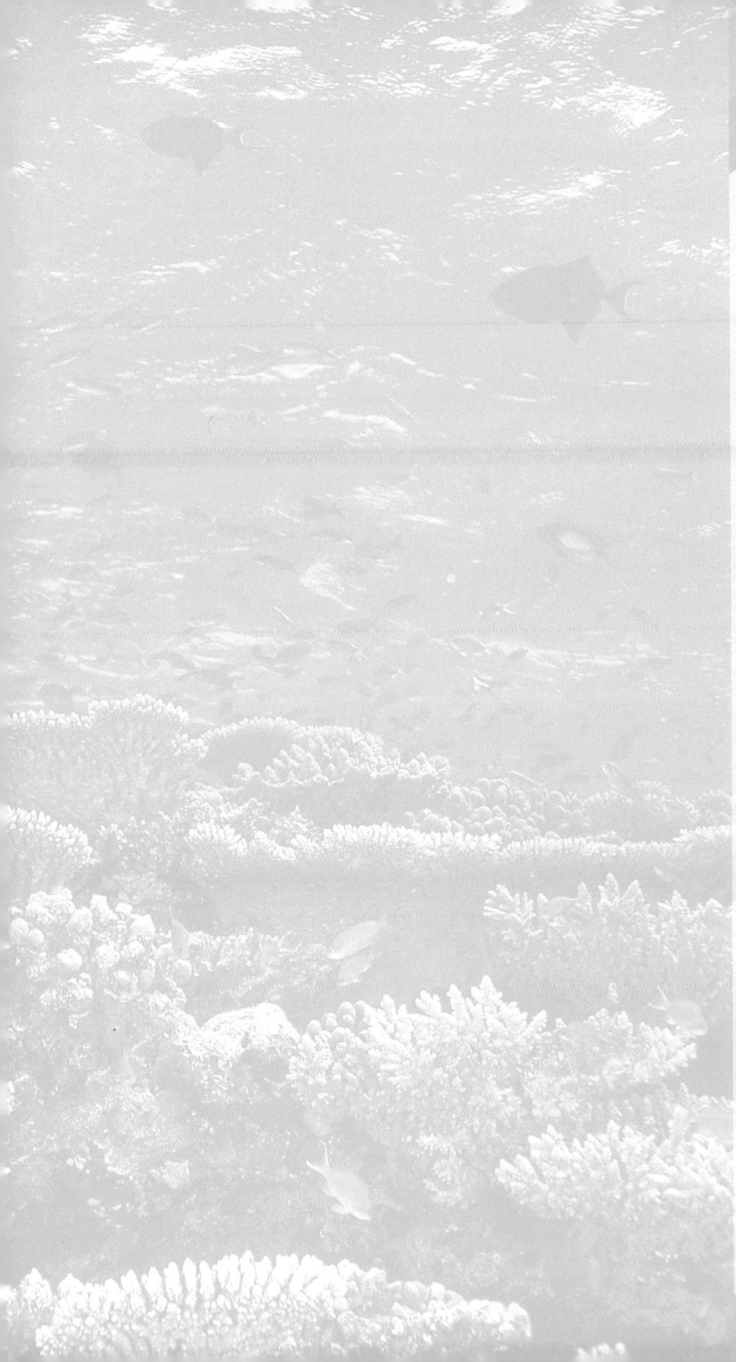

Index of Common Names

A

B

C

G

H

I

J

L

Index of Scientific Names

~ Photo Credits

marinethemes.com
Kelvin Aitken:
page 56 bottom,
57 top and middle,
58 middle,
62 bottom,
63 top and bottom,
64 bottom,
65 top,
68 top,
135 bottom,
136 bottom,
243 top,
449 middle and bottom,
452 top.

marinethemes.com
David Glennie:
page 59 bottom.

marinethemes.com
Mark Conlin:
page 62 top and middle,
63 middle,
64 middle,
82 middle,
241 bottom,
379 bottom.

marinethemes.com
Rob Torelli:
page 68 middle.

marinethemes.com
David Muirhead:
page 91 bottom.

marinethemes.com
Mary Malloy:
page 127 bottom.

marinethemes.com
Akos Luminatzer:
page 137 bottom.

marinethemes.com
David Fleetham:
page 234 bottom.

marinethemes.com
Ken Hoppen:
page 418 bottom right.

Ketrick Chin:
page 94 bottom,
271 top,
315 bottom,
316 top,
325 top,
326 top,
388 top.

Thomas Gutmann:
page 109 bottom.

Franco Pozzi:
page 115 bottom.

Claudia Pellarini:
page 360 bottom.

Tony Wu:
front cover/dolphins,
page 450-451, 452
middle and bottom,
page 453 all.

All other photographs are by the authors.

THE AUTHORS

World-famous marine photographers and nature writers, Andrea and Antonella Ferrari have published many photographic books and magazine articles on travel and marine life. Their books - published in Italy, France, Germany, Holland, Spain, Great Britain, the Usa, Malaysia and Japan - include *Malaysia Diving Guide* (1997), *Malaysia - An Underwater Paradise* (1998), *Reef Life* (1999), *Sharks* (2000), *Layang Layang - The Island of Dreams Come True* (1998), *Top Nature and Dive Resorts of Borneo* (2001) and the coffee-table volume *Oceani Segreti* (2004), which was awarded the prestigious World Grand Prize at the Festival of the Underwater Image in Antibes. This is their second volume in Nautilus' Diver's Guide series after *Underwater Malaysia Macrolife* (2003).

Reef